Sounds of War

ANNEGRET
FAUSER

Sounds of War

Music in the United States

during World War II

OXFORD
UNIVERSITY PRESS

OXFORD
UNIVERSITY PRESS

Oxford University Press is a department of the University of Oxford.
It furthers the University's objective of excellence in research, scholarship,
and education by publishing worldwide.

Oxford   New York
Auckland   Cape Town   Dar es Salaam   Hong Kong   Karachi
Kuala Lumpur   Madrid   Melbourne   Mexico City   Nairobi
New Delhi   Shanghai   Taipei   Toronto

With offices in
Argentina   Austria   Brazil   Chile   Czech Republic   France   Greece
Guatemala   Hungary   Italy   Japan   Poland   Portugal   Singapore
South Korea   Switzerland   Thailand   Turkey   Ukraine   Vietnam

Oxford is a registered trademark of Oxford University Press in the
UK and certain other countries.

Published in the United States of America by
Oxford University Press
198 Madison Avenue, New York, NY 10016

Library of Congress Cataloging-in-Publication Data
Fauser, Annegret.
Sounds of war : music in the United States during World War II /
Annegret Fauser.
    p. cm.
Includes bibliographical references and index.
ISBN 978-0-19-994803-1 (hardcover : alk. paper)
1. Music—Political aspects—United States—History—20th century.
2. Music—Social aspects—United States—History—20th century.
3. Music and state—United States—History—20th century.
4. World War, 1939–1945—Music and the war.   I. Title.
ML3917.U6F38 2013
780.973'0904—dc23
2012047880

ISBN 978–0–19–994803–1

This volume is published with the generous support of the Dragan Plamenac Fund
of the American Musicological Society.

9 8 7 6 5 4 3 2 1
Printed in the United States of America
on acid-free paper

In memory of my father, Johannes Albert Fauser

CONTENTS

ACKNOWLEDGMENTS

The genesis of this book owes a great deal to colleagues, friends, students, and institutions in the United States and Europe. My research was generously supported by a Summer Fellowship and a Faculty Research Fellowship from the National Endowment of the Humanities, which sponsored the project under the "We the People" initiative. Without the freedom offered by these invaluable grants, my archival work would have been dramatically curtailed. Most of the book was written in Berlin, where I spent a wonderful year as a fellow at the Wissenschaftskolleg; more ideal and congenial writing conditions could barely be imagined than in this glorious enclave in the Grunewald. And yet, it was a poignant place to write this text, for the house in which I worked and lived had once been owned by a German Jew who perished at the hands of the Nazis. My stay in Berlin was partially funded by a Marie Curie Fellowship from the European Union, for which I am deeply grateful. I wrote the final chapters during a research and study leave from the University of North Carolina at Chapel Hill—a treasured sabbatical that made all the difference. These fellowships and leaves were vital in so many ways, not only financially but also in the encouragement they carried with them. I offer my deepest gratitude for such precious assistance.

Among the greatest joys of my journey into the musical realms of World War II was conducting research in the Music Division of the Library of Congress, a treasure trove of documents and a truly welcoming place for scholars to explore those riches. I cannot thank its staff enough for sharing leads to documents and working with me on identifying often uncatalogued materials that were essential for my project. When I received an e-mail in Berlin that a set of as yet uncatalogued documents we had searched for the previous year had been identified, I realized once more the exceptional qualities of the library's staff. I cannot express enough how grateful I am to each and every one of them. It was a privilege to work there.

I also owe thanks to Dave Stein at the Weill-Lenya Research Center in New York for his tireless and thoughtful help in sharing newly discovered materials about Weill's wartime activities. At Yale University, Richard Boursy and Emily Ferrigno (Irving S. Gilmore Music Library), and Susan Brady (Beinecke Library) eased my access to archival materials through their more than generous help. At the New York Public Library, Jonathan Hiam worked wonders in a system that can defy a reader with limited research time. The staff at the National Archives and Records Administration (College Park, Maryland) also helped make my frequent visits there a delight. Furthermore, I am grateful to Naomi Bishop, Stephanie Challener (Musical America Worldwide), Nicole C. Dittrich (Special Collections Research Center, Syracuse University Library), Robert Frank, Scott Hankins (Ackland Art Museum), Stephen Hassay (Visual Information Coordinator/Archive Assistant, U.S. Navy Band, Washington, D.C.), Lucy Kostelanetz, Lisa R. Marine (Wisconsin Historical Society), Philip Langner, Daniel Milhaud, Martha Robertson (Archives and Special Collections, Library of the Marine Corps), Gabryel Smith (New York Philharmonic Archives), John Snelson (Royal Opera House Covent Garden), Alice Standin (New York Public Library), Hans-Jürgen Winkler (Paul Hindemith Archive), and Heidy Zimmermann (Paul Sacher Foundation) for their help with illustrations and other documents.

From the outset, Mark Evan Bonds, Suzanne G. Cusick, Hermann Danuser, Ralph P. Locke, and Carol J. Oja supported this project with wise counsel and thoughtful commentary; without their encouragement, this book might never have been made a reality. Kevin Bartig, George Ferencz, Don Harrán, Barbara Kelly, Neil Lerner, and Manuela Schwartz shared important information and source materials, and Chris Wells contributed as my research assistant in the project's early stages. During my year in Berlin, I benefited greatly from regular discussions with Reinhart Meyer-Kalkus, who challenged my conclusions and assumptions relentlessly and inspired further reflection. The Wiko Study Group dedicated to "The Fatigue of Avant-Garde Movements and the Emergence of New Paradigms in Art and Culture in the 1930s" (led by Boris Gasparov and Galin Tihanov) proved an important discussion forum that helped focus my ideas, and the research seminar "Music in World War II: A Transcultural Exploration," which I was able to organize at the Wissenschaftskolleg in June 2010, provided a vital transnational context to the topic. I am grateful to its participants: Esteban Buch, Tim Carter, Stephen Downes, Albrecht Dümling, Marina Frolova-Walker, Boris

Gasparov, Reinhart Meyer-Kalkus, Fiamma Nicolodi, Albrecht Riethmüller, Dörte Schmidt, and Manuela Schwartz.

My research on this book has filtered into my teaching on both graduate and undergraduate levels. Presenting this material and engaging with smart and inquisitive students were pleasures all in themselves, and I am delighted that several master's theses and a doctoral dissertation emerged from these seminars. My warmest thanks go to the students for sharing this journey into a past whose presence was noticeable in a U.S. state brimming with military bases. I am also grateful to my colleagues in the Department of Music and elsewhere in the University of North Carolina at Chapel Hill for their inspiring conversations about the topic, especially Brigid Cohen, David García, Karen Hagemann, Mark Katz, Stefan Litwin, Jocelyn Neal, Severine Neff, and Philip Vandermeer. The staff at the UNC Music Library has been wonderfully helpful with my many requests and calls for help. As the book took shape, friends and colleagues, especially Kevin Bartig, Carol A. Hess, Kim Kowalke, Erin Maher, Howard Pollack, Elsa Rieu, Alex Ross, Manuela Schwartz, and Giselher Schubert, read and commented on the text. I thank them for their generosity. I am also very grateful to Barbara Norton, whose copy-editing skills I have come to admire, and the team of Oxford University Press for putting together a beautiful book.

Tim Carter, my best friend, colleague, and husband, shared this entire project and its genesis. No one could have been more supportive as both a spouse and a scholar. Reading every word of this book and sharing his brilliant mind and miraculous editorial abilities were most precious gifts. I also owe thanks to the menagerie—without y'all, there would not be a book.

I dedicate this book to the memory of my father, Johannes Albert Fauser, whose youth had been shaped by World War II. His life as a Protestant pastor was devoted to the principles of tolerance, love, and peace. As I started research on this book, our conversations turned to our biographies and the ways in which our own lives were marked by this war. He did not live to see the book completed.

General Abbreviations

ABSIE	American Broadcasting Station in Europe
AFM	American Federation of Musicians
AFN	American Forces Network
ASCAP	American Society of Composers, Authors, and Publishers
CBS	Columbia Broadcasting Society
CIA	Central Intelligence Agency
FBI	Federal Bureau of Investigation
FMP	Federal Music Project
FTP	Federal Theatre Project
NAB	National Association of Broadcasters
NBC	National Broadcasting Company
NGO	Non-Governmental Organization
NNOC	National Negro Opera Company
OCD	Office of Civilian Defense
OCIAA	Office of the Coordinator of Inter-American Affairs
OSS	Office of Strategic Services
OWI	Office of War Information
SHAEF	Supreme Headquarters Allied Expeditionary Force
USO	United Services Organization
WAVES	Women Accepted for Volunteer Emergency Service
WPA	Works Progress (Projects) Administration

Archival, etc. Abbreviations

ACC   Aaron Copland Collection, Library of Congress,
Music Division

AKC   Andre Kostelanetz Collection, Library of Congress,
Music Division

DTP   Deems Taylor Papers, Yale University, Irving S. Gilmore
Music Library

ESCC   Elizabeth Sprague Coolidge Collection, Library of
Congress, Music Division

HCC   Henry Cowell Collection, New York Public Library,
Music Division, *ZB-4189

JANC-NARA Records of the Joint Army and Navy Committee on
Welfare and Recreation, National Archives and Records
Administration, RG 225

JANCSM   Archives of the Subcommittee on Music, Joint Army and
Navy Committee on Welfare and Recreation, Library of
Congress, Music Division

LEC   Lehman Engel Collection, Yale University, Irving S.
Gilmore Music Library

MBA   Marc Blitzstein Archives, State Historical Society,
Madison, Wisconsin

MCTP   Mario Castelnuovo-Tedesco Papers, Library of Congress,
Music Division

MGP   Morton Gould Papers, Library of Congress, Music Division

NARA   National Archives and Records Administration, College
Park, Maryland

NNOCC   National Negro Opera Company Collection, Library of
Congress, Music Division

NSC   Nicolas Slonimsky Collection, Library of Congress,
Music Division

NYpM   New York Public Library, Music Division

NYpT   New York Public Library, Billy Rose Theater Division

OHC   Oscar Hammerstein II Collection, Library of Congress,
Music Division

OWI-NARA   Archives of the Office of War Information, National
Archives and Records Administration, RG 208.

PHC   Paul Hindemith Collection, Yale University, Irving S.
Gilmore Music Library

RHP   Roy Harris Papers, Library of Congress, Music Division

SKC	Serge Koussevitzky Collection, Library of Congress, Music Division
VTP	Virgil Thomson Papers, Yale University, Irving S. Gilmore Music Library
WcM	Library of Congress, Music Division
WLP	Kurt Weill and Lotte Lenya Papers, Yale University, Irving S. Gilmore Music Library
WLRC	Weill-Lenya Research Center, New York

Sounds of War

On January 20, 2009, moments before Barack Hussein Obama was sworn in as the forty-fourth president of the United States, "Simple Gifts"—a Shaker tune made famous by Aaron Copland's ballet *Appalachian Spring* (1944)—sounded in an instrumental arrangement by Copland's student John Williams. The tune was significant enough, but still more was its source, given the new president's well-known appreciation for Copland.[1] The previous week, at the start of the inauguration festivities, the actor Tom Hanks had narrated Copland's *Lincoln Portrait* (1942) on the steps of the Lincoln Memorial. The composer's *Fanfare for the Common Man* (1942) was also performed on this occasion. These iconic works of World War II were played, over six decades later, during the inauguration of a U.S. president who not only inspired worldwide enthusiasm but also inherited a protracted war.[2] For American and global television audiences alike, the musical choices during the 2009 presidential inauguration made audible a connection, however unintended and unacknowledged, between what has come to be seen as America's "good" war in 1941–45 and the positive musical identity that was forged in its cauldron.

World War II was, indeed, a defining moment in American history, when ideas about national identity were consolidated both in internal discourse and in internationally oriented propaganda. Although the 1920s and '30s were rife with social, racial, and political tensions, the attack on Pearl Harbor pushed Americans together in a wave of patriotic fervor that swept the nation, creating "a unanimity of purpose that was shared by the government and people and extended solidly to the men on the fighting front."[3] Radio programs, presidential speeches, movies, and magazines celebrated the "American way" as a shining beacon of human civilization and cast U.S.

involvement in the war as a noble act of defense thrust upon a peace-loving, enlightened society by barbaric enemies abroad. Until postwar McCarthyism and the unfulfilled promises of the civil rights movement broke this national covenant apart, America did indeed appear to be "the beautiful."

The United States formally entered the war the day after Pearl Harbor, on December 8, 1941, more than two years after Germany had set in motion what would quickly escalate into a global conflict through the invasion of Poland on September 1, 1939. Tensions had been brewing even before that attack, starting with Mussolini's invasion of Ethiopia (1935), the Spanish Civil War (1936–39), and the Japanese invasion of China in early July 1937. The United States had kept its distance in accordance with the isolationist Neutrality Acts, although it offered tacit support to its allies by way of the Lend-Lease Agreement, signed into law on March 11, 1941; the United States also instituted its first peacetime draft (in 1940) and increased its defense budget exponentially. The Axis powers—Germany, Italy, and Japan—made rapid gains upon the British, French, and other Allied forces (as well as those from British Commonwealth countries), including the invasion and fall of France and the Low Countries in May–June 1940, primarily because the Molotov–Ribbentrop Pact kept the USSR neutral by dividing Eastern Europe between Germany and the Soviet Union.

The equation changed dramatically with the launch of Operation Barbarossa, Hitler's invasion of the Soviet Union in June 1941, which pushed it into the Allied camp through an alliance with the United Kingdom. After Pearl Harbor, not only the United States but also China—which had been fighting since 1937—formally joined the Allies, so that the war was now fought in Europe and northern Africa, on the one hand, and the Far East and Asia, on the other. The next year, 1942, looked bleak for the Allies as the Axis gained victory after victory; the tables turned, however, with Field Marshal Bernard Montgomery's victory in El Alamein in November 1942. In 1943 Allied forces started to gain ground, from China and the South Pacific to the Soviet Union and Sicily. With Mussolini's fall that year, the first of the three Axis leaders was vanquished. By 1944 the tide had turned decisively, and on May 8, 1945, the war in Europe was over. Three months later—soon after the United States dropped atomic bombs on the civilian targets of Hiroshima and Nagasaki in August 1945, killing close to a quarter of a million men, women, and children—Japan surrendered, and World War II was over.

These bare details cannot do justice to a conflict that also generated unspeakable war crimes in countries from China to the Soviet Union and led to the genocide of the Holocaust. Bombings had destroyed cities on both sides of the war, from London and Rotterdam to Berlin and Tokyo, killing millions of civilians. The death toll among the armed forces on both sides was staggering. A few of the warring nations—mainly the continental United States, Canada, and Australia—remained untouched in territorial terms, though all paid a bitter price in the lives lost in battle and in prisoner-of-war camps. It was a global war that defies any kind of summing up, a war fought with every means, from weapons to words.

Music also played a role in the battle. Whether as an instrument of blatant propaganda or as a means of entertainment, recuperation, and uplift, music pervaded homes and concert halls, army camps and government buildings, hospitals and factories. A medium both permeable and malleable, music was appropriated for numerous war-related tasks. Indeed, even more than movies, posters, books, and newspapers, music sounded everywhere in this war, not only in its live manifestations but also through recordings and radio. So far as the United States is concerned, even today musicians such as Dinah Shore, Duke Ellington, and the Andrews Sisters populate the sonic imaginary of wartime. Whether performed by "all-girl" groups such as the International Sweethearts of Rhythm or by military bands conducted by Glenn Miller and Artie Shaw, swing and boogie-woogie entertained civilians at home and GIs stationed abroad.[4] Numerous films created to boost both civilian and military morale—from *Star Spangled Rhythm* (1942) and *Stage Door Canteen* (1943) to *Anchors Aweigh* (1945)—featured star-studded numbers presenting country sounds, barbershop quartets, swing, sentimental ballads, and hot jazz, among other styles. Likewise, nostalgic songs such as "I'll Be Seeing You" (1938) and bellicose tunes as "Praise the Lord and Pass the Ammunition" (1942) had their place on popular radio programs, United Services Organization (USO) shows, and V-Discs.

Star Spangled Rhythm, for example, brings together all the popular styles for which this period is so well-known, and indeed they are often regarded as iconic for the era. However, it does so in what might sometimes seem surprising ways, if with obvious programmatic intent. The big production number "Swing Shift," set in an aircraft factory, combines jazzy swing with traditional barn dances, musical and dance styles that might otherwise have been criticized as incompatible. Another number merges the style and performance of the African American vocal group the Golden Gate Quartet with the more sentimental duet "Hit the Road to Dreamland" (marked as "white" by both its performance style and its crooning arrangement), performed by Mary Martin and Dick Powell. Hot jazz is represented, inevitably, by a Harlem street scene featuring the legendary African American dancer Katherine Dunham. And just as inevitably, the film ends with a patriotic number, "Old Glory," in which Bing Crosby, in the front of a crowd standing before a stage set of Mount Rushmore, sings in praise of the U.S. flag, engages with a doubting Thomas, and leads representatives of the states (including a gospel group from Georgia) into a choral hymn of patriotic solidarity.

Yet that final number has still more surprises to offer, given its obvious, and no doubt deliberate, echoes of another well-known patriotic piece, John Latouche and Earl Robinson's *Ballad for Americans* (1939). Here we move from "popular music" in the direction of a repertoire that was, and is, often labeled "classical." I use that term with all due caution—and mostly for lack of anything better—without asserting value judgments on its superiority over other musical forms and acts. Nor do I limit my inquiry to elitist, "highbrow" domains: indeed, one of my points is that wartime classical music is not at all highbrow—just as popular music is not lowbrow—but instead does its cultural work in differently configured social spheres. However, for all the scholarly emphasis on popular culture in the wartime period, what in fact distinguished musical life in the United States during World War II from other times of war was the significant role assigned to classical music: in 1940s America it had a cultural relevance and ubiquity that is hard to imagine today.

The nation's out-and-out involvement in the war meant that all music was to serve its needs, and that included types of music that had already gained a significantly broader presence in U.S. culture during the 1930s. This new prominence was achieved in New Deal America—and we shall see how New Deal institutions transferred to wartime ones—especially through music appreciation courses in schools and colleges, nationwide radio broadcasts of major orchestras and the Metropolitan Opera House, and phonograph catalogs that offered a repertoire of classics for the middlebrow household. Through these educational and marketing initiatives, classical music from symphonies to Schubert songs carried added value as cultural capital that moved beyond popular musical entertainment. Also at stake, however, was the United States' role as not just a military power, but also a force for civilization. In the composer Henry Cowell's words, musicians of all stripes were "shaping music for total war." Indeed, no other event in U.S. history mobilized and instrumentalized culture in general, and music in particular, so totally, so consciously, and so unequivocally as World War II.

Musicians—from the singing cowboy Gene Autry to the Metropolitan Opera's John Carter—saw themselves as cultural combatants. Copland was just one of many classical composers deeply involved in the war effort. Marc Blitzstein, Elliott Carter, Henry Cowell, Roy Harris, and Colin McPhee all participated in the propaganda missions of the Office of War Information

(OWI). Earlier, in the summer of 1942, Blitzstein had become attached to the Eighth Army Air Force in London, where he was commissioned to compose his *Airborne Symphony*. Samuel Barber also served in the Army Air Force (but stationed in the United States), writing both his Second Symphony and his *Capricorn Concerto*, "a rather tooting piece, with flute, oboe and trumpet chirping away" and thus fitting for the times, as he assured Copland.[5] Civilian commissions for new music focused on patriotic and "martial" subjects, most famously the series of fanfares that Eugene Goossens, the chief conductor of the Cincinnati Symphony Orchestra, requested from American composers and from European musicians in exile: Copland's *Fanfare for the Common Man* is a still much-performed result. Similarly, the League of Composers (financed by the Department of the Treasury) commissioned seventeen works on patriotic themes, including Bohuslav Martinů's *Memorial to Lidice* and William Grant Still's *In Memoriam: The Colored Soldiers Who Died for Democracy*. Classical music was heard on the radio and in film scores, whether Yehudi Menuhin playing Schubert's *Ave Maria* in *Stage Door Canteen* or Victor Young infusing the entire score for *Frenchman's Creek* (1944) with Claude Debussy's *Clair de lune*. Concert music was performed in the armed forces, for example by the Camp Lee Symphony Orchestra or the U.S. Navy Band String Quartet; it even played a role in the work of the Office of Strategic Services (the predecessor to the CIA), whose director, General "Wild Bill" Donovan, was known not only to support experiments in using music as a cipher, but also to involve himself in music-related propaganda efforts.

This rich field of Western classical music and its musicians during the war years in the United States forms the center of the present book. This is not to say that it existed in isolation from other musical styles, or that jazz, Tin Pan Alley, and country music played a less important role in the war effort. But numerous studies have already explored with great authority the role of jazz and other popular musics during World War II,[6] including their extensions into either the concert hall, such as Duke Ellington's "jazz symphony" *Black, Brown, and Beige*, or Broadway musical theater, in the case of Richard Rodgers and Oscar Hammerstein's *Oklahoma!* (both 1943).[7] In contrast, research on classical music in the United States during these years has been limited in its scope and focused mainly on the experiences of such European émigrés as Arnold Schoenberg, Igor Stravinsky, and Kurt Weill.[8] Only recently have we begun to scratch other surfaces with specific case studies involving in particular the music of Samuel Barber, Aaron Copland, and William Schuman.[9] For the most part, classical music in America during World War II has only been addressed either as a chapter in broader studies, such as Barbara A. Zuck's *A History of Musical Americanism*, or as a short interlude in studies and biographies dedicated to composers and performers such as Blitzstein and Arturo Toscanini.[10]

This paucity on the one hand, and the relative lack of coverage of the United States in broader studies of music during World War II on the other, raise more difficult questions. American music during these years developed within a politicized framework similar at least in rhetoric and intent to those of Germany, the Soviet Union, and Great Britain, for example. Like their counterparts in other Allied and Axis powers, American musicians found themselves in a cultural field ripe with contradictory demands from government institutions and the military, from the general needs of day-to-day musical life at home, and from their own private desire to continue composing and performing. And like music in the Soviet Union, American concert music gained new status as a direct result of world events. Musical life was shaped by the complex intersections between musical production and consumption and the political, social, and economic environment within the United States on the one hand, and their relationship to European countries—whether Allied or Axis—on the other.

If one were to believe both wartime propaganda and cold-war musicology, music composed in Nazi Germany and Fascist Italy should and did sound markedly different from that written in democratic America, fiercely resistant Great Britain, and the socialist Soviet Union. As Pamela Potter has pointed out, however, wartime classical music may be more homogeneous than its different origins might lead us to expect.[11] Likewise, a simple transposition of moral and aesthetic positions (e.g., the modernist avant-garde as socially progressive, neoclassical and neoromantic music as politically repressive) is inappropriate for a repertoire that was expected to fulfill precise political, social, and cultural functions.[12] In the decades since the end of the war we have come to understand the propaganda value that music held for Nazi Germany, both in nation building before the war and in the years after 1939, whether of Carl Orff's medievalizing *Carmina Burana* (1937), Elly Ney's and Wilhelm Kempff's Beethoven performances at the German front, or Richard Strauss's nostalgic opera *Capriccio* (1942).[13] Similarly, recent research by Kiril Tomoff and Marina Frolova-Walker has shown how nationalist concerns and Soviet ideology merged into an all-consuming revival of Russian pan-Slavicism in order to strengthen a positive cultural identity in the face of the Nazi invasion.[14] Musical culture in Fascist Italy and under the Vichy government in France has elicited deep scholarly engagement with exploring the complex webs of political ideology and musical production.[15] The apparent reluctance of scholars of American music (and, to a lesser extent, of British music as well) to engage in similar investigations raises intriguing questions. It also has a precedent in the times.

Allied propagandists during World War II tended to claim the ideological high ground typically by avoiding any engagement whatsoever with ideology. It is easy to accuse Fascist regimes of abusing music as an instrument of nationalist propaganda; it is harder to acknowledge that such forces were at work—with not so dissimilar results—on the other side of the wartime fence. While the Allies may never have overtly condemned "degenerate" music—defined by style or by ethnic origin (or both)—its production was strongly discouraged save in certain highly controlled circumstances. In both Allied and Axis spheres of influence, the typical prior instruments of musical internationalization (for instance, the International Society for Contemporary Music) declined sharply in favor of such bilateral organizations as the Council of American–Soviet Friendship and various German–Japanese cultural associations. And the tendency of the postwar West to deride the results of socialist realism as a sign of intolerable artistic oppression hardly squares with the mandates imposed upon and willingly accepted by Western composers as a necessity of, and for, war.

No less complex, and running no less counter to traditional historical narratives, were the questions raised by the patterns of musical migration across national boundaries and political spectra. Whereas during the 1920s and early '30s the Western focus of music (and art in general) was on internationalization, during the war such transnational cross-fertilizations and migrations became problematic, and it was not clear whether they were to be embraced (as a sign of inclusivity or even cultural preeminence) or rejected (as a source of contamination). Thus the tensions between the international and the national—and even between the regional and the local—entered not just the battlefield of political domination but also, and necessarily, that of the moral high ground.

With the United States during World War II deeply immersed in these cross-currents, any exploration of American music making finds itself faced with a balancing act that acknowledges both national developments and their transnational context. Furthermore, musical life in the United States was shaped by institutions and individuals as much as by political and aesthetic trends. In particular, such bodies as the armed forces and the OWI were formative in this context because their centralized national reach was unprecedented in U.S. history (the country's short and limited involvement in World War I had far fewer consequences in this respect). The agendas of government employees, orchestra conductors, individual composers faced with the draft, propaganda warriors, and medical professionals in military hospitals wove a complex fabric of musical production in which serendipitous alignments and ideologically crossed purposes could lead to musical commissions, their performances, and their cancellations in ways that sometimes defy logic. Both Barber and Blitzstein found themselves freed from day-to-day military duties in 1943 to write symphonies dedicated to the U.S. Air Force. Yet whereas Barber's Second Symphony (1944) was performed to great acclaim in Boston, shifting priorities in the European war theater, where Blitzstein was stationed, impeded the planned première of his *Airborne Symphony*, delaying it for two years until 1946. Thus the complexities of civilian and military musical life—with its interconnections, contradictions, and rivalries—form an important part of exploring U.S. music during these years.

These institutional interconnections, personal rivalries, and aesthetic trends of the war years grew, of course, out of the musical and cultural developments of the 1930s. Three interconnected strands of musical practice in particular provided the foundation for the most characteristic developments of concert music in the United States during the war: the increased predominance of an accessible style—one that Copland dubbed "imposed simplicity"—among modernist composers from William Grant Still to Roy Harris; the institutionalization of a nationwide concert, opera, and dance infrastructure through the WPA, especially the Federal Music Project (FMP) and the Federal Theatre Project; and, finally, the impact, after 1934, of FCC regulation on radio broadcasts that encouraged "educational radio," including the programming of "serious" music.[16] When the United States joined the war in 1941, it had a cultural system in place that permitted, for the first time in U.S. history, a centralized implementation of cultural politics that—despite regional idiosyncrasies, political differences, and individual resistance—reached both music makers and consumers across the nation. Radio shows that delivered "serious" music to American citizens during the Depression, and FMP programs that had put into place music-educational mechanisms favoring so-called good music, could be transformed almost wholesale into music programs for the new military. Elements of these emerging political, institutional, and aesthetic practices that at first glance might be seen as specific to a world war—stylistic simplification, nationalist retrenchment, and the politicization of musical composition—are in fact a continuation and culmination of trends that already dominated American music in the 1930s. Yet pressures increased—not least owing to the need for propaganda and the short time frame in which it was to be produced—and changes occurred.

There are other challenges facing any musicological engagement with World War II.[17] Rainer Werner Fassbinder's *Lili Marleen* (1981), Steven Spielberg's *Saving Private Ryan* (1998), and Bryan Singer's *Valkyrie* (2008) are just three iconic films of the past thirty years that have shaped what our senses associate with these wartime soundscapes. In telling the stories of those six years between 1939 and 1945, films and documentaries have for over half a century added countless layers of invented, reconstructed, and recovered sound to this slice of history, creating a sonic imaginary whose vivid immediacy provides an acoustic framework not only for moviegoers but also for scholars who engage with the period's music. In this respect, World War II is unique. Earlier historical periods rely on different representational imaginaries where sound can sometimes become fleetingly symbolic but more usually remains subordinate to the visual and verbal. Since World War II, on the other hand, recorded sound has become so commonplace that it has lost its historical specificity. Songs may still stand for a period—the Beatles' "I Want To Hold Your Hand" or Joan Baez's version of "We Shall Overcome" are heard as embodying the 1960s—but these postwar soundscapes remain open and often fragmentary. World War II as a period, however, has been fashioned into a total soundscape of acoustic and musical signifiers fusing the sounds of war, oppression, and propaganda with those of the radio, concert hall, and opera house. The voices of Hitler, Roosevelt, and Stalin remain in our ears and merge with those of such actors as Colin Firth as he recreates King George VI's address to the nation, underlaid with the Allegretto slow movement from Beethoven's Symphony no. 7 in the Oscar-winning film *The King's Speech* (2010). Analyzing the acoustic history of World War II thus poses unique problems that bring into sharper relief the broader concerns of anyone seeking to engage with sound, music, and culture.

There are two key issues in this study. The first is the challenge of defamiliarizing the soundscape of this period by reintroducing—or at least acknowledging—the topic's historical, cultural, and sonic distance. Because of the sonic immediacy of modern media experiences, the chasm between the imaginary soundscape of postwar films and the lived sonic experience of that world war often remains unrecognized. A case in point is the soundtrack of *Saving Private Ryan*.[18] In the DVD's bonus material, members of the production team describe in striking detail how they worked on turning the acoustic representation of battle into an "authentic" experience in the cinema, the soundtrack acting as a "transporter" into historical reality that might seem to make time travel come true. Whereas we have learned to distance ourselves cognitively from the visual experience of film—we remain aware that Private Ryan also goes by the name of Matt Damon—the reception of soundtracks tends to be, for the most part, subliminal and unreflected. Therefore, the musicological commonplace of the impossibility of period listening—the fact that our ears are not historical ones, and that our listening experience has little or nothing to do with that of the 1940s—becomes an acutely important distinction for the acoustic history of World War II.

The second issue is that scholarship on the music of World War II also needs to face the political, cultural, and even acoustic exceptionality of this global conflict in terms of the deliberate employment of music, and of sound technology, within the military and for propaganda purposes. World War II was the first war in which modern media played a key role: radio, phonograph, and film allowed for the strategic distribution of sonic materials in entirely new ways. These sonic remnants pose different challenges to scholarship from text-based archives, especially when one seeks to emphasize the chasm between our own ears and those of the past. And then, the music itself hovers in the interstitial space between a past manifestation in performance, its notated form as score, and its continued reception in concert hall, recording, and advertising. Witness how Copland's *Fanfare for the Common Man*, *Lincoln Portrait*, and *Appalachian Spring*, for all their popularity today, owe everything to the time in which they were composed. And while they may have lost their wartime resonances—or perhaps not—the reconstruction of that context allows for a better understanding of how such musical identity markers were shaped. Add to that the complicated history of concert music in the United States, with its unique anxieties over European influence and national identity, and the musical fabric of this period becomes quite difficult to weave.

Thus at the heart of this book lie several thematic strands: the transnational complexities and nationalist trends of music during World War II, the institutional and individual forms of musical practice, and the past's sonic and experiential alterity. My text is in two large parts: the first (chapters 1 and 2) treats the people and institutions that created, performed, and listened to this music; the second (chapters 3–5) explores its sonic manifestations. Chapter 1 focuses on individuals, both Americans and foreigners, and their musical activities during the war. It explores how men and women dealt with this global conflict, whether they were musicians in uniform, performers providing wartime entertainment, composers working on music appropriate for this time, or musical mediators such as radio hosts and newspaper critics. Chapter 2 flips the perspective from individual to institution. Music became a tool of choice in the cultural war that the United States fought in concert with its military campaign. Musical diplomacy aimed at winning the hearts of Allied and neutral nations; morale and propaganda operations employed classical music to uplift and impress; the military was faced with contradictory ideologies and agendas when it came to musical performance and education; and music therapy flourished in the desperate fight to "recondition" those soldiers whom trauma had left unable to return into combat or to reintegrate into postwar civilian society. Yet chapter 1 also addresses such organizations as the OWI and the USO in terms of the ways individual musicians tried to forge their own paths through the institutional matrix of the time; and individual performers and composers feature in the stories in chapter 2 about the institutions they served in and helped to shape. These two chapters thus form a dynamic pair with themes echoing across both.

The second part of the book then turns to the "classical" music that was composed and performed in the United States during the war. This section encompasses—to draw on Irving Lowens's foundational formulation—both "music in America and American music."[19] Although this dichotomy, as Lowens himself acknowledged, does not allow for the many subtle hybridities in the repertoire, it offers a distinction between music that was conceived self-consciously as "American" and music whose universalist appeal or deliberate otherness had its own place in wartime concert life, independently of whether it was composed in or imported into the United States. Although each of the chapters in the second section approaches this repertoire from its own perspective, all share a concern with trying to reveal what was considered "American" in music. This is by no means an attempt to distill a distinctly national musical trait; rather, I show how musical signifiers are identified and instrumentalized in this nationalist endeavor in general and by individual musicians in particular. By looking at music composed for the American market both by Americans (chapters 3 and 5) and by European exiles (chapter 4), these markers of identity start forming a matrix of musical signifiers that can be seen codifying, well beyond the war years, the trope of American music.

Chapter 3 explores the historical underpinning of American music during the war, including how this conflict reframed the debate about a "usable past," the appropriation of folk music, and strategies to Americanize European opera and employ it for "racial uplift." These were not new issues in the history of American music, but with the country's sharpened need for national delineation, the war intensified and crystallized the debates. Chapter 4 focuses on the music of foreign musicians who arrived on American soil as refugees from the war in Europe. As they continued to write music, they faced a new world in both their musical and their everyday lives. Discovering the United States through the eyes of exile composers offers a perspective on American music that breaks apart a number of familiar stories, including the often overplayed dichotomy between European progressiveness and American conservatism. Indeed, this chapter is equally about "American" music as filtered through exile musicians' appropriations and about the individual responses to "America" by these composers in exile.

The final chapter tackles the music with the worst reputation in twentieth-century historiography: intentionally nationalist works including such blatantly obvious Americana as Morton Gould's *American Salute* (1943) or Roy Harris's Symphony no. 6, "Gettysburg" (1944). But Americana are made up of a much broader set of signifiers, especially in works of commemoration such as Still's *In Memoriam*. Presenting these works at the end of my journey allows for a deeper contextualization that goes beyond a facile dismissal as nationalist trifles or bombast and instead shows that, for all their topicality, these works also responded to more sophisticated and long-standing concerns about musical and national identities in the United States.

Although the transnational context of American wartime music remains a constant frame throughout this study, my narrative privileges a U.S. perspective. Much of the material is presented here for the first time, filling an important gap in the historiography of American music between the well-researched developments of the 1920s and '30s and those of music during the cold war.[20] Archival work provides the foundation of this project, and my interpretations are anchored in a range of methodologies drawn from music history and theory, aesthetics, reception history, and cultural history, as well as exile and diaspora studies. They are more broadly informed by my previous work on musical identity, race, nationalism, cultural transfer, and gender studies, especially with respect to notions of masculinity in music.[21]

Any attempt to address so substantial a topic will be defined as much by what is left out as by what is included. I have been able to focus on one set of repertoires rather than offering a more ecumenical overview embracing others precisely because of the scholarly studies of popular musics, jazz, and musical theater noted earlier. Similarly, recent work on Schoenberg, Stravinsky, and Weill in their U.S. exile enabled me to concentrate more strongly on others less frequently considered in this context, including Darius Milhaud and Bohuslav Martinů. Many of the composers discussed in this book (including Blitzstein, Copland, Thomson, and Weill) wrote film music during the war years—a subject that I hope will soon attract much-needed scholarly attention but that lies beyond the scope of this inquiry.[22] Opera, too, sits on the margins—although I discuss some features of the repertoire—largely because it was less mobile and more foreign, and because its canon was more firmly fixed. Furthermore, the United States is a sizable nation, with numerous local traditions and activities that all deserve attention in their own right; but because so many of the institutions, concert halls, and radio stations were located on the East Coast, this book focuses mostly on that region. Inevitably, some of my choices of what to cover and what not were personal as much as professional, and sometimes (though rarely) I was hostage to archival accessibility.

At first glance, some potential protagonists may seem underrepresented in this book, especially those musicians whom we count as minorities by reason of either gender or ethnicity. Some of this absence has to do with U.S. cultural politics of the 1930s and '40s, which limited access to concert halls and stages especially for African American concert artists and opera singers and led to a noticeable lack of visibility and presence of African American musicians, particular within such institutions as the State Department and the OWI. This circumstance is highlighted by my narrative strategy: I have chosen not to segregate African American and American Indian musicians into their own subsections. Rather, I have integrated composers (e.g., William Grant Still and Ulysses Kay); educators (e.g., Chauncey G. Lee); and performers (e.g., Dorothy Maynor) into my broader narrative about institutions, composition, performance, and cultural politics. Because of the cultural landscape of the United States during the war, therefore, minority musicians cannot be but underrepresented in this book: in that segregated and racist society, more often than not African American musicians remained ghettoized in Negro production units or even barred from performance altogether, whether in the USO or the armed forces. The picture that emerged from the archives and libraries was overwhelmingly white, even though some African American leaders considered the contributions of singers such as Marian Anderson and Paul Robeson vital to the war effort. But for African Americans, transgression into white territory could have dangerous results. When the world-renowned tenor Roland Hayes protested the shabby segregationist treatment of his wife and daughter in a shoe shop in Rome, Georgia, in 1942, he was beaten and jailed by police. The *New York Amsterdam News* reported that Mrs. Hayes had protested: "This sort of thing is out of place at a time like this. You ought to go over there with old Hitler."[23] Marian Anderson, for her part, was treated worse than German prisoners of war in Birmingham, Alabama, where she had to stay outside a train-station waiting room while enemy soldiers were allowed to come in.[24]

As a feminist scholar, I kept looking for women in this musical war world. As performers, women were very active, especially in civilian endeavors from USO shows to radio programs, although—as we will see in chapter 1—a small group of performers enlisted to form the Marine Corps Women's Reserve Band. Unlike in other professions, where Rosie the Riveter presented alternate models of female accomplishment, in music we find an entrenchment of traditional gender concepts that valued "feminine" qualities in female performers—from glamorous beauty to nurturing maternity. These seemed to preclude women being active composers during the war to a significant degree. Ruth Crawford Seeger spent the war years promoting folk song in nursery and primary schools, which culminated in her volume *Folk Songs for School Children* (1948).[25] Marion Bauer wrote only a few compositions and worked mainly as a music educator. Others, such as Vivien Fine, who came to prominence in the postwar years, were primarily heard in their capacity as performers, even though she wrote a small number of compositions, including *Rhapsody on a Russian Folk Song* (1943) and *Songs of Our Time* (1943) in support of American–Soviet activities.

This book also represents a personal journey. For me, a scholar of German origin, the study of music during World War II remains a painful undertaking, given that it engages with a musical culture forever altered by a war started by the Axis powers. Encountering exile and death, devastation and loss, through the raw immediacy of historical documents was as challenging as the need to develop resistance to the often brilliant propaganda I found in the OWI archives, the power of which remains, after seven decades, undiminished. In addition, I teach at an American university located in an area with a large number of military bases. In Chapel Hill, the current war is a reality: many of my students are touched by this conflict, either directly (because of their own ROTC status or because of family) or indirectly, and I have been humbled by, and have learned from, their willingness to reflect deeply on the role of culture in wartime, if at a somewhat safer historical distance.

I have also taken comfort from recent scholarly trends. Since the U.S.-led invasion of Iraq—one of three nations that the former president George W. Bush called, in a direct play on World War II rhetoric, the "axis of evil"— literature about music and war has exploded. Some contributions tackle current events head-on, most prominently Suzanne Cusick's eye-opening work on the abuse of music for torture and as a weapon.[26] Others engage with music and war more broadly, most often in essay collections.[27] World War I and the American Civil War have also attracted renewed interest.[28] As musicologists, we have begun to write, speak, and teach about war. The present book, too, is part of this broader network of reflective discourse concerned with the uses of music as a morale booster and source of comfort and consolation; as a signifier of individual and national identities; and as a political tool, instrument of propaganda, and military weapon. In World War II, as it is today, music was an agent in a global conflict. The performance of Copland's Americana during a wartime presidential inauguration in 2009 was, indeed, a political gesture rallying Americans through these familiar sounds while projecting these sonic markers of identity across the globe to both enemies and allies. To understand how it could do so is the main aim of what follows.

CHAPTER ONE | "We, as Musicians, Are Soldiers, Too..."

O N THE DAY after Pearl Harbor, the director of the Group Theatre, Harold Clurman, wrote to his cousin, Aaron Copland: "So you're back in N.Y.... ready to defend your country in her hour of need with lectures, books, symphonies!"[1] Clurman's wit notwithstanding, Copland would be one of numerous composers, performers, and critics in the United States who actively contributed to the war effort as musicians by carving out professional roles for themselves in government and private organizations and by mobilizing music for the needs of their country at war. Thus Samuel Barber, Marc Blitzstein, Elliott Carter, Copland, Henry Cowell, Roy Harris, Colin McPhee, and Kurt Weill were all involved in the propaganda missions of the Office of War Information (OWI). Performers from Yehudi Menuhin to Lily Pons played and sang for soldiers stationed in army camps at home and deployed to the front. Scholars and educators, including Alfred Einstein, Alan Lomax, Paul Nettl, Lilla Belle Pitts, Charles Seeger, and Harold Spivacke, used their publications, research, and committee work to integrate music into the nation's war efforts. Instrument makers, record producers, radio hosts, patronesses of music clubs—all joined forces in the great patriotic cause. Indeed, every aspect of musical production and reception was retooled for the new circumstances lest music—and especially classical music—be considered irrelevant in the shifting priorities of a global war.

"We, as musicians, are soldiers, too," Serge Koussevitzky exhorted in 1942, "fighting for the ever-growing spiritual need of the world. If music is our life, we give it joyfully to serve the cause of freedom, for the victory of freedom is also the victory of truth."[2] Koussevitzky's rousing call to

musical arms, however, betrays an unease similar to that which the carica-
turist George Hager captured in a series of drawings published in *Musical
America* in February 1942 under the heading "So Music Wins the War." Not
only was music's true effectiveness as a weapon somewhat in doubt—witness
the cluster of cheerful trombonists attacking their enemies with their instruments in Figure 1.1a—but musicians themselves might in fact prove lacking

(a)

The Brass Goes Into Action

(b)

"And Just Think—One Year Ago We Were Playing Mozart Quartets"

FIGURE 1.1 George Hager, two cartoons from a series titled "So Music Wins
the War." *Musical America* 62 (February 10, 1942): 20.

a. "The Brass Goes Into Action"

b. "And Just Think—One Year Ago We Were Playing Mozart Quartets" when employed as soldiers. The group in Figure 1.1b clearly hankers after their Mozart quartets while suffering in the field—a portrayal that plays on popular ideas of musicians as rather wimpish creatures who might not be cut out for the manly pursuit of war. Classical music and musicians thus had to prove their usefulness in the exceptional circumstances brought about by World War II—a need for justification that pervaded much of the discourse about music's place in the war.

How musicians in their professional capacity could play some part in this new patriotic enterprise became an urgent question early on in the conflict. Two musical administrators—Ross Lee Finney, of Smith College, and Claire Reis, of the League of Composers—sent out questionnaires to composers across the nation to find out what they could contribute to the war effort. Finney's questionnaire asked the more philosophical question—"What do you feel is the composer's war-time function?"—which led to a fascinating range of responses about whether or not music could (or should) be utilized for the specific needs of the U.S. military and for American propaganda.[3] Some—such as Richard Donovan (who taught composition at Yale University) and Theodore Chanler (a composer and music critic in Boston)—openly addressed the underlying fear that there was not "any burning need" for composers "right now." Others speculated on how music could indeed make a contribution. Whereas Earl Robinson's declaration that "songs *can be bullets*" (pointing out that "La Marseillaise" "was worth in its time several regiments of men, machines, and guns") pushed the boundaries of musical activism to the extreme, numerous composers saw their art as somehow serviceable.[4] Marion Bauer's pragmatic response, asking her colleagues "to compose works that would be timely, principally choral numbers, that might be used in the U.S. Treasury or other concerts throughout the country," was as much about instrumentalizing music for the war as was Isadore Freed's more ideological answer, according to which he "wrote 'Appalachian Sketches' (my first venture in American Folk Lore) as a direct result of my consciousness that America is a better way of life than Fascism or Nazism."[5] Two composers, however, pointed to the competing demands of war work and composition: both Barber and Lehman Engel explained that they had, for the time being, stopped composing because they had been drafted and were, in Barber's words, "unable to work on music due to military duties."[6]

In contrast to Finney's broader approach, Reis tried specifically to identify musicians' individual abilities so as to be "of help in placing these composers in line for work they could do in defense activities." Her targets were composers who either would be drafted and, with the help of the questionnaire, could be identified for service in a musical function (for example, in an army band) or could be asked to lend their talent in a civilian capacity for "films which need music, broadcasts, inter-cultural developments, music for propaganda, new music for bands, conducting, transcribing, etc."[7] To that end, she asked about musical skills, from arranging to composition, and included such practical questions as "Can you teach a band instrument?" Most composers—including Samuel Barber, John Cage, Elliott Carter, Aaron Copland, R. Nathaniel Dett, Morton Gould, Ernst Krenek, Richard Rodgers, William Schuman, and William Grant Still—answered that last question in the negative, though William Handy, Werner Janssen, and Earl Robinson said yes, Henry Cowell admitted he could but "not too well," and Arnold Schoenberg answered "I guess." However, in most of the composers' answers they emphasized their experience as arrangers and their compositions for bands, radio, and film. Reis's plan—which, in the end, was unsuccessful—was to use the responses to identify for music something akin to a national talent pool on which both military and civilian agencies could draw.[8] Her endeavor also highlights both the practical issues that musicians faced during the war and the complicated intersections between individuals and institutions, and between military and civilian contributions to the war effort.

Musicians in Uniform

It is a commonplace that war strengthens centralized bureaucracies and leaves the individual to find her or his way within (or despite) the institutional juggernaut. Nowhere was this more noticeable in the United States during World War II than in the military, whose ranks swelled from about 900,000 inductees in late 1941, by which point the draft had been in effect for a year, to over ten million by the end of 1945.[9] Like other men between the ages of eighteen and forty-five, able-bodied musicians—whether nationally known concert performers such as the pianist Eugene List or local musicians and teachers such as Haskell Harr, who had taught at the Vandercook School of Music in Chicago before being stationed at Camp Forrest in Tennessee—were liable to be drafted into military service.[10] The War Manpower Commission made no exception for musicians on the basis of their profession; neither musical performance nor composition was deemed vital enough for civilian morale to count as an alternative to military service. Health problems spared some musicians, such as Arthur Berger and Elliott Carter, from the draft; others, including Cage, Copland, and Menuhin, were classified as low priority because they were deemed the sole economic providers for their families. Most male musicians, however, were not spared military duty.

In contrast, female musicians could only volunteer for general military service: Betty Brandel, a member of the Tucson Symphony Orchestra, was commissioned as a major in the Women's Army Corps in 1943.[11] Specific musical duties in the armed forces, however, became available very rarely for women musicians. One such exception came in late 1943, when the Marine Corps Women's Reserve enlisted musicians for its only band. Stationed in Camp Lejeune, North Carolina, the forty-two players came from all over the United States and were led by Master Technical Sergeant Charlotte Louise Plummer, who in civilian life had conducted a school band in Portland, Oregon (Figure 1.2).[12] They played concerts for troops and war-industry workers, and they performed for military ceremonies such as "trooping the line."[13] And they were trailblazers for women in their new gender roles, just as much as women working in munitions factories or on the farm. But such high-profile assignments remained the exception for women in the armed forces. They were involved, if at all, mostly in choirs and on a voluntary basis. Women thus usually sang (though rarely played) in addition to their

FIGURE 1.2 Marine Corps Women's Reserve Band, conducted by Charlotte Plummer, in a concert at the Camp Theatre, Camp Lejeune, North Carolina, June 1944. Courtesy of the Archives and Special Collections, Library of the Marine Corps.

main, nonperforming duties, which could even include work as music copyists in military film units, like that performed by the four WAVES assigned to the U.S. Naval Photographic Science Laboratory in Washington, D.C.[14]

It would be as unreasonable to impute lofty motives to those who enlisted as it would be to attribute ignoble ones to those who waited for the draft or somehow managed to avoid it, although many in the last group demonstrated their need to compensate for the awkwardness of their position. Enlisting did have some advantages in terms of providing a modicum of influence over the enlistee's in-service assignment. Whether they were enlisted or were drafted, however, male conductors, percussionists, and wind or brass players had a decent shot at duty in a military band, whereas singers, string players, and pianists were a less obvious match for the institutionalized forms of music making in the armed forces (although they could be assigned as chaplain's assistants). Composers, on the other hand, and so-called classical composers in particular, found themselves confronted with the question of how their talents might be used, if at all, in the context of the American military.[15] The letters of the young African American composer Ulysses Kay tell of the problems he faced during his time at the band of the U.S. Naval Air Station in Rhode Island. He had enlisted in the navy on August 1, 1942, in order to beat the draft. At that time, musicians could still enlist specifically for band duty in the navy and the marine corps, whereas those drafted into the army had "no assurance of an inductee's being assigned to band duty."[16] As Kay explained to Aaron Copland, life in the navy was better than anything he could have gotten in the army. This came, however, at a price: he was primarily there as a saxophone player in the military concert band and as a pianist in the dance orchestra at Quonset Point. Yet, as he pointed out, he had not played the saxophone since high school and had to work hard to gain his dexterity back.[17] Performing in this navy band and completing the odd musical arrangement for that ensemble constituted his assignments over the next three years. While at first Kay claimed to enjoy this task, within the year he was mentioning his "very dull and seemingly useless" routine in letters.[18] Nevertheless, his duties eventually allowed him enough time and mental space to compose a number of works, such as the Quintet for Flute and Strings (1943) and his concert overture *Of New Horizons* (1944). The Sonatina for Violin and Piano was premièred in January 1943 on a "Program by Composers in the Armed Forces" that the League of Composers put on in the New York Public Library.[19] As Claire Reis recalled, the composer had been given leave to attend the première, after which he was "called to take a bow, and as he stood there in his Navy uniform, I thought what a poignant memory he would carry back to camp with him, and perhaps into battle."[20]

Of New Horizons also had its première in a concert dedicated to the armed forces, this time by the New York Philharmonic in Lewisohn Stadium and "attended by high-ranking Army and Navy Officials" as well as an audience of over nine thousand listeners who cheered Kay's new work.[21]

Whereas Ulysses Kay, like many other fledgling composers, including Cecil Effinger, Homer Keller, and Ellis Kohs, was able to draw on his musical skills by performing in a band and composing on the side, more seasoned and better-known composers such as Barber, Blitzstein, Copland, and Lehman Engel negotiated more prominent roles for themselves within the institutional context of the armed forces. From the outset, Copland was in discussions with the army about becoming a so-called music advisor, a specialist assignment created to implement musical policies formulated in Washington in the various camps in the continental United States and, increasingly, in the overseas war theaters. After the forty-two-year-old composer passed his physical "with flying colors," the paperwork started to wind its way through the bureaucracy. Copland's correspondence with Harold Spivacke, chief of the Music Division of the Library of Congress, reflects both the pitfalls of a large bureaucracy and the composer's individual concerns about the impact of military life on his art. Spivacke, a prominent musical administrator in the nation's capital, was at that time the chair of the Sub-Committee on Music of the Joint Army and Navy Committee on Welfare and Recreation, and he served as a key mediator between the country's musical community and the military.

Copland's chief concern was how to keep up his creative work. As he put it in a letter to William Schuman, "I hate like hell the idea of giving up composing—at least until New York is under attack."[22] On August 21, 1942, Copland brought this up in a letter to Spivacke when he sent in his application to become a Special Services officer: "As I told you on the phone, I contemplate the giving up of my composing activities with the greatest reluctance, but if I must be used in the war effort, I wish to be as useful as possible."[23] Spivacke responded reassuringly: "I admit that you will not have as much time for composing as you had in civilian life but I see no reason why you will have to give it up entirely. No matter what branch of the service you end up in, whether as a commissioned officer in the Army Specialist Corps or even as a buck private in the Infantry, there will be time for composing. It may be difficult but it will be important that you carry on."[24] Copland was reassured:

> Your letter cheered me up considerably—I mean the part about composers in the Army being given "time for composing." You can't imagine how right I hope you are. But I should warn you that "composing" to me means a private room with a piano and some consecutive time

for writing. (Unlike Beethoven and Hindemith I don't work in the fields.) If the Army can provide that, its set-up is even more intricate than I thought. Well anyway, I'm only too happy to take your word for it that army life and composing are not incompatible.[25]

But Spivacke then had to interject a note of reality:

I do not want you to get a false impression of the possibilities of composing while in the Army. It will be up to you to find the opportunity and facilities for composing. Please do not expect the Army to make any special arrangements for you, as I fear you will be disappointed. (Perhaps you had better start learning to compose on something portable like an accordion rather than rely on the pianos you will find in the camps. Some of those I have seen would produce a very peculiar harmony when an ordinary C major chord was played on them.) At any rate, you will certainly have a better chance of finding an opportunity to compose as an officer than you would as a private. I think you had better start preparing yourself for some very peculiar experiences no matter what happens.[26]

As this correspondence continued, Copland's papers went missing in their transfer from the Joint Army and Navy Committee on Welfare and Recreation to Special Services, and soon thereafter Copland was reclassified by the Draft Board as 3-A (deferred because of hardship to dependents).[27] He remained a civilian throughout the war but, as we shall see, found other ways to mobilize his craft as a composer.

Although the exchange between Copland and Spivacke ended up casting composition and army life as fundamentally at odds with each other, Barber and Blitzstein were able to have their composing designated a military activity. Both composers were released from other duties and assigned to compose a symphony, and both were later assigned to the Office of War Information so as to lend their expertise in modern music to its propaganda missions. Once drafted, Private Samuel Barber started out in the army, in September 1942, as a frustrated desk jockey in the Second Service Command of Special Services in New York, which allowed him to compose only at night.[28] One of his most popular works of that period, the *Commando March* for military band, was the result, and its première in May 1943 led to a highly successful series of performances and recordings. Barber became known nationwide as a composer in uniform, which helped his personal campaign to be assigned, as his military duty, the composition of a symphonic work related to the air force.

Although air combat had developed into an operative branch of the military in World War I, it came fully into its own during World War II. Reconfigured in June 1941 as the United States Army Air Forces, the newly unified and, by March 1942, autonomous branch of the army counted as the most modern element of the armed forces. The mystique and danger of aviation and air combat made it a favorite topic in the arts. Indeed, as early as on the eve of World War I, Claude Debussy declared that the "century of aeroplanes has a right to a music of its own."[29] In the interwar years, the worldwide fascination with flight grew with the feats of Amelia Earhart and Charles Lindbergh, the latter's crossing of the Atlantic commemorated among others by Weill and Bertolt Brecht in 1929 in the cantata *Der Lindberghflug*. As Barber put it in 1943, flight was a subject that is "of great fascination to the public and is being celebrated in all the arts."[30] It was therefore a logical, if not entirely disinterested, strategy on Barber's part to propose a major musical work on the theme.

Barber convinced army headquarters to transfer him, on August 30, 1943, to the army air forces with the assignment of composing a symphony. Between September 1943 and March 1944, he escaped the barracks and instead lived at home in Mount Kisco, New York, while developing his new work, then known as the "Flight Symphony." Aside from sending biweekly progress reports to a colonel at West Point, composing the symphony was all he was expected to do. Barber's letters speak with pride about the piece: as he explained to Sidney Homer, the first movement tried "to express the dynamism and excitement of flight," whereas the second, with its "lonely sort of folk-song melody for English horn," evoked a "solo flight at night." After the première, Barber was particularly proud that "pilots and A.F. men" responded to and therefore validated his work.[31] But Barber considered military life an obstacle to his creative work—"I cannot compose in this regimentation," he said—that needed to be worked around.[32] To escape the threatened return to the barracks on completing his symphony, he exploited his many social and professional connections and finally was transferred as a music advisor to the OWI Overseas Bureau in New York. There was certainly a degree of special pleading in his claim (a misleading one, we shall see in chapter 2) that he should continue to compose because this is "the first time the Army has allowed any serious music." Yet after his move to the OWI in May 1944, he took the business of arranging and recording music for the agency very seriously, even if he remained less unfettered than he might have wished: he wrote the *Capricorn Concerto* for the OWI but, as he explained to Aaron Copland, "under much pressure" from Daniel Saidenberg, the music director, who wanted the work performed and recorded.[33]

Whereas Barber's sometimes reluctant military service was the result of his having been drafted, Blitzstein enlisted on August 29, 1942: he had just been reclassified by the Draft Board as 1-A (available for unrestricted military service).[34] He was assigned almost immediately as an entertainment specialist with the Eighth Army Air Force.[35] Life in the service, Blitzstein wrote in 1942, was "exactly what I want, need for realization: the chance to do my own work, fused into the stream of the most terrifying events of our time, and right at the field of operations!"[36] After his month-long basic training at Bolling Field, just outside Washington, D.C., he was stationed in London, where from October 8, 1942, to May 22, 1945, he served in a number of capacities (Figure 1.3). According to his discharge papers, he composed "musical scores for concert, radio and film. Directed U.S. Army negro [*sic*] chorus. Directed music of American Broadcasting Station in Europe (OWI). Music director of Anglo-American film project. Wrote movie and radio script[s]."[37] Blitzstein was in his element in the pressure-cooker atmosphere of wartime London. The left-wing activist of the popular front had turned into a soldier in the democratic fight against Fascism, using his music

FIGURE I.3 Publicity still of Marc Blitzstein in London, 1943. With permission from the Wisconsin Center for Film and Theater Research.

passionately both against the enemy and in support of his own political and aesthetic agendas. Honed through his experience with the Federal Theatre Project and other left-wing causes in the previous decade, Blitzstein operated with ease inside the institutional context of the military and the OWI in London and was able to thrive with his projects, ranging from the composition of a major propaganda work, the *Airborne Symphony* (parallel to Barber's), to the advancement of the emancipation of African Americans.

Lehman Engel also brought his WPA experience to his military service. After enlisting in the navy, he was put in charge of the bands at Great Lakes Naval Station near Chicago, the main training facility for that branch's musicians. As Engel explained in a letter to Harold Spivacke, there was a "large music department" of about 125 men, "all professional musicians." Engel was mainly responsible for the sixty-eight-member concert band with whom he rehearsed "three times weekly for two concerts. The rest of my time is spent making arrangements."[38] These concerts took place in "a fine modern auditorium."[39] Once the band was up and running, its concerts became a magnet for renowned artists, from Vladimir Horowitz to Paul Robeson. The band's own repertoire ranged from arrangements of the "Prelude and Love-Death" from Richard Wagner's *Tristan und Isolde* to selections from George Gershwin's *Porgy and Bess*. Engel found two ways to incorporate the famous soloists into the programs. Usually, such musicians would perform their solo program as interpolations between band numbers: on July 16, 1943, Robeson sang to piano accompaniment excerpts from Mendelssohn's *Elijah* and Mussorgsky's *Boris Godunov*, songs by Roger Quilter, and arrangements of spirituals in between the band's performance of Richard Rodgers's *Slaughter on Tenth Avenue* (from the 1936 *On Your Toes*) and Tchaikovsky's *"1812" Overture*, among others. Sometimes, however, musicians would also appear together with the band: Yehudi Menuhin played Bach's E Major Violin Concerto (with Adolph Baller as continuo player on the piano) with a formation of the band designated the "U.S. Naval Training Station Orchestra." Rudolf Ganz, on the other hand, performed the first movement of a perennial favorite, Tchaikovsky's Piano Concerto in B-flat Minor, accompanied by the concert band in an arrangement by Dick Wilson.[40]

Engel's success as conductor, arranger, and concert manager did not go unnoticed, and by the spring of 1944 he found himself commissioned a lieutenant (junior grade) in Washington, D.C., to head the Music Division of the navy's Photographic Science Laboratory, where he worked on the production of training and propaganda films. As he later recalled, he and his musical collaborators worked under high pressure: "As soon as we completed the composing, arranging, and copying of a film score, the Navy Symphony

Orchestra, which contained some of the finest musicians in America, recorded it."[41] But even with all his film-music duties, Engel was able to write a number of concert works, some of which were clearly related to the performance opportunities his position had brought. He composed a Concerto for Viola and Orchestra for Emanuel Vardi, a well-known violist who was at that time a member of the U.S. Navy Band Symphony Orchestra.

Both the navy and the marine corps supported symphony orchestras in Washington, D.C., which during the war years played weekly concerts for the swelling ranks there of service personnel and government employees. But in contrast to the Marine Band Symphony Orchestra, which had been founded in 1899 and given regular concerts since the 1930s, the Navy Band Symphony Orchestra was a direct result of the influx of musicians into the armed forces. It was founded in 1942 by the band's leader, Lieutenant Charles Brendler, within a couple of months after Pearl Harbor. For performers such as the well-known violinist Oscar Shumsky (the orchestra's concertmaster), this became a perfect opportunity to turn war service into an extension of his civilian life. Like Ulysses Kay before him, Shumsky proactively enlisted in the navy in October 1942 in order to ensure that his military service would be musical (Figure 1.4). In addition to orchestra duty and playing in the U.S. Navy Band String Quartet, he appeared as a soloist both with the orchestra and elsewhere, playing Mendelssohn's Violin Concerto with the National Symphony Orchestra in June 1943 "by permission of the Navy Department."[42] As Ray Brown, the music critic for the *Washington Post*, explained to the readers of his column, the navy orchestra's sound was transformed "since the selective service brought many young and talented musicians into the personnel. The roster of musicians now contains the names of men who were formerly listed as members of several of our major symphony orchestras"[43]—Emanuel Vardi had played viola in the NBC Symphony Orchestra under Arturo Toscanini before enlisting in 1941, and Mason Jones, who joined the U.S. Marine Band, had been principal French horn with the Philadelphia Orchestra. Nor was Shumsky the only musician to have had a solo career before enlisting. Both the cellist Bernard Greenhouse and the pianist Earl Wild had performed as soloists with such top-ranked ensembles as the New York Philharmonic, the Baltimore Symphony Orchestra, and the NBC Symphony Orchestra (Figure 1.5).[44]

The Navy Symphony Orchestra's programs followed the well-trod path of mid-twentieth-century urban concert seasons. The majority of concerts consisted of an opening orchestral piece, a concerto, and a symphony, pieces almost always drawn from the long nineteenth century. Works by Johann Sebastian Bach were as rare as those by Roger Sessions. Special programs

FIGURE 1.4 Publicity photograph of Oscar Shumsky, concertmaster of the U.S. Navy Band Symphony Orchestra, in uniform (1943). Courtesy of the U.S. Navy Band.

included an all-Tchaikovsky concert on May 12, 1944 (with Shumsky's performance of the Violin Concerto, op. 35), and an "all American" one on January 12, 1945, in which Hugh O'Meager played his own Piano Concerto in B Minor, a work based on three poems by Walt Whitman.[45] If any bias can be detected in the repertoire, it would be for French music; included in this selection were such works as Hector Berlioz's *Harold en Italie* (with Vardi), César Franck's Symphony in D Minor, Claude Debussy's *Prélude à l'après-midi d'un faune*, and Maurice Ravel's *La valse* and *Rapsodie espagnole*. Even Igor Stravinsky's *Firebird Suite* was announced by its French title, *L'oiseau de feu*. German repertoire was still well represented, however, by everything from extracts from Wagner's *Parsifal* to the symphonies of Johannes Brahms.

Similarly, the U.S. Marine Band Symphony Orchestra held concert seasons that featured the familiar repertoire of contemporary symphony concerts, if with a slight twist. Music from Allied and American composers clearly took precedence, given the prominent link of the orchestra to the U.S. presidency. A concert in January 1942 started with the American Philip Dunn's 1924

FIGURE 1.5 The U.S. Navy Band Symphony Orchestra in 1943 at the Departmental Auditorium, Washington, D.C. The conductor is Lieutenant Charles Brendler. The pianist to the right is Earl Wild. Courtesy of the U.S. Navy Band.

Overture on Negro Themes—"a robust and vigorous work," according to the pre-publicity—followed by Joseph Haydn's Symphony no. 104 in D Major ("London"). Other works on the program were the British composer Arthur Hinton's *Three Orchestral Scenes from "Endymion,"* Tchaikovsky's *Romeo and Juliet* Overture, and Debussy's *Rapsodie pour clarinette et orchestre*, thus combining composition from (or about) Great Britain, France, Russia, and the United States.[46] Three months later, Captain William F. Santelman and his "brilliantly uniformed Marine musicians" presented a "concert of music of the Americas" in honor of "Pan-American Day" on which were represented Argentinian, Bolivian, Brazilian, Cuban, Ecuadoran, Mexican, Peruvian, and Uruguayan composers.[47] If France was the Allied country favored by Charles Brendler (conductor of the U.S. Navy Symphony Orchestra), Santelman emphasized compositions by Soviet composers, especially Prokofiev and Shostakovich, in his regular concert programs during the war years.

But performance opportunities for musicians in the two ensembles did not stop with the regular concert season and band duty. Vardi and Wild performed in Washington's National Gallery of Art in a chamber concert that included works by Brahms and Hindemith as well as arrangements for viola and piano of works by Frédéric Chopin, Girolamo Frescobaldi, and Benedetto Marcello. Vardi was also, with Shumsky, a member of the U.S. Navy String Quartet, which presented its first radio broadcast on February 14, 1943, with Antonín Dvořák's String Quartet in F Major, op. 96 (the "American"), and made its concert debut on April 11 at the National Gallery with Beethoven's String Quartet in F Minor, op. 95, next to "shorter works by Bridge, Hugo Wolf, Haydn, and Dvorak." At the same time, the Junior String Quartet of the Navy Band gave its debut with works by Haydn, Debussy, and Joaquín Turina.[48]

String quartets in the armed forces were not limited to the official ensembles of the U.S. Navy Band. On August 20, 1944, Isabel Morse Jones reported in the *Los Angeles Times* on the Santa Ana Army Air Force Base String Quartet, which "kept the soul of music alive for themselves and others." She then went on to inform her readers that the "orchestra of the A.A.F. directed by Eddie Dunstedter has many musicians of high standing. They include four concert masters, any of whom could take his place in any major orchestra of the United States, and they comprise the quartet. One is Bronislaw Gimpel, former concert master of the Los Angeles Philharmonic. Another is the violinist, James Getzoff, also from the Philharmonic. With these, and Edgar Lustgarten, cellist from Toscanini's N.B.C. Orchestra, and Louis Kievman, who played viola with the Musical Art Quartet, the unit in Santa Ana has produced a string quartet of the first rank."[49] Other quartets and chamber-music ensembles were formed for short periods at a time in the context of various bands in the armed forces, such as the string quartet comprising Ira Baker, Irving Nussbaum, Jascha Bernstein, and Julius Baker at Fort Dix (Figure 1.6).[50] Conversely, one professional quartet was able to enlist as a unit: all four members of the Manhattan String Quartet were assigned as pit musicians to Irving Berlin's hit show *This Is the Army*. After the show's successful run in the United States in the summer of 1942, the four quartet members joined the overseas unit sent to the United Kingdom. But as the violinist, Nathan Gottschalk, reported from Manchester, "I am happy to say that the quartet is still intact but only as part of the orchestra of the show."[51]

Whereas band duty was the most likely task assigned to drafted and enlisted professional musicians, some performers and composers chose (or were assigned) nonmusical responsibilities. The African American baritone William Veasey was motivated by his flight from the German troops across Belgium (where he had been performing at the Royal Opera House in Brussels) and France to join the army so as to get in "a few licks at the Germans and Japs."[52] The well-known American Indian concert singer

FIGURE 1.6 The Soldier String Quartet at Fort Dix, New Jersey (1943): Ira Baker, Irving Nussbaum, Jascha Bernstein, and Julius Baker. *Musical America* 63 (February 10, 1943): 7.

Ish-ti-Opi (Wesley Le Roy Robertson) became a Special Services officer with the rank of captain in the Eighth Air Force and was involved in intelligence and code work (Figure 1.7). While in Europe he sustained severe injuries that ended his musical career.[53] Another singer, the German-born bass Doda Conrad, enlisted in the army in May 1942, where he moved through the ranks from private to lieutenant, serving in war theaters from Algeria to Marseilles before becoming a member, in the summer of 1945, of the army's Monuments, Fine Arts, and Archives Division in Berlin.[54] The composer Ross Lee Finney also spent much of his service in Europe, where he became a high-ranking officer with the OSS and earned a Purple Heart for injuries sustained in France: his wartime letters to his family report about daily life during his European deployment but contain almost no reference to music.[55]

On the other hand, some performers in the armed forces ended up with very high-profile musical assignments. The most famous were, of course, two popular bandleaders, Glenn Miller (who led the Army Air Force Band until he was shot down over the English Channel in December 1944) and Artie Shaw (who enlisted in the navy to form a service band and toured the Pacific theater in 1943–44). But renowned performers of classical music could also

FIGURE I.7 The baritone Ish-ti-Opi (Captain Wesley Robertson) in uniform, 1943. He was "with the Eighth Air Force and the Eighth Bomber Command under the direction of Lieut. Gen. Ira C. Eaker, from whom he received a citation for 'outstanding services.'" *Musical Courier* (December 20, 1943): 22.

be assigned to musical duty outside the realm of bands. Military service developed into a major opportunity for the New York–based pianist Eugene List. The twenty-six-year-old had been drafted and was inducted into the army on March 1, 1942, starting out as a private in the Transportation Corps at the New York Port of Embarkation in Brooklyn.[56] He had just wowed audiences as a soloist in concerts with the New York Philharmonic, first with the première of Carlos Chávez's Piano Concerto on January 1, and then with the Schumann A Minor Concerto two days later. List's musical rise in the army reveals not only how one person negotiated his musical career within an unwieldy institution, but also how the military used his broad appeal in the world of classical music to present a wholesome and cultured face to the American public. Readers of the *New York Times* as well as of illustrated music journals such as *Musical America* and the *Musical Courier* could follow List's well-publicized exploits, including his romance with the violin prodigy Carroll Glenn. Their wedding was attended not only by the Who's Who of American music but also, as the *New York Times* reported, by fellow musicians from the army, including (then) Corporal Doda Conrad as one of the ushers.[57]

List concertized both within army camps and in civilian contexts, but, as Olin Downes pointed out in his review of List's performance of Rachmaninoff's Piano Concerto no. 2 in C Minor with the New York Philharmonic in June 1943, he did so "in the regulation uniform required." Furthermore, photographs of List in uniform, often with his wife, were liberally added to illustrate articles about the handsome pianist for American newspaper readers. Combined with the ubiquitous references to his military rank in articles and concert reviews, List served as a poster child for the contributions of a "musician-soldier" to the nation's morale. After a year with the Transportation Corps, during which he gave some concerts in New York, List became a member of the Special Service Office of his unit and could now focus officially on his performing. Newspaper reports took care to point out that he served as a magnet to attract his "fellow service men" to concerts of classical music: during yet another performance of the Rachmaninoff concerto at Carnegie Hall, some of the many soldiers attending "stood two rows deep at the rear of the hall."[58]

His army years offered a major boost to List's career. He was broadcast all over the United States and in the overseas theaters; his national and overseas concert tours were organized by the army and the USO; in the summer of 1944 he recorded Tchaikovsky's Piano Concerto no. 1 in B-flat Minor as a V-Disc for the army; and the next summer, a serendipitous set of circumstances made him the "unofficial court pianist" of the American president, when he played at a Sanssouci state dinner during the Potsdam Conference for Winston Churchill, Joseph Stalin, and Harry Truman. In April 1946 *Time* reported that List had played "five times at Potsdam" and after his army discharge "at two Truman dinners in Washington."[59] Even Hollywood called right after his return to civilian life and cast the eye-catching musician as the pianist-hero in the 1946 comedy *The Bachelor's Daughters*.

Performing for Victory

Eugene List may have been in uniform, but he was not alone in devoting his virtuoso talents to the war effort. After Pearl Harbor, numerous performers in the United States cast their music making as a form of war service. Like movie stars from Merle Oberon to Marlene Dietrich, famous musicians contributed their glamour and talent to raising funds for the cause. Concert performers and opera singers provided entertainment for troops and civilian war workers and even used their programs as a means of pro-Allies cultural diplomacy. They walked a tightrope between patriotic commitment and professional opportunism, for the increased need for both propaganda and entertainment brought new opportunities for musicians of all ranks. Women musicians found openings in orchestras and bands that had hitherto been closed to them because of prejudice against their gender.[60] Similarly, the war years cut off the international supply of musicians to the United States, so that all-American ensembles became a necessity that, in turn, was celebrated as a national and nationalist achievement. Olin Downes counted as a "blessing" the fact that the Metropolitan Opera engaged only American singers for its 1942–43 season: "Up to the present time the Metropolitan has imported its principal stars from overseas. This season there has not been a single importation from Europe."[61] As early as October 1939, *Newsweek* had published an article with the headline "War Expected to Make U.S. the World's Music Center": "Today, with Europe's musicians reaching for guns instead of violins and trumpets, with opera houses and concert halls dark in many foreign cities, the United States is expected to experience an even bigger music boom. Professional and trade leaders predict that the war may make America the world's music leader."[62] Indeed, a thriving culture of musical performance was presented as an indicator of the nation's superiority and was supported, to that end, by government agencies, civilian organizations, and the military.

This shifting focus on American achievement came at a price for some musicians, in particular those foreign performers whose careers had long been centered in the United States but who suddenly found themselves cast as adversaries. Audience favorites such as Lotte Lehmann and Ezio Pinza were declared enemy aliens, forced to register as such with the authorities and to ask for permission when traveling outside their places of residence. The *New York Times* reported that Lehmann, "Wagnerian soprano of the Metropolitan Opera Company, was one of the persons to call at the Foley Square Court house yesterday. She declared her intention of opening a concert tour with a trip to Raleigh, N.C., a week from Monday. As an Austrian citizen she had to fill out some twenty questionnaires, listing the points to be covered on her tour."[63] For many, being transformed into an "enemy alien" also shaped their interactions with colleagues and friends. Paul Hindemith and his wife felt that they had to warn a former pupil, now in the military, not "to say a word about any of your occupations": "we are now *registered aliens* and you know how many of them are suspect."[64] For some, especially musicians in exile from their home countries, the sudden change from displaced person to enemy alien was a difficult adjustment: Ernst Krenek's diaries tell of being "confounded by the discrimination against 'enemy aliens' which I feel as a personal injustice done to me."[65] Others tried to come up with ways to show their loyalty actively and openly. As early as 1940 Weill, for example, had come up with the idea of an "Alliance of Loyal-Alien Americans" with the stated objective of demonstrating their allegiance to the United States.[66]

Whoever could acquired American citizenship, but even naturalization did not always prevent persecution. Ezio Pinza had already received his first citizenship papers when he was arrested by the FBI under the suspicion of being a pro-Fascist sympathizer, probably as the result of what Pinza suspected was "an anonymous denunciation" by a "fellow bass."[67] The news was splashed across the front pages of the *New York Times* on March 13, 1942: "Ezio Pinza Seized as Enemy Alien; FBI Takes Singer to Ellis Island." Although exonerated in the end, Pinza was forced to spend almost three months in detention, together with 126 other interned New Yorkers. "Many of us," he recalled, "were bewildered and frightened, desperate for solace and despairing at our helplessness. Our misery was still further intensified by the untidiness to which we were reduced: all suspenders, belts, shoelaces and other objects that might help a would-be suicide had been taken away from us."[68] During Pinza's internment, fellow musicians and political leaders (including New York's mayor, Fiorello LaGuardia, and the prominent anti-Fascist publicist Carlo Tresca) interceded on his behalf so that, on June 4, he could be freed to return to his position as "first bass" at the Metropolitan Opera for the next season.[69] Nevertheless, the Pinza affair, following hard on Pearl Harbor, reflected the ever-present anxiety about a fifth column of enemy aliens and spies and the fear of an attack on mainland America, in those early months of the war: Alfred Hitchcock's movie *Saboteur*, for example, was released in April 1942, just over a month into Pinza's detention.

Even before Pearl Harbor, music's role in the expanding war in Europe had become a topic of broad interest for American music lovers. Regular reports on Myra Hess's free lunchtime concerts at the National Gallery in London praised their morale-boosting effect, while the continuation of concert life in Brussels in the face of the Nazi invasion was celebrated as a sign of courage, when "music lovers ignored the heavy bombardment and waited at the door of the Musée Royal in the mad hope that their daily musical food would be provided despite all catastrophe."[70] In the United States, musicians rallied to give benefit concerts in support of war-torn countries from China to Poland. In November 1939 Artur Rubinstein and Jan Kipura performed works by Chopin and Moniuszko in a sold-out Carnegie Hall, with the future OSS director William J. Donovan addressing the audience about the logistics of the Polish war relief effort.[71] Moreover, war-related musical activities in America between 1939 and 1941 united musicians and organizations whose political differences would otherwise have defied collaboration; this was a different and much more demanding situation than that of, say, support in the United States for the anti-Fascist cause in the Spanish Civil War from 1936 on. Just as the hawkish Donovan had contributed to the Polish war relief concert, so could an outspoken left-wing activist such as Blitzstein perform at a benefit in support of China.[72] Even when such activities were separated along political lines, they all shared a newfound commitment to using music to support the global struggle.

Therefore, when the United States entered the war in December 1941, the musical groundwork had already been laid, and music had been turned publicly into a "wartime weapon."[73] Just two months after Pearl Harbor, a letter to the nation by Eleanor Roosevelt, published in *Musical America*, exhorted her compatriots to continue making music, since it was "one of the finest flowerings of that free civilization which has come down to us from our liberty loving forefathers." She also described music as "a force for morale" (Figure 1.8).[74] The same month Fiorello La Guardia addressed America's musicians in his new position as director of the Office of Civilian Defense and complimented them for not waiting "to be told what to do for national defense. Thousands of them have already contributed substantially to the broad program of civilian defense."[75] The Victory Concerts initiated by the Juilliard School's Dean Ernest Hutcheson in February 1942 at the Metropolitan Museum were "patterned on those being given in London by Dame Myra Hess."[76] In January 1943 the fiftieth program in the series was presented to an audience of nineteen hundred listeners that "almost doubled the seating capacity of the hall."[77] Throughout the country there were benefit concerts aplenty, though not all were quite as openly political as the one advertised for March 18, 1942, at Carnegie Hall, in which "Artists of 16 Anti-Axis Lands" appeared in "a Music Festival of Allied Nations."[78] Often one or several famous musicians—Marian Anderson, Vladimir Horowitz, Lotte Lehmann, Yehudi Menuhin, Lily Pons, Arturo Toscanini—headlined these occasions to attract the largest possible audience; and sometimes special events, such as the concert in Carnegie Hall in June 1943 under the sponsorship of Crown Princess Martha of Norway celebrating the centenary of Edvard Grieg's birth, served to raise funds for specific national causes.[79] Throughout the war years, the fact that such performers aided either the American government (by selling war bonds) or Allied charities counted as a significant patriotic contribution by musicians to the national effort. Music's function was, so Hutcheson said, to "meet evil with a superior morale."[80]

Vol. LXII, No. 3

PRICE
$1.00

MUSICAL AMERICA

February 10, 1942

Founded in 1898 by JOHN C. FREUND

THE WHITE HOUSE
WASHINGTON

At all times music should be part of our
lives, and I think in times of strain, such as this
present period, it is more valuable than ever.

Music is one of the finest flowerings of that
free civilization which has come down to us from
our liberty loving forefathers, and we have come
to regard it as an essential of the heritage of
a country that has cherished the genius of the
great composers and the musical artists of all
lands and peoples.

Music is a force for morale, and it
contributes to the happiness and well-being of
the millions who turn to it for enjoyment, relaxation,
consolation and spiritual renewal. It should go on,
fulfilling its mission.

Eleanor Roosevelt

Music Should Go On!   A MESSAGE FROM
THE FIRST LADY

FIGURE 1.8 Eleanor Roosevelt, "Music Should Go On! A Message from the First Lady." *Musical America* 62 (February 10, 1942): [3].

Indeed, the slogan "music for morale" served as a two-fold justification for the performance of classical music during the war. On the one hand, it shared in the general task of entertaining the armed forces; on the other, its morale-boosting factor provided the added value of putting "better music than ever...within the reach of the multitudes who will need its divine solace in grave days to come."[81] For this reason, both the armed forces and civilian agencies put significant stock in presenting Western classical music to all its constituencies. Performers bought wholeheartedly into this dual strategy by adapting their repertoire and performance styles to their new audiences while simultaneously framing their music as spiritual sustenance. If Koussevitzky called for American musicians to become "new bards, new Orpheuses—inspiring, invigorating, ennobling and consoling," Jascha Heifetz chose a far more pragmatic metaphor when he said about Bach's works for solo violin that "in musical language this is spinach. Whether you like it or not—it's good for you."[82] In particular, the successful presentation of classical music to the whole spectrum of servicemen (and -women) in the context of USO tours became a badge of honor for musicians engaged in the more official duty of war entertainment.

Although the USO was a civilian agency, its activities were inextricably intertwined with the American military. Chartered in February 1941, it replaced the diverse and often competing efforts of six agencies (including the YMCA and the National Jewish Welfare Board) that performed morale-boosting work for the armed forces after the reinstatement of the draft in 1940. Perhaps the most visible pursuits of the USO were their entertainment offerings, which were managed by a separate branch within the organization. This entity, USO–Camp Shows, was founded in October 1941 "to provide theatrical and concert entertainment on military and naval reservations, posts and stations."[83] By the end of the war, thousands of entertainers had made their way courtesy of the USO across the United States and in overseas war theaters to perform in military camps and hospitals. Organized in so-called units, performers were usually grouped together to maximize the entertainment value of their offerings. The predominantly classical Unit #79, for instance, combined seven artists who presented a varied program of "the vocal, instrumental, and saltatorial" (as one publicity text characterized them) offerings of "the finest music of great composers, in addition to the best in modern music and dance." Starring the Spanish dancer Phyllis Olivia and the "world's greatest saxophone player, Sigurd Rascher," the unit performed as the Cavalcade of Music.[84] Other musicians in this group included the cellist Signe Sandstrom, the pianist Cynthia Earl, and the tenor Sergei Radamsky.

Unit #79 was one of a number of classical groups managed by the concert division of USO–Camp Shows, created in the fall of 1942 under the direction of Gino Baldini, a concert manager from New York.[85] As the unit's composition suggests (despite the publicity hyperbole), and typical of USO camp shows in general, real stars were the exception rather than the rule: the USO president declared in 1945 that "98 percent of the troupers are the 'little people.'"[86] For these regular performers, the USO provided steady and well-paid employment with wages that were "union scale and even above."[87] Indeed, the war was a boon for rank-and-file musical (and theatrical) professionals who in the 1930s had suffered severely from the pressures of the Great Depression and from the inroads of the new broadcasting and recording industries. As the military-industrial complex was to discover, albeit on a far greater scale, war was good for business. Moreover, the demand for female entertainers meant that the USO circuits offered increased concert opportunities for numerous female musicians—not just in the famous all-girl bands whose deployment gave women the opportunity to play jazz for the first time in venues and before audiences comparable to those usually reserved for male entertainers, but also for classical pianists, violinists, and singers who toured nationally and overseas. To emphasize the intrinsic value of concert music in its own right, however, the USO and other commentators were quick to point out that soldiers' enjoyment of classical music was not linked solely to the sex of the performer, however appealing that might be. A report about Unit #275 (Figure 1.9) stressed the fact that one concert during their tour of the southwestern Pacific had soldiers sitting on the "jagged sharp edges of the coral reef" during a program of arias, chamber music,

FIGURE 1.9 "Members of Concert Unit No. 275 in Their Rough and Tumble Traveling Attire. (Left to Right) Ralph Lear, tenor; Leah Effenbach, pianist; Ruth Terry, contralto; Ann Buckley, soprano; and Dolf Swing, bass-baritone." *Musical America* 65 (February 10, 1945): 280.

and some lighter fare. Leah Effenbach, the unit's pianist, pointed out that their successful program consisted of "good music that was familiar."[88] The commentator then emphasized that it was "extremely unlikely that even GIs who hadn't seen a white woman in 16 or 18 months, would sit for an hour and a half on anything so uncomfortable as coral rock, if they hadn't been attracted by the music as well as by the unaccustomed sight of three women in evening dress."[89]

Similarly, Chaplain Theodore B. Mitzner reported from an advanced fighter base in the South Pacific about Unit #223 that featured (alongside the baritone Frank Richards) three female musicians: the pianist Loreland Kortkamp, the violinist Rena Robbins, and the cellist Marsha Barbour. Mitzner wrote that the "program of semi-classical and modern music was well selected and splendidly performed. Many of the men agreed it was refreshing relief from the usual type of program that has been coming to this Base." Moreover, "Any charming American girl looks mighty good to men overseas, but it is a mistaken notion that refinement and quality of accomplishment are not appreciated in those who take part in the shows that are sent out here."[90] Yet, as Sherrie Tucker has pointed out, women performers in the service of the USO found themselves in a dilemma: on the one hand, they stood for the all-American "good girl" whose idealized image formed part of the national mythology; while on the other, women's patriotic obligations as entertainers without question encompassed some form of "comfort" for those "all-American boys" laying their lives on the line for their protection.[91] Given the cultural cachet of classical music, however, female concert performers seem to have encountered expectations rather different from those faced by musicians in jazz bands. As one seaman put it in the case of (classical) Unit #368, it was the women's "friendly, wholesome personalities" and enthusiasm that "added up to the typical American girl."[92] This unit consisted of five female performers whose music, according to the same seaman, touched everyone: "As Miss MacNeill sang 'Ave Maria,' accompanied by Miss Mitchell on the electric organ and Mrs. Chapman on the violin, every heart and mind was flooded with the warmth and tenderness of her soft, clear voice." Instead of emphasizing the (sexual) attraction of the female entertainers, the surviving documents about women musicians in the classical domain focused on a different aspect of feminine gendered behavior: that of emotional nurture.

It was not a foregone conclusion that performers of concert music would become so important a part of the USO enterprise; on the contrary, some officials at the USO doubted that "our drafted men would appreciate the singing of classical arias by an operatic star" and sought to limit musical offerings to popular entertainment.[93] One memo to Colonel Marvin Young (Special Services Division) put it quite bluntly: "With the exception of Marian Anderson, Jascha Heifetz and people of that caliber, I do not recommend offering concert people to posts.... Women might be more acceptable (because they are women), but men would not be wanted." To his credit, Young disagreed entirely: "I think we should encourage more use of concert artists."[94] Indeed, it seems that the demand among the troops for performances of classical music was so strong that some military companies started to contract directly with concert artists, bypassing the USO, because the organization "does not send them classical music and representative concert artists for which they are 'starved.'"[95] One reason for the interest in classical music was diagnosed as the draft's having brought a large cross-section of the male population into the armed forces, including those music lovers whose tastes ran to concert music and opera; therefore, it was paramount to provide "music of the highest quality to that small percentage of servicemen...who needed it badly."[96] But in keeping with the ideologies of cultural hierarchy still prevalent in the 1940s, classical music was also cast as a mighty force for moral and emotional uplift that by its intrinsic power could affect listeners across all social and educational strata, even the seaman from the Bronx who famously commented on Yehudi Menuhin, "Jeez! Dat guy c'n do more wit' a G-string dan Gypsy Rose Lee!"[97]

Such musical prowess could be harnessed also for political ends. After a USO tour that took him to the United Kingdom, Menuhin advocated the need for famous American artists being sent more often to the troops deployed overseas: "This is a spiritual war," the violinist declared, "which means that our troops, like the British, are very serious-minded these days.... They would like to hear Marian Anderson and Horowitz and similar artists."[98] If for Menuhin the presence of such performers was vital on a transcendental level, the journalist Elmer A. Carter invested "eminent artists" with political capital in the African American civil rights struggle. Writing for the prominent African American newspaper the *New York Amsterdam News*, he saw the potential USO tours abroad of "a great Negro artist such as Marian Anderson or Roland Hayes or Dorothy Maynor" as contributing "so much to give the Negro soldier that sense of pride and loyalty which repeated humiliation, the inevitable consequence of discrimination, tends to rob him of. The presence of artists such as these would have a salutary effect on America's white soldiers too, many of whom have never heard of or seen a great white concert artist let alone a Negro."[99] During the war years, the USO increased its concert offerings by African American performers to both integrated and segregated military bases. Dorothy Maynor was much in demand when the

Concert Division of USO–Camp Shows organized a series of recitals in the United States in the fall of 1943. Marian Anderson, however, declined to perform under the auspices of the USO so as to retain control over her dignity as much as over her performance venues, even though she sang for African American troops in, for example, Tuskegee.

One prominent USO music advisor active in Tuskegee who had been hired "to soothe ruffled Negro feelings" found that his musical activities contributed to calming "Negro–white relationships" in Alabama.[100] The famous African American composer, conductor, and pianist R. Nathaniel Dett was among the first seven USO music advisors hired by Raymond Kendall in February 1943. In an article that celebrates music as a "potent weapon against race hate," Alfred Smith tells the story of Dett's USO achievements, where "Whites and Negroes flocked to his community sings, concerts, and lectures, sitting completely intermingled and crowded together, unmindful of the southern traditions. They sang together, listened together, played together."[101] Just as Elmer Carter saw eminent concert artists such as Maynor and Hayes as ambassadors for African American musical achievements across the racial divide in the United States, so Dett considered music an art that could make "race prejudice and antagonisms vanish miraculously." That power of music to speak for his ethnic group, he said, was reason to take up his USO duties, even though he had just resigned from his position as musical director at Bennett College (in Greensboro, North Carolina) to gain more time to compose. "I was spurred on . . . by knowledge that while Catholics and Jews are specifically represented in the USO, Negroes have only incidental representation through the composite organizations." Soon thereafter, on October 2, 1943, Dett died of a heart attack (just short of his sixty-first birthday) while on duty at a USO clubhouse at Fort Custer in Michigan; his dream of fostering greater visibility for African American concert music while contributing to the war effort as a USO music advisor and conductor died with him. Here a prominent African American musician had engaged with the USO not so much as a concert performer (as most musicians would do), but as a cultural mediator with a powerful civil agenda, although the outcome remained mixed at best.

Like their counterparts in the movie industry, the more famous concert artists donated their services to the USO and performed, sometimes for months in a row, without payment and under harsh conditions. Many sang and played in the continental United States, but a surprising number of them also faced the dangers of war zones around the globe. Though often directly in harm's way on the battlefield, performers such as Menuhin, Heifetz, Isaac Stern, Nelson Eddy, and Lily Pons traveled for the USO into "combat areas, right behind the front lines."[102] Their exploits found their way into both contemporary newspaper reports and later (auto-)biographies, where they read like fabulous adventure stories starring the brilliant performers as intrepid heroes and heroines. Yet even when these were cast as blatant self-promotion after the fact, most of these musicians suffered real physical hardships during their deployment and risked their health and sometimes their lives in their musical contributions to the war effort: Menuhin, for example, was in a plane crash, though he walked away unharmed.[103] However, none of the concert artists suffered the fate of musicians from other branches of USO entertainment who were killed or severely injured during their service, including the Broadway stars Tamara Dreisen and Jane Froman.[104]

As the press releases and official newsreels show, the apparent self-promotion of musical stars on USO assignment was, in effect, a joint effort that involved not only private press agents hired by the performers, but also the USO itself, in a mutually beneficial arrangement.[105] These artists appeared patriotic to the American public, and the USO accrued prestige and support from the reflected glamour. Not everyone agreed, however, with this approach; one irate lieutenant colonel assured a military colleague that "every effort is made by the Entertainment Section of the Special Services Division to minimize the amount of personal publicity received or sought by individual performers." He lamented the fact that even his military colleagues in the War Department and the combat zones overseas were complicit in this exploitation of war service for personal gain; it was unfortunate that "the most important guest stars who offer themselves for these tours and who are most eagerly desired by the men, are the greatest offenders in the matter of publicity."[106] The frustration of the memo writer is palpable when he contrasts the stars with regular performers: "Such offenses among minor entertainers rarely arise—because they are less newsworthy—and can be more readily suppressed—because they are under the financial control of USO–Camp Shows, Inc." He admits, however, that the GIs would rebel if the military stopped accepting the "services of great and newsworthy stars who are the principal offenders but who are also the greatest morale boosters," or if one were to turn these "and all similar breaches of oath to the Judge Advocate General for action." Performers certainly had to sign an oath of secrecy before starting their tours, but a mere lieutenant colonel was not going to be able to hold them to it.

The notion of the arts and the military having a common purpose in their fight against the barbarian hordes of both east and west was a powerful one. In 1944 Isaac Stern wrote in a private letter from his USO tour in the Pacific that he was amazed at "the way the idea of music and the value of music in war is [*sic*] so superbly integrated with the war effort here."[107] Yet his private comment resonated publicly: readers of such magazines as *Musical America* and the *Musical Courier* were offered richly illustrated stories, the content of which often closely matched USO press releases, with pictures coming from official sources and even the military itself.[108] The members of Unit #264, headlined by Isaac Stern and Frederick Jagel, are pictured in their USO uniforms (and one evening dress) just before one of their performances in the South Pacific (Figure 1.10); Yehudi Menuhin is seen as a cultural ambassador when learning from a Chinese fighter pilot how to play the *jinghu*, a two-stringed Chinese fiddle (Figure 1.11); and GIs at Fort Monmouth, in New Jersey, flocked to hear Albert Spalding (Figure 1.12).

The ways in which individual agendas and institutional needs intertwined varied from case to case. Menuhin performed tirelessly for the troops both under the auspices of the USO and independently whenever his concertizing took him in the vicinity of an army or navy post. His own reasons might

FIGURE 1.10 "'Unit 264' as the Artists Are Classified Pauses for a Picture. (Left to Right) Isaac Stern, Alexander Zakin, Frederick Jagel, Polyna Stoska and Robert Weede." *Musical America* 64 (August 1944): 9.

FIGURE 1.11 "Yehudi Menuhin has a lesson on the 'Hu Chin,' or Chinese violin, after appearing in a concert for American and Chinese flyers at Thunderbird field in Arizona. Cadet Hsi Kung Huang is instructing the eminent virtuoso." *Musical Courier* (February 1, 1943): 10.

FIGURE 1.12 "Albert Spalding Plays at Fort Monmouth." *Musical America* 64 (February 10, 1944): 19.

have been a complex mixture of feelings of patriotic zeal, civic responsibility, and guilt over not having been drafted despite his excellent health. As one journalist put it when Menuhin and his pianist, Adolph Baller (designated as Unit #222), spent time in the Aleutians from March 13 to April 11, 1944: "For Menuhin, it took courage to expose his obvious 27-year-oldness to draft-conscious men who, for the most part, have not seen their families for two years or more." Yet the journalist was quick to assure his readers that Menuhin's "complete mastery of his instrument, the awe of his approach, his apparent ease and 'stage presence' combined successfully to combat any snide attitude his audiences might have brought with them."[109] By this point, Menuhin was a veteran at entertaining the armed forces with a repertoire that included not only that all-time favorite, Schubert's *Ave Maria*, but also works by composers ranging from Bach to Kreisler. In a letter to his father-in-law from mid-1942, the violinist reflected that playing for soldiers had given him something that he had not known before: thanks to these performances, he had finally come to know his "American brother" and his own generation. It is a poignant remark from a Jewish musician and former child prodigy long cloistered within a virtuoso career. Concertizing in this environment was an experience in immediacy, one unobstructed by the usual "concert-like ceremonial."[110] In retrospect, Menuhin credited his years playing the army bases with having "cracked open many inhibitions" through the "rigors of traveling, the masculine free-and-easiness."[111] His fellow concert artists, from Isaac Stern to Nelson Eddy, felt similar satisfaction at proving themselves in the masculine world of the military. Others noted the benefits of adding "prestige to the profession, which has so far been outstripped by the film and radio industries in this particular."[112]

Few concert artists so enhanced the image of classical music in the USO as Lily Pons, the glamorous French coloratura soprano who had made the United States her home since the early 1930s. She had wowed American audiences not only on the stage of the Met, but also in a number of Hollywood movies such as *I Dream Too Much* (1935), where she played the lead opposite Henry Fonda. Even before Pearl Harbor, the singer was active in supporting her native France through benefit concerts and publicity appearances. As soon as the United States entered the war, Pons was photographed selling war bonds in the Met during intermission, and she performed frequently for the Armed Forces Radio Service with repertoire that ranged from Henri Duparc's *Chanson triste* to one of her signature pieces, Gilda's "Caro nome" from Giuseppe Verdi's *Rigoletto*. In May 1944 Pons and her husband, the equally famous Russian-born conductor Andre Kostelanetz, embarked on a much-publicized USO tour to the Allied fronts in Africa and the Persian Gulf

(Figure 1.13). They left on May 8, 1944, and returned, after a little more than three months of travel, on August 16. Their programs clearly aimed at representing Allied inclusiveness. Besides her signature coloratura arias, Pons performed British and Latin American music, while Kostelanetz conducted his arrangements of popular Red Army songs such as "Polyushko Polye" (Meadowland) and popular American compositions (including Gershwin's *Rhapsody in Blue*). One of their concerts was given in Iran for the Soviet troops. In the audience was Lev Knipper, the composer of "Meadowland," and that concert inspired him to write a Russian song for Pons titled "Song of a Young Iranian Girl." This musical goodwill exchange was, of course, exploited immediately in a radio broadcast for the U.S. public and armed forces.[113]

FIGURE 1.13 Lily Pons (soprano), Frank Versacchi (flute), and Andre Kostelanetz (conductor) in Teheran, June 1944. Courtesy of the Andre Kostelanetz Estate. The inscription above the stage, in Russian, reads "Трудящиеся всех стран соединяйтесь для борьбы против немецко-фашистских захватчиков!" (Trudiashchiesia vsekh stran soediniaites' dlia bor'by protiv nemetsko-fashistskikh zakhvatchikov!), which translates as, "Workers of all nations unite in the battle against the German Fascist aggressors!" I am grateful to Kevin Bartig for his help with this text.

The pair went on a second, even longer USO tour in December 1944 that took them from India, Burma, and China to Italy and France, and finally even to occupied Germany in April 1945. A press release after their return summed up their achievements: "Their first concert on this tour was given on Christmas Eve in Calcutta, India and their last concert before returning to the United States occurred in the Paris Opera House with the U.S. Army band providing orchestral accompaniment.... Miss Pons and Mr. Kostelanetz estimate they have entertained more than two million GIs on this trip.... The Kostelanetzes have traveled by plane, jeep, tank, automobile, carriage, and by boat. A bomb inscribed by the musical couple was dutifully dropped on the Japs in Burma" (Figure 1.14).[114] Kostelanetz's travel diary reveals what the two artists wrote: "Lily and I autographed a 500 pound bomb with an inscription, 'Greetings to Japan.' I am sure that it was delivered speedily and accurately."[115] Or rather—as he wrote to his brother Boris—he hoped "it

FIGURE I.14 In the absence of a photograph from Burma, this U.S. government still presents Lily Pons signing a "152-mm. brass shell case, the longest of its kind and the first made in the U.S. for the differently calibered guns of the French Navy, as a gesture of Godspeed on its future missions against the enemy of the United Nations." National Archives (111-SC-20305).

blasted the hell out of the Japs."[116] The Japanese were not the only ones at the receiving end of the couple's enmity. When she crossed into Germany on the heels of the invading American troops, Pons "leaned out of the car and spat on the first foot of this enemy territory."[117] Kostelanetz himself shared these sentiments when he reported to his brother: "Now that we are deep in Germany, we are even more pleased with the devastation—most cities are level with the ground or at least not habitable" (Figure 1.15).[118]

Nevertheless, the reports about the pair's exploits, their letters home, and their travel notes show a more complex set of motives behind their unquestionably strong commitment to serving the American armed forces. For Kostelanetz, who had fled the Russian revolution in 1922, the USO tours were a substitute for combat duty: by the time he and Pons started their tours, the conductor was too old to enlist. He pushed for their musical

FIGURE 1.15 Lily Pons and Andre Kostelanetz in Cologne, March 1945. Courtesy of the Andre Kostelanetz Estate.

entertainment to be as close to battle zones as possible, and his letters and diaries are replete with references to his direct (albeit musical) involvement with combat troops. He reported to his brother that such troops were "great audiences" and that "to see your public in full battle regalia is an amazing sight."[119] At times the musical soundscape was invaded by that of battle, whether of bombers taking off airstrips in India and Burma or anti-aircraft cannons in Germany, which provided "a reasonable replica of the bass drums in the most unexpected moments during the concert."[120]

For Kostelanetz and Pons, the concerts presented a unique opportunity to make a difference through music. Kostelanetz reported from Iran to members of his CBS orchestra that anyone "who sees and hears the rapt attention and wild enthusiasm of our audiences will realize what music means to our fighting men."[121] Pons marveled at the fact "that these vast audiences of fighting men, many of whom have never listened to a coloratura soprano, sit so intently and reverently as I sing."[122] Kostelanetz found it particularly satisfying to be playing for the members of the 20th Bomber Command in India, who joined the concert after long missions and made "some of the most appreciative listeners.... The expression on the faces of the fliers, who this very day faced the maximum of dangers, is a study and inspiration. Rapt, smiling and highly attentive."[123] In a set of diary notes scribbled during the tour, the conductor observed that "music and good music is appreciated by [the] soldiers. When they were surrounded by enemy in Burma, [the soldiers] wore out the record (most requested) of *Peter and the Wolf*. Listening to BBC from London and quiet music."[124] Moreover, both Pons and Kostelanetz took pride in the fact that their accompanying musicians were active fighters, especially in the Pacific theater. Their letters brag that their assistant conductor (and pilot) Lieutenant Don Taylor had over three hundred combat hours, and that the orchestra was made up of pilots, copilots, navigators, and gunners. On the tour, an upright piano traveled with the musicians in the plane's bomb bay.[125] Pons and Kostelanetz themselves thus became crucial members of the armed forces, their music making a special form of military support, keeping the minds and souls of the troops in shape just as a ground crew would service the bombers that flew into battle. In a published commentary in 1944, after his return from Africa and the Persian Gulf, Kostelanetz contrasted the calming, enjoyable, and therapeutic effects of their music with the apparently less effective forms of jive and jazz—clearly supporting highbrow prejudices about the inherent superiority of classical music.[126] For Pons and Kostelanetz, a concert artist's contribution to the war effort could thus become an educational, uplifting, and even heroic undertaking, not only because of their daily encounter with the rough conditions on tour but also in terms of their extraordinary musical feats: daily concerts for weeks in a row in the often unforgiving climates took their toll especially on the forty-six-year-old diva, who prided herself on performing to the same standards for the soldiers as she would in Carnegie Hall.

Though less fraught with danger, troop entertainment in the continental United States also counted as a vital contribution toward keeping morale up among service personnel. Again, famous concert artists competed with Broadway entertainers and film stars in their artistic patriotism by performing for free across the nation. Some areas, such as the camps around New York, Chicago, and Los Angeles, were better served than others on account of their proximity to major concert venues. Fort Monmouth in New Jersey was located just across Raritan Bay from New York City and could be easily reached by entertainers who were either visiting the metropolis or based there. The classical concerts given there from February to May 1943 reveal a series that would not have been out of place at Carnegie Hall (Table 1.1). The importance of Horowitz's appearance at the camp (May 25) can also be gauged by the telegrams from Fort Monmouth requesting that a theater show be canceled to allow the famous pianist's concert.[127] Not surprisingly, the local USO representative sent a glowing report: "To comment on this particular concert would be gilding the lily; suffice to say that this was an outstanding and magnificent musical event, at which the response ran extremely high."[128] The auditorium was filled to its 1040-seat capacity, with hundreds of servicemen taking advantage of standing room. Other stars could count on similar numbers: on May 20, twelve hundred listeners

TABLE 1.1   USO Concerts at Fort Monmouth, New Jersey, Spring 1943[129]

February 15	New York Philharmonic Orchestra, conducted by John Barbirolli
February 23	John Charles Thomas (baritone), Irra Petina (soprano), Carroll Hollister (accompanist)
March 11	Richard Binelli (baritone), Dorothy Kirsten (soprano), Nathan Milstein (violinist), Henry Jackson (accompanist), Max Lenner (accompanist)
April 1	Ballet Russe de Monte Carlo
April 16	NBC Television Opera (dir. Luigi Rossini), performing *Pagliacci* [in costume but without scenery]
May 4	Winifred Heidt (soprano), Walter Cassel (tenor), Emanuel List (bass), James Quillian (accompanist), Paul Berl (accompanist)
May 20	Lawrence Tibbett (baritone), Stewart Wille (accompanist)
May 25	Vladimir Horowitz, performing with the Fort Monmouth Signal Corps Symphony Orchestra under Thor Johnson

enjoyed Lawrence Tibbett's presentation of mostly operatic arias. Even less well-known artists such as Walter Cassel, Winifred Heidt, and Emanuel List (May 4) commanded a respectable audience of nine hundred, the smallest crowd at any one of these classical concerts; most of them were filled beyond capacity—a large number who showed up on February 15 for a concert by the New York Philharmonic Orchestra had to be turned away at the doors. The Ballet Russe de Monte Carlo's performance of Copland's *Rodeo* (April 1) was such a highlight that the local USO officer judged it "highly desirable to arrange for many future appearances."[130] Whether or not the glowing reports back to USO headquarters embellished the positive reception of the concerts, at least in terms of numbers they proved a significant success.

If performing for service personnel, charities, and (we shall see) war workers in factories was perhaps the most obvious war contribution of concert artists, their responses to events can also be gauged by their musical choices for more regular concert presentations. Contrary to what one might expect, they tended to feature the same repertoire as they had during the 1930s: a significant portion of Germanic music from the long nineteenth century, compositions from other European countries, and a small percentage of American works. These programs were far more ecumenical than was common on either side in Europe and included music from both Allied and Axis sources. But as we shall see in chapter 2, this rather traditional Eurocentrism with its emphasis on German and Italian music could also be used to score significant political points in U.S. propaganda by demonstrating an ability to rise above national enmities in matters of culture. A few concerts were dedicated entirely to politically inspired programs, as for example when, in March 1942, the Detroit Symphony Orchestra presented a "Festival of Allied Music."[131] More frequently, orchestras turned to American works to express patriotic commitment. After Pearl Harbor, Hans Kindler, the conductor of the National Symphony Orchestra in Washington, D.C., announced at the beginning of each season how many and which American works would be performed.[132] A particularly newsworthy event was Toscanini's decision to conduct his first all-American program on November 1, 1942, with Charles Martin Loeffler's tone poem *Memories of My Childhood*, Paul Creston's Choric Dance no. 2, Morton Gould's *A Lincoln Legend*, and George Gershwin's *Rhapsody in Blue* with Earl Wild as the soloist.[133] Few conductors in the United States had such strong anti-Fascist credentials as Toscanini, which made his gesture all the more powerful.[134] Gershwin's *Rhapsody in Blue*, the keystone of the program, was also—as Olin Downes noted—proof of Toscanini's full commitment to American culture, for his performance was fit to be judged by "the curious music-lovers of the nations, not only symphonists but jitterbugs and musical American-firsters," as so successful as if the maestro had "spent his life with the denizens of Tin Pan Alley."[135] Other newspapers raved about "Hepcat" Toscanini having turned the NBC Symphony Orchestra into "Symphonic 'Jivesters.'"[136] Such enthusiasm over Toscanini's outstanding performance might also indicate, however, that his record in this respect was rather dismal in terms of his (all-too-brief) conversion to American music.

It is, of course, illuminating that Downes and, for that matter, Toscanini still felt it necessary to make the point. It was a strength to be exploited, and a weakness to be counteracted, that of all performers in the United States, it was the famous and usually foreign-born conductors of the major symphony orchestras who were perhaps the most influential. Eugene Goossens (born in England), Otto Klemperer (from the "safe" Silesian region of Germany), Andre Kostelanetz and Serge Koussevitzky (Russia), Pierre Monteux (France), Eugene Ormandy and Fritz Reiner (Hungary), Leopold Stokowski (England, although he claimed Poland), Toscanini (Italy), and Bruno Walter (Germany, but a Jewish exile)—the low proportion of Germans was no doubt a convenience—had become the arbiters of symphonic taste in the nation.[137] They did so not just by means of the prestigious orchestras under their baton, but also because of their influence over, and even manipulation of, the broadcast media. That they were aware of their roles can be seen in a number of ways, including their presentation of music in the service of the war effort. Stokowski no doubt had his tongue in his cheek when he suggested privately to Goddard Lieberson, of Columbia Records, that Lieberson learn to play that all-American instrument the alto saxophone so that he might single-handedly "win the war with it. When the Germans and Japanese hear your saxophone, they will be so charmed, they will lose all desire to kill anyone, and a statue will be erected to you in Central Park, disguised as Orpheus with his lute."[138] But these conductors, like their fellow musicians, set great store by the orphic powers of music and contributed through performance for charities and military by their prestigious ensembles. A visit to an army camp by the New York Philharmonic or Philadelphia Orchestra counted among the highlights of any USO-sponsored performance series. During the war years, however, conductors could do still more to push a national agenda: such broadly publicized events as the U.S. première of Shostakovich's Seventh Symphony—for which several conductors competed, only to be beaten out by Toscanini—were instrumentalized as highly visible gestures of cultural diplomacy by the American press and propaganda agencies.[139] Yet it was not just the performance of music by the Soviets and other Allies that fit the agenda of a vital musical life. One soldier exhorted Koussevitzky to preserve the whole range of concert music for the sake of the fighting men when he wrote to the conductor in April 1942 that it was "good to know that we have men who still uphold our culture and our treasured progress of civilization."[140]

This "progress of civilization" in the United States prompted a number of star conductors to include, commission, and perform new music by American and Allied composers. Among the most active was certainly Koussevitzky, who in wartime fostered a large number of symphonic compositions by such composers as Copland, Harris, Martinů, Schuman, and Stravinsky. But if Koussevitzky tended to leave issues of genre and style to the composer's wishes, other conductors took a stronger hand. Copland's *Fanfare for the Common Man* was composed for a series of patriotic fanfares commissioned by Eugene Goossens in August 1942 from a number of well-known composers from both the United States—for example, Roy Harris, Walter Piston, and Virgil Thomson—and other Allied nations, such as Darius Milhaud and Martinů. They were to be "stirring and significant contributions to the war effort," and Goossens himself suggested such possible titles as "A Fanfare for Soldiers" and "A Fanfare for Airmen."[141]

Kostelanetz was perhaps the first conductor to respond to Pearl Harbor by commissioning, on December 18, 1941, his series of musical portraits "of some outstanding Americans" from Copland, Thomson, and Jerome Kern.[142] While Copland and Kern chose two key figures of the Civil War period—Abraham Lincoln and Mark Twain—Thomson settled on two contemporaries: the mayor of New York, Fiorello LaGuardia, and (eventually) the writer and journalist Dorothy Thompson. In order to facilitate the personal "sittings" of Thomson's subjects (on which the composer insisted), Kostelanetz interceded with the mayor on his behalf. His letter to LaGuardia, written on December 30, 1941, is revealing for its eloquent defense of newly commissioned music as a contribution to the war effort by keeping "great American patriots" in the minds of the "great mass of American people." Kostelanetz argued that music was "one of the most potent means" to reveal what "America and Americanism stands for," and could indeed contribute "as a tremendous patriotic force."[143] Even if he was exaggerating so as to secure LaGuardia's participation, Kostelanetz's line of argument bound the role of the performer as cultural mediator intimately with the ideological underpinning of works that—as these portraits were characterized elsewhere—were a musical "reaffirmation of the democracy in which we live and the people who have made our country great."[144] In contrast to Eleanor Roosevelt (Thomson's first choice, but she declined), LaGuardia agreed on the condition "that the portrait is not translated into syncopation, swing or modernistic music!"[145] As far as Kostelanetz was concerned, these musical portraits were an unadulterated success for his patriotic enterprise. Both concert and radio audiences were highly appreciative of compositions that he intended—as he explained in the program notes of their premières—"to mirror the magnificent spirit of our country."[146]

Composition in the War Effort

Kostelanetz's portrait commission was accepted by all three composers—Copland, Kern, and Thomson—with alacrity. The generous honorarium of $1,000 may have helped, plus the series of guaranteed public performances with fees for performing rights attached ($25 for each one).[147] Yet Kern's letters to Kostelanetz reveal that such a commission so close to Pearl Harbor also provided a compelling means for composers to use their very specific abilities to contribute to the war effort. Indeed, Kern laid everything else aside because of his "tremendous enthusiasm for our project, which, for the past forty-eight hours or so, has made me well-nigh breathless."[148] Thomson and Copland similarly considered these works patriotic contributions: in his first draft of the program notes Copland described *A Lincoln Portrait* as embodying "the spirit of American democracy," and in his memoirs he explicitly cast the work as patriotic wartime service.[149] Through their musical responses to the Kostelanetz commission, the three composers positioned themselves at the forefront of wartime musical patriotism. These programmatic (in several senses) tendencies were soon followed by, on the one hand, such historically oriented compositions as Harris's Symphony no. 6 ("Gettysburg") and Weill's Whitman songs, and, on the other, works relating to current events, including Robert Russell Bennett's *Four Freedoms Symphony*, Harl McDonald's symphonic poem *Bataan*, and Marion Bauer's choral work *China*.

Like performers, composers could participate through benefit concerts and contribute in official roles. The difference from other musical professionals, however, lay in their creative output. A composer's artistic contribution carried the potential of inscribing into the sonic fabric of music itself his or her political and social response to the war, just as Beethoven's *Wellington's Victory*, op. 91, reflected the Napoleonic battles of his time. Beethoven's piece has often since been charged with being trivial *musique d'occasion*, and the tension between possible accusations of banality and irrelevance on the one hand, and the need to reflect on the conflict within their very own medium on the other, formed the background of U.S. composers' musical engagement with the war. Many composers tried to tread the fine line between music tailored to the present circumstances and music whose scope would be unequivocally universal.

Contemporary composers, even more than performers, needed to validate their professional pursuit as an essential contribution to the war effort, lest its esoteric marginality be reinforced rather than disproved. As almost a ritual incantation, the trope of music as a weapon returned regularly in composers' writings. Blitzstein wrote in May 1942, just a few months before he enlisted, that "music no less than machine guns has a part to play, and can be a weapon in the battle for a free world."[150] Other composers—from Cowell and Harris to Lazare Saminsky and William Grant Still—echoed this sentiment with similar emphasis. Newly composed music was celebrated as an active contribution to the war effort, if just to resist defeatism: only a strong culture could continue to produce art that mattered. As Arthur Berger explained, keeping music flourishing in all its diversity was a matter of pride for "a nation which likes to distinguish itself from the enemy in its superiority to the crude practice of suppressing whatever is not materially instrumental to military force and world domination...As such, [music] offers a direct antithesis to Nazi materialism."[151] Berger thus turned the tables on Nazi Germany: the land of music had lost its culture, and America had taken its place. In Finney's summary account of his survey of composers, the act of composing itself was framed as a contribution to the war effort, one that "[kept] alive the spark of creative work."[152] The Soviet Union served as a particular point of reference—a friendly competitor whose commitment to classical music could be held up as a mirror to musical practice in the United States. After the collapse of the Nazi–Soviet pact in June 1941, Shostakovich and Prokofiev were constantly cited as model composers who purposefully wrote symphonic and other concert music that was a deeply appreciated contribution to the war.[153] The *New York Times* published Prokofiev's New Year's greetings in January 1943; his peroration predicted "that the great struggle against the Nazi hordes is finding reflection in the works of American composers."[154] Whatever the reality in the Soviet Union, U.S. wartime discourse celebrated its support of music even under the most adverse circumstances as a sign of true civilization.

What Prokofiev may have considered appropriate rhetoric in wartime had already become contested ground among his colleagues in the United States. Roger Sessions was perhaps the most outspoken critic of instrumentalizing art for political ends, characterizing this attitude as a form of quasi-Fascism.[155] Berger was similarly cagey when he worried that composers might begin to limit their expressive freedom by elevating "one facet of art into a unique value."[156] Conversely, Saminsky advocated self-censorship when he wrote that a composer now needed "to suppress as much as he can the peculiar emotionalism and parochialism of musicians. He must take on a complete awareness of his duty as a citizen of this country."[157] Warren D. Allen chastised current musical diversity, in particular the "rich, sensuous music" on the radio, and, in an unapologetic call for the masculinization of American music, demanded that choices of repertoire and new composition should be oriented toward, and restricted to, "the strong, vitally pulsating music which nourished our forefathers."[158]

For most composers, however, the key issue concerning music's wartime role was what one might call the paradox of freedom. If freedom was the foundational value of American democracy, then it was paramount to inscribe creative freedom into the discourse about musical composition.[159] Berger even went so far as to express his fear that the exigencies of war meant that "we will not always be supporting the freest expression, as we believe we are doing, when we support music. So much of it will have lost its freedom."[160] In a sharply ironic observation, he claimed that "the war's concept of freedom" generated oppressive tendencies, for "even the finest music composed in the vein of democratic idealism betrays the impetus which might have originally given rise to the movement."[161] Similarly, Blitzstein confronted the dilemma of defining wartime music's specific character in the ideological framework of free cultural expression which (and herein lies the paradox) negates any such determination. After conjuring up—almost like a catechism—the notion that a "free world implies free peoples, and free democracies, and free cultures," Blitzstein nevertheless identified the music appropriate for this crisis as one that emphasized communication with the audience: "For if music is not communication, it is nothing."[162] Blitzstein thus retooled his activist aesthetic, sharpened during his involvement with the popular front in the 1930s, into a prescriptive and populist wartime program that defined music through the democratic and freedom-promoting value of communication. Downes used a similar argument when he suggested that the wartime composer should leave his "aesthetic seclusion" so as to "address his fellow man in terms of sincerity and reality. This is needed in art."[163] Blitzstein and Downes thus let stylistic prescription in through the back door by defining freedom as a democratic system whose core value could be called on to judge specific works as either communicative (and thus embodying democratic freedom) or self-centered and therefore "undemocratic." Even Berger fell prey to this argument when he rejoiced that Schoenberg had turned "from his normal esoteric content of ghoulish and stifled personal anguish to make a timely setting of Byron's *Ode to Napoleon*."[164] Owing to the moral imperative of a global crisis, then, the war heightened the ideological tensions, prevalent in the interwar years, between the ideal of unfettered creative freedom on the one hand and community-based artistic populism on the other. Yet in contrast to the more dogmatic wing of mid-1930s popular-front thinking in the United States—with its May Day songs and workers' choruses—wartime circumstances on the Allied front allowed, if not encouraged, more advanced and even sometimes abstract musical idioms as a sign of liberal progressiveness running counter to Fascism's condemnation of such idioms and their racial origins as "degenerate." For composers, these poles marked out a negative dialectical framework (in the Adornian sense) whose unresolved paradox opened a creative space that, in the end, could encompass with equal justification such diverse works as John Cage's *Credo in US* (1942) and Morton Gould's *American Salute* (1943).

These aesthetic challenges were compounded by the strange no-man's-land in which most (male) composers found themselves stuck after Pearl Harbor—between active military duty on the one hand and more or less benign indifference from the government and the media on the other. In contrast to performers, who slid almost effortlessly from civilian musical life into morale-boosting concert and recording activities, classical composers had to work hard to generate and define talent-specific wartime contributions. In August 1943 a rather irritated Copland wrote to Berger: "In general, damn little has been done to make use of the talent of serious composers in the War effort."[165] This neglect often put the onus on them to find a way to insert themselves into the American war effort specifically as composers if they were not to follow the example of Percy Grainger and turn their efforts in other directions (Grainger was active mostly as a pianist for the USO during the war years). As we shall see in chapters 3 and 5, concert composition continued to provide a solution. But as the wartime activities especially of Milton Babbitt, Elliott Carter, and Henry Cowell reveal, composers' expertise could also be put to the service of specific civilian government agencies.

Babbitt and Carter found themselves in similar situations, if with different outcomes. Exempted from military service by their respective draft boards, they tried to find other ways in which to take part in the war. Writing in October 1942 to Spivacke (again in the latter's role as chair of the Subcommittee on Music of the Joint Army and Navy Committee on Welfare and Recreation), the twenty-six-year-old Babbitt tried to build a case for why the Army Special Services should make use of his talents. He explained that he had already done "work in secret communications under the direction of the Signal Corps Intelligence" and would now like to enter "the armed services by way of the Specialist Corps." His list of achievements included not only his teaching experience in music history and theory at Princeton University, but also his knowledge of radio and recording technology, and "experience performing in bands, both military and popular."[166] Babbitt's attempts to join the army remained unsuccessful, but his quest to contribute to the war effort led him eventually to still-secret government work in Washington, D.C.[167] Carter, for his part, applied to government intelligence organizations but was turned down because he was deemed "unsuitable for decoding and other intelligence work."[168] As he wrote to Copland in May 1943, his hopes of being actively involved in the war effort had been dashed so far. Soon thereafter, however, Carter finally joined the New York branch of the OWI as a music specialist for about a year, until June 1944; there he produced recordings (including that of the première of Schoenberg's Piano Concerto in February 1944) and provided music for radio programs.[169] His and his colleagues' specifically musical expertise became an integral and increasingly important part of American propaganda efforts that at the same time afforded them an opportunity to further the cause of American music to a global audience. One of Carter's final tasks during his OWI assignment was to work on an essay to be called "Music in America at War," in which he outlined both its history and its current production, emphasizing its democratic diversity.[170] Carter's individual agenda—which combined the promotion of contemporary American music with wartime patriotism—thus found an ideal outlet in the OWI's propaganda machinery. The same might be said for Barber, Copland, Cowell, Harris, and Weill, each of whom put his professional skills to OWI service.

Weill's relationship with the OWI and similar institutions was less straightforward than that of his American-born colleagues, because of his precarious situation as someone "formerly German" who, together with Lotte Lenya, became an American citizen only in late August 1943.[171] The pressures and enticements of exile (as Adorno put it) created a different, more self-conscious framework for Weill when he engaged in the American war effort, for just below the surface of his work to that end was the need constantly to demonstrate his loyalty.[172] Even before the United States entered the war, Weill agonized about figuring out "our, the refugées', position" in his new home in order to "to avoid being mixed up with the Fifth Column elements when the anti-alien feeling is growing stronger." The crux for him was "to prove to our American friends that we are loyal citizens of this country."[173] Although Weill had made many positive efforts to assimilate into American life and culture, there remained an undercurrent of fear about his alien status that inevitably increased as a result of wartime pressures. A month after Pearl Harbor, he declared in an interview, "I completely feel like an American."[174] But clearly he now sensed that the burden of proof for pro-American sympathies lay with him and his fellow refugees from Axis countries. Via his musical compositions, writings, and other wartime contributions, he involved himself frenetically in the war effort time and again in what now seems almost a desperate attempt to prove himself above suspicion.

Contrary to the self-conscious alienation of a Bertolt Brecht or Theodor W. Adorno (one of Weill's harsher critics after 1945), Weill's successful assimilation to life in the United States may give the retrospective impression that the urgency of exile, to borrow Bharati Mukherjee's words, had blended into the serendipity of expatriation.[175] Yet American identity was made up of different components from those with which a secular European of the early twentieth century would have been familiar, given that in the United States both ethnicity and religion played crucial roles. In constructing this new American identity, Weill needed to identify himself not only as "formerly German" but also as Jewish.[176] This local custom—in addition to his parents' escape from the Nazis to Palestine—may explain in part the notable increase in Weill's Zionist activities during this period, which coincided with fervent American patriotism and contributions to the war effort.[177] Thus, in his self-transformation into an "American," Weill had not only to assimilate to his new cultural environment, but also to foreground different markers of identity by explicit reference to both a religious affiliation and a point of ethnic origin.[178]

These markers and their complex interplay shaped Weill's musical work during the war. His relationship to his German past remained ambiguous. According to the composer himself, he thought of America as "the continuation of Europe."[179] This positive slant can be traced in his *Four Walt Whitman Songs* (1942–47), whose texts stand for American patriotism but whose musical idiom harks back to German art song.[180] Nazi Germany, in contrast, was the enemy, against which Weill fought with deep fervor and conviction. He not only sought to distinguish himself in American eyes from the German Reich and its sympathizers, but also serviced the propaganda machinery of the OWI and the OSS by providing arrangements and compositions for recordings and broadcasts. The outstanding musical manifestation of Weill's Zionist engagement during the war was the pageant *We Will Never Die*, a "Memorial Dedicated to the Two Million Jewish Dead of Europe," which Billy Rose produced in Madison Square Garden. The performance, in March 1943, was sponsored by the Committee for a Jewish Army of Stateless and Palestinian Jews (at a time when Weill himself was still stateless). The lion's share of Weill's wartime activities, however, could be characterized as affirming his new national identity both politically (in such morale operations as the *Lunchtime Follies*) and culturally, in particular in his work for Broadway with the lighthearted, elegant musical *One Touch of Venus* (1943). Weill's specifically war-related output was both anti-German and pro-American, marked simultaneously by a complex play of past and present.

The *Lunchtime Follies* (originally "Lunch Hour Follies") was an operation of the American Theatre Wing War Service aimed at using entertainment to encourage productivity in war plants (Figure 1.16). Together with Moss Hart and Aline McMahon, Weill founded this series of shows in the spring of 1942 and acted as chairman of its production committee.[181] After successful tryouts at the Wheeler shipyard in June 1942, the civil-morale operation quickly developed into a large enterprise that entertained often thousands of workers as they broke for a meal, whether (depending on their shift) at noon, 8 p.m., or 4 a.m. As Weill explained, sometimes, the shows had to be timed down to the second, just like a radio show: At the Curtiss-Wright Corporation plants, for example, performances took place from 12:03 to 12:18 p.m., 8:03 to 8:18 p.m., and 4:03 to 4:18 a.m.[182] Once the idea became a reality, the American Theatre Wing actively sought out material. In September 1942 Weill addressed members of the Hollywood Writers Mobilization with "a pep talk on the need for material for the 'Lunch Hour Follies,' which supplies original shows for the defense industries."[183] In August the Theatre Wing's Carly Warton had sent letters to such well-known lyricists as Oscar Hammerstein II to solicit humorous contributions "reflecting the lives and problems of the workers, and to inspire them with the idea that they too are soldiers."[184] Hammerstein replied that there might, in effect, be a new number suited for this project: "Kurt Weill and I wrote a song called 'Hello There, Buddy, On The Night-Shift' which I think might be developed into a very good number for this purpose. If you would be interested in hearing it, let me know and I will get ahold of Kurt and we will play and sing the number. If it sounds good when we play and sing it, it will have met the acid test of all time."[185] Hammerstein and Weill's jazzy, catchy song was indeed included in one of the *Lunchtime Follies*, as were other songs that Weill composed for them, such as "Schickelgruber" (lyrics by Howard Dietz) and "Song of the Inventory" (lyrics by Lewis Allen). The latter's breathless refrain, tying the worker in the shipyard through a chain of industrial activities to "the bomb that dropped on Hitler," was a hit with audiences.[186] Another prolific composer for the shows was Harold Rome (of *Pins and Needles* fame), whose song "The Lady's on the Job" was received with particular enthusiasm.

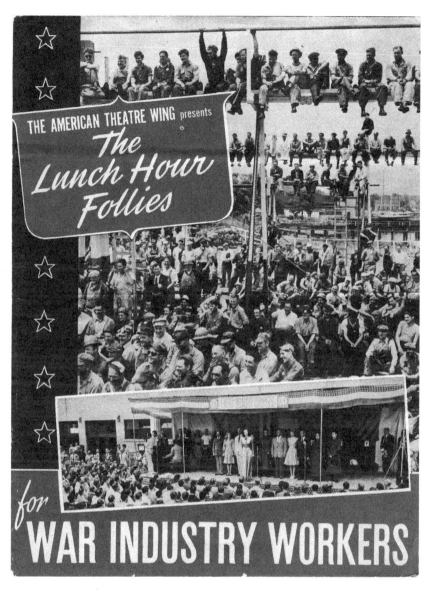

THE AMERICAN THEATRE WING presents

The Lunch Hour Follies

for WAR INDUSTRY WORKERS

FIGURE 1.16 Cover for the "Lunch Hour Follies" brochure featuring Kurt Weill's productions for war-industry workers, 1942. Courtesy of the Weill-Lenya Research Center, Kurt Weill Foundation for Music, New York.

Weill was involved in this project as both a producer and a composer, and his aims were ambitious. Like the USO camp shows for the military (to which the enterprise was often compared)—and as almost inevitably needed to be claimed in order to secure official support—*Lunchtime Follies* was conceived not only to provide entertainment and morale boosting for civilian workers, but also as an educational opportunity. Weill explained to the writer and Librarian of Congress Archibald MacLeish that, beyond the shows' contribution to the war effort, "we felt that this might become the birthplace of a real people's theatre."[187] Samuel Grafton, a critic who had witnessed one of the early performances at Wheeler shipyard, picked up on this agenda: "here is their theatre, reborn, the theatre that has served man for three thousand years, suddenly sprung up again, the kind of theatre that is as natural as a tree, and as hearty as a cookstove."[188] The typical rhetoric of the Federal Theatre Project had now found a more urgent force. The claim of developing a new form of truly popular theater, and of simultaneously gaining new audiences for traditional theater, can be found in numerous newspaper articles that reported on the *Lunchtime Follies* during its heyday in 1943.

Alas, what had started so well, as far as Weill was concerned, soon hit several roadblocks. His letters to Ruth Page mention the heavy workload, and he complained to Ira Gershwin in April 1943 that "everybody has deserted me on that project, and practically all by myself I produced 15 little shows for defense plants."[189] More troublesome, however, was the fact that Weill—as a putative enemy alien—often could not enter the heavily guarded defense plants, where performers were sometimes assigned armed guards just to go to the bathroom. This inevitably impeded his effectiveness as a producer, a fact that both Weill and his supporters at the American Theatre Wing used as a reason for accelerating his naturalization. While there is no doubt about Weill's commitment to the *Lunchtime Follies*, it did provide a well-publicized means not only of showing his loyalty, but also of claiming preferential treatment in his citizenship application. Once it was successful, Weill reduced his work for the *Lunchtime Follies* almost immediately to concentrate on preparing the première of *One Touch of Venus* in October 1943 and on the composition for the anti-Nazi film musical *Where Do We Go from Here?* between November 1943 and January 1944. Although the latter was intended as a patriotic celebration of American ideals by invoking key moments in U.S. history, such as the battle at Valley Forge, OWI officials found that the lighthearted, satirical approach of the book could "confuse and be misinterpreted by overseas audiences."[190] Musically, however, the film broke new ground by including the longest vocal number thus far recorded for the silver screen and thereby heading toward Weill's ideal of a through-composed musical for Hollywood.[191] Just as with the *Lunchtime Follies*, where he envisaged a new people's theater, Weill again had greater artistic ambitions, pointing in an interview conducted in June 1945 to opera as a model for new ways of thinking about music in film.[192]

In 1944 Weill became involved in two other war-related projects by contributing to the soldier show *Three Day Pass* and by writing the score for the OWI documentary *Salute to France*, which he described to Ira Gershwin as "a big job for the government."[193] Directed by Jean Renoir and produced by Burgess Meredith, *Salute to France* was one in a series of OWI documentaries linked to the invasion of Europe in 1944–45 (in some cases using military footage), either presenting Allies such as France in their best and bravest light or showing the United States as a freedom-loving, civilized nation. Weill was only one of several illustrious musicians recruited by the OWI for their production. Indeed, the first in the series (released in 1944) presented Toscanini conducting Verdi's *Hymn of Nations* (adapted by Toscanini to include the "Internationale" and "The Star-Spangled Banner"); later, Virgil Thomson contributed the music for *Tuesday in November* (1945), a documentary about democratic election procedures in the United States (taking 1944 as an example), and Aaron Copland composed the score for *The Cummington Story,* which chronicles the integration of refugees into a rural community in New England.[194]

Whether in composing for film, writing patriotic music, contributing to civilian and military morale operations, or organizing concerts, Weill's activities were akin to those of many U.S. composers. He was, however, one of only a very few composers in exile to engage so self-consciously and fully in the American propaganda war. Others, such as Milhaud and Martinů, chose to contribute patriotic compositions but by presenting their own Allied identities in such works as *Memorial to Lidice* or *Suite française*. For the "formerly German" Weill, however, his new musical identity had to be consistent with musical Americanism, perhaps even more than in the case of any native composer. This shines through in particular in one of his earliest war works, the orchestrations for Helen Hayes's recitations on the recording released in 1942 under the title *Mine Eyes Have Seen the Glory*. Hayes recites four famous American texts over Weill's adaptations of "America," "The Battle Hymn of the Republic," "The Star-Spangled Banner," and his own music for Walt Whitman's poem *Beat! Beat! Drums!* They are fascinating for their sophisticated orchestration combined with modernist touches in rhythm and harmony that claim artistic currency. Not for nothing did Weill maintain in his notes to the recording that he had, in effect, composed new songs for the familiar words, "as if they were fresh material." In this process of recomposition, he made the songs "part of my own form," and therefore, by implication at least, made his "own form" genuinely American.[195] Again, Weill also sublimates the topical specificity of patriotic wartime work into the more rarefied strata of Western classical music—he refers to opera and art song as his compositional framework—transferring these validating concepts of a canonic tradition into the new context of creation. By 1942 this strategy of transfer was new neither to Weill nor to those of his fellow American composers striving toward a populist modernism, or at least those who were also in some sense outsiders: William Grant Still, for example, considered the fusion of blues and symphonic form in his *Afro-American Symphony* (1930) as "elevating" African American forms such as the spiritual "to higher artistic planes."[196] Weill, for his part, also referred to new, hybrid forms for Broadway, starting with his first American project, *Johnny Johnson* (1936), some of the music for which he reused in *Salute to France*.[197] But Weill's crossover works were more than just a case of opportunistic assimilation: they had, on the one hand, deep personal significance and, on the other, far broader political import, as claims about rejuvenating European traditions in the United States took on fresh urgency in a global conflict in which music was declared a weapon on all sides.

Of those American composers in the United States who remained civilians during the war, perhaps Copland, Harris, and Elie Siegmeister came closest to Weill's breadth of patriotic engagement through both composition and arts administration. Copland acted as a cultural ambassador by visiting Latin America and as a musical advisor to both to the State Department and the Joint Army and Navy Subcommittee on Music. He wrote music for a propaganda film (*The North Star*, 1943) and an OWI documentary and was involved in concert planning, in particular for an OWI festival (ultimately abandoned) of American music in liberated Paris. His compositions from *Lincoln Portrait* to his Symphony no. 3 reflected and sublimated world events during the war. Yet while Copland's activities ran the gamut of patriotic musical work, they lack the aura of overcompensation enveloping Weill and (as we will see in chapter 2) Henry Cowell. On the contrary, secure as the dean of American music, Copland did not need to validate his own national identity; his task, instead, was to prove the newfound worth of America and her art.

Cultural Mediators and Educators

The musical war effort included not only performers and composers, but also music administrators, educators, journalists, and amateurs. Sometimes conflicting interests and personal ambition led to turf wars, as when various New York–based individuals tried to take control of a national wartime music program after the Office of Civilian Defense (OCD) was set up under the leadership of Mayor LaGuardia. Two meetings at the house of Walter Damrosch, on January 10 and January 24, 1942, pitted the meeting's organizer, the composer Samuel Barlow (head of the Independent Citizens Committee for the Arts, Sciences, and Professions in New York and a regular contributor to *Modern Music*), against several other representatives of musical organizations, including Aaron Copland (for the American Composers Alliance), Edwin Hughes (president of the National Music Council), Horace Johnson (New York WPA), Jacob Rosenberg (Local 802 of the American Federation of Musicians [AFM]), and Blanche Witherspoon (for USO camp shows). Three obviously biased letters by Edwin Hughes to his friend and colleague Harold Spivacke paint a vivid picture of the jockeying for position in the first meeting by the "almost totally uninformed" Rosenberg and Witherspoon, on the one hand, and Barlow, on the other, who "seemed to have no knowledge of wartime musical activities that are already going on."[198] Hughes himself represented a national conglomerate of thirty-six music organizations from music-related industries, education, and performance—for instance, the American Composers Alliance, ASCAP, the Music Publishers Protective Association, the Music Teachers National Association, and radio stations such as CBS. To Hughes's claim that "the Council was in a position to coordinate all national musical activities for wartime use," Witherspoon responded "that she thought the Council was not composed of important enough people!"[199] To salvage the situation, Barlow suggested a second meeting, but within hours he had revealed details of the first one to Howard Taubman, one of the music critics of the *New York Times*, who presented the ideas of Barlow's Citizens Committee as if they were supported by the whole group.[200] After that attempt at media manipulation (which left Claire Reis, of the League of Composers, "quite indignant"), the group's cohesion was even more fragile than before.[201] The second meeting made it clear to Hughes that it was naught but a "plan to resuscitate the WPA and to put it under the OCD, with full charge of all wartime cultural and art activities." Hughes was informed "that all musical, art and cultural projects were to be combined in one office under Dean Landis in OCD," sidelining the National Music Council into an "advisory capacity"—or rather, as Hughes put it, "left outside, holding the bag."[202] A week later Hughes received a letter from Eleanor Roosevelt, the patron of the OCD, in which she informed him that "there will soon be a division in charge of all artistic participation in the Office of Civilian Defense."[203] In the end, the OCD never became a wartime equivalent of the WPA, which by now was probably too tarnished by its associations with the New Deal. Instead, wartime musical and other artistic activities were supported either by non-governmental organizations (for instance, the National Music Council or the USO) or the newly founded OWI. But as this episode reveals, the lack of central control at the beginning of the war led to sometimes bitter infighting about responsibilities, resource allocation, and decision-making power between the various individuals and institutions seeking to shape America's musical landscape. We shall see more of this in chapter 2.

Perhaps the outstanding individual, rather than institutional, initiative related to classical music was the founding of the Armed Forces Master Records by the record collector and amateur musician Harry Futterman, an accountant by profession. Like many individual schemes, Futterman's concerned a cause dear to his heart and one that the war gave him the impetus and opportunity to realize. A great believer in the power and necessity of "good music" for the enjoyment and uplift of servicemen, Futterman gathered a handful of friends to create record libraries of classical music to be sent to army camps and service posts. By April 1942 the idea had gained traction, with well-known musicians from Toscanini to Koussevitzky sponsoring the purchase of these libraries (Figure 1.17). The group was incorporated on May 14, 1942, and registered with the President's War Relief Control Board in June.[204] When Deems Taylor became involved, he used his popular radio shows to support the project, and a misprint in Harold Taubman's report in the *New York Times* raised the stakes when he announced that Futterman and his colleagues were going "to set up 500 library units of at least 100 disks each"—instead of the fifty libraries Futterman had planned.[205] Futterman reported in a letter to *Notes* that he was surprised both by the strongly positive response of the armed forces, with requests pouring in faster than he could organize libraries, and by the fact that his "simple and easily adoptable" idea was not "taken up by some already organized national music organization." As he wrote to Spivacke in May 1943: "We still are dreaming of some sort of national super-duper music group of which we can be a small part."[206] Yet the Armed Forces Master Records remained a unique and independent enterprise, and Futterman continued to head a mushrooming association that by the end of the war had distributed over 1800 record libraries to the armed forces both in the continental United States and in war theaters from the South Pacific to Africa.[207]

Futterman's charitable enterprise closely matched the goals for education and morale in the forces, and his reports abound with quotations from letters he had received from soldiers, chaplains, and medical officers, emphasizing that "this music was one of the mainstays of their morale."[208] Some soldiers reported about the specific use made of libraries. One example came from a unit stationed in Papua New Guinea, where the chaplain described a concert

LIBRARY	DONOR	DESTINATION
1	Arturo Toscanini	Iceland (no acknowledgment received -- tracer through)
2	" "	U.S.Navy - Third District Command
3	Harry Futterman	Fort Hamilton, New York
4	AWVS	Fort Dix, New Jersey
5	Howard Hanson	Fort Livingston, La.
6	David Hall	Fort Slocum, New York (Hall giving weekly concerts here and will sponsor library unit)
7	Dr. Frank Black	Moody Field, Ga.
8	NBC Staff Orchestras	Fort Monmouth, New Jersey
9	Lawrence Tibbett	U.S.Navy,Third District X 1-2-3
10	Don Goddard	Shaw Field, No. Carolina
11	Dr. Rogatz	U.S.Navy, Third District
12	No.Shore Long Island Committee	Camp Upton, New York
13	Edna Purcell	U.S.Navy Command
14	Jerome Pastene	USS Albemarle Y 4
15	Amy L. Hopkins	Sheppard Field, Texas
16	William Rosenthal	JWB-USO Abilene, Texas
17	Lennerd Seim	Fort Croft, So. Carolina
18	Lyn Murray and the Lucky Strike Hit Paraders	Fort Meade, Md.
19	CBS Symphony Orchestra	Fort Wadsworth, New York
20	N.Y.Philharmonic Symphony Orchestra	U.S.Navy Command #3
21	N.Y.Philharmonic Symphony Orchestra	HMS(unknown)Lt.Gillespie X 5
22	March of Time	Fort Crowder, Mo.
23	Rudolph Wild	Fort Warren, Wyoming
24	Mark Warnow and the Hit Parade Orchestra	Fort Riley, Kansas
25	Martin Dickson Co.	Fort Charles Wood, New Jersey
26	Rudolph Wild	U.S.Navy X 6
27	Fred Waring	U.S.Navy X 7
28	Lennerd Seim	U.S.Navy X 8
29	NBC Staff Orchestras	U.S.Navy X 9
30	Prince Chavchavadze -- Eric Leinsdorf	U.S.Navy X 10
31	C.K. Etherington	Scott Field, Ill.
32	Gladys Swarthout	Marine Base, New River,No. Carolina
33	Martin Dickson Co.	U.S.Navy X 11
34	Washington D.C.Committee	Aberdeen Proving Ground, Md.
35	" "	Langley Field, Va.
36	WOR Staff Orchestras	Dale Mabrey Field, Miss.
37	Dallas Committee	Fort Wolters, Texas
38	Ben Grauer	U.S.Navy X 12-Construction Batt #23
39	No.Shore Long Island Com.	Fort Totten, New York
40	G.T.Weymouth	Fort Bragg, North Carolina
41	Frank S. Levy	No. Carolina Camp -- Levy now in army and contact lost temporarily.
42	National Orchestral Assn.	Maxwell Field, Ala.
43	" "	U.S.Navy X 13 Lt. Miner
44	Mrs. H.H. A. Beach	USO Hyannis,Mass.(partial library)
45	Andre Kostelanetz	Fort Jackson,Base Hospital,So.Carolina
46	Yehudi Menuhin	Camp Rucker, Ala.
47	Alexander Steiner Boston Victor dealer	U.S.Navy Bldg.(Fargo)Boston

FIGURE 1.17 Armed Forces Master Records, List of record-library donors, July 1943, Archives of the Subcommittee on Music, Joint Army and Navy Committee on Welfare and Recreation, Library of Congress, Music Division, Box 6.

he had organized with programs that combined semiclassical and classical music, including Mozart's *Eine kleine Nachtmusik* and Johann Strauß's *Emperor Waltz*. To his surprise, when he turned the programming over to the enlisted soldiers, they chose a "collection of heavies," starting with Elisabeth Schumann's recording of Johann Sebastian Bach's "Bist du bei mir" (BWV 508) and ending with Edward Elgar's *Enigma Variations*; their choices also included Beethoven's Fifth Symphony and Richard Strauss's *Rosenkavalier* waltzes.[209]

These reports from the field, and the fact that soldiers and units augmented the original libraries with records of their own, played a significant role in the group's fund-raising. One flyer pointed out that "our armed forces constitute a citizen's army" and therefore included music lovers from across the nation who would appreciate "good music."[210] In the attempt to mobilize audiences for two benefit concerts in Hollywood, the *Los Angeles Times* quoted from the letter of an armed-guard commander: "I wish you could see the effects that good music has on the frayed nerves of men coming in from battle stations or from arduous hours of standing watch in a North Atlantic convoy."[211] Donations came from individuals (often musicians), orchestras, organizations such as the Metropolitan Opera Guild, some businesses, and even high schools. One school in Shorewood, Wisconsin, raised $100 specifically for a record library for the men on the *USS Wisconsin*, whom they had adopted.[212] One donor, a Mrs. Whitney Briggs, wanted her libraries to go to submarines; another, from Lexington, Massachusetts, asked that the records be sent to an African American army post.[213] Usually the distribution of record libraries was left to Futterman, however, who responded to hundreds of requests sent from the various branches of the armed forces. To supplement individual donations, Armed Forces Master Records organized four major concerts in collaboration with ASCAP that raised between $4000 and $6000 each, enabling the purchase of several hundred libraries; the first, a Rachmaninoff memorial concert on June 1, 1943, netted about $5000, and "libraries were distributed to such widespread areas as the Aleutians, Alaska, the Antilles, North Africa, the South Pacific, Australia, etc., etc."[214] Another major event was a tribute to Lorenz Hart on March 5, 1944, organized jointly by ASCAP and the American Theatre Wing, in which, Futterman explained, "Broadway has joined with Toscanini." According to a promotional letter by Futterman's coorganizer, Oscar Hammerstein II, the performers ranged from Frank Sinatra and Paul Robeson to José Iturbi and Morton Gould.[215] A similar ploy—this one billed as Hollywood joining forces with classical music—had already proven successful in January in two concerts organized in the Shrine Auditorium in Los Angeles. Isabel Morse Jones, the music critic of the *Los Angeles Times*, made this concert her personal mission: it received extensive coverage in the pages of the newspaper and, in effect, sponsorship.[216]

Even though Futterman's musical initiative touched an important nerve of American musical culture during the war, rallying numerous supporters from Yehudi Menuhin to the students at the Western Pennsylvania School of the Deaf, it depended on the music-loving accountant for its success. He was driven by two personal motivations: his own experience in the Medical Corps during World War I, where he "had been starved for music," and his belief in records as a modern medium of musical enjoyment and education.[217] He insisted, for example, that records sent in these libraries be "only the best in character and condition. Nothing less befits the merits of the service man or the dignity of the donor."[218] Futterman's initiative was still active in late 1945, even though V-Discs had started to incorporate small amounts of classical music in their offerings; when he died suddenly, on December 10, 1945, however, his project came to an abrupt end.[219]

Whereas records may have been the safest way of transmitting approved music overseas, on the home front the radio remained the medium of choice for disseminating classical music while also pushing the purchase of defense bonds (later called war bonds) by discerning listeners. During the war years, the activities of such popular radio personalities as Deems Taylor multiplied, and Taylor used them to support those musical causes he deemed patriotic and suited to the "American way." His two most influential programs were a weekly broadcast for the Mutual network on Saturday evenings from September 6, 1941, to May 30, 1942, with the title *America Preferred*; and the intermission commentaries for the CBS broadcasts of the New York Philharmonic Orchestra.[220] The scripts for both programs shared the overarching theme that American music's pluralism reflected U.S. democracy as a superior political system. *America Preferred* presented "those musical artists of foreign birth who have elected America their homeland."[221] Playing ironically with Nazi rhetoric in one broadcast, Taylor described these weekly presentations as "a reminder of the welcome and loyal host of foreign-born musical artists who have found in America not only what Mr. Hitler calls *Lebensraum*—'room to live'—but also room to breathe, to breathe the fresh air of American tolerance and individual liberty."[222] One might read Taylor's choice for the composition immediately following this comment as a deliberate response to Hitler's racial politics: a performance of the Scherzo from William Grant Still's *Afro-American Symphony*. At the very least, this work fulfilled a second aspect of Taylor's agenda: the presentation of contemporary American music to a broad radio audience. As he announced in the first broadcast, his program would also serve to give its listeners "some idea of what our native composers have accomplished."[223] In general, however, Taylor's programming of contemporary American music tended to be restricted to neoromantic composers, including Barber, Eric Delmarter, and Leo Sowerby.

Taylor reached an even broader audience with his intermission talks for the broadcasts of the New York Philharmonic Orchestra, which, he pointed out, went out to "approximately 7 percent of the population of the United

States."[224] Unlike Nicolas Slonimsky, for example, whose radio scripts for the Boston Symphony Orchestra are best characterized as oral program notes, Taylor used these broadcasts to address larger issues of American cultural politics.[225] Especially in the early stages of the war, Taylor lobbied for musical pluralism as a conscious American cultural choice, hoping to head off a ban on so-called enemy music like the one that had affected U.S. concert life in 1917. As he explained in February 1942, "It's a Nazi technique to smash records and burn books. Don't imitate those barbarians."[226] He had used this plea even before Pearl Harbor, having declared in April 1941: "Let's not be Nazis. Let's not be a nation of witch-burners; let's not burn books, either literally or figuratively; let's not boycott artists, because of the race to which they belong." Drawing a parallel with American hospitality to such living composers as Schoenberg and Weill, Taylor asked his listeners, "Have we then no room for Haydn, and Mozart, Beethoven, Weber, Mendelssohn, Schumann, Wagner, Brahms?"[227]

The debate over "enemy music" reached dramatic heights on February 15, 1942, when the *New York Times* published a letter by the exiled author Erika Mann (daughter of Thomas) in which she accused Americans of being oblivious to the politically murky side of some of their favorite German musicians, in particular Richard Strauss. Mann had been one recipient of Weill's letter on how German "refugees" might best behave in the United States so as not to alienate their host nation.[228] But rather than keeping a low profile so soon after Pearl Harbor, she came out with guns blazing. "Why listen to Hitler's man?" she asked; "Strauss, it may be argued, has put his genius at the disposal of the enemy of mankind. At this moment he is apt to conduct for the benefit of Mr. Hitler's storm troopers in order to inspire them in their murderous assault on civilization."[229] Her argument hinged, somewhat cleverly, not just on Strauss's political affiliations, but also on the payment of royalties, seeing that as giving succor to the enemy. Readers responded quite heatedly, in particular the young Samuel F. Pogue, of Cambridge, Massachusetts, who, blind to Mann's own history (and to her point on royalties), judged her letter as "an indication of how political anti-fascism can be carried to the extreme of actual intellectual fascism."[230] For his part, Taylor took the lead among Mann's critics by accusing her not only of advocating Nazi-style book burning, but also of frivolously attacking some core values of American civilization, namely liberty and plurality. "Our kind of civilization is at stake," he argued. "Let us not think of [music] as the private property of any man or any country. Let us rather thank God that there exists an art so pure that it cannot be corrupted—even by its creator."[231] Hundreds of listeners wrote to Taylor supporting his argument, yet he chose—in the name of democracy—to quote from the handful who disagreed with his "plea for cool-headedness and tolerance in the field of art." He selected his extracts carefully to emphasize their irrational zeal: German music was "Wertherian welter [concealing] the werewolf," and Wagner was "indelibly associated with his valkyrie vomitings." This form of extremism, Taylor cautioned his listeners, could cause America to lose the cultural war between the Axis and the Allies by becoming just like the Nazis, with "their utter refusal to separate the work from the worker, the art from the artist."[232] In response to Taylor's attack, Mann asked CBS for an invitation to speak in the next intermission broadcast, only to be refused. Instead she tried to calm the waters in a fifteen-minute slot late at night.[233]

Taylor's disagreement with Mann touched on the question of who should be the appropriate arbiter of musical taste and practice in the United States, especially with respect to the music and art imported from abroad. Mann spoke with the voice of a cultural authority grounded in German artistic life, and also in the experience of exile, and she was no stranger to moral dilemmas and their political consequences. Taylor, on the other hand, bullishly defended music as a universal art divorced from the context of its creation and therefore not owned by any specific nation. From his perspective, Mann's claim of authority threatened the American project of cultural transfer that had characterized a significant segment of musical life in the United States since the eighteenth century.[234] Here Taylor's individual perspective fit into a broader American consensus about music's universalism and immanent value that (as we will see in chapter 3) could easily subsume Wagner's music, for example, as a symbol of freedom in the American context, even in the face of Hitler's predilection for the composer. Mann was silenced even before she spoke.

Taylor's voice as a radio commentator joined a rich, if often problematic, web of discussion about the roles and practice of music during wartime that traversed the media landscape. Both radio and print media—that is, newspapers and periodicals—became spaces in which music journalists, musicologists, and musical amateurs entered into a lively dialogue. In addition to being the source of debates on hot topics such as Mann's *New York Times* letter and the journalist's mainstay of music reviews and reporting, these media also served as a forum in which to address musical politics and history, now with an emphasis on the United States and its music, on the one hand, and on the musical cultures of its Allies, on the other. In particular, two foreign-born music historians found in journalism and related spheres a platform from which to question the prevailing American ideology of music's universalism and hence its political innocence. Paul Nettl explained in an article about national anthems that music can "play a great part in polit-ical history," and he provided not just a lesson in music history, by tracing the sources of various anthems and fighting songs, but also anti-Axis propa-ganda, by emphasizing the inferiority of such melodies as the Italian Fascist hymn "Giovinezza," which Nettl characterized as "trash," and the Romanian national anthem ("a potpourri of trivialities").[235] Here and elsewhere Nettl focused both on political influences on musical composition and on the polit-ical impact and power of any and all music, from simple songs to Wagnerian music drama. Such works as Mozart's *The Magic Flute*, Nettl argued, were products of their political context—in that case representing "the close of an extraordinarily important phase in the political history of Austria when the liberalistic period of Joseph II came to an early close with the monarch's death. 'The Magic Flute' is nothing more than a song of praise to the period."[236] Whether writing about Mozart or Wagner, Nettl's historicizing narrative was entirely the opposite of Deems Taylor's detached transcendence.

Paul Henry Lang also used such widely read papers as the *New York Times* and the *Saturday Review of Literature* to convey his ideas about music and poli-tics to his American readership. Just six weeks after Pearl Harbor, in January 1942, he took Americans to task over their "outmoded" musical practices. Only an informed look at music history would allow one "to understand the infinitely more complicated conditions which prevail today."[237] From this historical perspective, Lang denounced American musical institutions as duplicating obsolete European models of the nineteenth century. In order truly to democratize American musical life, the production of new music needed to be decentralized to avoid the continued control of these ossified institutions, especially in New York. Lang contextualized music in its insti-tutional and political framework so as to emphasize its intimate interconnec-tion with the civilization within which it was generated and/or received. Not for nothing was Lang's mammoth 1941 music history titled *Music in Western Civilization*: with not a single notated music example in sight, this was to be read less as a plea for music's civilizing force than as an account of how civil societies might have influenced the course of a supposedly pure art.[238]

The mediating role for music historians during the war years was not new: the publication of music-appreciation books had mushroomed dur-ing the 1930s to the point where Virgil Thomson described it, in 1939, as a "racket."[239] However, as Lang's 1945 article "Musical Scholarship at the Crossroads" shows, music historians now felt called upon to use their spe-cific abilities—and in this they were no different from composers and per-formers—to contribute to the cultural challenges posed by the war, not only in redefining their scholarly discipline but also with respect to the issues needing to be addressed.[240] The extent to which Lang saw musicology as a political tool becomes evident in his essay "Background Music for 'Mein Kampf,'" wherein he analyzed Wagner's writings and music and characterized the composer as "the musical architect of an incurable disease."[241] The difficulty for these émigré musicologists, as for Erika Mann, was that, while unmasking Axis ideology was acceptable up to point (no one was going to argue over the Romanian anthem), the closer they got to the core of the canon, the more fiercely Americans would resist their arguments, grotesquely twisting an anti-Fascist argument into a pro-Fascist one. Weill's warning had found a perverse reality: Mann and other critics of contemporary musical practice in the United States could be interpreted as a fifth column, erecting roadblocks in order to impede music's forward march along the American way as it was understood by such critics as Olin Downes, Oscar Thompson, and Deems Taylor.

American-born musicologists and music educators such as Warren D. Allen seemed to be more concerned about placing music history in the service of more pragmatic ends. In the spring of 1942, he developed a highly successful lecture-recital entitled "Our Marching Civilization" with the revealing subtitle "A Musical Interpretation of History." He created a narrative of the history of the musical march from its early "rudiments" through the Protestant Reformation (presumably marking the beginning of modern democracy) and heroic abstraction to a modern form in the "work-song idiom, in China, Russia, and America, suggesting that peace and progress mean devoted, incessant toil with realistic good humor."[242] The argument and its presentation could have come straight out of a trade-union lecture in the mid-1930s—although the politically correct inclusion of the Chinese and Russians had an additional wartime edge. Allen suggested that the march be revived as the ideal (and virile) expression of democratic art. In a letter to Spivacke, he proclaimed his lecture-recital the "greatest success of anything I've done publicly."[243] A year later he expanded its text into a monograph published by Stanford University Press under the same title, but with a new subtitle: *An Introduction to the Study of Music and Society*. Allen's goal had shifted, and he now used history to justify the creation of a new national march genre worthy of "our pioneer ancestors," who had "marched through the wilderness suffering all sorts of hardships" while singing march music.[244] In this new version of the narrative, the Axis countries played the expected role of abusers of the genre (even though the Germany of idealist philosophy and Beethoven symphonies remained a positive plot point). The modern Japanese were shown to be developing a "new type of unscrupulous warfare" while simultaneously borrowing and building upon "our march music and our other arts connected with war." The Germans, however, had fallen back to marching "brutally with sentimental enthusiasm" to musical idioms typical of the Thirty Years' War.[245]

Allen's blatant chauvinism offers one of many possible examples of how writers shaped historical narratives in the United States to fit the prevailing rhetoric of the time. He shared this approach, if not always such apparent naivety, with colleagues in other segments of music education, from Lilla Belle Pitts to Charles Seeger, who each saw his or her specific field as something that could be used to strengthen public morale, diplomatic mediation, and military action. In numerous articles published in the *Music Educators Journal*, Pitts offered advice on how schoolteachers could use their activities to teach democratic values and national pride through song. For Seeger, the war lent new urgency to his work in the Pan-American Union—given the new emphasis on U.S. "good neighbor" policies—whether it related to the creation and exchange of music libraries, the facilitation of travel by musicians across the Americas, the publication of Latin American folk-song collections, or student exchange programs. Indeed, Seeger became involved in a significant number of wartime government committees as a leading specialist in Latin American music and would make use of these assignments to further his long-range goals.

Seeger's ambitions, like those of many of the musicians discussed in this chapter, may have been modified to suit wartime purposes, but they did not necessarily change substantially: there are as many continuities with as discontinuities from prewar America. Lehman Engel's commission at Naval Station Great Lakes, in Illinois, was different in function but not in kind from his prior work for the Federal Music Project. Likewise, the composer Gail Kubik's work for the domestic branch of the OWI, writing and coordinating music for documentaries and propaganda films, hardly changed after he was drafted into the army save in terms of his affiliation and, no doubt, his living conditions. Seeger's involvement in various government agencies also reveals a side of the coin so far only touched upon in the present study. As in any other social context, musical life during wartime was shaped by the interplay between institutions and individuals who were (or were not) able to negotiate a path toward goals defined by personal ambition on the one hand and patriotic need on the other. While the most colorful stories in history tend to focus on the individuals strong enough to make it—we have already seen some shining examples in Menuhin, Pons, Weill, and Futterman—the bureaucracy of war reached unprecedented heights in the United States from 1941 to 1945. This administrative machinery did not emerge from thin air: in particular, the New Deal's WPA offered organizational patterns and mechanisms for their operation without which many cultural and other aspects of the American war effort would have been much slower to get off the ground. Any account of music in the United States during World War II can plausibly begin with its main players: composers, performers, critics, and educators. But it must also identify the institutions (and their administrators) that aided or impeded their ability to become "soldiers, too."

CHAPTER TWO | "Shaping Music for Total War"

I N HIS ARTICLE "Shaping Music for Total War" (1946), Henry Cowell recounted his experience as a senior music advisor for the Office of War Information, the U.S. propaganda agency during World War II.[1] On the one hand, the use of music in warfare, he argued, had served to open channels of communications so as to win over the hearts and minds of the citizens of Allied and neutral countries; on the other, it had contributed to creating a positive view throughout the world of the United States as a cultured and peace-loving nation whose rich and sophisticated musical life was reflected in both performance and composition. Cowell rejoiced that "we have succeeded in introducing American music to many people who have never heard it before."[2] Indeed, within just over a year after Pearl Harbor, the OWI had become one of the most important institutions in the United States in utilizing music for the war effort. Yet, its endeavors were but one strand of a complex fabric created by the often competing musical activities of a range of American government agencies and NGOs during World War II, including the State Department, the military, the USO, the Pan-American Union, and the Red Cross.

These wartime agencies were not created from scratch. While some were already an established part of the U.S. government, they and others also drew significantly upon the federal and local organizations established under the auspices of Roosevelt's New Deal WPA. In particular, the four federal projects concerning the arts (covering theater, music, visual art, and writing)—for all the political problems they faced in the late 1930s—already had strong bureaucracies in place both in Washington, D.C., and at the regional and state levels; they had a clear mission of putting the arts to political, social, and cultural use; they had the infrastructure and the personnel to carry it out; and they had a strong degree of popular approval, if not always government support. It comes as no surprise that many agencies involved in U.S. wartime efforts in the arts, including music, read like the WPA in another guise, for all that the focus was on a more clearly defined goal. It also comes as no surprise that many of the individuals who came to prominence in and through the federal projects reappear in the same or similar capacities, albeit now in a context working for war.

The agencies' collective, if sometimes conflicting, goals encompassed propaganda, morale, diplomacy, education, entertainment, and the rehabilitation of wounded service personnel through the fledgling discipline of music therapy. Whereas popular music and jazz counted as winners in particular in the realm of troop entertainment, classical music (and to some extent folk music as well) was considered to serve a far broader spectrum of purposes because of the strong aesthetic, social, and emotional values ascribed to it. The main reason for favoring classical music, which dominated the discourse about music in the armed forces, lay in the belief that "good music" (as it was then termed) could affect its listeners not just by immediate impact—for example, as a means of neuropsychiatric rehabilitation by providing "a new inner harmony, a greater peace of mind" to wounded service personnel—but also in the longer term, by educating soldiers, especially those from underprivileged backgrounds, and thus improving their upward social mobility in the brave new world after victory.[3] Another aim was to prove wrong those who criticized the American people as being uneducated and lacking in high culture. Charles Seeger noted that the Germans and Italians "had been using music as one of the ways of discrediting the United States. 'Oh they're nothing but money grubbers and jazz addicts, drinkers. If you want to study music you come to Italy,' say the Italians. 'If you want to study music, you come to Germany. All good music is either German or Italian.' That sort of thing."[4] Therefore it became vital to demonstrate that classical music was flourishing in the United States. No less influential, however, were the comparisons made with the uses of music by and within other Allied and even Axis nations. Indeed, throughout the musical war, the American gaze was turned outward as much as inward, and music was politicized and reified to the point (in Cowell's words) of "very precise exploitation."[5]

Music in the Service of Propaganda: The Office of War Information

When the OWI was established by Franklin D. Roosevelt on June 13, 1942, with the well-known CBS news reporter Elmer Davis as its director, music was slated to play only a very limited role in it, if any.[6] The OWI's mission consisted primarily of war-related information management. While some of its mandate included intelligence gathering, the OWI served predominantly to shape public opinion through mass media (print, radio, and film) both at home and abroad. To that end, the agency was divided into two branches, domestic and overseas, with headquarters located in Washington, D.C., and New York, respectively. Given that the OWI was firmly in the hands of writers and journalists, the written word dominated its activities at the outset. If music was perceived as having any use, it was to facilitate the transmission of verbal messages. A secret memorandum, for instance, reveals discussions in October 1942 between an agent of the Office of Strategic Services and Louis B. Cowan, acting chief of the OWI's radio bureau, about the possible use of music to include "cipher messages" as a means of communicating intelligence in enemy territory.[7] Otherwise, although the OWI was starting to establish itself as a serious contender in the competitive context of U.S. government agencies, music was barely present. Yet, ironically, it was through music that the fledgling propaganda bureau hit the American national press within weeks after it was founded.

In early June 1942 James C. Petrillo, president of the American Federation of Musicians, announced that his 140,000 unionized musicians would adopt a ban on making commercial recordings as of midnight on August 1.[8] Although on December 27, 1941, Petrillo had pledged the AFM's support for the war effort through the use of "music for morale," the threat posed by a recording industry taking jobs away from, and refusing to pay royalties to, rank-and-file performing musicians meant that union responsibilities now took precedence.[9] It seems likely that Petrillo, at least in the first instance, was using the proposed ban as a bargaining chip, hopeful, perhaps, that his claim for music and morale would place significant pressure on the record companies to give way. Their refusal to do so meant that the ban remained in effect for over twenty-seven months, until November 11, 1944, when the last of the major record companies signed contracts with the AFM. Not only did this ban press a number of hot buttons in the first year of U.S. involvement in the war; it was also the first major public issue in which the OWI was prominently and visibly involved.

It might seem strange for the OWI, a wartime propaganda agency, to have become mixed up in a national labor dispute. On the surface, and in public, the OWI justified its involvement in the disagreement by reference to its mission of information management, in which radio stations proved to be key collaborators. Without the ability to play recorded music, the argument ran, many smaller stations in particular had only limited local resources for broadcasting music, a circumstance that would threaten their existence. Elmer Davis, on behalf of the OWI, sided with the recording industries and radio stations, all the while claiming to speak "on behalf of the people of the United States" as well as the military and a number of government agencies that ranged from the War Department to the Office of Civilian Defense. He made two points. The first concerned the fact that "the ban was not only contrary to the 'music-for-morale' pledge made by Mr. Petrillo in December but would hinder the dissemination of vital war information by forcing many small radio stations to close." The latter, second point was ostensibly Davis's reason for intervening: as he said in a public statement to Petrillo, "since several hundred small, independent stations which are cooperating wholeheartedly with the government in the war depend for their major sustenance on electrical transcriptions, your order may well force them out of business and thus seriously interfere with the communication of war information and messages vital to the public security." In addition, Davis raised the specter of strikes and court fights that would "curtail musical services to the public in the critical months ahead—months which may well decide the fate of the country's war effort."[10] Predictably, Petrillo rejected Davis's arguments, claiming that he was sorely misinformed: AFM members would continue to make recordings for government agencies such as the OWI and the armed forces; the ban concerned only commercial recordings for public broadcast.[11] That argument was somewhat disingenuous—Davis's statement concerned, precisely, public broadcasting—although it showed Petrillo to be at least sensitive to the broader wartime issues. In the subsequent battle— which involved an antitrust lawsuit against the AFM brought by the Justice Department, hearings in front of a Senate subcommittee, the intervention of the War Labor Board, and even a direct plea by President Roosevelt to end the ban—the OWI remained firmly on the side of the recording industry. However, in his testimony before the Senate subcommittee, Davis was careful to point out that he was not involving himself in a labor dispute: his concern extended only to the war-related effects of the ban: "I was officially informed that the War Department has received representation from commanding officers at various war zones calling attention to the fact that a cessation of this supply of recorded music—and I quote from the letter of a commanding general—'will jeopardize the complete morale and propaganda broadcast structure' at combat zone points."[12]

Documents in the OWI archives reveal, however, that Davis's involvement was less disinterested than he claimed. A former star radio reporter, Davis and his staff were actively plotting with the National Association of Broadcasters (NAB) to end the recording ban as quickly as possible.[13] The

NAB in effect recruited the OWI for this task through a concerted campaign of telegrams sent by radio stations. In fact, shortly before Davis went public with his plea in July 1942, the OWI was flooded with close to a hundred telegrams containing such remarks as, "Suggest you use influence against Petrillo in order that this station may continue to serve the OWI." One telegram even compared Petrillo's recording ban to Hitler's Blitz: "Radio stations war effort assistance and public service in danger. Exercise influence prevent Petrillo music Blitzkrieg."[14] The OWI was actively involved in the preparation of the lawsuit that the Department of Justice brought against the AFM, and Davis's office also supported a publicity campaign directed against Petrillo, in which his actions as union chief were compared to those of the European dictators that the United States was currently fighting abroad. The style of the campaign is clear from an article in the notoriously antiunion *Los Angeles Times* on August 3, 1942: "There is a second front. It's right here in our house. It isn't against the Nazis, the Fascists or the Japanese, but against a man who, to our way of thinking, combines the unloveliest features of each of these groups. We refer to Mr. James Petrillo, that czar of the xylophone, that martinet of the mandolin, that Fuehrer of the reed winds, that Duce of the clarinet, trumpet and tenor sax."[15] Only when Petrillo's lawyers denounced Davis's own conflict of interest did the OWI cease to support the anti-Petrillo fight, at least in public.

Save for its involvement in the Petrillo affair, the OWI's Washington branch had a fairly limited interest in music, presumably because it had no national interest in doing more. The chief exception was outreach to rural and African American communities. The person chosen for this task was Alan Lomax, who had been employed as a folk-music specialist at the Library of Congress before he was transferred to the OWI's Bureau of Special Operations in Washington in 1942.[16] Paid at the rate of an army captain ($3,800 per year), Lomax was part of a group assigned to "prepare war information material designed for special groups—Negro groups, religious groups, and certain groups not reached adequately by ordinary information media."[17] During his year at the OWI, Lomax was involved mostly in "collecting contemporary wartime songs in the folk style" both for purposes of research and for propaganda. Indeed, he planned to use recordings of these songs by "hillbilly and race stars" in regional broadcasts.[18] But the Petrillo debacle set limits on the OWI's Washington operation, and by April 1943 "all music activities in this office" ceased; soon thereafter Lomax, who had been drafted in December 1942, was inducted into the army.[19]

In a classic case of bureaucratic double-dealing, however, while one part of the OWI was engaged in a very public fight with Petrillo, another was quietly negotiating a separate agreement with the AFM in early 1943 that guaranteed a steady supply of recordings, especially for the broadcasts of the OWI's Overseas Branch.[20] As the *San Francisco Chronicle* reported in an illustrated one-page spread in March 1943, the OWI embarked on a major recording program destined to "employ American music and America's music makers as a significant element in America's wartime message to the world." Inspired by the sensational results of the Soviet Union's propaganda efforts, the OWI set out to make and broadcast records and to establish libraries of American music in foreign countries. And as the newspaper proudly reported, "it seems to be a bigger, broader and better balanced attempt than that of the USSR."[21] The recordings featured sixteen major American symphony orchestras and encompassed works by composers such as Copland, Roy Harris, William Grant Still, and Robert Russell Bennett. Among the "specially recorded" works were Harris's *Folk Song Symphony* and Still's *Afro-American Symphony*. If Harris's work represented the American melting pot writ large, the promotion of Still's composition carried symbolic power for the OWI's wartime propaganda for a society that—unlike Nazi Germany—was committed to racial equality. Both its composer and the symphony's program served the agency's purpose in painting a far rosier picture than was actually warranted by American life, with its pervasive systemic racism. But the recordings also used Allied music for propagandistic ends: Milhaud's *Hommage à Debussy* (1920) was recorded for broadcast on March 25, 1943, to "all French-Speaking countries" to commemorate the twenty-fifth anniversary of Debussy's death.[22] The recording project was overseen by the Broadway and film composer Macklin Marrow, the first music director appointed to the OWI's Overseas Branch, where the lion's share of musical activities took place for the remainder of the war.

Because of radio's central role in the global propaganda war, music found its principal home in the OWI's Overseas Branch, operating out of New York and, to a lesser extent, San Francisco. The first music specialist hired by the New York branch in late 1942 was Bess Lomax Hawes (sister of Alan), a young folk-music scholar and singer who performed during those years with the Almanac Singers and was also associated with the Seegers and Woody Guthrie (Figure 2.1). Hawes was to be the one constant music presence in the OWI for the entire war, whereas some of the other advisors and directors changed every few months. She recalled later that between 1943 and 1945 she was "acting director of the music programs...five or six times because people would take the job and then quit in a couple of months." By May 1944 she was signing her correspondence "Assistant Chief of the Music Section."[23] As she clarified in a letter to Harold Spivacke, chief of the Music

FIGURE 2.1 Bess Lomax Hawes, the assistant chief and often acting director of the OWI's Music Section in New York and a member of the Almanac Singers, photograph from ca. 1943. Courtesy of Naomi Bishop.

Division of the Library of Congress: "I was appointed Chief of the Music Unit, pending the arrival of our new chief, Mr. Daniel Saidenberg. Right now I am assistant boss."[24] The OWI followed traditional gender lines in its employment strategies, with Hawes in effect running the music section but with a number of male musicians rotating in the position of director.

Hawes started out her tenure at the OWI by organizing the Overseas Branch's record library, which grew within three years into a collection that, in Cowell's assessment, contained "more folk music of the world's peoples and more symphonic works by serious American composers than any other I know."[25] The library consisted of around 50,000 items by the end of 1942 and had expanded to at least 200,000 by early 1945.[26] This was the heart of the OWI's music operations, because it provided the raw materials both for the agency's propaganda broadcasts and for the promotion of U.S. musical culture (and especially contemporary American concert music) to the world at large. In her memoirs, Hawes made the point that, in institutional terms, the OWI followed in the steps of the WPA "with another attempt by the federal government to bring the ordinary citizen in the flow of communication, which was growing faster every day—including the presentation of art for the people."[27] This new wartime agency, however, had very clear objectives insofar as music's role in this communication flow was concerned, especially once it had become obvious from early blunders that listeners responded to music even in news programs. The public was quick to ridicule the use of an extract from Jean Sibelius's *Finlandia* in a broadcast to the Soviet Union during the months when the Soviets were at war with Finland and the presentation of "Maryland, My Maryland"—a *contrafactum* of the German Christmas carol "O Tannenbaum"—as an American folk song.[28] It became paramount to consider carefully the appropriate use of music for propaganda, a problem based on the insight "that there was no possible way in which music could ever be thought of as nonpolitical," because it inevitably lent "its emotional authority to every context in which it occurred."[29]

To tame the genie that careless newscasters had let out of the bottle, the OWI did not just hire Hawes but soon thereafter also created the position of Director of Music, filled at first by Macklin Marrow. Whereas Hawes was a specialist in American folk music, Marrow was at home on Broadway and in the movie industry. Therefore the agency still lacked expertise in two crucial areas: world and concert musics. The administrators asked Harold Spivacke, perhaps the best-informed musician in government service, whom they should approach for the position of music specialist. Spivacke proposed Henry Cowell, certainly a prominent American composer, if also notorious for his conviction and imprisonment on a morals charge. Cowell's wife, Sidney Robertson Cowell, later recalled rather pointedly that "Harold was responsible for Henry's OWI job in 1943–45, and it has always intrigued me to know how he got a man 3 years out of San Quentin on to a gov't payroll!"[30]

Following his release from prison in 1940, Cowell had headed the Music Distribution Project of the New School for Social Research. He met with Hawes and Marrow on February 2, 1943, in New York to discuss a possible association with the OWI. Six weeks later, his position as a part-time music consultant was approved "by their personnel dept. (with full knowledge of my past) and if the FBI investigator gives his ok, I'll become a gov't official soon. Very funny!"[31] Inducted into the OWI on June 23, 1943, he started working at the Overseas Branch almost immediately. He was paid the consultant rate of $10 per day, which, given that the position almost immediately turned into regular employment, provided a secure income until the beginning of April 1945, when Cowell, who had been made a senior music consultant in May 1944, abruptly resigned.[32] According to Hawes, the resignation was forced by "some kind of security check problem."[33] This was almost certainly triggered by Cowell's attempt to gain the civil service rating that he would have needed to be appointed as the next music director after Marrow. It put him back on the radar screen of government officials, who by now were increasingly targeting the notoriously left-leaning OWI employees in proto-McCarthy purges against "un-American activities" (however defined).[34]

Aside from Hawes, Cowell was the longest-serving musical professional in the employ of the OWI and without doubt the most influential, given his ability to straddle Western and non-Western musical repertoires. His ideas about world music shaped the agency's recording and broadcasting strategies, and his long experience in New York's new-music scene aided the promotion of contemporary American music. Three other American composers were also employed by the New York bureau as music consultants: Samuel Barber (1944), Elliott Carter (1943–44), and Colin McPhee (1945). Daniel Saidenberg, who followed Marrow as music director in May 1944 after the latter joined the Radio Corporation of America, was a cellist and conductor (Figure 2.2); after he was drafted into the army in the spring of 1945, he was replaced by the composer Roy Harris, whose tenure lasted only a few

FIGURE 2.2 *Left to right:* Henry Cowell, Samuel Barber, and Daniel Saidenberg (chief of the OWI's Music Section in New York) studying a score prior to a concert recorded and broadcast by the OWI. This promotional still was published in *PM* on October 6, 1944. National Archives (208-PU-42KK-2).

months, until the operations of the Overseas Branch ceased.[35] In addition, in 1944 the army air forces had seconded Marc Blitzstein as music director of the OWI's London branch, and numerous other composers and musicians, from Aaron Copland to Kurt Weill, lent their expertise for specific OWI projects or commissions.

For the OWI, music counted as "very friendly propaganda" that crossed "international boarders at will" and made "friends out of strangers" by reaching "the natives' feelings with music."[36] The target groups for this friendly propaganda were four distinct sets of listeners. Perhaps most important, the OWI addressed neutral countries to present the United States as a cultivated, forward-looking, powerful, and democratic nation. A second target was Allied countries such as Great Britain and France, which received similarly positive messages, including musical programs that celebrated their country's musical heritage through performances by U.S. musicians. The OWI Overseas Branch also broadcast music programs, in particular American concert music, to U.S. soldiers serving abroad. Finally, the OWI aimed its message at enemy listeners, too, for whom music was to serve as a signifier of American sophistication and freedom. One show targeting Germany was called *Music with Margaret*, featuring "fifteen minutes of popular or serious American music with a running commentary by 'Margaret,' a lady who specializes in passing witty, burning remarks concerning German Government leaders. From underground reports the OWI has found out that this is one of the most successful programs."[37] It is not entirely clear whether the effectiveness of this program hinged on "Margaret's" ability to gain listeners or on the music programmed by the OWI, but its catholic use of both popular and concert music was a well-noted feature.

For the most part, these various programs were recorded in either New York or San Francisco, sometimes in multiple languages from French and Russian to Mandarin, and then sent as discs to various OWI or military transmitters, both in the continental United States and overseas.[38] According to Marrow, broadcasting was "separated into two divisions: short-wave transmissions from America and medium-wave broadcasts from local stations abroad. By the use of these two media... we are able to cover the entire surface of the globe."[39] The OWI's premier broadcasting conduit was the Voice of America, located on West Fifty-seventh Street; in Europe, the OWI and the Supreme Headquarters Allied Expeditionary Force (SHAEF) operated the American Broadcasting Station in Europe (ABSIE), whose headquarters were in London.[40] But OWI programs also found their way to such diverse stations as the British Broadcasting Corporation (BBC) and the American Forces Network (AFN).

In order to reach these diverse audiences, the OWI's music specialists collected and recorded music from across the world, including American folk music, Western concert music, and so-called world music. Cowell, for example, organized recording sessions with Vietnamese, Iranian, Chinese, and other nationally diverse musicians who lived in the United States and tried to secure recordings from various sources such as the American Embassy in liberated Paris (which was charged with procuring copies of the recordings made at the Colonial Exposition in 1937) and his own circle of friends. Colin McPhee said that he had "loaned the office my collection of Javanese and Balinese records for recording, some two hundred and fifty titles, rare, excellent, and for the most part the only copies in this country. I suppose that even in the Indies they will have been lost by this time."[41] In addition to the broadcasting of traditional musics to non-Western nations, Cowell also devised a deliberately cross-cultural approach through the strategic use of what he called "hybrid forms."[42] These consisted of either Western music performed on non-Western instruments, to accommodate the taste of the local population, or works that incorporated both Western and non-Western musical styles. Cowell cites as an example the Chinese song "Chee Lai," which he identified as being "in westernized style" but which was apt to "establish the bond between East and West."[43] "Chee Lai" had become famous in the United States as an Allied war song, in particular through Paul Robeson's 1941 recording, in which he sang in both Chinese and English; in the fall of 1943 it would be among the first songs released on V-Disc (see below).[44] Cowell's own compositions also engaged with the hybrid model, for example in *Philippine Return: Rondo on a Philippine Folk Song* (1943) and his collection *United Nations: Songs of the People* (1945). Robertson Cowell gave the credit for Henry's ethnomusicological awareness to, among other influences, his studies with the comparative musicologist Erich Moritz von Hornbostel during his Guggenheim year (1931–32) in Berlin.[45] Although Cowell may have enjoyed repaying what was now the enemy in kind—especially since Hornbostel was forced to flee the Nazis in 1933—this circumstance also emphasizes the role of their earlier German experiences in certain Americans' wartime developments.

As for American concert music itself (and journalistic reports on it), it served the OWI as a marker not just for U.S. artistic accomplishment, but also as a sign of civilized superiority. Here the OWI's particular target was those European nations subjected to Axis propaganda claiming the United States to be "a barbaric country without culture or taste."[46] Joseph Goebbels and his Reichsministerium für Volksaufklärung und Propaganda repeatedly made the point that the United States had neither any music of its own nor any other indigenous form of high art, putting his finger unerringly on America's sore point: dependence on European imports of both music and musicians.[47] To refute this charge of cultural inadequacy, the OWI counted especially on concert music (both contemporary and classical) "to show music critics, music societies and lovers of music that, contrary to Nazi propaganda, America has a real musical culture."[48] One memo suggested answering "German-made charges that America is culturally backward by showing our appreciation and development of serious music."[49] By March 1943 the New York office had already produced programs in twenty-two languages containing "representative American music…for distribution and broadcast to specific regions of the world."[50] As the pace of production increased over the next two years, such programs incorporated American performances of traditional concert repertoire from Mozart to Ravel, recordings of contemporary American music, and notable premières, for example of Harris's Fifth Symphony and Schoenberg's Piano Concerto. The latter was performed by Eduard Steuermann and the NBC Symphony Orchestra under Leopold Stokowski on February 6, 1944, with Elliott Carter producing the recording for the OWI.[51] "In other words," Cowell explained in January 1945, these programs broadcast "everything that goes to make up the musical life of America, including the excellent standards of performance of classics by American artists and orchestras."[52] What Cowell and his colleagues did not share with the worldwide audience of such programs, however, was that U.S. patrons and colleagues could also turn against such performances. Stokowski paid a high price for the high-profile première of Schoenberg's Piano Concerto: he lost his position with the NBC Symphony Orchestra, and among his key adversaries over his championing of Schoenberg was none other than Arturo Toscanini.[53] These developments, however, were not part of the rosy and inclusive image projected by the OWI's propaganda warriors.

Classical music could also be integrated into radio series that catered to a broader audience—for example, in such programs as *As You Like It* (1944), one episode of which paired Edward Elgar's "Land of Hope and Glory" (based on *Pomp and Circumstance March* no. 1) with a number of lighter tunes, or *Everybody's Music* (1945), on which Beethoven's *Egmont* Overture shared a program with the popular tune "La Paloma." Another wildly diverse program of *Music for Indonesia* (to be announced in either Dutch or Malay) combined such works as Tchaikovsky's *Elegy* with traditional musics from Indonesia and John Philip Sousa marches. In contrast, some broadcasts were dedicated exclusively to classical music; these were often produced in several languages. *The Concert Hour* presented programs with a repertoire typical of American concert halls, with works such as Mozart's violin concertos,

Brahms's *Academic Festival Overture*, the Prelude to Wagner's *Die Meistersinger von Nürnberg*, Tchaikovsky's piano concertos (with Vladimir Horowitz), and Georges Enesco's *Rapsodies roumaines*. Announcements were in the language of the targeted audience, even if that was Mandarin.[54]

Two broadcast series in particular make the agenda clear. *Radio Symphonies of America* presented the NBC Symphony Orchestra (conducted by Toscanini) and other major orchestras and was "accompanied by a script that describes the cultural life of a different American city on each show."[55] *Contemporary American Music* focused on twentieth-century music by such composers as Barber, Robert Russell Bennett, George Chadwick, Copland, Cowell, and Wallingford Riegger.[56] One program that Voice of America broadcast in early 1945 combined Cowell's *Hymn and Fuguing Tune* no. 2 with Barber's *Capricorn Concerto*. In September 1944 the OWI prepared a seventieth-birthday broad-cast for Charles Ives that—as Cowell informed the composer—was "being sent to various parts of the world for radio use."[57] As early as December 1943, Cowell had organized a fifteen-minute program on Ives "in which the announcer gives an outline of your work and accomplishment as a composer, and the *Charlie Rutledge* [*sic*] and the Fugue from the 4th Symphony are heard. This is then recorded, and the records used for broadcasting many times over. This program is up to now accepted for broadcasting to Italy and Persia, and probably for Arabia and Sweden; it will doubtless be used by the other nations as well."[58] Ives's Symphony no. 4 had by then acquired the status of a possible contender for the "Great American Symphony," especially among those of an avant-garde bent, and was therefore particularly suited to be presented on this kind of propaganda program.[59] Ives's 1921 adaptation of the folk song "Charlie Rutlage," on the other hand, grounded the composer sonically in the American soil of cowboys and farmers. Cowell's choice of repertoire for this broadcast thus combined the down-to-earth American Ives with the daring symphonist into a programmatic embodiment of avant-garde Americana.

One of the biggest musical coups for the OWI in 1944 was a propaganda film that featured Arturo Toscanini conducting Giuseppe Verdi's overture to *La forza del destino* and the same composer's *Hymn of Nations*. As Howard Taubman reported for the *New York Times Magazine*: "The other day the OWI began a new experiment with music as a propaganda weapon—a movie in which the emphasis is on music. The star is Arturo Toscanini, who once declined a Hollywood offer of $250,000 for a single motion picture, but who has made a movie for the Government without any fee at all."[60] The Toscanini film explicitly linked the maestro's music making to his fight against Fascism. It was produced in late 1943 and released early the next year, in tandem with the fall of Mussolini and Italy's invasion by Allied troops. This link to current events is clearly reflected in the musical arrangement, in which Toscanini added to Verdi's medley of national anthems his own orchestrations of the "Internationale" and "The Star-Spangled Banner." Alas, the portion of the performance containing the "Internationale" was later cut by U.S. film censors during the cold war, although one can now see it restored to its rightful place.[61] In this film music and musicians were fused into a powerful message about the inclusivity of American culture. The camera repeatedly highlights the African American alto in the front row of the chorus, and the Italian maestro is filmed voicing the words of "Italia" and "The Star-Spangled Banner." The rousing finale, with its five national anthems, carried a sonic message that even the most superficial listeners could decipher, especially after the commentator's initial explanation of their roles as positive signifiers of national identity. This commentary was reproduced in twenty-three languages, including Afrikaans, Arabic, Chinese, French, Serbo-Croatian, and Turkish.[62]

No other OWI film made a protagonist of classical music in quite this manner, but the Motion Picture Division of the agency placed significant weight on music in its documentaries, which contained often long stretches of images underscored only with music.[63] Twenty-eight-year-old Gail Kubik served as director of music for the OWI's Domestic Film Bureau before being drafted into the army in March 1943 (where he would fill a similar position).[64] His first OWI film was *The World at War* (released in September 1942), in which the score played a prominent role. A 1943 article described this film as taking "advantage of music as a powerful, emotional medium in a way in which few documentaries have attempted." The *New York Times* lauded its "eloquent" score, and several music critics devoted independent articles to Kubik's music.[65] Kubik himself discussed music's role in propaganda films as an "emotional commentary" that serves "as the voice of Democracy."[66]

During his tenure at the OWI, Kubik continued to write film music but also drew on composers such as Morton Gould and Paul Creston to score the documentaries. In addition to commissioning original scores, the film-music division could also dip into the vast library of government-film scores: for example, *Japanese Relocation* (released in November 1942) recycled music that Virgil Thomson had written for earlier government films.[67] As was the case with radio, after 1943 the focus of OWI documentary production shifted to the Overseas Branch in New York, where (as we saw in chapter 1) OWI filmmakers continued to draw on the cream of American composers, including Blitzstein, Copland, Thomson, and Weill (Table 2.1). As Kubik pointed out, OWI documentaries were an attractive medium

TABLE 2.1 Selected OWI-produced Documentaries

Date	Film Title and Director	Composer
1942	*The World at War* (Sam Spewak)	Gail Kubik
1942	*Ring of Steel* (Garson Kanin)	Morton Gould
1944	*Hymn of Nations* (Alexander Hammid)	Giuseppe Verdi/Arturo Toscanini
1944	*Salute to France* (Garson Kanin, Jean Renoir)	Kurt Weill
1945	*Tuesday in November* (John Houseman)	Virgil Thomson
1945	*The Cummington Story* (Helen Grayson, Larry Madison)	Aaron Copland
1945	*The True Glory* (Garson Kanin)	Marc Blitzstein

because they offered composers significantly more creative freedom than the traditional Hollywood motion picture. He celebrated this stylistic openness as a democratic feature, or a "force in the fight against Fascism.... The music of the documentary film is, to my mind, more distinguished for its essential democracy than the music of other types of films because composers in the documentary field have more often been allowed the luxury of writing what *they* felt than have our colleagues in the more commercial field."[68]

Though the OWI's emphasis was on music in radio and film, the agency also became involved in other forms of musical propaganda. In late 1944 concert music starred in a major OWI project when Blitzstein started planning to present American music in Paris, which had been liberated just that August. He envisaged a festival for the following spring that would present American orchestral music, chamber music, film music, and jazz in five concerts in Paris that would be destined for widespread radio broadcast. Not only were American composers to be featured in these programs, but also works by "great composers who have taken refuge in America since the emergence of the Nazi tyranny." Works he suggested for the American concert included such stalwarts as Copland's *Billy the Kid* and Harris's Third Symphony, as well as music by David Diamond, Walter Piston, and William Schuman. For the concert of works by composers in American exile, he included Stravinsky, Schoenberg, Martinů, Hindemith, Weill, and Milhaud, among others. And for the jazz concert, his memorandum of November 29 proposed Glenn Miller and his AEF Ensemble—barely two weeks before the bandleader's death.[69] By the end of December, Blitzstein had started negotiations with Duke Ellington instead.[70]

When Blitzstein was reassigned to work on the film score for the documentary *The True Glory*, he passed the Paris project to Copland, who was appointed to the OWI as assistant representative of the Overseas Branch in New York. Plans for the festival—now expanded to seven concerts—were revealed to the press, which reported that the festival's purpose was to stress musical progress in the United States. As Daniel Saidenberg explained, the aim was to show how contemporary American music had "progressed during the last five years. We are presenting these concerts...not so much to provide entertainment for the French people as to show what we have done in this country. The inclusion of music by European composers now living in the United States will give Frenchmen an accurate picture of how the music of foreign artists who took refuge in our country has grown during this period, and what effect our way of life has had on their work."[71]

Once Copland was on board, he started to mobilize his contacts. In a letter to his former teacher Nadia Boulanger he wrote: "Forgive me if I jump from the above to the enclosed clipping in to-day's paper. Imagine how excited I am! It is a unique opportunity to bring back to Paris at such a moment some of the fruits which were nourished there. You must give me all your ideas as to what would be most effective from a French point of view. We are planning to present Stravinsky's Symphony [in C] as part of the Festival."[72] In the end, however, all these plans came to naught, mainly because the OWI could not secure congressional funding for the project, and the festival was cancelled only six weeks after it was publicly announced. Wrote Copland to Boulanger: "Just between ourselves I feel the OWI made something of a mess of its own plans."[73] The OWI did sponsor a concert in Paris later in October, but the project was far more limited in scope—a swan song for the agency's musical propaganda mission—featuring music by Stillman Kelly, Schuman, and Thomson.[74] By the time the concert took place, the OWI had ceased to exist.[75]

While Copland worked on the festival's repertoire, Elliott Carter was assigned to write an essay for the program book to be titled "Music in America at War." This outline reflects OWI propaganda guidelines by emphasizing inclusiveness, diversity, and democracy. Carter proposed to elaborate on how "local differences in cultural minorities [were] not obliterated.... No élite or clique has been able to dominate the country and dictate trends."[76] European composers in American exile received as much attention as did the role of Boulanger in the education of American composers (including, of course, Carter himself). America's music—in Carter's presentation—was cosmopolitan while at the same time being firmly grounded, for the most part, "in native American materials." Carter named Copland, Cowell, Gershwin, Hanson, Harris, and Thomson as proponents of this tendency, although he counted Barber, Piston, and Sessions among the internationalists. It was a festival intended—in Carter's summary—to show "America becoming one of the important cultural centers of the West."[77]

Such overtly propagandistic use of music was also the intention of Roy Harris when he tried to find out from a number of American colleagues whom they would include among "the ten composers of symphonic and chamber music...most worthy to represent American culture to European nations."[78] Among those who answered, Thomson responded rather sarcastically that by asking for ten names, Harris set too broad a parameter, for this would "leave room for everybody," whereas Copland took his response more seriously by relating specific individuals to a target audience: "For example, for a broad radio audience I would prescribe RR Bennett or M. Gould rather than R. Sessions, although from a purely cultural standpoint I think the latter more significant. But of course the significance would only be apparent to an elite public."[79] In their response to Harris, neither Thomson nor Copland questioned the instrumentalizing of concert music for propaganda purposes, nor did any other composers who worked for the OWI. In effect, Cowell addressed the issue head-on in his comments to the Greater New York Chapter of the fledgling American Musicological Society by explicitly linking classical music and propaganda: "Propaganda is rather a new word, and we do not often think of it in connection with classic music; yet any music which serves a definite purpose may be said to have some propaganda aspect."[80] Similarly, Gail Kubik defended the inclusion of music in "the counter-offensive in propaganda," especially in film, because composers not only could serve as "the finest symbol of man's dignity" but also were "the men best equipped to support with music these messages to the world, of Democracy at work."[81] Here the majority of U.S. musicians stood in strong contrast to such film directors as John Ford, who eschewed both the word and the concept of propaganda, not only because of general U.S. suspicion of the ideology of propaganda since World War I, but also because of such problematic models of Nazi film propaganda as Leni Riefenstahl's infamous documentary *Triumph des Willens* (1935).[82] On the contrary, as Blitzstein, Harris, and others pointed out repeatedly, the propaganda victory of Shostakovich's Symphony no. 7 ("Leningrad") offered a positive model for American composers to join forces with the OWI specifically as musicians, in the process coopting symphonic and other concert music as an appropriate propaganda medium.

With the end of the war, the OWI came under increased scrutiny. Politicians and journalists alike had never been quite convinced of its usefulness, and rivalry with the OSS and the State Department created additional obstacles. As Harold Talburt's caricature from May 24, 1945, shows, music's power as a weapon of war took on the traits of an operetta plot rather than serious business, a sure sign of the OWI's declining status (Figure 2.3). Yet music's increasingly prominent role in the agency reflected and even affected developments in the United States both musically and aesthetically, not just during the war but also in American cultural politics in the first years of the occupation of Germany.[83] The uses of music in the OWI were certainly both pragmatic and programmatic, but there was more to this than just rallying the troops with music they might enjoy. The perceived view of America as a culturally deficient country demanded a concerted effort in the propaganda war to show its cultural achievements. The musicians chosen for this task combined their own personal tastes with the demands of this mission, so that by 1945 a canon of American music was ready to be shared with the world at large and with audiences at home. Until the ground shifted again with the cold war and McCarthy's witch hunt, American musicians came out of the war with a strongly positive identity as cultural winners.

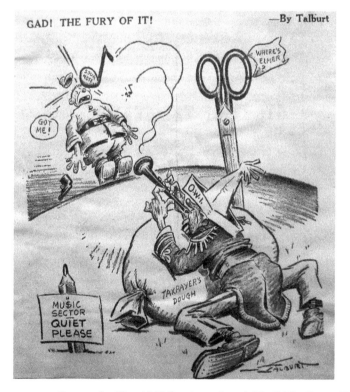

FIGURE 2.3 Cartoon by Harold Talburt, captioned "Gad! The Fury of It!" *Washington Daily News*, May 24, 1945.

Crossing Borders: Music, Diplomacy, and the State Department

Other U.S. government branches also discovered that concert music was eminently suited for their political objectives. In part this was due to their common, if not always shared, agendas; in part it was because key individuals were often called to serve in multiple administrative or advisory capacities. The State Department, for example, considered music "a medium through which whole peoples might be put in touch with each other."[84] In contrast to what it considered the OWI's "use of music for war and short term objectives," however, the State Department deemed its mandate to be "the contribution of music to international relations and principally for long term objectives."[85] This comment, made in 1943 by Charles A. Thomson, the chief of the State Department's Division of Cultural Relations, is revealing. The dichotomy that he established between propaganda's war-driven ends and diplomacy's idealistic internationalism mirrored an institutionalized ideological conflict between Roosevelt's Executive Office and the State Department that had shaped arts diplomacy in the United States since the late 1930s.[86]

Whereas music and the other arts had often played a significant role in the cultural politics of European nations such as France, Germany, Italy, and the Soviet Union, American diplomats and politicians traditionally steered clear of government-funded musical activities in the international arena. This changed dramatically with Roosevelt's establishment, on August 16, 1940, of the Office for the Coordination of Commercial and Cultural Relations between the American Republics, and his appointment of Nelson Aldrich Rockefeller to be its head.[87] By now the Roosevelt administration had become increasingly worried about Axis aggression and was taking protective countermeasures, most evidently with the reinstitution of the draft through the Selective Training and Service Act in September 1940. With its internationalist stance and focus on diplomatic equanimity, the State Department had failed, in the president's eyes, to counter the influence of Axis propaganda in the Latin and South American republics, even though its modestly funded Division of Cultural Relations had been in place since July 1938.[88] Therefore—as he would in June 1942 with the OWI in order to maximize the U.S. information flow—Roosevelt created an organization that would be under his direct influence in order to translate his Pan-American policies into action. Reconfigured a year later, on July 30, 1941, as the Office of the Coordinator of Inter-American Affairs (OCIAA), the new government office was set up to push Roosevelt's "Good Neighbor" policy aggressively, by both economic and cultural means.

Rockefeller considered his new agency as counteracting, through the arts, the Axis's "intellectual imperialism," which be considered "just as serious a threat to the security and defense of the hemisphere as the possibility of a military invasion." In contrast to the State Department's insistence on "reciprocity in relationship to other American republics," Rockefeller shifted the OCIAA's emphasis toward "interpreting the United States to Latin America rather than vice-versa."[89] The trigger for using the arts in this competition for public opinion in Latin America was the Fascist program for musical propaganda in the Americas, developed as early as 1934 after Adriano Lualdi's visit to South America in 1932. Reporting on his fact-finding tour through South America from June to October 1940, Carleton Sprague Smith (chief of the Music Division at the New York Public Library) warned about the significant German and Italian influence there. Many South American nations remained neutral throughout most of the conflict (Argentina and Chile, for example, joined the Allies only in 1945), and some were known for their sympathies with the Axis. In Brazil, which remained neutral until August 1942, when it joined the Allies, Smith discovered that "German and Italian subsidies still function despite the war," with money being used "in subtle ways to influence intellectuals and important men." In contrast to American inertia, "the German and Italian ministries of cultural propaganda and the publishing houses (especially Breitkopf & Härtel, Simrock and Ricordi) send review copies of their latest orchestral publications to practically all conductors in Latin America."[90] In short—as Smith's colleague Charles Seeger pointed out—in Latin America, the German and Italian "plans for furtherance of fascist ideas through music were extensive."[91]

To thwart this influence, Rockefeller threw significant resources toward his vision of arts diplomacy. Music alone was allocated $100,000 in the Office's first fiscal year (1940–41) and saw its budget multiplied to $600,000 for 1941–42.[92] Compared to Rockefeller's overall budget, these sums were relatively small, but in contrast with the State Department's modest allocation for culture they seemed princely.[93] Among the OCIAA's first musical activities was the establishment in November 1940 of a Music Committee, chaired by Carleton Sprague Smith, that was in charge of selecting the projects to be financed by the organization, one of which led to the formation in February 1941 of the Inter-American Music Center, a key operating unit that was placed under the organizational umbrella of the Pan-American Union, directed by Charles Seeger.[94] The OCIAA financed the center for the first three years to the tune of $20,000–$30,000, to which its Music Committee added supplementary project funds. Furthermore, the Carnegie Foundation and other private sponsors augmented significantly its operating budget.[95]

Both Smith and Seeger had gained extensive arts-administrative experience with Roosevelt's WPA before their involvement in Pan-American activities: Seeger had been the deputy director of the Federal Music Project from 1937 to 1941. Indeed, some of their programs for the OCIAA—including educational initiatives, folk-song collection, surveys, and concert programs—had obvious roots in the WPA's cultural activism.

Yet the OCIAA and its music program had little opportunity to develop independently from the State Department, given that Sumner Welles, the Under Secretary of State and one of Roosevelt's closest advisors, forced a showdown in early 1941 over foreign-policy control.[96] The president sided with Welles in this dispute with Rockefeller, which led in effect to a division of labor between the State Department (which was in charge of policy decisions) and the OCIAA (which controlled the money and was responsible for the specific implementation of programs). In order to formulate music-related policy, the State Department established its own Advisory Committee on Music in May and June 1941. In contrast to the OCIAA's Music Committee (a so-called operating committee), the State Department one was to be strictly "advisory" and would neither "manage nor execute programs."[97] Some of its membership overlapped with the Music Committee of the OCIAA, either ex officio, such as Smith and Seeger, or because individuals were appointed to both committees, as was the case with Copland. When Copland raised the question of his dual membership, everyone agreed that this arrangement had "many advantages."[98] Soon thereafter, in October 1941, the OCIAA's Music Committee was folded into the State Department's Advisory Committee, whose purpose was now to advise both the State Department and the Coordinator of Inter-American Affairs "regarding the stimulation of musical interchange among the American republics and the coordination of activities in this country which concern inter-American music."[99]

Even though the two institutions collaborated on cultural programs as the focus of U.S. arts diplomacy turned toward "influencing other American republics in the way of better appreciation of the United States," the difference between the State Department's ecumenical internationalism and the OCIAA's aggressive focus on national security continued to pull these agencies into two different directions.[100] With respect to music, the two contrasting positions became clear, for example, in a discussion about "the value of culture as a national asset." From the toned-down wording of the minutes it can be assumed that OCIAA pushed for the active promotion of U.S. music in Latin America, whereas the State Department questioned the "advisability of the United States attempting to transplant its music into other countries." In the end, the committee "generally agreed that American music was not to be imposed but exchanged."[101] While the OCIAA was more aggressively in favor of propaganda, the State Department's emphasis on exchange reflects the deep-seated distrust of any form of indoctrination during the interwar years. Propaganda's positive alternative, as Harold D. Lasswell pointed out in 1935, was education and constructive information; the State Department's inter-American music program reflected this bias not only in allocating significant sums to student-exchange programs and music education, but also in promoting Latin American guests and their music during their U.S. visits.[102] As one example among many, a press release from June 1, 1943, drew attention to the "tour of musical and educational centers" of the Dominican musician Enrique de Marchena as a guest of the State Department.[103]

The inter-American music exchange, sponsored by the OCIAA and the State Department, went beyond exchange programs and sponsored visits to the creation of lending libraries of American music in several South American capitals; the support of concert tours by U.S. ensembles such as the Yale Glee Club and the American Ballet Theatre; the recording of folk music in Latin and South America; the production of radio programs such as the fifty-two half-hour broadcasts titled *Music in American Life*; and the financing of fact-finding missions across the Americas—most famously Copland's four-month tour through Colombia, Ecuador, Peru, Chile, Argentina, Uruguay, Brazil, and Cuba in the fall and winter of 1941.[104] The OCIAA's budget for 1941–42 reflects the variety of musical activities that fell under the mandate of cultural diplomacy (Table 2.2), and also the key role Seeger's Inter-American Music Center played in their realization. What stands out in this budget is the allocation of substantial funds for the reciprocal visits of Latin-American musicians (especially $100,000 for a yet-to-be-determined major ensemble) on the one hand, and for scholarly projects on the other.

In musical terms, the focus of U.S. arts diplomacy was on folk and contemporary concert music. This was reflected in the makeup of the Advisory Committee, which included not only Seeger and Smith, but also Olin Downes, Melville J. Herskovits, Alain Locke, and Harold Spivacke, all of whom had a pronounced interest in the recording, study, and dissemination of folk music.[105] Copland (who was replaced by Howard Hanson in 1944), Seeger, and Deems Taylor all had extensive experience in the promotion of contemporary American music (Table 2.3). Both folk and concert music could serve two interconnected purposes by fostering cultural exchange, on the one hand, and by creating national as well as hemispherical identities, on the other. In a statement from May 1944 on the music program of the State Department, the war was credited as "promoting a kind of musical nationalism in all of the American republics."[106] The previous year Seeger had

TABLE 2.2 1941–42 Budget Allocation to Pan-American Music Activities, Office of the Coordinator of Inter-American Affairs, approved by the Advisory Committee on Music to the Department of State

Allocated Budget	
$15,000	Grant for Inter-American Music Center (additional funds for "smaller research projects")
$100,000	American Ballet Theatre Tour
$6,000	Yale Glee Club Tour to South America
$6,000	Survey of School Music by Dr. John Beattie and Dr. Willard Curtis (handled through the Inter-American Music Center)
$3,200	Survey of Carnivals in Brazil and Central America by Evans Clark
$1,200	Exchange of folk material by the Music Division of the Library of Congress with the Discoteca of São Paulo (Brazil).
$1,000	Purchase of 200 copies of the *Boletín Latino-Americano de Música*, vol. 5, by the Inter-American Music Center
$1,500	Bibliography of music books and reference materials (Inter-American Music Center)
$617	Deficits of concerts of Latin American Music, performed by Hugo Balzo and John Kirkpatrick in New York City, the University of North Carolina at Chapel Hill, and Oberlin College (underwritten by the Inter-American Music Center)
$2,500	Lecture concert tour by Domenico Santa Cruz through the United States (also handled by the Inter-American Music Center)
$15,000	Composer-player concert tour in Latin America (15 concerts)
Projects under Consideration	
$100,000	To send music phonographs, books, and records (Carnegie sets) to key institutions in Latin America (to be "supplemented later with sets containing exclusively United States works")
$30,000	Projects of the Inter-American Music Center
$100,000	Tour of Latin America by the Goldman Band ("or some other outstanding Band")
$100,000	Importation of some important concert group from Latin America
$30,000	Folklore expedition
$50,000	General music student exchange program
$50,000	Exchange of North and South American music works
$50,000	Project in popular-music field
$50,000	Project in operatic field
$10,000	Employment of reliable music agents on the East and West Coasts
$20,000	Contingency fund

Source: Minutes of the Meeting on June 13, 1941, of the Advisory Committee on Music, Division of Cultural Relations, Department of State, pp. 8–10. Records of Interdepartmental and Intradepartmental Committees (State Department), *NARA*, RG 353.3, Box 30.

TABLE 2.3 Membership of the Advisory Committee for Music, Department of State, 1941–44

1941–42	1942–43	1943–44
Warren D. Allen		
	James Angell	
Marshall Bartholomew		
John W. Beattie		
William Berrien		
		Clifford V. Buttleman
		Gilbert Chase
Samuel Chotzinoff		
Evans Clark		
Aaron Copland	Aaron Copland	
	Olin Downes	Olin Downes
		Nathaniel Finston
	Benny Goodman	
		Howard Hanson
Melville Herskovits	Melville Herskovits	Melville Herskovits
	Edwin Hughes	
	Alain Locke	
Earl Moore		
Russell W. Morgan		
		John G. Paine
	Lilla Belle Pitts	
	John Sengstack	John Sengstack
Carleton Sprague Smith	Carleton Sprague Smith	
Davidson Taylor	Davidson Taylor	
	Deems Taylor	
Ex officio		
Charles Seeger	Charles Seeger	Charles Seeger
Harold Spivacke	Harold Spivacke	Harold Spivacke
Charles A. Thomson	Charles A. Thomson	Charles A. Thomson

pointed out that all twenty-one American republics had become conscious that, after Pearl Harbor, they were "on their own feet, musically speaking." Although he noted that there was still some dependence on Europe ("especially in respect to the monuments of the occidental art"), he also subscribed to the widely held belief "that the contribution of the New World to music may be substantial."[107] The anti-European undertones of Seeger's comments reflect not so much the State Department's traditional position as that of Rockefeller's OCIAA, but—as the 1944 comment above on Pan-American musical nationalism reveals—such attitudes slowly crept into the discourse of the State Department as well.

Music's assumed ability to speak "without the need of an interpreter" by appealing "directly to the emotions as well as the intellect" counted as its unique power, in the context of arts diplomacy, to build bridges where words held no sway.[108] Furthermore, in Downes's opinion, such a contribution to "the development of international understanding" not only fostered positive relations but also had the added advantage of serving as an "antidote for anti-American antagonism."[109] As Herskovits pointed out in a letter to Charles A. Thomson in May 1943, "exchanges of various 'art music' forms would tend to acquaint these other countries, already greatly impressed by our technological achievements, with the fact that there are other values in our civilization worth their knowing."[110] The rhetoric of the Music Advisory Committee echoed similar discourses in the OWI about the promotional value of presenting U.S. culture to neighboring nations. The difference, so far as the State Department was concerned, lay in the continued focus on exchange, even though the exigencies of war shifted the emphasis from education to propaganda. Nor were the Advisory Committee's decisions about which music to promote uncontested. In 1942 Seeger criticized his committee comrades as "intellectually snobbish" and "academically clubby"; William Berrien—who represented the American Council of Learned Societies in the Advisory Committee and (though not a musician) had published a book entitled *Latin American Composers and Their Problems* in 1937—accused them of a "certain cliquishness."[111] A year later Downes suggested that the musical exchange was too narrow because it was "entirely too much characterized by the production of certain cliques of the allegedly 'advanced' musical minds of the two continents and their music." Furthermore, the selections needed to "include a much larger percentage of the folk music in its genuine original simple forms of the respective nations." Downes leveled heavy charges against the "self-propagandists" on the Advisory Committee as having "seized avidly the opportunity of exploiting their own wares" instead of choosing "compositions of proved value and likewise melodic attractiveness" that would constitute an "enlivening influence."[112]

The progress of the war brought with it another dramatic change of focus for the Advisory Committee by broadening the scope of the State Department's cultural activities to include not only the Soviet Union and China but also so-called non-European nations, for example in the "African zone."[113] The impulse for this shift was a meeting of three committee members—Seeger, Charles A. Thomson, and Davidson Taylor (the head of music programming at CBS)—in March 1943, where Seeger suggested expanding the scope of the Advisory Committee to include the whole world.[114] This development coincided with the decision to transfer, as of July 1, 1943, the "music and arts activities of the Coordinator of Inter-American Affairs" to the State Department.[115] At the meeting of the Advisory Committee on June 24, 1943, this new direction for arts diplomacy provided grounds for extensive discussion, initiated by Herskovits, about the role of music in cultural relations with different countries around the globe. The committee members brought examples "both of antipathy and appreciation on the part of various nationalities toward different types of American music. This led to a discussion of the possible dangers in attempting musical interchanges in geographical areas with regard to which the music traditions are not understood."[116] As a consequence, the Advisory Committee voted to set up three subcommittees of specialists to prepare models of arts diplomacy with "areas of non-European culture," the Soviet Union, and China. The minutes of this meeting reveal, however, that the State Department's Division of Cultural Relations had already been active with respect to the latter two. As far as music relations with the USSR went, the State Department, in cooperation with the OWI, had sent the Soviet Union "microfilm copies of contemporary American compositions and transcriptions [i.e., recordings] of the NBC Symphony Orchestra and the Metropolitan Opera." With respect to China, activities ranged from recording Chinese music for American audiences to "shipping recordings of American music to China."[117]

On the heels of the much-publicized tour of the United States in 1943 of Madame Chiang Kai-shek (Soong May-ling), the wife of China's generalissimo and "first lady of China," the State Department's renewed focus on China matched the increased pro-Chinese sentiment in 1943, which culminated in the repeal of the Chinese Exclusions Acts in December 1943.[118] She was the first Chinese national, and only the second woman, to speak before Congress: her address in the Capitol, on February 18, 1943, was broadcast across the United States, igniting nationwide support of China War Relief. She had been educated at Wellesley and was a Christian, and she was considered a modern woman. This pro-Western identity prompted even Eleanor Roosevelt to declare "a great feeling of pride in her achievements," and Madame Chiang was the perfect ally.[119] One fascinating photograph, taken on her fund-raising tour in Boston and published in both *Musical America* and the *Musical Courier*, represents arts diplomacy at its most poignant (Figure 2.4). Standing next to Madame Chiang is the American Indian

FIGURE 2.4 Madame Chiang Kai-shek (*front*) with soprano Mobley Lushanya in Boston, March 1943. *Musical Courier* (March 20, 1943): 1. The caption identifies Lushanya as an "Indian soprano" who was "chosen to sing the National Anthem as a representative of the oldest culture on this continent, and appeared in Chickasaw ceremonial dress as a Princess of that nation."

soprano Mobley Lushanya, who had opened the rally with "The Star-Spangled Banner." The caption in *Musical America* identified the performance as a sign of "the sympathy and support of Americans like Mobley Lushanya, Chicksaw Indian Soprano," thus emphasizing simultaneously the exotic aspect of the visit and the inclusive side of the war effort.[120]

The State Department must have been delighted with the image. Its Division of Cultural Relations had established a China section with money from the president's Emergency Fund to expand its cultural activities from Latin America to China in 1942 and the next year in the Near East.[121] The China section's policies were a direct descendant of American cultural and educational efforts, which had been dominated, since the mid-nineteenth century, by missionaries. Raymond Fosdick, the president of the Rockefeller Foundation, had declared in the late 1930s that the object of such American initiatives was "to make over a medieval society in terms of modern knowledge."[122] The State Department's twin goals for China were modernization and democratization (along the lines of the American model), and as in the case of Latin America, student exchange and cultural diplomacy were considered powerful means of achieving these aims. In a report to the State Department, two American China specialists explored how music could serve to foster cultural relations. After discussing traditional Chinese music and Western-influenced songs ("Chee Lai" comes to mind), the authors addressed the question of which kind of music could contribute "to China's desire to know and understand us better" by exploring which "types of American music would be acceptable to the Chinese." As far as "purely American music" went, the authors found that "Negro spirituals strike a highly consonant chord with their hearts," whereas "American jazz is distasteful to them," an assessment that probably reveals more about U.S. prejudices against a "medieval" people than Chinese taste (by assuming that the Chinese, as members of a preindustrial society, would prefer music associated with rural slavery over that of urban modernism). With respect to Western concert music, the list of "acceptable" composers became problematic, for all but Debussy were Austro-German, with Bach, Brahms, and Mozart at the top of the list. On the contrary, music perceived as "overbalanced emotionally such as Tschaikowsky, Wagner, Chopin, Liszt, was not well liked," again suggesting a problematic essentialism in this assessment of China.[123] But with no comment on contemporary American music, the outcome of this report was practically worthless for the musical program of the State Department. China disappeared from the purview of the Advisory Committee as fast as it had been introduced, probably because traditional forms of musical exchange (concert tours and folk-music research) were perceived as tricky given contemporary prejudices about Chinese music. Instead, and in what smacks of a classic case of passing the buck, American musical programs directed at China were placed in the hands of the OWI, even though other programs such as student and teacher exchanges continued to thrive in State Department hands.

In contrast to this diffidence over arts diplomacy with China, the Advisory Committee's second new musical target, the Soviet Union, received significantly more attention once it entered the reckoning in 1943. Even at the height of pro-Soviet sentiment during World War II, the nature of U.S. relationships with the USSR remained ambiguous. The Molotov-Ribbentrop Pact of 1939 had cemented the fear of "red Fascism" in numerous American minds, and the attacks on Finland and Poland had painted the Soviets as aggressors alongside Nazi Germany. Despite a tremendous amount of pro-Soviet rhetoric from the Roosevelt administration after the German invasion of the USSR in June 1941 and the United States' military alliance with the Soviet Union after Pearl Harbor, the United States never trusted its Soviet allies to the extent that they did either Great Britain or China.[124] Furthermore, even though Moscow, in July 1943, suggested that cultural relations between the United States and the Soviet Union be strengthened, the actual implementation of policies and programs to that end stalled, especially on the Soviet side.[125] The Advisory Committee on Music, however, took a special interest in the issue: after all, Russian music and musicians—whether conductors such as Serge Koussevitzky or composers such as Sergei Rachmaninoff—were a staple of American concert life, and Russian war music had stirred its U.S. audiences, from the much-loved recordings by the Red Army Chorus to Shostakovich's widely disseminated Symphony no. 7 ("Leningrad"). In June 1943 the committee emphasized its "especial interest in bringing about a closer relationship in musical interchange between the United States and Russia."[126] Charles A. Thomson wrote to Loy W. Henderson of the Division of European Affairs in order to clear the establishment of a new committee devoted to the matter: as he pointed out, "This sub-committee will work quietly and without publicity."[127] Once Thomson had the go-ahead, he invited Olin Downes to form his Sub-Committee on Musical Interchange with the USSR during the fall of 1943, with the directive that its membership was to remain confidential.[128]

Downes constituted a committee of composers, performers, and administrators (including Allen Wardwell, chairman of the Russian War Relief Fund), which met in New York in February, March, and May 1944 and reported back to the State Department's Advisory Committee in June. Whereas Downes, in a letter to Thomson, went into such details as to who should be invited to the United States (the Red Army Chorus and the Soviet Ballet) and who should be sent over (the Boston Symphony or the "unique *Oklahoma!*"—the latter being "a genuine and cultural project"), the subcommittee's report remained on the level of abstract policy recommendations.[129] The proposal emphasized the State Department's antipropaganda ethos of education and exchange, and the first suggestion was a reciprocal agreement between the two governments on musical copyright, which would constitute an essential element "to end the present chaotic situation" and therefore encourage further exchange. Other reciprocal projects were translations of important music books into Russian or English and the exchange of artists, students, teachers, and printed music and records. "Finally," Downes concluded his report, "the Committee has under consideration a plan for commissioning a book on Music in America" that would not only target the

Soviet market but "is needed at home" and "if properly executed, may be considered for translation into several languages."[130]

The subcommittee, however, was not without its institutional and political idiosyncrasies. Several of its members—including Copland, Howard Hanson, and Serge Koussevitzky—overlapped with the Music Committee of the National Council of American–Soviet Friendship, whose pro-Soviet stance was inspired and condoned (if only for about two years) by the wartime alliance.[131] Just like its official counterpart at the State Department, the National Council's music committee met to discuss musical exchange with the Soviet Union.[132] In addition, it organized the concert for the three-day conference in November 1943 marking the tenth anniversary of diplomatic relations between the United States and the Soviet Union with a performance—among others—of quartets by Prokofiev and Shostakovich by the Budapest String Quartet.[133] Parallel attempts to promote American music in the Soviet Union bore fruit in May 1944 in a concert in Moscow by the State Symphony Orchestra. The program ranged from Roy Harris's Symphony no. 5 to Jerome Kern's "Smoke Gets in Your Eyes."[134] This concert, attended by numerous diplomats and broadcast in the Soviet Union, clearly fused the efforts of the State Department and the private initiative of the National Council of American–Soviet Friendship, and it constituted what was probably the high point of U.S.–Soviet musical relations before their deterioration during the cold war.

The Soviet Union and China expanded the State Department's musical horizons away from its intense earlier focus on Latin America. Likewise, a third initiative that began in 1943 led to the recruitment of the young anthropologist Richard Waterman to conduct research on non-Western music based on sources available in the United States. Waterman had just completed his Ph.D. at Northwestern University (advised by Herskovits), and he spent most of 1944 on this project, financed by the State Department. Letters between the State Department and the OWI reveal that the propaganda agency, with its extensive record collection, became, in effect, Waterman's main resource for his study.[135] Furthermore, by the summer of 1944 the State Department was allotting funds for musical exchanges in an ever-increasing territory, including Iran, Afghanistan, and India; it also started to prepare itself for musical diplomacy after the end of the war, especially in European countries.[136] But throughout this expansion, the State Department's inter-American music exchange continued—if on a smaller budget—and included the financing of concerts in Latin and South America, exchange programs, or simply diplomatic assistance, as when Carlos Chávez's scores for his 1943 concerts in the United States were transported in diplomatic pouches.[137]

The Singing Army: Uplift and Education for a Nation

If the State Department saw music as a means of cultural diplomacy in which the act was sometimes more important than the result, the armed forces considered it first and foremost a weapon. Indeed, as the popular entertainer Joe Jordan wrote during his time as a music advisor at Fort Huachuca, Arizona, "a singing army is a winning army." Raymond Kendall, the music coordinator for the USO, put it more bluntly: "Within the armed services . . . singing is primarily a weapon, a medium through which men march straighter, give better commands, fight harder, work longer and move co-ordinately."[138] In order to justify music as "an effective weapon," military personnel and civilian advisors explored not only the benefits of the practical applications of singing and band music in training, combat, and recreation, but also the broader social implications of music education on both amateur and professional levels.[139] During the war, music was increasingly considered a civilizing force in the American military, even though both music and musicians faced prejudices rooted in stereotypes, especially at first. One was—as one advisor commented in February 1942—"the traditional American suspicion that there is something 'sissy' about music for men,"[140] a trenchant remark in the context of a military that screened its draftees for sexual orientation and considered homosexuality a "deviation" disqualifying one for armed service.[141] Music was also perceived as a racial marker: over and over again, reports about music making in the armed forces commented that "colored troops sing," whereas "white troops are half-hearted singers."[142] This stood in sharp relief to the much-publicized employment of music by the German military. As Howard Bronson, the Army Special Services officer in charge of music, pointed out in his address to a group of morale officers, "mass singing is a part of daily routine" in the German army.[143] For Caucasian Americans, who made up about 90 percent of the American military during World War II, music making and singing had (according to Bonson's assessment) little place in day-to-day life outside church services and variety shows; the aim of military music programs was to change that situation.[144]

Although the American military, especially the U.S. Navy and the Marine Corps, had remained a standing (albeit reduced) organization between the wars, most of the U.S. Army had to be reconstituted through the Selective Training and Service Act of September 14, 1940 (the navy and the marines relied on volunteers until the end of 1942). The draft brought a wide cross-section of the male population into the armed forces.[145] This differed from the situation in 1917–18, when almost 80 percent of enlisted men had indicated "grade school and under" as their educational background, and only 9 percent were either high school or college graduates. While "college men," at 10 percent, still constituted the smallest proportion of draftees in World War II, the remainder was equally divided between high school graduates, high school dropouts, and grade schoolers.[146] Such a breadth of educational and musical backgrounds meant that soldiers' recreational needs were far more diverse than in World War I. It caught the military leadership by surprise that the musical tastes of their new recruits included not only swing and popular but classical music as well, and that to an unexpectedly large degree.

From the outset of conscription in 1940–41, officers in charge of recreation considered music a strong antidote to the more nefarious leisure activities of the men, a desirable alternative to frequenting prostitutes. Participatory musical entertainment therefore even became part of the military's moral and medical campaign in its fight against venereal disease.[147] From the nineteenth century on, communal music making had been a by no means unusual strategy in the moral mission of armies and industry: from the English mining and textile magnates who sponsored brass bands as part of the temperance movement to the number of European armies with active singing programs, music was often seen as an alternative, healthier form of pleasure. Commentators who wrote in support of music in the American military turned to just such precedents to make their case for music as a builder of morale. Fairfax Downey, writing for the *Los Angeles Times*, cited Napoleon's insistence on music for his regiments, and the World War I veteran and Metropolitan Opera star Lawrence Tibbett reached back to "the time of the ancient Greeks, whose warriors gave so much attention to choral song" to justify the contemporary emphasis on music.[148] Even the German Imperial army was cited as being among the victorious troops who valued music as a key factor in forging strong soldiers and an *esprit de corps*.[149]

Oversight of soldiers' activities outside their specific military duties lay with the Joint Army and Navy Committee on Welfare and Recreation, which quickly appointed a Subcommittee on Music, under the leadership of Harold Spivacke, to formulate "good programs" for the army that "involved all branches of musical activity."[150] Constituted in September 1941, this group of musical professionals, drawn from private, government, and military organizations, was remarkably effective in the establishment of musical activities for and in the military. It served as a clearinghouse for numerous issues ranging from questions of copyright to the establishment of music advisors in the army and set up a number of successful programs in close collaboration with the Army Special Services, including the distribution of songbooks and pocket-sized instruments to enlisted soldiers and the organization of long-distance music courses. As Spivacke commented in the fall of 1943, he had started out "hesitant to put forward much in the way of serious music and leaned over backward in my effort to disseminate popular music. I soon ran into considerable resentment on the part of men in the service toward such an attitude."[151]

At Spivacke's instigation, the Research Branch of the Army tried to quantify the musical tastes of American soldiers through a study undertaken in the spring of 1943. The report, "based on a survey of 4296 white enlisted men in eight camps," was considered important enough to be classified as restricted for containing "information affecting the national defense of the United States."[152] The researchers found that classical music ran a close second to swing and jazz in soldiers' preferences overall, and that men over thirty and college graduates preferred classical music over all other types. In a second survey, completed in January 1944, classical (and semiclassical) music again came out second only to swing and jazz. Modern popular music was ranked in third place, and band music in fourth: the least favorite genre was hillbilly/western.[153] This survey also tackled the question of singing. Eighty-seven percent of soldiers answered that they liked to sing, especially "with a few fellows." Asked specifically about whether they would like to hear more classical music in armed forces radio programming, 41 percent of the men answered in the affirmative. Even granting the likelihood of distortion in such surveys (people often respond in ways they think are expected of them), these results are quite extraordinary.

Official schemes for musical activities and entertainment in the armed forces therefore came up against soldiers whose musical tastes defied conventional wisdom and to which they had to be adapted. Thus music making in the military developed and changed over the four years of American involvement in the war. It became associated with a highly diversified cultural and educational program shaped by a complex set of parameters such as contemporary notions about "good music," traditional beliefs about desirable activities for soldiers (e.g., group singing), prejudices about so-called highbrow music, the missionary zeal of concerned citizens, and the individual tastes and preferences of enlisted men. That jazz and swing formed the centerpiece of musical entertainment in the armed forces was never in doubt; rather, as one of the officers in charge of music put it, the question lay in the mix of things: "My boys have souls in their hearts and jive in their bones; so if you want to make them happy, feed them both."[154] Providing this musical mix in the appropriate proportions was the core mission of the American armed forces' musical programs. This explains why such prominent musicians as Artie Shaw and Glenn Miller headed their own, prestigious bands in the navy and the army air forces respectively, while commanding officers also supported symphony orchestras, string quartets, and concerts of classical music and choirs in their camps both in the United States and overseas. Yet beyond music's recreational value, the armed forces also considered the educational significance of classical music in terms of a self-imposed institutional mandate of social uplift, in the spirit of the New Deal. Classical music thus intersected with the military's goals in both pragmatic and ideological terms.

In order to translate policies into specific activities, the Special Services employed so-called musical advisors with the task of coordinating music in military camps (Table 2.4). Although many of these music officers (as they were called after 1942) had experience in music education in civilian life,

TABLE 2.4 U.S. Army Music Advisors, Status as of October 1943

Name	Rank in 1943	Birth	Background
Bronson, Howard C.	Lieutenant Colonel	1889	Band musician (army and civilian)
Bachman, Harold R.	Major	1892	Instructor of music and director of band, University of Chicago
Bainum, Glenn C.	Captain	1888	Instructor of music and director of band, Northwestern University
Barnard, Eugene A.	2nd Lieutenant	1915	ROTC; supervisor of music in Franklin, NY
Baum, Donald E.	2nd Lieutenant	1902	Instructor at Upper Iowa University; bass soloist
Bostwick, Harold	1st Lieutenant	1915	Dance-band pianist (Leo Reisman's Orchestra/Bob Chester's Band)
Broman, Carl	Captain	1904	Concert pianist and conductor; director of the Department of Music at Hampden Sidney College, VA
Campbell, George W.	Captain	1892	Nationally known song leader; director of music for Kiwanis International
Carr, George W.	Captain	1893	Vaudeville manager and performer; band musician
Carter, Alan	Captain	1904	Concert violinist; conductor, Vermont State Orchestra; professor of music, Middleburg College

(continued)

TABLE 2.4 *(Continued)*

Name	Rank in 1943	Birth	Background
Ely, William H.	2nd Lieutenant	1909	Organist; administrator
Ferguson, Lester J.	2nd Lieutenant	1917	Tenor with Philadelphia Opera Company
Grant, Richard W.	Captain	1887	Glee club and choral director; head of music, Pennsylvania State College
Gridley, Aldus E.	Captain	1914	Private piano teacher; personnel supervisor, National Youth Administration
Haller, George	2nd Lieutenant	1915	Member of Tom Coakley's Orchestra
Held, Enos R.	2nd Lieutenant	1901	High school chemistry teacher; band and glee club conductor
Howard, George S.	Captain	1903	Director of band, orchestra, and chorus, Pennsylvania State College
Huguelet, Adalbert	Captain	1899	Concert pianist, conductor, and composer
Hunt, Arthur S.	Captain	1890	Nationally known song leader; conductor of NBC Radio Choir; editor
Isham, Ralfe C.	2nd Lieutenant	1903	Concert pianist (stage name: Ralfe Chritman), conductor
Jordan, Joe	Captain	1882	Preeminent arranger, songwriter and publisher
Keating, John R.	Captain	1913	Concert manager, Columbia Concerts Corporation
Koval, Michael J.	1st Lieutenant	1917	Saxophonist; pit violinist; bandleader
Kucinski, Leo	2nd Lieutenant	1904	Concert violinist; head of Morningside College, Iowa
Manning, John A.	2nd Lieutenant	1912	Music and dramatic arts teacher
Marriner, Guy V. R.	2nd Lieutenant	1898	Concert pianist; director of music, Franklin Institute, Philadelphia; lecturer, University of Pennsylvania
McAllister, Forrest L.	1st Lieutenant	1912	Band director
McClure, Marion	2nd Lieutenant	1909	Band director

(continued)

TABLE 2.4 (*Continued*)

Name	Rank in 1943	Birth	Background
Mear, S. R.	Captain	1894	Cornet player and bandleader; instrumental supervisor, Whitewater, WI
Mills, Clarence L.	2nd Lieutenant	1915	Band director and teacher
Morrissey, John L.	Captain	1906	Conductor, arranger, and composer; head of Department of Music, Tulane University
Multer, W. L.	Captain	1898	Bass and choral conductor; director of music, Grove City College, PA
O'Connell, Thomas	2nd Lieutenant	1919	Violinist and clarinetist; band director
Peter, Fred D.	2nd Lieutenant	1918	Pianist, choir and band director
Petrie, Charles H.	Captain	1899	Cornet player; owner and director of band camp at Winona Lake; director of Petrie's White Hussars Musical Company
Prescott, Gerald R.	Captain	1902	Bandleader and educator; director of band and music instructor, University of Minnesota
Privette, Josef	2nd Lieutenant	1906	Pianist; music teacher at Gilman County School
Quinto, O. Lenard	2nd Lieutenant	1913	High school music teacher, composer, orchestrator
Reese, Ulmont K.	Captain	1897	Band director and music educator
Robinson, Frederick H.	2nd Lieutenant	1912	Opera and concert singer
Rosenberry, Claude M.	Captain	1889	Music educator and song leader; chief of music education, Commonwealth of Pennsylvania
Ross, Lanny	1st Lieutenant	1906	Radio and film star (including *Stage Door Canteen*, 1943)
Rubinstein, Berryl	Captain	1898	Concert pianist; director of the Cleveland Institute
Salter, Harry	Captain	1898	Leading radio conductor
Schumann, Walter	1st Lieutenant	1914	Choral arranger and conductor (Andre Kostelanetz; RKO Studios)
Skornicka, Joseph E.	Captain	1902	Music educator and bandleader; orchestra musician

(*continued*)

TABLE 2.4 (*Continued*)

Name	Rank in 1943	Birth	Background
Smith, Robert A.	2nd Lieutenant	1919	Orchestra and band musician (bass horn and bass viol)
Stacy, King G.	Captain	1890	Military and civil bandleader
Stewart, Henry W.	2nd Lieutenant	1913	Professor and college organist, St. Lawrence University
Thayer, Lynn W.	1st Lieutenant	1904	Director of music, Louisville, KY
Thomas, Arnold R.	2nd Lieutenant	1913	High school music teacher and bandleader
Tremaine, Eric Paul	2nd Lieutenant	1901	Popular bandleader and performer
Vincent, George R.	Captain	1900	Sound engineer (Thomas A. Edison; RCA); curator, National Voice Library, Yale University
Watters, Lorrain	Captain	1899	Music educator and conductor
White, Lawrence R.	1st Lieutenant	1907	Percussionist, Boston Symphony Orchestra
Wright, Harold C.	2nd Lieutenant	1905	Resident baritone soloist, Roxy Theatre, NY; Broadway performer
Zobel, Edgar H.	Captain	1883	Music educator and band director

Source: "History, in Brief, of the Music Section, Athletic and Recreation Branch, Special Services Division, Army Service Forces," October 1943, *JANCSM*, Box 24.

others were concert soloists and orchestra players, sound engineers, church organists, and even (in the case of Lanny Ross) a well-known crooner. Stationed both in the continental United States and in overseas war theaters (in particular the South Pacific), they were "assigned to Service Commands and overseas installations for the purpose of developing and carrying into effect song leader training courses, instruction in the playing of small instruments, [and the] assist[ing of] band leaders, chaplains and special services officers in all matters pertaining to music."[155] In addition, they were to report back to Washington about the state of music within their service commands, addressing not only their specific activities but also the question of whether music making was encouraged or hindered by military personnel in the field. Whereas most of the music advisors were deployed in camps, two officers were assigned on the production side of things in New York and Washington: Captain George R. Vincent, a distinguished recording engineer in civilian life, was put in charge of V-Discs for both the continental United States and overseas, and Captain Harry Salter was responsible for the publication and distribution of the *Army Hit Kit*.

The *Army Hit Kit* was an extension of the army's first musical step: the publication in March 1941 of the *Army Song Book*, which contained a selection of "service, patriotic, nationality, folk, sacred, ballad, and old favorite songs."[156] Published "by order of the Secretary of War," the *Army Song Book* established the format of military music publications, which would later include, for example, the *Women's Army Corps Song Book* (1944) and the *Navy Song Book* (1945). The *Army Song Book* came in two versions: one just with lyrics and—for each thirty copies of that edition—a score for voice and piano. Army regulations demanded that each enlisted man be handed a copy of the text-only edition, but as reports and complaints from the field showed, this remained a lofty goal, even though millions of copies were distributed during the war. Also issued were song slides, which projected the words on the walls of mess halls and other communal spaces, and song shorts (films to sing along to). As army promotional material reveals, the aim was to have soldiers join harmoniously in joyous song (Figure 2.5).

FIGURE 2.5 Army publicity still from 1942. Archives of the Subcommittee on Music, Joint Army and Navy Committee on Welfare and Recreation, Library of Congress, Music Division, Box 14.

The *Army Hit Kit* built on this model by extending the repertoire to popular music and offering a selection of songs on a monthly basis (Figure 2.6). As Claude Rosenberry, one of the senior music officers, explained: "The widespread distribution of the *Army Song Book* and the training of Army song leaders did much to encourage group singing, but naturally the men in the ranks wanted to sing the current song hits that they hear on the air."[157]

FIGURE 2.6 *Army Hit Kit* for June 1943, piano-vocal edition. Archives of the Subcommittee on Music, Joint Army and Navy Committee on Welfare and Recreation, Library of Congress, Music Division, Box 1.

By 1944, 2.4 million copies of the text-only edition were being distributed each month, along with 71,000 piano-vocal scores and 3500 sets of orchestra and band arrangements. Furthermore, because these publications were considered a patriotic necessity, the Music Publishers Protective Association waived copyright fees so long as text and music were used solely within the armed forces.[158] As with the *Army Song Book*, promotional photographs emphasized community building (Figure 2.7).[159] But the *Army Hit Kit* did more than simply reproduce popular radio hits. Each edition also contained a "favorite song of any of our Allies," with a triple text underlay: English translation, original language, and phonetic transcription.[160] As with most musical initiatives, entertainment, education, and wartime politics thus remained tightly interwoven. Yet soldiers made use of the *Hit Kits* as they saw fit. Though originally "planned to stimulate mass singing," they served increasingly for small-group and band entertainment and for soldiers to remain "acquainted with what is being sung at home." As one staff sergeant reported, "when the going gets tough, we like to pick up a song sheet and

FIGURE 2.7 Three soldiers performing from the text-only edition of the *Army Hit Kit*. U.S. Army Special Services publicity still, 1943. Archives of the Subcommittee on Music, Joint Army and Navy Committee on Welfare and Recreation, Library of Congress, Music Division, Box 14.

sing again some of the songs we used to sing with our friends, families and loved ones at home."[161] In a brilliant move to insert the *Army Hit Kit* into soldiers' routine, the song sheets were distributed during mail call, so that even those soldiers who did not get any letters received the *Army Hit Kit* text edition at least once a month.

Four months after the launch of the *Army Hit Kit*, in July 1943, Special Services, under the guidance of Captain Vincent, started its next major music project, the V-Discs. These recordings included a wide range of repertoire, such as "current and favorite songs, the most popular dance bands, symphonic, semi-classical, sacred and patriotic music." Pressed on a new medium—"12-inch practically unbreakable plastic platters"—the recordings were shipped in waterproof boxes, "each containing 20 records and 200 needles."[162] In the two years between the summer of 1943 and the summer of 1945, more than three million copies of records were produced and shipped around the world. The first two V-Discs were recordings of tunes from the *Army Hit Kit*, including "It Ain't Necessarily So" (recorded by Bing Crosby and Dinah Shore) from George Gershwin's *Porgy and Bess* (released on V-Disc no. 2). But V-Disc no. 3 contained a medley of the most successful Broadway show of that year, Rodgers and Hammerstein's *Oklahoma!*, performed by Andre Kostelanetz and his orchestra. V-Disc no. 5 had "United Nations Marching Songs" (according to its label), with four songs from the Soviet Union, China, Great Britain, and the United States (Figure 2.8). In general, swing, jazz, and popular music dominated the V-Disc offerings, although some classical music made its way into the collection—for example, recordings of Hector Berlioz's "Rácóczy March" from *La damnation de Faust* and of the ballet music of Franz Schubert's *Rosamunde*, performed by Serge Koussevitzky and the Boston Symphony Orchestra (V-Disc no. 153, March 1944); or Mischa Elman performing "several concert favorites of mine," as he explained at the beginning of the recording (V-Disc no. 142, also March 1944).

The question was raised, however, over whether Captain Vincent was producing the right mix of classical and popular music to suit the army's institutional guardians of music, who had emphasized in their initial press release of December 1943 the inclusion of classical music in the selection.[163] A memorandum from Doris Goss of the Joint Army and Navy Committee on Welfare and Recreation to Harold Spivacke seems to indicate a discrepancy between Vincent's more entertainment-centered view of the repertoire and the more educational one of Howard Bronson, the Special Services Officer in charge of music. Bronson "realized the need for including classical records in their V-disc program and . . . had discussed it with Captain Vincent," whom

Typical V-Disc set for Army Installations in the U.S.

	Title	Artist
	PUT YOUR ARMS AROUND ME HONEY	Bea Wain
1.	COMIN' IN ON A WING AND A PRAYER	" "
	BLUE SKIES	Tommy Dorsey
	IT AIN'T NECESSARILY SO	Dinah Shore and Bing Crosby
2.	HOME ON THE RANGE	John Charles Thomas
	TAKE ME BACK TO MY BOOTS AND SADDLE	" " "
3.	"OKLAHOMA" MEDLEY	Andre Kostelanetz
	IN MY ARMS	Eddie Cantor
4.	JOHNNY ZERO	Marion Hutton
	"MURDER" HE SAYS!	Dinah Shore
	Music for Marching Men:	
	MEADOWLAND (Russia)	Mark Warnow and the Lyn Murray Singers
5.	CHE LI (China)	" " "
	I'VE GOT SIX-PENCE (British)	" " "
	WHEN THE YANKS GO MARCHING IN (U.S.A.)	" " "
6.	MAN TO MAN	Fred Waring
	THE CAISSONS GO ROLLING ALONG	Fort Slocum Band
	THE ARMY AIR CORPS	Alvino Rey

- 5 -

24-61451

FIGURE 2.8 List of V-Discs nos. 1–6, attached to "V-Disc Records to Supply Wide Variety of Music to U.S. Soldiers Everywhere," press release, Joint Army and Navy Committee on Welfare and Recreation, December 8, 1943. Records of the Joint Army and Navy Committee on Welfare and Recreation, National Archives and Records Administration, RG 225, Box 9.

he then asked "to work out a program in which classical music would be included."[164] Indeed, Bronson and the members of the JANCWR (including its Subcommittee on Music) held distinct views on music in the military that shine through in both their discourses and their programs.

Among the key issues was an official emphasis on the promotion of what was generally termed "good music" and its use in cultural education. "Good music" and popular entertainment seemed to serve different functions in the armed forces. One the one hand, active music making by soldiers was considered such a top priority that the end justified the means: popular hits found their way prominently into the *Army Hit Kits* to stimulate singing, even if they did not always count as "good music" in official eyes. Similarly, popular

music and jazz, seen as keeping up morale, were staples in recreational entertainment. On the other hand, music in the armed forces was also used for
moral and social uplift and education, as well as consolation and relaxation,
and here the catchall category of "good music" played a significant role. Its
definition was influenced by a Western musical canon as it had developed
in the United States in the late nineteenth and early twentieth centuries
through educational and cultural programs in schools, congregations, government institutions, and radio.[165] It included primarily the symphonic concert repertoire, opera, and—as a form of apparently authentic expression of
the people—folk music. A second, interrelated ideological framework, however, became increasingly prominent in the discourse swirling around music
considered suitable for the armed forces, with the straightforward Platonic
correlation between the right music and the right emotional affect being the
guiding principle. In 1942, for example, rough criteria for the selection of
recordings to be sent to army camps were drawn up, and "it was agreed that
too many sentimental 'sob' songs should be avoided and that an effort should
be made to select forward-moving, stimulating songs."[166] Yet even mellow
music had its Platonic part to play in combat situations as a calming and
soothing agent.[167]

Soldiers who preferred the classical repertoire seemed to have consisted
of two groups: those who attended concerts and opera in civilian life—
constituting, as Spivacke wrote, "a minority, but from all reports, a large
group"—and those whose tastes shifted in the course of overseas deployment.[168] Yehudi Menuhin related this broader shift toward classical music to
the danger of war: "A change occurs . . . when men are taken into the army and
sent overseas. That change makes them something more contemplative, emotional and nostalgic. They are different human beings. They need inspiration,
need more than a joke."[169] Menuhin's intuitive observation corresponded to
the polls conducted by the OWI of soldiers and civilians, which reflected a
significantly higher preference for symphonic music among soldiers than in
the general American public.[170] In response, Army Special Services proposed
to take action by programming classical music especially for overseas troops
in a new twice-weekly program called *Soldiers' Symphony*: "Research indicates a high degree of interest in good classical music among overseas troops.
Fighting men, faced with the actualities of war, find spiritual encouragement
in symphonic music. It gives them 'something to hang onto.'"[171] Here classical music was cast as a source of spiritual sustenance *eo ipso* that could calm
the emotional stress especially of soldiers in combat zones. Bill Hammerstein
wrote in 1944 to his father, Oscar Hammerstein II, about the almost painful beauty of listening to a symphonic broadcast on deck of his navy ship:

"Above to hear Toscanini with the NBC Symph. It's very, very seldom that I get the chance to hear music + it sounded wonderful. Very satisfying + restful but at the same time causing pangs of frustration."[172]

Especially in the South Pacific, classical music was a rare and coveted treat. One soldier, stationed in New Guinea, was married to Spivacke's secretary, Frances C. Gewehr. She explained to Harry Futterman of the Armed Forces Master Records (see chapter 1) to what extent classical music was craved by those who enjoyed it: "You see, my husband Corporal Hamilton D. Gewehr, has been there for a year, and frequently has written that he would *so* enjoy hearing some good music. For a while he had access to a radio and was occasionally able to dial in some faint symphonic music from Australia but at present there is no radio and the only music is of two types: (1) That which the fellows concoct themselves and (2) very old popular recordings played over the amplifying system before the presentation of movies."[173] Gewehr used her connections with Spivacke to try and have a classical record collection sent to her husband's camp, but soon thereafter he was moved to a different island where conditions were even less conducive to listening to music: "Honey, we don't even have tents here, much less phonographs, so I'm afraid the record library would do some other group more good.... Needless to say, the tent situation was remedied, but the lack of phonographs remains the same. I think you should feel free to direct it to some outpost where there *is* a machine."[174]

Access to recorded and broadcast music was, indeed, a problem in combat zones in this era before iPods and CD players. Music was available only when there were functioning radios and record players in a camp or on a ship. With electricity a sporadic commodity in the war theaters, hand-cranked and battery-operated machines in good working order became essential musical tools. One air force officer pointed out in 1943, for example, that "victrolas [*sic*] and records were vitally needed for small units in Africa."[175] Therefore, the charitable gifts sought out by such groups as the National Federation of Music Clubs to support soldiers included not only records but also record players and needles. In addition, the armed forces purchased machines for their units so as to enable musical recreation among the soldiers.

Contrary to camps in the continental United States, military posts in war zones did not have auditoriums. There the space designated as the chapel would generally serve for weekly concerts of recorded classical and "semiclassical" music, whose persuasive powers were enhanced by the sacralized setting (Figure 2.9). Such "concerts" depended both on the available recordings and on the tastes of the organizers. Sometimes they were mounted by the army's music officers: for example, Captain Arthur S. Hunt described

FIGURE 2.9 "Soft candle light sets the tone for the weekly Candle Light Musicale" in unspecified war-theater chapel where "classical and semi-classical music is played." Archives of the Subcommittee on Music, Joint Army and Navy Committee on Welfare and Recreation, Library of Congress, Music Division, Box 14.

a typical program of that kind as consisting of *"The Rite of Spring* [by] Stravinsky, *Zampa Overture, Meditation, Finlandia, Voices of Spring*, and selections by Mischa Elman."[176] Special Services supplied its music officers with a set of program notes to be "read, posted or made generally available wherever records are played" and "designed as an aid to recorded programs," providing short comments on those works that were "most often included in camp record libraries."[177] This set of notes included such staples of American concert life as Franck's Symphony in D Minor, Rimsky-Korsakov's *Sheherazade*, and Schumann's Piano Concerto. The first composer presented was, however, "the democratically minded Beethoven" and his Symphony no. 5. In this work, the program notes insisted, "Beethoven, himself always a champion for freedom, has furnished us with a strong symbol in the present war."[178] It is striking that of all the works described in these program notes, only Beethoven's was singled out as the sonic embodiment of the universal value of liberty so profoundly associated with American ideals.

Although these prefabricated program notes provided a starting point, some music officers were more ambitious in relating their educational role to the situation of their listeners. In Fort Huachuca, which had African American troops, for instance, Captain Joe Jordan organized a series of concerts in the division chapels of the camp. His "Music Appreciation Hour" was "a big success." Jordan delegated the preparation of the program notes to the guitarist Chauncey Lee, who was attached to Special Services and who threw himself into the task with fervor. As his notes reveal, the army's goal of education meshed with his own notions, similar to those of W. E. B. Du Bois, of education as a means of racial uplift. Lee's first set of program notes, for a program dedicated to Brahms's Symphony no. 2 on June 20, 1943, was clearly aimed to guide his African American audience from what he considered more familiar music to an appreciation to Brahms. He began with the claim that musical enjoyment depended on getting to know a repertoire: "It is definitely true that in order to appreciate the more serious music one must have some knowledge of what it is."[179] After addressing the "younger portion of the audience" and their predilection for swing, he compared swing's modernity and freedom to that of contemporary American art music, written "by men who are young and unhampered by say old world restrictions." But even if—Lee wrote—"music, like any other art, must progress," he claimed that true appreciation was founded on understanding "the old masters whose works have endured through the Centuries."[180] For the section on Brahms, Lee relied mostly on Charles O'Connell's *Victor Book of the Symphony* (1941), from which he quoted appropriate passages as he first introduced the theme(s) of each movement, then played the movement before continuing to the next. In conclusion, Lee announced the next "Music Appreciation Hour" for the coming Sunday, invited his audience to make use of Fort Huachuca's record library, and then expressed his hope that these sessions "might be able to interest a few of those who heretofore have never taken time to acquaint themselves with this type of music. It is my belief that most of the beauty of music is to be found in orchestral music."[181]

Lee's next lecture, the following Sunday, was dedicated to Beethoven's Symphony no. 3, the "Eroica." But before he engaged with Beethoven, he launched into a defense of tonal music against musical modernism, "whose reproduction of everyday sounds and scenes is robbing modern music of most of its beauty."[182] Nor, he said, could music "paint pictures." In his example, a composer who tried to depict a battle might succeed in having those who had experienced battle recall that soundscape; but those who had never been in war might only envision a train wreck or similar violent event. Abstract beauty, for Lee, was the hallmark of great music; it allowed the transcendence of everyday banality and even misery. Proof lay with Beethoven's "Eroica," which was then introduced, again with the help of O'Connell's music-appreciation text. Beethoven also starred on the following Sunday, with his Symphony no. 5: Beethoven "was the most democratic, the most daring, and the most powerful figure in musical history"—a born revolutionary; he also "liberated music from the indignation of being carried on by lackeys."[183] After another passionate rejection of experimental and atonal music, Lee then presented Beethoven's Fifth as the pinnacle of true beauty, once more with the trusted support of O'Connell's book. Over the months, "Music Appreciation Hour" continued presenting mainstream concert repertoire in Fort Huachuca as one of many musical activities sponsored by the installation's music officer, broadening soldiers' education and forming their musical taste.

Individual members of the military in personal possession of classical recordings also put together concerts to educate their fellow servicemen. For example, Lieutenant Franklin Miner, the armed guard commander of a navy gun crew and, in civilian life, the manager of the Indianapolis Symphony Orchestra, worked passionately to convert his crew of twenty-eight men to classical music.[184] Starting out with "a battered USO phonograph and a few recordings of the Indianapolis Symphony Orchestra," Miner began to present onboard concerts of recorded music. After six months, he had taught all his men—including a reticent gunner's mate—to appreciate classical music. His ship docked in New York, donors were moved to offer $700 worth of recordings, and it then "set sail to North Africa." By the end of that voyage, the Toscanini-Heifetz recording of Beethoven's Violin Concerto had become the seamen's favorite record. Then, however, "his crew was changed. He found himself right back where he had started. The crew frankly admitted they would prefer to spend their time in the brig than listen to his brand of music." Again, Miner persevered in his mission, and "gradually Beethoven won out" over dance music and boogie-woogie. His story ended when on "one dark night, shortly after a record concert, a torpedo struck and the ship began to go down.... The $700 record library is on the bottom of the Atlantic, but a number of Navy men are now converted to good music." Few stories from this era embody the ideology of educational and moral uplift through exposure to "good" music as fully as this one. Indeed, Beethoven's "winning out" over popular music could not but prove the validity of the dominant Western cultural hierarchy in the eyes of classical music's devotees.

Requests for records swamped the desks of Spivacke, Harry Futterman (of the Armed Forces Master Records), and others perceived as being able to help with such needs. Alvin Josephy, a marine sergeant and combat correspondent, and in civilian life a screenwriter and historian, was one of many who wrote to Spivacke about the joy he and his fellow marines were deriving from a set of records:

> Every night we have crowds of people in our tent, listening to the symphonies, over and over again. They are starved for good music, and our arrival with such luxuries was hard at first for them to believe. Now there is a cry for more. The records we have are becoming well-worn. Is there a chance that some kind of agency can see its way to sending us another boxful—or two? I assure you they would be gratefully received and appreciated by many hard-working Marines. If we could presume further to suggest what we would like, here they are: Tchaikowsky's 4th, 5th, and 6th symphonies and piano concerto; Beethoven's 5th and 6th symphony; an album of Strauss waltzes played by a Pops or symphony orchestra; Sibelius 2nd and 5th symphonies, and an album of best-known opera arias.[185]

Josephy was also described, in another letter to Spivacke, as the sergeant on guard willing to keep the electricity running until 4:30 in the morning— three hours beyond its usual shut-off point—so that music-hungry marines could listen to the new records. As another marine officer recounted:

> Saturday night I asked my two tent mates if they would like to hear some good music. Yes. We brought down the machine and some of the wonderful records which you sent along. Lowbrowly, we first put on Dinah Shore singing that tantalizing *Mood Indigo*. It wasn't on three minutes before a Major came tumbling in from a nearby tent demanding to know what kilocycles we were on; he had been frantically trying to get the music on his radio. We laughingly explained what it was all about. Off he rushed to turn off his machine and back he came to stay all evening. A helter-skelter programme proceeded. While *Finlandia* (cracked but acceptable) was playing, a Lieutenant wandered in. His favorite. He stayed all evening. Bizet brought another Major. He stayed. Soon the tent was crowded.[186]

Individual musicians and music lovers also developed initiatives that led to concerts and other performances in camps both in the United States and overseas. Lieutenant Charles Bacharach, a music librarian, reported back from North Africa to his friend Edward Waters at the Library of Congress that he was "able to carry on with my music in a way never dreamed of. Some months ago I started a series of concerts, which have been continued ever since, more or less regularly."[187] These concerts featured both amateur and professional musicians drawn entirely from service personnel, including a choir founded and conducted by Bacharach. As he explained: "Originally planned as informal musical gatherings around an old beaten-up piano, these concerts have become well-publicized, formal functions, attracting many civilians as well as members of the armed forces." A typical program contained a remarkably wide range of piano music and four-hand arrangements, spirituals, and choruses, from Carissimi to Gilbert and Sullivan (Table 2.5). For Bacharach, however, his concerts served more than his fellow soldiers; they were also a means of cultural diplomacy: "The local population seems quite impressed with these musical activities. I am constantly being asked when the next concert

TABLE 2.5 Transcription of the Program of a Soldier Concert (Unspecified Military Camp in North Africa), February 23, 1944.

CPI CITIZENS' CLUB PRESENTS: Seventh Musical Evening Wednesday, February 23, 1944	
Fantasie in C Minor	Bach (1685–1750)
Intermezzo in C Major – op. 119, no. 3	Brahms (1833–1897)
Aufschwung (Fantasiestücke no. 2)	Schumann (1810–1856)
Lt. Giddings, piano	
Three Negro Spirituals:	Arranged by H. T. Burleigh
Weepin' Mary	
My Lord, What a Mornin'	
Oh, Didn't It Rain	
Lt. Cuttino, bass	
Lt. Bacharach, piano	
A *Midsummernight's Dream*: Overture	Mendelssohn (1809–1847)
Lt. Bacharach, piano	
Lt. Burns, piano	
Plorate, Filii Israel	Carissimi (1604–1674)
Crucifixus	Lotti (1667–1740)
Judas Maccabeus: Halleluia, Amen	Händel (1685–1759)
CPI Chorus	
Lt. Werner, piano	
INTERMISSION	
Spanish Dance, op. 12, no. 3	Moszkowski (1854–1925)
Boabdil: Scherzo–Waltz	Moszkowski
Boabdil: Malagueña	Moszkowski
Lt. Bacharach, piano	
Lt. Burns, piano	

(continued)

TABLE 2.5 *(Continued)*

Four Negro Spirituals:	Arranged by H. T. Burleigh
De Gospel Train	
I Want to Be Ready	
Every Time I Feel de Spirit	
Go Down, Moses	
Lt. Cuttino, bass	
Lt. Bacharach, piano	
Etude in E Major, op. 10, no. 3	Chopin (1810–1849)
Nocturne in F# Major, op. 15	Chopin
Ballade in G Minor, op. 23	Chopin
Lt. Giddings, piano	
Two Italian Folk Songs	Arranged by A. T. Davison
Canto di caccia	
Tu mi vuoi tanto bene	
Patience—Four Choruses	Gilbert (1836–1911) and Sullivan
1. The Magnet and the Churn	(1842–1900)
2. Oh, List While We a Love Confess	
3. When I Go out of Door	
4. After Much Debate Internal	
CPI Chorus	
Lt. Werner, piano	
Lt. Schniering, piano	

*****

CPI CHORUS	
First Tenors:	Lts. Burns, Esser, Marino
Second Tenors:	Lts. Donadino, Lundin, Nuner, Schidley
Baritones:	Lts. Holtman, Lombardi, Pauly, Pino
Basses:	Lts. Cuttino, Gioielli, Wikender
Director:	Lt. Bacharach

The audience is requested to join in the singing of *La Marseillaise* and *The Star-Spangled Banner*.

Source: Charles Bacharach, letter to Edward Waters, 15 April 1944, *WcM*, Old Correspondence.

will take place. It is a real satisfaction for me in that these people are thus able to see a cultural side of American life, of which they probably are not so aware as they are of the more material achievements of the American people."

Bacharach's initiative was but one example of numerous soldier-sponsored concerts, choirs, and orchestras. Few units went so far as the Army Air Forces Command stationed at Chanute Field near Rantoul, Illinois, who performed a fully staged production of Leoncavallo's *Pagliacci* in the sold-out Auditorium Theater of the Chicago Servicemen's Center on April 8, 1945.[188] Yet several camps had standing soldier-organized symphony orchestras that played with a regular conductor and local soloists, or even, on special occasions, worked with "Mischa Elman, Andre Kostelanetz, Lily Pons, Ania Dorfmann, Osi Renardy, Alec Templeton, Dorothy Kirsten, Nan Merriman, Oscar Levant and other famous artists and conductors."[189] Such orchestras had been formed at, among other places, Boca Raton Field in Florida, Camp Shanks in New York, and Fort Monmouth in New Jersey.[190] Perhaps best-known, however, was the Camp Lee Symphony Orchestra (near Petersburg, Virginia), where one of the army's two Band Replacement Training Centers was located.[191] Their concerts featured soloists such as Eugene List and Rudolf Firkusny, and their enterprising conductor, George Hoyen, even tried to put on a ballet spectacle with the dancer José Limon, who was stationed at Camp Lee as well.[192] Obtaining the specific scores needed for this performance proved impossible: Limon had hoped to choreograph Manuel de Falla's *Ritual Fire Dance* and Igor Stravinsky's *Petite Suite*.[193] While much of the programs consisted of staples such as Dvořák's "New World Symphony," Hoyen also turned to current works, including Bohuslav Martinů's *Memorial to Lidice*, which the Camp Lee Symphony Orchestra performed in December 1943, barely two months after the work's première in New York.[194] In other cases, however, symphony orchestras and chamber ensembles had the opportunity to draw on the former WPA/FMP music-lending libraries, now administered by the USO and other institutions such as Chicago's Newberry Library.[195]

It is easy to see the tours of concert artists under the auspices of the USO and similar organizations as the flagship operation insofar as classical music in the armed forces was concerned (see chapter 1). What emerges from the present discussion, however, is the sheer extent of grassroots music making for and by members of the military themselves, both at home and abroad. Communal performance, on the one hand, and listening, on the other, played huge roles in terms of morale, bonding, and even reminding those in battle just what they were fighting for. The coverage of such activities in contemporary newspapers and similar sources also acted as proof to those on the home front that the military remained a force for civilization. But while such accounts clearly have an agenda, one should not discount their individual human significance: the notion of Beethoven's Violin Concerto's being voted the favorite work of gunners onboard a ship making its way to North Africa, or of a movement-by-movement lecture on Brahms's Second Symphony being listened to intently by soldiers in an army camp, is quite extraordinary. An official report by the Joint Army and Navy Committee on Welfare and Recreation may have had a broader point to make: "Men and boys, who used to impatiently flip the dial if by accident serious music should emanate from their radio sets, are forming groups to listen to the Metropolitan Opera Hour, the NBC Symphony, and the Philharmonic Orchestra on Sunday afternoon."[196] Countless personal testimonies, however, suggest not just that this was the truth, but also that it mattered.

Music Therapy and the "Reconditioning" of Soldiers

As the war dragged on and the American military was faced with increasing numbers of wounded and traumatized soldiers returning from combat, the armed forces became interested in music for another reason: its healing powers could be harnessed for therapeutic ends. In this respect, the same concepts of "good music" and Platonic aesthetics that underlay the general music program in the military converged with modern experimental music psychology and developments in neurophysiology in order to identify music's curative potential and develop institutionalized programs in military hospitals. Whereas music had been used, for example by the Red Cross, for the purpose of recreation in hospitals since the beginning of the war, the military's turn in 1943 toward music therapy as a medical discipline, at the instigation of the Surgeon General, profoundly changed both the theoretical discourse and the practical strategies surrounding music in reconditioning. This reorientation "proved a watershed for the development of a more clinical approach to music therapy."[197] Yet even in this paradigm shift, the older Platonic and Galenic correspondences between music and emotion that had shaped European and American theories about music's healing properties throughout the late eighteenth and nineteenth centuries remained a strong and deep-running undercurrent.[198] Indeed, the exploration of music and emotion's complex interrelation was what underpinned this shift from intuitive to scientific engagement with music therapy.[199] In order to validate the concept of music's influence on human behavior, authors repeatedly tried to explain that music did indeed have powers of persuasion that were intrinsic to the medium. The music educator John Warren Erb argued in 1943 that "today we must begin with the realization that music is the expression of emotional experience. It is a language derived from the audible, spontaneous reactions of primitive man to joy, anger or sorrow or primitive emotions."[200]

As in the case of the army's general music program, the experiential and ideological roots for institutionalized music therapy lay in the 1930s, and in particular in the programs of the WPA, which tried to reach untraditional audiences through concerts and music making in schools, communities, factories, and even prisons. These activities were aimed not only at music education and moral uplift, but also at using music to alleviate twentieth-century American social ills aggravated by the Great Depression. The *New York Times* reported in March 1938 on a Federal Music Project initiative spearheaded by Harriet Ayer Seymour, who for the previous three years had organized music activities and classes in seven New York hospitals and two women's prisons. The article claimed that "listening to Beethoven helps relieve mental tension, anemia and paralysis" and noted Seymour's experiments, based on the "theory that by classifying song material under the headings of stimulants, tonics, sedatives, and narcotics, music may be administered to relieve various types of diseases."[201]

The notion that music possesses intrinsic qualities generating clearly definable emotional and mental effects—to stimulate or sedate, for example—relates back to the third book of Plato's *Republic* and has floated through Western music theory for more than two millennia. The line that can be drawn from Greek antiquity, in particular Plato and Timotheus, to Ficino in Renaissance Italy, to *Affektenlehre* in seventeenth- and eighteenth-century Germany, and to the experiments of Hermann von Helmholtz highlights some of the familiar reference points in both theoretical and populist discourses about music's emotional power.[202] During World War II, this historic lineage and its grounding in Greek antiquity were repeatedly evoked in the United States in order to bestow a historical depth on the therapeutic use of music, thereby protecting it from the suspicion of frivolousness, on the one hand, or modish novelty, on the other. In 1944 Doron K. Antrim traced music's "healing qualities" not only to Plato but also to Homer, Hippocrates, and Aristotle before presenting their modern offspring in the shape of contemporary medical practitioners such as Willem van de Wall and Joseph H. Pratt.[203] Even when philosophers, for their own reasons, were pursuing more abstract formalism, the argument still held some sway: in 1942 Suzanne K. Langer rejected the traditionally assumed cause and effect between music and emotion but still maintained that there was some kind of interconnection, given that "the real power of music lies in the fact that it can be 'true' to the life of feeling in a way language cannot."[204] The composer Howard Hanson took a music-theoretical perspective in exploring music and emotion, explaining to members of the American Psychiatric Association in 1942 the basics of harmony and rhythm in Western music so as to illustrate "the influence of music, both benevolent and malevolent, in the lives of people."[205] Yet even though both the ancient Greeks and conventional music theory kept their places as historical authorities in the broader discourse about music and emotion, validation of the therapeutic legitimacy of music was sought—especially in the context of the armed forces—through modern neurophysiological experiments. While this new emphasis on the laboratory and clinical trials as sites of knowledge had its roots in the turn of the twentieth century, the large-scale application of neuropsychiatric research for music therapy was specific to medical developments that originated in the United States during World War II.[206]

Unlike other medical and psychiatric specialties, American music therapy between 1900 and 1940 was firmly in female hands and therefore carried the gendered stigma of amateurism and professional feminization.[207] Three women in particular were influential during those decades, not only through their individual work but also because of their roles in the founding of professional associations. Eva Augusta Vescelius was active between 1900 and 1917 and established the National Society for Musical Therapeutics in 1903. She was influenced by New Thought principles—based on the ideas of Phineas Parkhurst Quimby and Ralph Waldo Emerson—and considered both rhythm and timbre the key factors in classifying music's healing effects. Isa Maud Ilson started out as a nurse, but her experience in military hospitals during World War I led her to music therapy. In 1919 she accepted the position of lecturer in "musico-therapy" at Columbia University—the first time that the subject was taught as part of the regular curriculum at an American university; her first class comprised twelve students. In 1926 she founded the National Association for Music in Hospitals, which, in its early years, attracted a great deal of media attention. A third female music therapist, Harriet Ayer Seymour, entered the scene in 1915; she too had experience with soldiers in World War I. Like Vescelius, she was strongly influenced by the New Thought movement. Around 1935 she became affiliated with the Federal Music Project, and in 1941 she established the National Foundation for Music Therapy. The two male researchers and practitioners of music therapy during the 1930s, Willem van de Wall and Ira Altshuler, both had a stronger institutional footing at New York University and Michigan State University, respectively, but Vescelius, Ilson, and Seymour had a far higher public impact: their lectures drew large audiences, and their work was reported in newspapers and popular journals.

In 1939 Seymour published an introductory text titled *How to Use Music for Health*. Following traditional Platonic patterns, she distinguishes three levels on which music can influence human conditions. On the lowest, the physical level, sound waves affect the patient's body through vibration. "The second level," she explains, "is the emotional."[208] The third level, finally, is the "higher or spiritual plane." Seymour suggests that music be used, for example, "to wipe out emotional disturbances," so that "all that causes disease is dropped from the mind and peace is restored." But, she cautions, "do not use modern music for people who are ill. The irregular pulse and lack of form is more disturbing than healing. Jazz stimulates, but on a low level, and a little goes a long way."

In 1943 Seymour focused specifically on what music therapy could do for soldiers who had returned from battle with severe trauma. Her brochure *Music Answers the Call* opens with a narrative that presents the power of music over even the most hopeless cases:

> Tom, a recently wounded soldier, lay tense and miserable on his bed in a military hospital. The piercing din of falling bombs was still ringing in his ears, sleep was seemingly impossible, and in his intense pain the ardor of sacrifice had been weakened by his suffering. Despair had engulfed him. Presently, soft music floated over the ward. At one end of the room a gentle-looking girl, with a particularly soothing voice, was softly singing the *Ave Maria*. The influence of the music was at once perceptible. He closed his weary eyes and as he recognized the familiar music his relief was so great that all outward appearance of pain vanished as his body became more noticeably relaxed.[209]

Schubert's soothing and calming music is then credited with the complete transformation of Tom from a hopeless case into a soldier on the way of recovery. Seymour's narrative brought forth a lively response among musicians, who signed up by the dozen for her courses at Steinway Hall in New York City to become qualified as therapists.

One reader, however, had a much more negative reaction. Harold Spivacke, writing as the chairman of the Subcommittee on Music of the Joint Army and Navy Committee on Welfare and Recreation, complained to Raymond Fosdick: "Following our recent conversation on the subject of the possibility of organizing a study on musical therapy, I am taking the liberty of sending you the enclosed three booklets. I do not expect you to read all of these, but I do hope you will read the first paragraph of *Music Answers the Call*. If I see much more of this kind of stuff, I fear that I shall become violent even before my admission into one of the mental hospitals."[210] Given that Spivacke was an intermediary between the musical and military worlds, his comment opens a window into the mindset of military and government institutions, where emotional appeals to music's healing powers, without scientific proof of them, were looked upon with suspicion and even contempt. Such an intuitive approach flew in the face of the new paradigm of controlled scientific studies in medicine championed by Thomas Parran, Jr., the Surgeon General of the Army. Although the recent history of the scientific method is usually associated with large-scale trials for such diseases as malaria, tuberculosis, and syphilis (including the notorious Tuskegee syphilis study), Parran also instigated large-scale research studies related to mental-health issues, including a systematic examination of music therapy. Spivacke's almost visceral reaction to Seymour's openly emotional account—casting her in the role of an incompetent amateur—meshes with other strategies through which he tried to masculinize and professionalize music in the context of the war.

For Spivacke, music therapy was a particularly tricky issue, as his response to another female music therapist reveals. He took such offense at Esther Goetz Gilliland's article "Music for the War Wounded," published in the *Music Educators Journal* in 1945, that he threatened to resign from its editorial board: "To say that I was shocked by this article, would be putting it very mildly. It would be much more accurate to say that I am incensed. The second footnote on page 25 sounds just like the old snake oil advertisements, and I feel sure that if you had printed this as an advertisement for a patent medicine you would have run afoul of the law. Furthermore, I do not feel that the statement you have in the box in the upper right quarter of page 25 is sufficient to atone for printing such a piece of quackery."[211] The offending footnote in the article explained that "while the treatment of psychiatric cases seems to offer the richest field in music therapy, many other diseases, we are told, can be similarly benefited, such as certain heart ailments, tuberculosis, orthopedics, nervous indigestion, paralysis, as well as insomnia, pain, and any other symptoms due to emotional conflicts."[212] Gilliland's psychosomatic and holistic understandings of medical conditions were anathema to Spivacke, and her unfortunate conflation of different uses of music—from physical exercise for hand injuries by playing the piano to influencing somatic states through passive listening—made this list look like an absurd hodgepodge.

Spivacke was not alone in considering especially female practitioners of music therapy to be little more than quacks. For William van de Wall, "it was high time to do something about" Seymour's National Foundation of Music Therapy, which he hated as a "downright phony music undertaking"; what was really needed was proper research conducted under his supervision.[213] Raymond Kendall, the music coordinator of the USO, joined forces with Spivacke to attack the music therapist Frances Paperte (who had been commissioned to conduct a study of music therapy at Walter Reed General Hospital in 1944), with the result that she dropped her previous claim to heal through music and instead "changed the name of her organization to the Institute of Applied Music and is soft-pedalling the therapy throughout."[214] Around the same time, Kendall took great care "to warn our USO professional workers against the charlatans who are doing so-called music therapy." As far as Spivacke, Kendall, and others of their ilk were concerned, the claims made by such therapists as Seymour were to be treated with deep suspicion: "Any program for hospitals designed in accordance with current theories of music therapy will be inconclusive if not actually dangerous and will of necessity remain so until medically controlled tests have developed objective evidence."[215] Such objective research, it was argued, would go far toward alleviating the fear implicit in the discourse of government, military, and NGO officials that music-therapy activities could be considered "sissified."[216] The clear subtext was that they also needed to be put in male hands.

The armed forces started their engagement with music therapy by documenting and assessing current practice. To this end, in 1943 Lieutenant Guy V. R. Marriner conducted, on the orders of the Office of the Surgeon General, a survey of music-therapy programs already in place in military installations.[217] It is unclear why Marriner, a concert pianist in civilian life, was selected to spearhead this initiative, but he remained the Special Services officer in charge of music-therapy programs for the rest of the war. After this initial exercise, Marriner developed research programs in collaboration with Willen van de Wall, first at LaGarde General Hospital in New Orleans and then in numerous others, including Walter Reed. As Van de Wall explained, his research in New Orleans followed "the principle of medical direction and control....My program of music therapy at La Garde has found acceptance by the local Army medical authorities because it is based on the same principles. It is for the present confined to the Neuropsychiatric Service being understood as a demonstration of scientific method and not as a service to promote music activities. The program, however, is capable of extension to other medical services, although the neuropsychiatric patients are in the greatest need for the psychotherapeutic help derived from this treatment."[218] Once the original study was successfully completed, not only military hospitals across the United States but even hospital ships became sites of the medical use of music in what was generally referred to as "reconditioning."[219]

Harry S. Etter, the officer in charge of rehabilitation at the U.S. Naval Hospital in Bethesda, Maryland, was typical of the many medical personnel who were faced with soldiers suffering from severe posttraumatic stress disorder and similar conditions, and who grasped at music therapy as a gentle form of mental therapy. He viewed classical music in particular (if inevitably) as especially promising: "In music that is really music, there is procedure....One phrase leads to another and all forms a continuous whole. There is a mental satisfaction in the consecutive approach to music. It is this that provides a new inner harmony, a greater peace of mind, a more lasting mental strength."[220] Altshuler's neuropsychiatric research added new physiological explanations into the mix. He explained music therapy's success through music's power over the thalamus, the part of the brain considered "the seat of emotions, sensations and feelings—even aesthetic feelings such as reactions to music." In his opinion, music was a "unique agent for mental therapy" because it could "gain access to the mind of the patient via the thalamus.... Once music has found its way into the lower brain, it is comparatively easy for it to reach up into the higher, conscious strata. The discovery of this 'back door' to the conscious mind and the realization of music's ability to enter through it obviously are matters of great moment in psychotic treatment."[221]

One might fairly argue that Altshuler's neurophysiological account simply adds a layer of medical sophistication to Seymour's anecdotal account of the traumatized soldier. For that matter, Seymour's views on "good music" and its power to shape human emotions for the better resurfaced in numerous documents generated in conjunction with the army's clinical studies. A 1944 program for "Music in reconditioning...adopted in Army general hospitals in the continental United States" still kept the dreaded jazz and boogie-woogie out of locked neuropsychiatric wards, favoring instead "quiet classical, semi-classical and folksong music" to calm the patients.[222] The authors of the War Department's technical bulletin on music in reconditioning soldiers contend that "'Jive' or 'Boogie-Woogie' may have an overstimulating effect on certain types of closed-ward neuropsychiatric patients."[223] Indeed, even in the more clinical context of "music in reconditioning" under the auspices of self-proclaimed scientific researchers, emotion remained the key target for the therapeutic use of music, given that feelings were considered particularly susceptible to stimulation by its means. In the same technical bulletin, right on the first page, music's emotional power is explained in terms familiar, once again, to the reader of Plato:

> Much of the benefit derived from a well-planned music program comes from the emotional appeal of music. All countries, civilized or not, have folk music which has endured because it grew out of the emotional life and moods of the people. Although folk music has the most universal appeal, all types of music have value. A rousing march generally quickens the pulse; tired troops are refreshed by a song.... In contrast to this, music may be an emotional sedative, for instance: a baby is soothed by a lullaby.... Moods may thus be influenced through the proper use of music, while pent up emotions are often released.[224]

This passage harks back to Seymour's Platonic taxonomy of songs as sedatives or stimulants, albeit reconfigured for the military technicians. The earlier music therapists and their more flowery prose had disappeared without a trace from governmental discourse, yet their core tenets remained at the heart of the new discipline.

Nevertheless, in 1945 Marriner, by now chief of the Hospital Section of the Special Services' Music Branch, cautioned his compatriots with a distinction that would increasingly influence research into music therapy and music psychology after the war: "The emotional values of music are not to be confused with their effects upon hearers, as probably no two listeners listen to or absorb music the same way. Many people assume that the emotional reactions to music are evidence of the therapeutic value of music." In contrast, he pointed out, "medically controlled tests and experiments have not proven 'Music Therapy' to be a scientific fact."[225] In Marriner's and the army's postwar world, alternative forms of therapy had to measure up to recently developed standards of scientific and medical research that sought to isolate causes and quantify effects. But now there was also a broader agenda in play. The increasing suspicion of a direct connection between music and emotion was rooted not only in the new paradigms of medical research: once it had become clear to what extent such regimes as the Nazis had instrumentalized music for political gain, music's emotional side became deeply suspect and demanded careful investigation.

Even during the war, the broader rhetoric advocating the benefits of music for morale and uplift tended to downplay its purely emotional elements. In part this was because everyone knew that they were playing with fire, not just because of music's essential intangibility but also because of its evident use on both sides of a war that could have only one just and proper outcome. While it was easy to distinguish between "good" and "bad" music in terms of fitness for purpose, the question for classical music in particular was whether one could also distinguish it on moral or other grounds in terms of its origins and intrinsic features. What constituted "good" classical music for U.S. wartime purposes, and what was "bad"? Answering that question posed significant challenges to composers, performers, and critics, and also served to configure a new "American" music in very different ways.

| "I Hear America Singing..."

I N MAY 1942 the Los Angeles City College A Cappella Choir presented a concert that started with Johann Sebastian Bach's *Magnificat* and, for its second half, included a number of traditional American folk songs before finishing—in front of a "gigantic American eagle [that] spread his wings over the choir from the backdrop"—with the performance of George Kleinsinger's cantata *I Hear America Singing* (1940), with text by Walt Whitman.[1] The program could be considered emblematic for the pursuit of national musical identity in the United States during World War II in the way it unselfconsciously mirrored three key tenets of the country's musical life that formed a unique referential web during those years. First, Bach's work brought into play both the European concert repertoire that had been performed in America since colonial times and the wartime rhetoric that portrayed the New World as the (sole) custodian of the arts in a time of global crisis. Secondly, the folk songs as well as the text of Whitman's famous poem (first published in *Leaves of Grass* in 1867) powerfully encapsulated a renewed focus on the people's music as the true embodiment of American culture. Finally, by including a recently composed, patriotic work that represented musically the pluralistic voice of the nation, the program connected the creation of new music in the United States to American concert life's dual heritage. This triangulation of European repertoire, native folk music, and contemporary composition had its roots in the nineteenth century (if not in William Billings's Revolutionary-era rhetoric). Yet, because the establishment of a singular and mainstream autochthonous lineage was tenuous at best in so heterogeneous a population, when faced with the cultural challenges posed by allies and enemies alike during the war years

American musicians found themselves in an acute quandary about their specific national musical identity.

By the nineteenth century, the notion that music could embody the essence of a group's identity—whether national or ethnic—had been established as a commonplace in Western music. This kind of musical chauvinism peaked before and during World War I but then receded again during the 1920s. In its place arose such postwar institutions as the International Society for Contemporary Music, which promoted international musical exchange "regardless of the nationality, race, political views, or religion of the composer."[2] Fueled by the cosmopolitanism and (especially left-wing) internationalism of that decade, composers from France to Latin America threw themselves into this transatlantic world of music. Yet even in that decade, when a "League of Nations" spirit dominated international musical discourse, the quest for a specific national identity remained a constant, albeit less overt, factor in the search for a musical self, especially in the Americas—for example, in Copland's modernist Americana such as *Music for the Theatre* (1925) or the *Piano Concerto* (1927).[3]

The seismic political and economic shifts around 1930—most prominently in the Soviet Union, Germany, and the United States—reconfigured the construction of cultural identities worldwide, leading to a renewed focus on musical nationalism.[4] Whether in the United States or in numerous European nations from Germany and France to the Soviet Union and Italy, this turn to a deliberately national art shared several traits that culminated during the war years. In order to reground art (including music) in each nation's specific identity, it was not enough simply to draw on folk motives or local and national historic markers, although this strategy would rise to prominence during the 1930s through craft revivals (from quilting to ceramics), folklore research (in music, for example, through Béla Bartók or John Lomax), and the search for archaic roots and hence embodied history (as in the semantic paleography of Olga Freidenberg in the Soviet Union).[5] Perhaps even more essential to claims of national cultural preeminence, however, was the "great appropriation" of world culture during the 1930s.[6] In the Soviet Union, for example, high-profile edition and translation projects served to frame the heritage of Western literature in the context of the Marxist-Leninist ethos following the founding in 1931 of a new scholarly serial, *Literaturnoe Nasledstvo* (Literary Heritage).[7] Across the Atlantic, also in the 1930s, Mortimer Adler and Robert Hutchins started to push the "great books" program at the University of Chicago as a foundational curriculum of American higher education, soon popularized by Adler in his 1940 manual *How to Read a Book*.[8] Parallel to this appropriation of the world's literary legacy, the large-scale classicism of new representational architecture integrated the stylistic heritage of the past into the grand visual narratives seen in projects of the 1930s such as the Palais Chaillot in Paris, the Italian Embassy in Berlin, or the National Archives in Washington, D.C. Indeed, when President Herbert Hoover laid the foundation stone for the new National Archives, a neo-Palladian "temple" on the capital's Mall, it was intended "for one of the most beautiful buildings in America, an expression of the American soul," meant to provide a dignified frame for "the romance of our history."[9]

Just like classical architecture and literature, classical music played a significant role during that decade in the making of "middlebrow" (to use a term popularized in 1933 by Margaret Widdemer) culture in the United States.[10] Prepared by countless music-appreciation books and radio shows, American audiences consumed Beethoven and Rachmaninoff as the well-publicized products of the booming recording industry and the radio.[11] Indeed, by 1939 such Saturday afternoon programs as the Metropolitan Opera broadcasts and the NBC Symphony Orchestra reached more than ten million listeners across the United States, and the preparations for Walt Disney's music-appreciation movie, *Fantasia* (1940), were in full swing.[12] Besides the industry's promotion of classical music, the government, too, pushed concert music for the broader masses. Between 1935 and 1939 the Federal Music Project offered close to a quarter of a million free or low-priced classical-music concerts, intending thereby "to give such cultural values to communities that a new interest in music would be engendered and the audience base expanded."[13] FMP concerts crossed the bandwidths of art music, from Italian madrigals and Mozart symphonies to Copland's *El salón México* and Schoenberg's *Pelleas und Melisande*, even though the emphasis lay on the traditional classical and romantic repertoire. Lehman Engel presented Renaissance music with his Madrigal Singers, and the Los Angeles FMP dedicated an entire concert to Schoenberg and his American pupils.[14] The FMP also sponsored close to 250 music-teaching centers that included "layman's music courses," established by the pianist Olga Samaroff, for whom "the greatest things of the past and a vital interest in modern creative music" were inextricably linked.[15] Working toward lay fluency in the concert-music repertoire through education, appreciation, and public exposure thus became one way through which culture was democratized by Roosevelt's New Deal. In the effort to create a national artistic horizon, these programs included a deliberate push toward an "aesthetic melting pot."[16] Not for nothing was the FMP also deeply involved in folklore projects whose embrace went beyond the traditional forms of fieldwork and the publishing of song collections: the New Deal folklorists also tried to reintroduce folklore as a mainstream American form of music making.[17] Between the populist nationalism of the Roosevelt New Deal, on the one hand, and the commercialism of U.S. radio, the recording industry, and even Hollywood, on the other, by the late 1930s both classical and folk music were fully established as an integral part of American middlebrow culture. The melting pot was put to work especially with respect to classical music, for that ideology enabled the European classics to be considered a fully appropriated and "naturalized" tradition—in the words of the editors of *Musical America*, as having been "made a part of our American cultural life."[18]

Sounds of a Usable Past

The international cultural rivalry of the 1930s had prepared the ground for a nationalized culture through both competition over the classical world heritage and the turn to folklore and other historic residues of national culture, but the outbreak of World War II sharply exacerbated these tendencies in musical performance, composition, and scholarship in the United States. Classical music was hailed as "the heritage of all people regardless of race, color, creed and economic status."[19] Indeed, democratic concert music was seen as a force that had "within itself the power of persuasion to evangelize the consciousness of the world."[20] Because of the war that devastated Europe, American commentators constructed their country as the stronghold of world culture, for other Allied nations such as the Soviet Union were seeing their musical treasures pillaged and destroyed by the German army. Both the title of David Ewen's 1942 history of music in the United States, *Music Comes to America*, and his comments about the contemporary cultural landscape in Europe turned the United States into music's promised land: "The only music that can be heard in Europe today is the roar of the dive bomber, the cannon, the tank. While Europe is in cultural darkness, the musical lights in this country are burning brighter than ever, even though we, too, are in the war."[21] Some music lovers considered the cultivation of the European concert repertoire in the United States to be a sacred duty and even a reason to go into battle. A Private Bernard B. Ross wrote from Camp Shelby, Michigan, in April 1942 urging the Boston Symphony Orchestra to continue its work: "It is so good to know we have men who still uphold our culture and our treasured progress of civilization."[22] Serge Koussevitzky, himself a newly minted American, considered the preservation of the world's musical heritage to be his new nation's sacred duty during this war: "America holds her traditions and culture from the Old World and now has been given the flaming torch of all the suffering and suppressed peoples to carry, to keep burning until peace. And then, America will be able to restore the cultural wealth which was entrusted to her, and which she alone can save from destruction."[23]

Whereas Koussevitzky saw the United States in a dual role as both an owner and a custodian of classical music, Deems Taylor was far less sanguine about the notion of restoring music to Europe. For him, the nation's totalitarian enemies, Germany and Italy, had relinquished their claim to classical music: "As a matter of fact, it isn't theirs any longer. If there is any beauty or spirituality in whatever so-called axis music we elect to play, be assured that those are just the qualities that they of the axis have angrily repudiated."[24] Taylor's rhetorical sleight of hand attributed ownership of all classical music to the United States not only because it was part of the American concert tradition but also because Europe—and most important, Germany—had forsaken its moral claim to it. This strategy of emphasizing the United States' national and political ethos was widely used to justify American entitlement to the classical repertoire. On August 4, 1942, the *Boston Globe* published a review of a Tanglewood performance of Bach's *Magnificat* and Beethoven's Ninth: "The text of the *Magnificat* is a revolutionary hymn in church Latin, and Beethoven's music to Schiller's ode is a human-to-human brotherhood [*sic*]. . . . Had Bach, Beethoven, and Schiller lived in the Germany of today they would probably have perished in concentration camps."[25] Program notes, newspaper reviews, and radio comments celebrated Bach as "the universal genius of humanity" who rightly made his home in this last bastion of civilization, and the revolutionary Beethoven was turn ed into a truly American composer whose music embodied "the spirit of liberty."[26] Whether "trying to portray the brotherhood of man" in his Ninth or putting "into his quartets his great love of man," Beethoven stood as the musical equivalent of the American ideal.[27]

It comes as no surprise that entire concert series were dedicated to Beethoven, such as the cycle of six concerts marking the one hundredth anniversary of the New York Philharmonic Orchestra and conducted by Arturo Toscanini in April and May 1942 (Figure 3.1). The opening concert featured the *Missa solemnis*. In that concert, and contrary to the recent custom, the national anthem did not open the evening but was performed at its end. For Olin Downes, this sequence only emphasized the message inherent in the music: "The end of the mass, with the calls of the trumpets and drums, the cry for forgiveness of the sins of the world and the prayer for peace, can never be heard indifferently. Last night it had such connotations that the immediate succession of the singing of the nation's anthem seemed neither theatrical nor in a way inappropriate in the relation of Beethoven's thought

BEETHOVEN FESTIVAL UNDER THE DIRECTION OF ARTURO TOSCANINI

 SERIES OF SIX CONCERTS AT CARNEGIE HALL

I. WEDNESDAY EVENING, APRIL 22, at 8:45

    Missa Solemnis, in D major
    Florence Kirk, *Soprano*
    Bruna Castagna, *Contralto*
    Hardesty Johnson, *Tenor*
    Alexander Kipnis, *Bass*
    Westminster Choir

II. FRIDAY AFTERNOON, APRIL 24, at 2:30

    Overture to "Egmont," Op. 84
    Symphony No. 1, in C major, Op. 21
    Symphony No. 2, in D major, Op. 36
    Overture to "Leonore," No. 2

III. SUNDAY EVENING, APRIL 26, at 8:45

    Overture to "Coriolanus," Op. 62
    Symphony No. 4, in B-flat major, Op. 60
    Symphony No. 3, in E-flat major ("Eroica"), Op. 55

IV. WEDNESDAY EVENING, APRIL 29, at 8:45

    Overture to "Prometheus," Op. 43
    Symphony No. 6, in F major, Op. 68 ("Pastorale")
    Symphony No. 5, in C minor, Op. 67

V. FRIDAY AFTERNOON, MAY 1, at 2:30

    Overture to "Fidelio," in E major, Op. 72
    Triple Concerto, for Piano, Violin and 'Cello
    Ania Dorfmann
    Mishel Piastro
    Joseph Schuster
    Symphony No. 7, in A major, Op. 92

VI. SUNDAY EVENING, MAY 3, at 8:45

    Symphony No. 8, in F major, Op. 93
    Symphony No. 9, in D minor, Op. 125, with Final
    Chorus on Schiller's Ode, "To Joy"
    Florence Kirk, *Soprano*
    Bruna Castagna, *Contralto*
    Hardesty Johnson, *Tenor*
    Alexander Kipnis, *Bass*
    Westminster Choir

FIGURE 3.1 Advertisement for the New York Philharmonic Orchestra's Beethoven Festival under the direction of Arturo Toscanini, April 22–May 3, 1942. Courtesy of the New York Philharmonic Archives.

and the cause of humanity."[28] After several concerts that included the rarely heard Triple Concerto, the series concluded with "Beethoven in the Homeric vein" with his last two symphonies.[29] Another high-profile Beethoven series was the performance in the spring of 1944 of his complete string quartets in the Coolidge Auditorium of the Library of Congress by the exiled Budapest String Quartet, a chamber-music series that had audiences waiting for hours to secure a ticket. Nor did the war stop an eight-evening concert cycle in 1943 by the Coolidge Quartet dedicated to the chamber music of Johannes Brahms.[30] Indeed, more even than orchestral music, chamber compositions were considered manifestations of abstract universalism.

So it not surprising that historical models of classical music found their way also into American wartime composition, although the presence of such intertexts stands in no particular contrast to earlier compositional developments in the United States. Whereas some works such as Leo Sowerby's *Classic Concerto* for organ and string orchestra (1944) even resorted to the referential moniker, other composers turned to historical genres to ground works that were emphatically American in a universal tradition. Marion

Bauer's neoclassical Trio Sonata no. 1 for flute, violoncello, and piano (1944) combines thematic material inspired by American folklore, especially in the last movement, with thoroughly contrapuntal textures typical of the baroque genre that gave the piece its name. Sometimes specific works of the classical concert repertoire provided a reference point for new compositions, as in the case of David Diamond's String Quartet no. 2 (1943–44), composed with the third of Beethoven's Rasumovsky Quartets (op. 59, no. 3) as an intertext.[31] Especially in the final, third movement, the deliberately open texture and barn dance–like gesture of the beginning, which seems to parody Copland's manner in such Americana as *Rodeo*, quickly transforms itself into a fugue subject echoing the strings of eighth notes from Beethoven's last movement. Perhaps best-known among the American wartime compositions that use a well-known historical score as an intertext, however, is Samuel Barber's *Capricorn Concerto* (named after Barber's home), which in instrumentation and formal structure echoes Bach's Brandenburg Concerto no. 2 in F major (BWV 1047). Written in the politically charged environment of the OWI—Barber described it in a letter to Copland as a "rather tooting piece, with flute, oboe and trumpet"—the work self-consciously combined a modernist appropriation of a baroque prototype with a nationalist agenda.[32] Indeed, during the war this kind of play with models from an appropriated cosmopolitan history—be they genres or composers—claimed this universal heritage for contemporary American music.

Nevertheless, this form of cultural transfer fell short of rooting American concert music in an indigenous historical idiom of concert music. As the United States entered the war, the need for a "usable past" that did not incorporate the long-standing appropriation of European concert repertoire became increasingly critical. Van Wyck Brooks famously developed this proto-Hobsbawmian concept in 1915 in his book *America's Coming of Age*, and references to a "usable past" had become a catchphrase during the 1920s and '30s, in particular in the context of such national WPA projects as the "Index of American Design."[33] As far as music during World War II was concerned, as early as 1940 the critic Paul Rosenfeld grounded the history of truly American composition in the time of the Revolution, when composers such as William Billings and Francis Hopkinson not only wrote patriotic airs but also attempted "to embody national sentiment and subject-matter in music,"[34] and he offered the Bostonian Hans Gram's 1791 orchestral piece *The Death-Song of an Indian Chief* as an example of the latter strategy. Although such scholars as Oscar Sonneck and Carleton Sprague Smith had started national collections of early American music well before World War II, the impact of their work remained limited to a few insiders. Furthermore, their focus was as much on colonial America as it was on the Revolutionary period, if not more so.[35] Whereas Sonneck paid some tribute to the Revolutionary composers Hopkinson and James Lyon as early as 1905, Smith's particular interest was in colonial psalmody. His research led during the late 1930s to the employment of twelve FMP music copyists to establish, among other projects, scores of seventeenth-century American psalmody based on the partbooks preserved in the newly established Americana section of the New York Public Library's Music Division.[36] Some of this FMP repertoire found its way into a 1937 recording by Lehman Engel's Madrigal Singers; another WPA production, Paul Green's 1937 outdoor drama *The Lost Colony*, integrated into its incidental music Lamar Stringfield's and Adeline McCall's adaptations of psalm tunes and other early Elizabethan music that had probably been brought to the colonies.[37] After several editions of Billings and Hopkinson made in close proximity to World War I, only the occasional score with works by composers of the American Revolution was published between the wars, such as William Arms Fisher's 1931 anthology *The Music That Washington Knew*.

After December 1941, however, music associated specifically with the American Revolution gained considerable currency both as historical evidence of genuinely American creativity in art music and as nativist inspiration for contemporary composition. In 1937–38 Paul Green and Kurt Weill abandoned their attempt to bring Revolutionary music to the stage in the FTP-sponsored historical drama *The Common Glory*, which was never finished. Just four years later, however, editions such as *Seven Songs of the Early Republic*, published by Richard Franko Goldman and Carl Buchman (1942), gained the attention of critics in the *New York Times* and *Musical America*. The *Times* journalist pointed to history's relevance to contemporary events: "One of the things that fascinates the student of history is the way turns of contemporary events give new significance to records of the past. An example is the way the current crisis has suddenly made the popular songs of the early days of the United States have an almost topical impact."[38] Similarly, *Musical America*'s critic related the importance of the edition, which presented songs that "reflected the deep and spontaneous patriotic faith of such men as Hopkinson and Tom Paine," to current events when he claimed that "it would be difficult to imagine music more appropriate to our times."[39] Lehman Engel, also writing in 1942, considered these Revolutionary songs particularly fitting for "the present urgency," for they came "out of the heart of the war itself."[40]

William Billings's music was performed in wartime choral concerts and patriotic ceremonies, often in Clarence Dickinson's four-part arrangements.

His works were heard in New York at Lazare Saminsky's Three-Choir Festival, held at Temple Emanu-El in March 1942 and devoted to "Songs of War and Peace"; at the Town Hall Endowment Series in April 1944, when the Collegiate Choir "gave a concert of American choral music"; and in a concert of Edgard Varèse's Greater New York Chorus in June 1945.[41] The martial spirit of Revolutionary music also shone through in the dedication of a service flag in the Covenant First Presbyterian Church in Washington, D.C., in November 1942, when the offertory was "one of the earliest choral works written in America, William Billings's 'Be Glad Then America.'"[42]

One group in particular, Elie Siegmeister's American Ballad Singers, promoted music of the Revolutionary War era as part of its core repertoire of "native American songs" (Figure 3.2).[43] Siegmeister formed the group in 1939 with six singers, three women and three men (whose membership fluctuated because of the draft). After their New York debut on February 18, 1940, the ensemble toured the United States for long stretches each year until it was dissolved shortly after the end of the war.[44] In a 1943 interview with the *Washington Post*, Siegmeister attributed both his interest in early

FIGURE 3.2 "The American Ballad Singers in rehearsal for their annual Town Hall recital, December 21, under the sponsorship of the American Youth Theatre." *Musical Courier* (December 1, 1941): 19.

American music and the formation of the group to the scorn he encountered in Europe when the conversation turned to the history of music in the United States: "I lived in Europe from 1927 to 1930. Many times people taunted me about America having no native songs. It made me so mad that I decided to find out upon my return here. The result of my interest was the formation of the American Ballad Singers in 1939."[45] For Siegmeister, this American music embodied "typical and unquestionably native" qualities that stood in sharp contrast to the decadent sophistication and elegance prized by "many cosmopolitan esthetes."[46] As one critic wrote, a concert of the American Ballad Singers presented such "universally appealing" revolutionary songs, ballads, and other folk music that it "revealed more of the heart and soul of America than two dozen history books."[47]

Siegmeister's strategy in this context was twofold: for music whose origins lay in Europe, he claimed transformation into a native art through musical practice within a (proto-)democratic society; for music composed in America, especially that which originated during the Revolution, he posited a direct connection between national identity and musical content. The principle of alchemical conversion in the process of cultural transfer appears, for example, in Siegmeister's introduction to *Songs of Early America, 1620–1830* (1944), when he explained that psalms and ballads imported from Europe "were so radically changed in their transit from mouth to mouth that they became thoroughly American in spirit and form."[48] In his concert programs such appropriated works were represented by two tunes from the colonial *Ainsworth Psalter*, "Who Is the Man" and "Confess Jehova." But more important for Siegmeister was the music of Revolutionary America itself. Composers such as Francis Hopkinson—whose signature is on the Declaration of Independence—offered an embodied authenticity, "thereby forging a link between American music and the struggle for freedom that has never since been broken."[49] Siegmeister mythologized the Revolutionary songs as unadulterated expressions of "an independent American culture."[50] Music from the American Revolution, Siegmeister claimed proudly, had both ideological and musical value: "Besides telling us much about the thoughts and feelings of those who founded our American democracy, these songs have a musical quality all their own."[51] For a composer with strong communist leanings such as Siegmeister, rooting his national culture in the voice of the people carried political weight, too, especially given these songs' Revolutionary merits.

Billings's music in particular served to exemplify the earthy genius of Revolutionary musicians, who ventured daringly "into the realms of higher composition....Billings's music is often crude, to be sure, but it is not lacking in a genius of sorts, and a typical American enthusiasm and flair for the vigorous and unconventional."[52] Whereas Siegmeister claimed Billings's "Chester" as "the Marseillaise of the American Revolution," he declared the more delicate "A Virgin Unspotted" as probably "the very first original Christmas carol ever composed in America. At any rate, its archaic harmonies, its charming words and tune, and the contrast between the sustained slow verse and the jubilant lively chorus distinguish it as one of Billings's best, and a truly lovely piece of music."[53] In celebrating the old-fashioned immediacy of this repertoire, Siegmeister tapped into two intersecting discourse networks: on the international level, a fascination with archaic roots, emerging in the 1930s, as a culture-inherent form of nationalism that sought to validate national superiority through the traces of ancestral expression; and on the national level, the search for an original American art originating from a context defined as foundational in order to claim a cultural ancestry that was uniquely American. The 1942 compilation of Constance Rourke's writings titled *Roots of American Culture* specifically claimed the archaic aspect of Revolutionary art as a signifier of America's originality.[54] She stated that Billings was "as much a force in the democratic upheaval as the instigators of Shay's Rebellion" and lauded his "courage and ingenuity" in following his own homegrown musical impulse.[55] But the performance, editing, and scholarly presentation of Revolutionary music not only put into place an ancestral repertoire; it also served as a well of inspiration on "which the Americans of the future will be able to draw."[56] For composers, the rediscovery of this heritage could finally counteract the frequently invoked danger of sterility that came from looking to European traditions; instead—as Siegmeister put it—"we are discovering our roots in the present and past...depicting our native backgrounds, our traditions of democracy, our rich folk heritage."[57]

However, this wartime folk heritage not only homogenized diverse traditions into an all-American folk style, but also defined native music as bound to the land.[58] Any genre associated with modern urbanism was seen as alienated from these rural roots—a reasoning that turned jazz in particular into a suspect musical idiom when it came to identifying indigenous musical signifiers in American music. In effect, folk-music researchers started to characterize jazz tunes and spirituals as contaminated transformations of the "true folk music of America," as Lee Lyons Kaufman in 1945 called the ballads and other folk songs based on Anglo-Celtic roots. "American jazz lovers may not realize it," Kaufman explained, "but most of their favorite song hits of the last two decades have been 'hand-me downs'!"[59] Virgil Thomson, too, found it quite comforting that all American folk music was based on what he described (following George Pullen Jackson) as "White spirituals." In this account, the "precious heritage of modal melody" from pre-Elizabethan days survived in two strands of folk music that had thus far been seen as incompatible: the shape-note tunes in William Walker's *Southern Harmony* and the African American practice of florid embellishment, which—though "long thought to be an African survival of some kind"—was, according to Thomson, "nothing less than a continuation into our time of the old Presbyterian psalmody." Thus Thomson could celebrate the "ethnic integrity of American folk music" as an entirely white and British tradition.[60] Few were as outspoken in their whitening of American folk music, but the turn to an archaic heritage during the war years brought about a silencing of the African American idioms that had been appropriated—though not always without controversy—by musicians in the 1920s and early '30s as markers of an American identity. The musical models from the Revolution served a dual function: they embodied a preclassical sound world because of their modal texture, and they grounded this idiom in a foundational period of American history.

Indeed, with the onset of the war years, more and more composers in the United States—whether Cowell, Schuman, or Ross Lee Finney—turned to the repertoire and style of American Revolutionary music as an autochthonous form of early music. Even Otto Luening's orchestral *Prelude to a Hymn Tune by William Billings*—one of the first modern American works to refer to Billings, and one that he had composed as early as 1937—was not published until 1943. A set of variations over Billings's "Hymn to Music," Luening's work had been premièred at Bennington College, Vermont, in a program of early American and European music that included compositions by Stephen Foster and Giovanni Gabrieli.[61] But the year of its publication—Thomas Jefferson's bicentenary—brought other such works to light. Schuman's *William Billings Overture* (1943) used "several themes by that rugged individualist and pioneer of American composition" as the motivic basis for a work that Downes characterized as "written in lively and lusty fashion, with plenty of bounce and go, and gingery counterpoint in the free dissonant manner."[62] Premièred by the New York Philharmonic Orchestra in February 1944, Schuman's composition found its place in several wartime concerts, including an open-air summer program in Lewisohn Stadium in August 1944 on which it was featured along with Tchaikovsky's Symphony no. 4 and Wagner's Overture to *Tannhäuser*.[63] In 1943 Finney also turned to Billings as the foundation of an orchestral work titled *Hymn, Fuguing, and Holiday*. Based on Billings's hymn tune "Berlin," it consists of a hymnic statement of the melody, a set of eight variations, two fuguings (the second a kind of woodwind interlude), and a lively final section that concludes with the apotheotic restatement of the hymn.[64] By integrating such period compositional procedures as variations and fuguing into the formal conception of these works, the self-consciously historicist approach of Schuman and Finney differed from that of such earlier pieces as Thomson's *Variations on Sunday School Tunes* (1927), which were rooted in the composer's attachment to shape-note hymns. He commented later: "When you reach down into your subconscious, you get certain things. When Aaron reaches down, he doesn't get cowboy tunes, he gets Jewish chants. When I reach down I get Southern hymns."[65]

Thomson was kinder about Cowell's second *Hymn and Fuguing Tune* (1944), a work with a deliberately austere and monochromatic character thanks to its modal inflections and stark instrumentation for string orchestra, which create an archaic evocation of America's sonic roots: this was, Thomson said, "an extended and songful development in the diatonic modal manner practiced by our American back-country forefathers."[66] In contrast to Finney, Luening, and Schuman, who all used one or several of Billings's hymns as the thematic foundations for orchestral works and relied on contrapuntal variation as their compositional strategy within a predominantly tonal framework, Cowell tried his hand at a different form of compositional engagement with the "Yankee Tunesmiths," an informally defined group of early American composers that included Billings, Jeremiah Ingalls, Justin Morgan, Daniel Read, and Timothy Swan, among others. He explained in 1945, a year after his first *Hymn and Fuguing Tune* was composed, that this work "is written in a manner which is frankly influenced by the early American style of Billings and Walker. However, the early style is not exactly imitated, nor are any of the tunes and melodies taken from these early masters. Rather I asked myself the question, what would have happened in America if this fine, serious early style had developed?"[67] In these works, Cowell used stylistic elements such as modes and open chords that he derived from early American hymn tunes, but in a sparse, modernist, diatonic framework. For Cowell, the romance of homegrown American music played itself out not so much in the invention of a past as in the imagination of an alternate present. In a comment made a couple of years earlier, he described this approach as "an original development of materials suggested by the early American folk-hymn style."[68] Although his musical idiom had shifted toward a more traditional tonal language, Cowell's anti-European stance in fact remained consonant with his ultramodern Americanism of the 1920s. Furthermore, the "open and consecutive fifths and octaves" and "the sustaining of unaccented syllables and modes" that he discovered in American hymnody suggested for Cowell "a Celtic origin." Celtic references, as an autobiographical marker, had played a role in other works by Cowell, whether of this period (his *Gaelic Symphony* of 1942) or of his experimental phase, such as his well-known piano piece *The Banshee* (1925). By identifying the signature traits of American hymnody as Celtic, Cowell created a nationalist lineage anchored in his own Irish background. Whether or not his dual compositional rootedness at that time—in a universal Celtic ancestry and the American Revolution—was in any way related to reestablishing himself after his release from prison, it certainly fit broader wartime needs for a musical present whose past was grounded in "natal soil."[69]

Like Finney and Schuman, however, Cowell first engaged with the Yankee Tunesmiths in 1943, when he arranged two fuguing tunes (one by Jenks, the other by Billings) for military band and composed *American Muse*, three songs for two-part women's chorus in the "early American hymn-style."[70] That year brought the dedication of the Jefferson Memorial in Washington; saw early Federal America represented on Broadway with Sidney Kingsley's play *The Patriots* (which won that year's New York Drama Critics Circle award for best play because of "its thoughtful projection of a great American theme"); and occasioned the publication of numerous exhibitions, books, and newspaper articles about the author of the Declaration of Independence.[71] The theme running through the Jefferson celebrations—including Roosevelt's bicentenary address—drew parallels between the Revolutionary War against tyranny and the current one.[72] As one commentator put it: "Today's conflict is in essence the same fight against tyranny as that on which Jefferson staked his life, his fortune and his sacred honor."[73] Musically, the bicentenary led most prominently to a new composition, Randall Thompson's *Testament of Freedom*, a choral work with texts by Jefferson (1943).

Cowell's *American Muse*, the first work for which the composer claimed to have written new music in the style of early American hymns, seeks nativist authenticity based on the fact that—as a footnote in the score indicates—its musical elements "derive from rural American hymns."[74] All three songs are modal and use flatted leading tones, with the result that modal cadences predominate. The first of the three songs, of the same title as the set, is in white-note Dorian mode with B-naturals (except for the very occasional flat). Its opening sets the words "American muse" almost programmatically in a two-voice note-against-note style that starts strongly in unison and develops into sweet modal harmony, with the modal C♯ leading to B♮ in the soprano. The cadence (at "diverse heart") is markedly modal, with its move from C to D minor. The second song, "Swift Runner," is in A-Aeolian (with dissonances) and alludes to the jigs of early American dance music. The final song, "Immensity of Wheel," is in G-Dorian (with one flat in the key signature) and organized in a modified strophic form whose repetitive stanzaic structure echoes the hymns of federal America.

However, the texts that Cowell chose for this set of choral songs were neither Revolutionary poems nor contemporary texts about eighteenth-century America. Rather, he selected as his source the opening "Invocation" from Stephen Vincent Benét's Pulitzer prize–winning narrative poem, *John Brown's Body* (1928), considered the grand American epic about the Civil War. This choice offered not only a homage to the poet, who had just died at the age of forty-four, but, perhaps more important, allowed a fascinating fusion between the musical styles that Cowell associated with Revolutionary America and an iconic text about the Civil War, thus linking the two foundational narratives of the American struggle for liberty in a single artwork. The three extracts that Cowell chose from the opening segment of Benét's epic poem create a plot that originates in a grand, archaic world of the "native" land—in fact, "native" (the word concluding the first song) is blared out fortissimo on the melody's highest note. The second song presents the landscape of the frontier and leads in the third into the harsh world of industrialized war, whose machinery was "oiled with inhuman sweat / And glittering with the heat of ladled steel." Cowell had recently written a composition entitled *American Melting-Pot* (1941) and was soon to compose *Philippine Return: Rondo on Philippine Folk Song* (1943) and other hybrid works that extended this kind of musical identity politics to an almost imperialist appropriation of global cultures. In *American Muse*, however, he constructed a deliberately nativist argument through both music and text. Indeed, save for the two words "diverse" and "varied" in the first, well-known lines of the poem that he set as his opening song, the composer omitted all the verses in Benét's "Invocation" that referred to specific ethnicities and individual forms of existence. Instead the verses Cowell chose were those that commented "in strong and moving words on the special quality of American life"—on creating a homogeneous nation shaped by its soil and industries.[75]

Early American hymn tunes also played an important role in the works of other composers, perhaps most prominently in Aaron Copland's ballet *Appalachian Spring* (1944). His choice of the Shaker hymn "Simple Gifts" for a set of variations was far more programmatic in terms of its context than is usually acknowledged. Copland's instrumentation, his emphasis on open fifths in the ever-so-lightly modal idiom in these passages, his final fuguing treatment of the melody, and his use of variations to work through the song inscribe his treatment of the hymn fully in the context of the Billings variations by Schuman and Finney on the one hand, and Cowell's invention of an American modernism forged out of the idiom of the Yankee Tunesmiths on the other. In a letter to Arthur Berger, Copland characterized this musical language as "a home-spun musical idiom, similar to what I was trying for in a more hectic fashion in the earlier jazz works. . . . I have touched off for myself and others a kind of musical naturalness that we have badly needed."[76] Furthermore, Copland picked for his variation set a hymn that begins with the line: "'Tis the gift to be simple, 'tis the gift to be free." Far from being simply a pastoral reference, Copland's choice of a hymn that promises freedom—that ubiquitous word in war propaganda—and merges it with notions of simplicity, belonging to the land, and early American culture of a quasi-Utopian character fits perfectly with the overall casting during wartime of the United States as a nation wholly grounded not just in its soil but in its history. That this particular history was one of pacifism rather than nativism—Ann Lee, the founder of the Shakers, was arrested for treason during the Revolutionary War because she refused to take the oath of allegiance—was lost in translation, however, when Copland appropriated the melody for *Appalachian Spring*. By virtue of his adaptation, "Simple Gifts" became a signifier of Americana, albeit a quiet one.

Both Cowell and Copland appropriated early American hymn styles in the service of a modernism that posited this heritage as a native musical character trait, even though their individual forms of engagement with this "usable past" were mediated through their different compositional backgrounds. In their symbolic and idiomatic integration of this national musical past, Copland's *Appalachian Spring* and Cowell's *Hymns and Fuguing Tunes* could be interpreted as having elective affinities to works composed not only in the recent past—for example, Maurice Ravel's *Le tombeau de Couperin* (written during World War I)—but also in the wartime present. The affirmation of a nationally specific, contemporary compositional idiom as grounded in that country's treasure trove of preclassical "early music" can be traced in works that originated in countries as different as Fascist Italy and war-torn Britain, including Luigi Dallapiccola's *Tre laudi* (1937), Michael Tippett's *Concerto for Double String Orchestra* (1939) and *Fantasia on a Theme of Handel* (1941), André Jolivet's *Guignol et Pandore* (1943), and Wolfgang Fortner's *Music for Strings* no. 2 (1944). In each case, the archaic reference was nationally specific and served for validation: the anti-Fascist Tippett evoked William Byrd in his *Concerto*, whereas the (then still) Fascist Dallapiccola's intertext was thirteenth-century Italian polyphony.[77] Instrumentalizing one's own preclassical music for nationalist identity politics also had roots deep in the nineteenth century's early-music revivals in Germany, France, Britain, and Italy.[78] Moreover, it is clear that the United States had already participated in more conventional notions of a neoclassical revival: not for nothing were the two godparents of American modernism, Nadia Boulanger and Edgard Varèse, actively involved in the promotion and performance of preclassical music, a repertoire that played a central role in the aesthetics and teaching of both. The British music critic D. F. Aitken noted in 1936 that "the nineteenth century, in Mademoiselle Boulanger's view, has been a dangerous influence. We are only now getting back to the great tradition of the past—a tradition of order and restraint and discipline, in fact of classicism."[79] Yet by 1943 this universalist concept was no longer sufficient for U.S. composers. Instead, the Yankee Tunesmiths fit the bill of a genuinely American "early music" precisely because of their perceived crudeness and lack of erudition; theirs was a music whose essence lay in a much earlier era than the late eighteenth century, when it was actually composed, so that its archaic quality could rival that of a Tallis or Machaut while still serving modernist ends. By tapping into this idiom and dissolving the historical and stylistic distance that often self-consciously marked concert compositions citing folk melodies into a sonic immediacy, American composers developed an approach that jibed well with the aesthetic demands of wartime America, all the more as they claimed national uniqueness in the face of cosmopolitan neoclassicism.

Salutes to American Folk Song

The sublimation of the historically distant into a modernist musical idiom was only one form of compositional engagement with early American music in the wartime United States. Other musicians emphasized the historic depth of the country's traditional musics. One work in particular was intended to be emblematic in its search for authentic musical expression through the historic voices of the American people. Walter Kerr and Elie Siegmeister's *Sing Out, Sweet Land! A Salute to American Folk and Popular Music* premièred on Broadway on December 27, 1944 (Figure 3.3); its theme was "the story of the vital part music has always played in people's lives through the nation's development, from pioneer times to the present."[80] For Siegmeister, who professed in 1944 that he saw "no fundamental difference between folk music and classical music," this production sat squarely at the center of his quest for "discovering our roots in the present and past."[81] Yet it was not Siegmeister who was at the origin of *Sing Out, Sweet Land!*, but Kerr, a young playwright and drama professor at Catholic University who wrote and produced several shows each year at its drama department's thriving semiprofessional theater. The 1943–44 season presented a series of Americana productions that included, among others, David Belasco's *The Girl of the Golden West* and closed with

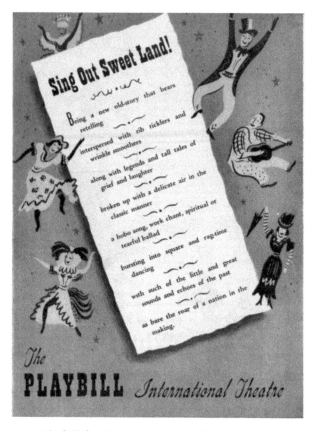

FIGURE 3.3 Playbill for *Sing Out, Sweet Land!* (December 31, 1944). The design of the playbill (and of the souvenir program) echoes the style and design details of that for *Oklahoma!*, which was on more than one level a model for and intertext of *Sing Out, Sweet Land!*[82] Courtesy of the Beinecke Rare Book and Manuscript Library, Yale University.

Sing Out, Sweet Land!, "an original musical comedy by Walter Kerr which dips in our folklore of dance and music."[83] Premièred on May 17, 1944, the Washington performances continued before an enthusiastic audience until June 4.[84] Just over a month later, on July 25, Kerr signed a contract with the Theatre Guild for a production of *Sing Out, Sweet Land!* on Broadway. The show had a run of 102 performances at the International Theatre before being taken on the company's national tour in April and May 1945.[85]

The Theatre Guild's Lawrence Langner and Theresa Helburn obviously meant to capitalize on their runaway success with Rodgers and Hammerstein's *Oklahoma!*, which had opened on March 31, 1943, and was still playing on Broadway and on tour. The question for them was how to find the right mixture of song, dance, and drama to repeat its creation of the "integrated musical." Siegmeister, however—whose involvement with *Sing Out, Sweet Land!* started only after Kerr signed with the Theatre Guild—clearly tried to put his own ideological stamp on a work aiming to tell the story of America through its music. As he explained: "Helburn, Langner, Kerr and myself had many a heated discussion as to how many of the show's songs should be of the familiar, well-known variety, and how many brand new, or at least unknown to most people. Kerr was for having the majority well known, on the theory that the public enjoys what it already knows; I plunked for new and unfamiliar ones." For Siegmeister, these lesser-known works were the "real roots of American music and theatre."[86] In contrast to the folk and popular songs used in Kerr's original version, the Broadway score included not only arrangements of folk songs, but also original compositions by Siegmeister as well as newly written pieces based on folk motives for the ballets and other incidental music, thereby "integrating the whole musical continuity of *Sing Out, Sweet Land!*"[87] Siegmeister thus took the keyword "integration" in a very different direction from what was claimed for *Oklahoma!*

Olin Downes was not convinced, claiming that in *Sing Out, Sweet Land!* the tail "has ended by wagging the dog," because the play seemed first and foremost structured to accommodate the music.[88] Certainly, Kerr had tried to create a dramatic plot that did more than just string things together: as he clarified in the souvenir program, "it was easy enough to put these things together into a kind of pageant, hanging traditional American songs and poetic atmospheres on an obvious historical outline. But who really wants to see a pageant? I don't, and I usually try pretty hard not to ask anyone else to look at something I wouldn't take for myself in the theatre."[89] Thus he invents the figure of Barnaby Goodchild, "an American youth of legendary proportions who everywhere makes Americans sing as he light-heartedly traverses this sweet, glorious and epic land."[90] But there is more than a little of the pageant in the result. In Barnaby's time travels, which include Puritan New England, the Oregon Trail, a Mississippi riverboat, a Civil War campfire, and a Texas railroad station, he encounters Revolutionary patriots, fiddlers, farmers, African American slaves, an American Indian girl, gamblers, and hobos, among others. In addition to dialogues, songs, and dance numbers, various characters recite poetry, as when the Revolutionary patriot in act 1, scene 2 answers his daughter's question of why Barnaby cannot stay with an excerpt from Stephen Vincent Benét's poem *Western Star* (1943), which opens with the line, "Americans are always moving on." Barnaby then leads the audience from one stereotypical American history locale to the next until things go awry in the decadent interwar years. During the Jazz Age, the lessons of true American cultural identity are forgotten in urban speakeasies with the consumption of commercial music: Barnaby enters a nightclub that he mistakes for a neighborhood gathering-place just after four chorus girls have presented "a brief but hot number to Gershwin's *I Got Rhythm*."[91] As always, Barnaby wants to share his songs "about out on the prairie, or nice blue skies," a proposition in response to which Maxie, the hostess, quips: "Now ain't that sweet! Whaddaya think this is—The Old Homestead? Last time these suckers saw sky was during the eclipse!"[92] Predictably, the patrons reject the homely fare, asking for "hot stuff," and Barnaby concludes that "folks don't like me no more."[93] However, this rejection is the point that pivots him toward the wartime present: Barnaby receives a letter from Uncle Sam drafting him into the armed forces, where his folk music once more contributes to American morale. The redemptive final scene takes place on an aircraft carrier, with a petty officer singing a sea shanty before everyone joins together in the show's patriotic finale, staged "in V formation."[94] "Sing out, sweet land," they entreat the audience, reminding listeners that "a country's more than a hill and a stream / And more than earth and trees / It's a poet's promise and the patriot's dream / And more than these." In an earlier version of the lyrics, the sounds of American folk music were celebrated as beacons of global freedom: "Men across the sea / Fighting to be free / Listen to America / Sing its melody (and) / Rise and fill the skies with music."[95] These propagandistic lines were omitted by the time of the première in favor of a more U.S.-centric view of the power of song: "The people are people like you and me / And if forty-eight states of us stay on key / The song should be kind of grand."[96]

Because *Sing Out, Sweet Land!* featured folk music, critics focused on the immediate connection between what was considered a desirable authentic expression of American ideals and a quasi-utopian past. The critic Richard P. Cooke, for example, made it clear that he saw a decline when the story reached the industrialized later nineteenth century: at that point, "the charm began to fade from the production."[97] For the theater critic Lewis Nichols, the flaw lay with Kerr's book: his decision to emphasize the burlesque and the "coy, cute and—to come right out with it—often childish" ran counter to the genuine folk spirit of the songs presented in the show. Indeed, "the show had its choice of burlesque or, by playing straight, to offer nostalgia, and the choice was wrong." Nichols posited the authentic folklore as an object of nostalgic desire and therefore criticized Kerr for inventing the rather anemic Barnaby Goodchild; instead, "American song deserved a real [Paul] Bunyan with vast ideas and vision."[98] This preference for the genuine fare of American folk shaped the reception of the show and its performers. Instead of becoming a vehicle for Alfred Drake (the first Curly in *Oklahoma!*),

who was cast in the leading role of Barnaby Goodchild, *Sing Out, Sweet Land!*
turned the folk singer Burl Ives—who had just started to become known
through his radio show, *The Wayfaring Stranger*—into a Broadway star. By the
time the touring version of the show reached Chicago in April 1945, Claudia
Cassidy raved that "Burl Ives makes music magic. . . . There's never enough
of him, nor would be, if he sang all night."[99] In Washington, where Kerr's
show had originated, the theater critic for the *Washington Post*, Nelson B.
Bell, celebrated in particular the work's "richness of American musical folklore": "A tribute to the power of song to weld a nation into a lighthearted
and courageous unit," *Sing Out, Sweet Land!* was appreciated for its "homely,
indigenous folk tunes that comprise the backbone of the music-drama."[100]
Despite the limitations of the book, the power of the apparently authentic
native musical voice swept audiences and critics off their feet.

Intimately linking folk music to American history, *Sing Out, Sweet Land!*
is a staged realization of Siegmeister's view that American folk music had
started with "daily life in colonial times" but received its "spark and fire"
in the days of the Revolution and from there developed into "a vast body
of music with distinctively American traits. Besides its sheer musical fascination, it tells us much of the life and spirit of the plain people of this
country."[101] Even though *Sing Out, Sweet Land!* played on Broadway and was
treated, at the time of its première, as the "latest of Broadway musicals to
draw its material from Americana," the generic context—at least insofar as
Siegmeister was concerned—was not popular music but concert composition
and opera.[102] His ideological framing of folk music as a historically anchored
"people's music" could both provide a deep lineage of American music and be
considered an inspiration for new composition, a development parallel to the
events across the Atlantic when "centuries ago, European musical theatres
grew out of the songs of just such wandering minstrels and troubadours."[103]
Even though his rhetoric allowed folk music's transatlantic roots, Siegmeister
nationalized the repertoire and its history through the notion of the melting
pot as the crucible in which a native culture is forged from diverse sources by
imbuing the very fabric of the songs with the American way of life.

In contrast to Cowell's imaginary present, which jumped over a century
and a half straight into vernacular modernism, Siegmeister constructed a continuous "usable past" both in his work with the American Ballad Singers
and in the score for *Sing Out, Sweet Land!* by historicizing early American
song and U.S. folk music in this archaeological enterprise, thus crafting a
direct musical line from Plymouth Rock to the present. Yet as a nationalized
repertoire, especially during the war years, folk song also carried within its
ideological underpinnings the aspect of a people's eternal present. A place of

symbolic memory, this institutionalized vision of folk song as embodying a native essence created a new form of patriotic homogenization. In the 1930s folklorists emphasized the diversity of folk music in the United States; wartime needs melded "these discordant voices into a single united chorus of nationalism. Folklore moved into the realm of propaganda."[104] The Librarian of Congress, Archibald MacLeish, highlighted this aspect of grandeur in his preface to John A. Lomax and Alan Lomax's folk-song collection *Our Singing Country*, which was published less than a month before the attack on Pearl Harbor. He compared folk song to the humanly created specificity of national landscapes, incarnating "the people's mark more even than the line of the roads in a country...and they last longer." He praised the edition as a "body of words and of music which tells almost as much about the American people as the marks they have made upon the earth itself."[105] This notion of folk song as the essence of America found its way also into the reviews of the volume—for example, in Horace Reynolds's claim that the collection expressed "America and the American spirit more fully and faithfully than any other art form."[106] William Schuman echoed these sentiments (in remarks on a collection by Siegmeister and Downes) when he extolled folk song as "the mirror of our national life as reflected in these unself-conscious creations."[107]

In the 1930s and '40s, folk song as a national heritage not only stood alone as a monument to authentic Americana, but also was considered the raw material of compositions that would embody in their very fabric the voices of the nation. John and Alan Lomax hoped that their volume was "merely a foretaste of what may grow into a fairly complete collection of American folk tunes, and of the books, symphonies, plays, operas for which it should eventually provide material."[108] Comments about the proper American form of folk-song adaptation in concert music drifted through the writings of composers and critics during the war years, and more than one shared Roy Harris's polemical rejection of any transfer of European models into American folk-song composition as un-American, in particular the use of sonata form: "This treatment of folksong is annoying to all discerning people except to those who are permanently conditioned to nineteenth-century German professional concert music."[109] Here Harris echoes his teacher Nadia Boulanger; he also betrays a debilitating anxiety over the influence and foundational role of Antonín Dvořák's "New World" Symphony.[110] Yet in this context, too, the war years brought a subtle shift in the long-established Western tradition of forging national identity in music through the use of folk art. Just as Cowell appropriated the musical characteristics of the Yankee Tunesmiths, so did composers who engaged with American folk music try to forge a synthetic national style in the face of cosmopolitan developments. Among the models repeatedly cited were not only Stravinsky but also Bartók, who also infused his own musical idiom with traditional sonic markers of his national identity.[111] In fact, Bartók considered absorption in folklore necessary to the formation of musical identity, something that—as he explained to an American journalist in 1941—required a composer "to command this musical language so completely that it becomes the natural expression of his musical ideas."[112]

The predominant theme of American folk music–based compositions was the mythology of the American frontier, a particularly apt topos for the wartime challenges of a nation fighting on foreign territory rather than at home.[113] The roots of this mythology went back to the 1930s, when composers such as Virgil Thomson turned to cowboy songs—for example, in his 1936 score for the Resettlement Administration's documentary *The Plow That Broke the Plains*—to claim authenticity in their representation of the rural frontier, a hardy space recently emphasized by the New Deal's sympathetic engagement with the agricultural pioneer.[114] Perhaps best-known among the musical representations of the frontier is Aaron Copland's iconic cowboy ballet, *Billy the Kid*, written in 1938 for Leo Kirstein's Ballet Caravan. After the outbreak of the war, the prairie and its cowboys featured in numerous concert works, including Norman Dello Joio's *Prairie* (1942), Eugene Goossens's *Cowboy Fantasy* (1942–44), Lukas Foss's *The Prairie* (1944), and Elie Siegmeister's *Prairie Legend* (1944) and *Western Suite* (1945). *Western Suite*, for example, celebrates the uncorrupted qualities of the early west in five movements based on easily recognized folk melodies. It begins with a slow crescendo mimicking the beginning of the day in the first movement, "Prairie Morning"; then come the lively "Round-up"; a lyrical middle movement, "Night-Herding"; and the energetic rhythms of the "Buckaroo." The final movement combines the tune "Trail to Mexico" with an increasingly emphatic lyricism whose heavy reliance on the full strings makes use of every trick of symphonic lushness in the service of a narrative program that leads "home to the ranch."[115]

One work in particular stands out in this accumulation of prairie folklore during the war years: Aaron Copland's *Rodeo* (1942), a stage work that entered the canon of American concert repertoire within a year after its première. Conceived by Agnes de Mille as an "American Ballet," the work presented "the story of the Taming of the Shrew—cowboy style."[116] In contrast to *Billy the Kid*—which was, according to Kirstein, a ballet about "the necessity of establishing law and order," with Billy a "symbol" in the "historical process of the developing Frontier"—*Rodeo* celebrated a static and idealized *ur*-American society to which the individual cannot but submit for both personal fulfillment and social continuity.[117] Outlaw Billy might have been an attractive figure for late 1930s audiences flocking to cinemas in prurient fascination with the gangster antiheroes that dominated the silver screen, but the war forced a different direction. From the outset, de Mille sought to stage not only the story of a cowgirl's surrender to social conformity but also the mythologized American frontier itself, represented by a small, isolated farm in the southwest. Her earliest scenario made clear her intent: "There are never more than a very few people on the stage at a time, and while they generate a lot of excitement between themselves, they are always dwarfed by space and height and isolation. One must be always conscious of the enormous land on which these people live and of their proud loneliness."[118] Oliver Smith's stage design for the production emphasized this frontier landscape, especially in the opening scene, with fences receding in the background and the orange-red sky almost overwhelming the rest of the set (Figure 3.4).[119] Costumes and a choreography "rooted in American folk dance" further contributed to the visual representation of the American frontier on the stage.[120]

FIGURE 3.4 Scene from Agnes de Mille's choreography of Aaron Copland's *Rodeo*, Ballet Russe de Monte Carlo, performing at the Naval Training Station, Newport, Rhode Island, 1942. The backdrop shows Oliver Smith's original stage design. Official U.S. Navy Photograph. Dance Division, New York Public Library for the Performing Arts.

De Mille wanted a congenial, folkloric score for her first high-profile choreography for the Ballet Russe de Monte Carlo in New York, and she approached Aaron Copland—with whom she had been acquainted since the 1930s—in April 1942 about the composition.[121] Although the composer was not entirely sure that he wanted to write another cowboy ballet, he accepted readily. De Mille supplied Copland with several cowboy tunes, including "one with a good 'riding rhythm,' one called 'Ground Hog,' and another from the waltz she had heard in Virgil's film, *The Plow That Broke the Plains*."[122] By the time Copland left for Tanglewood in May, he had most of *Rodeo* mapped out; he wrote to Benjamin Britten from the Berkshires, "I'm doing a frothy ballet for the Monte Carlo people on the usual wildwest subject—full of square dances and Scotch tunes and the like."[123] He finished the full draft on July 10, 1942, and started work on the orchestration while de Mille rehearsed the dances. The première, on October 16, 1942, was a major success. The ballet's music was broadcast less than two weeks later on New York's WQXR radio station, and by early November Copland was discussing with Serge Koussevitzky a possible performance of a concert suite based on *Rodeo*.[124]

Copland's music was also considered simply an "enchanting" and "vividly effective" soundtrack to the ballet as a whole. Primed by such earlier stage works as *American Legend* (1941), which contained a square dance choreographed and danced by Agnes de Mille, "wearing country manners," and the National Folk Festival that drew more than twenty thousand people to Madison Square Garden on May 11, 1942, the ballet's audiences and critics cheered *Rodeo* first and foremost as a "truly American ballet."[125] Hailed as something that grew "out of the American mind and the American landscape," with a dance style that was an "authentic blend of drawling ease and trigger quickness," *Rodeo* was celebrated furthermore as revealing "a real public appetite for genuinely American ballets."[126] The San Francisco critic Alfred Frankenstein contrasted the alienated (and alienating) efforts of foreigners toying with American topics with the authenticity of *Rodeo* in a chauvinist comment that turned de Mille's ballet into a war victory:

The [Ballet Russe de] Monte Carlo has often toyed with American themes, employing Russian choreographers and Russo-Parisian composers, and the results have been as close to the intention as were the results of those views of New York and London engraved a century ago by Japanese block printers who had never been outside of Tokyo. In *Rodeo* the Monte Carlo has its first American ballet by American artists, which does not mean simply that the work is correct in its details, but that it is the product of characteristically American imagination. It is much the kind of ballet that Mark Twain might have written if his mind had run to ballets.[127]

Not everyone, however, rejoiced in this straightforward nationalism. When the dancer Ted Shawn heard Copland's score during a rehearsal in 1942, he put his finger on the negative side of artistic nationalism when he distanced himself from this production, saying to Agnes de Mille, "it's because of music like that that we are having war."[128]

"Redolent of our American soil," according to de Mille's program notes for the première, *Rodeo* became an overnight, all-American success whose nationalist appeal as prairie folklore intersected with widespread nativist discourse about the work's American choreographer and composer.[129] This chauvinist impulse carried over into the reception of the concert suite that Copland extracted from the ballet score several months later, premièred by the Boston Pops Orchestra, with Arthur Fiedler conducting, on May 28, 1943. Copland's seamless fusion of the quoted and adapted cowboy melodies into his own, more and more finely tuned folk style led to an iconic score of musical Americana.[130] Yet the suite, entitled *Four Dance Episodes from Rodeo*, also invokes the four-movement symphony, with a fast first movement containing allusions to sonata form ("Buckaroo Holiday"), a slow second movement ("Corral Nocturne"), a dance movement whose slowness echoes the minuets or *Ländler* of classic models ("Saturday Night Waltz"), and a rondo-type finale ("Hoe-Down").[131] Copland's awareness of formal signifiers had been shaped through his studies with Nadia Boulanger and then honed through his teaching and such writings as *What to Listen For in Music* (1939), where he declared of the contemporary symphony that "one can safely say that the symphony as a collection of three or more separate movements is still as firmly established as ever. . . . If any fundamental changes may be discerned, they are likely to be changes of the inner structural setup of an individual movement."[132] Copland's decision to pare the ballet down to the proportions and movements associated with the classical symphony may well have been a deliberate attempt to present his own version of a "folk-song symphony" at a time when he was not only fully and enthusiastically involved in the U.S. war effort, but also had to face the journalistic division of his music into two styles, either "severe" or "simple." Copland rejected this dichotomy in a letter to Arthur Berger written at exactly the time that he was revising *Rodeo* for the concert hall.[133] But whether as ballet or quasi-symphony, it served as a musical embodiment of the American frontier myth. Copland's score was rooted self-consciously in the homegrown vernacular of cowboy music.

Voicing Opera in America

With the beginning of World War II, in the United States the question of cultural transfer in concert music suddenly became an acute problem because of the need to forge a national music with its own usable past in order to mark as intrinsically American both the international concert repertoire, from Bach to Brahms, and new compositions created in the United States. This process of appropriation consisted of two closely interrelated steps: the dissolving of any previous national signification into a universalist rhetoric of world heritage, crowned with the establishment of the United States as the sole and rightful heir to this art; and the identification of native traditions that could serve as distinctive national signifiers in the stylistic framework of international neoclassicism. While these trends played themselves out mainly in the concert hall, the operatic stage needed to rely on different strategies of transfer, because specifically American concerns about the musical stage intersected with the broader distrust of opera's contemporary relevance in the face of an established and increasingly hidebound performance repertoire. Indeed, although illustrious composers such as Taylor and Thomson had tried their hand successfully at composing "American opera," the canon remained almost exclusively European—and, worse, dominated by Axis composers such as Rossini, Verdi, Puccini, and Wagner.[134] As one self-professed music lover wrote to Thomson in April 1942, "It has always seemed to me that Opera can't pay in America because it is un-American. It remains a totally European form of art. It is slow, often stupid and ridiculous and extremely un-natural. By un-natural I mean that it not only fails to resemble nature, it doesn't even resemble our dreams or imaginings. (As the movies often do, for instance.)"[135] Clearly this was an extreme view: it pushed the charge of opera as an entirely European genre to its limit, and it also coded unnaturalness as un-American. Still, during the war years many commented on the genre's outsider status. This form of critique posed particular problems, however, if one hoped—to paraphrase Whitman—to hear America singing on the opera stage during World War II.

The roots of this issue, too, reached far back into the nineteenth century, when the translation and adaptation of European opera for U.S. audiences often placed the results in a field of reception somewhere between that of minstrel shows (so-called Ethiopian operas), English-language folk theater, and snobbish Europhilia.[136] Yet opera was regarded increasingly also as an art form that could be appropriated specifically for American musical life through translation and performance practice. During the 1930s in particular, this form of appropriation was tied to the New Deal ideologies of democratizing elite art.[137] Such a concept of opera as socially malleable and artistically transferable located the national character of opera as much on the production side of things as in the work itself. Both the FTP and the FMP flirted with opera and related music-theatrical genres, though often with little success because it lacked the resources, and the performers, to produce it effectively. But with the entrance of the United States into World War II, both the social aspect of opera as an institution and the question of national identity in the context of a European-born genre became crucial issues for validating opera's continuous relevance. Indeed, the cultural capital assigned to opera proved both attractive and problematic. Given that Americans purportedly had joined the global conflict in December 1941 in order to save democracy, the exclusive cultural practice associated with the institution of opera now became tricky. Access to what the masses perceived as highbrow culture could no longer be solely the social concern of New Deal agencies such as the FTP; instead, it was quickly turned into a national necessity.[138] Opera in wartime America had to respond to two interrelated issues: it needed to be both Americanized and democratized.

The issue of access to opera was intimately related both to performance strategies and to financial concerns, especially with respect to the Metropolitan Opera, which had evolved into a kind of national opera house because of its regular Saturday afternoon radio broadcasts.[139] Further, the Met not only made seats available for military personnel, but also lowered ticket prices for the 1942–43 season.[140] Olin Downes assessed this change positively in his retrospective of the season by observing that "in an unprecedented degree, the Metropolitan has made opera popular.... The audiences are not those of earlier seasons. They now involve a cross section of the general public of the city, rather than of the socially or even musically elect. The man on the street, the Broadway denizen, the visitor from out of town, large numbers of the armed forces quartered in and about the city, and plain people in every walk of life, frequent the performances."[141] Moreover, the New York City Opera was founded in 1943 on the express initiative of Mayor Fiorello LaGuardia—it opened at the newly restored City Center Theatre in February 1944 with productions of *Tosca*, *Martha*, and *Carmen*—and charged with the mission of bringing opera to wider audiences at low cost. Ticket prices and ease of access to "long-haired" entertainment (whether opera or classical music in general) remained a much-observed theme throughout these years, one directly related to the war-generated educational and propaganda discourses associated in particular with the OWI and the Subcommittee on Music of the Joint Army and Navy Committee on Recreation and Welfare. Whether at the Met or elsewhere, the war-related widening of access thus folded what for long had been accounted an elite ritual into the New Deal concept of middlebrow culture.

Advertisements and reviews point—sometimes rather desperately—to fresh translations, American singers, and up-to-date staging as key ingredients in the formula for turning European opera into an American art form. An advertisement for performances of Rossini's *Barber of Seville* and Bizet's *Carmen* in Pasadena, California, claimed: "Grand opera, Americanized by new English translations and young American singers, will be presented by the American Music Theater of Pasadena at the Civic Auditorium in that city next month."[142] In a review of a previous production of *Il barbiere* in 1942, one critic identified the "racy new English translation and... livelier tempo" as providing "a healthy argument for those who would refurbish old works for modern taste."[143] Newspapers announced a season of "Grand opera produced in the 'American way'" for Washington, D.C., in the winter of 1943.[144] Surprisingly, even the Metropolitan Opera responded to the call for English translations; it presented several productions in English, particularly of operas that incorporated spoken dialogue (where the vernacular could more easily be justified), ranging from *The Magic Flute* in 1941 to *Fidelio* in 1945.[145]

Indeed, it was the Met's production of *The Magic Flute* that rekindled public debate about opera in translation. Journalists praised Ruth and Thomas Martin's new English-language version of Emanuel Schikaneder's libretto as a model in its unadorned directness.[146] On February 10, 1942, the Metropolitan Opera Guild held a public event in which defenders of productions in the original language and advocates for opera in English squared off against each other. This was followed by a poll of the audience, which the original-language faction won by just 460 to 451.[147] What is significant about this debate, however, is not the result per se, but the fact that as apparently trivial an issue as the translation of European opera attracted a passionate audience of over nine hundred in the first weeks of the war.[148]

Around the same time, in the spring of 1942, another initiative directed at opera in English got into full swing when the National Committee for Opera in America worked toward a survey of English-language opera translations.[149] This was intended as a first step toward standardization, given that one impediment to opera in English "is the lack of good, standard translations. Those to be found printed in scores are usually stilted and unsingable, whereas the latest and best translations are usually unpublished."[150] Such translations would also solve the problem that singers faced of having to learn a new translation with each production.[151] For example, the committee found that eight previous productions of Bedřich

Smetana's *The Bartered Bride* used six different translations, whereas the six most recent *Carmen* productions relied on three separate English versions.[152] As sensible as this project of standardization might have been, it led to no immediate results. Instead, new and better translations became an advertising feature during the early 1940s—for example, when the Met promoted its new *Falstaff* as "using a new translation worked out by Sir Thomas [Beecham]."[153] Critics regularly addressed the quality of the translations in their reviews. The Philadelphia Opera Company's successful English versions in 1942–43 of *Il barbiere di Siviglia*, *Pelléas et Mélisande*, and *Der Rosenkavalier* earned high praise in general and positive comments on specific turns of phrase in particular. In the case of the 1942 production of *The Barber of Seville*, "about 5000 auditors enjoyed an experience unusual for even the most confirmed opera goers, that of hearing this familiar comic opera sung in English with a text so up-to-date as to contain such a phrase as 'take a walk around the block.' This use of the vernacular certainly met with the approval of the assemblage, as was evident by frequent outbursts of laughter and by salvos of applause directed as much at the neat rendering of a couplet as at the artistry of the singer."[154] If a translation was unsuccessful, however, critics could be merciless. An English-language version of Flotow's *Martha* in November 1942 at the Chicago Civic Opera House, for example, launched accusations of a "charade" contrived by "operatic saboteurs."[155]

It was not just the established opera companies that were turning to English-language productions. The fall of 1942 brought two Broadway shows that presented themselves as Americanizing European repertoire. Whereas *Rosalinda* (alias *Die Fledermaus*) was highly successful with a run of 611 performances between its première on October 28, 1942, and its final performance on January 22, 1944, *Once Over Lightly* (alias *Il barbiere di Siviglia*) folded rather quickly after its first performance on November 19, 1942.[156] Advertised as an "Americanization" of Rossini's opera, *Once Over Lightly* kept the Spanish location of the original; but the libretto, as the theater critic George Jean Nathan reported, regaled the audience "with such old Spanish locutions as 'what's cookin'?' 'I'll say it's a racket,' 'you'll get your dough,' 'it's my motto, never be blotto,' 'tell the world,' 'phony,' 'who in hell are you?' 'just a local yokel who made good in a big way running a clip joint,' 'for the love of bacteria!' and 'I'm the well-known barber of Seville who gets in everybody's hair,' along with stage deportment that the singing histrios apparently deemed suitable to the articulation of the academic pearls of speech."[157] Nathan had no "critical objection to Americanizing any such libretto," but he opposed language that he perceived as mimicking the fake dialect (or slang) of the blackface performer George Primrose and the vaude-ville star Junie McCree.[158]

Unlike *Once Over Lightly*, however, Max Reinhardt's adaptation of *Die Fledermaus* "for the American stage" was deemed much more successful, on account of the libretto's almost Gilbertian flavor.[159] *Rosalinda*'s famous watch duet, for example, starts out with the lines "Her whole bearing is delicious/ And her figure most propitious," while the rhymes in the third-act trio add to its comic character:

ROSALINDA / ALFRED	EISENSTEIN
In sad contemplation	In anticipation
Of this situation	Of this castigation
I feel desolation	I feel great elation
And sheer desperation!	And no exultation![160]

But even though this translation was deemed "jazzy" and "pepped up...to the newer standards," the plot remained largely the same, the locale still nineteenth-century Vienna. It seems that translation into smooth, middle-of-the-road English was the key to what was perceived as Americanizing opera.[161]

In addition to the use of functional and fluent translations in Americanized productions, the continuous touting of the successful employment of U.S.-born singers brought an openly chauvinist note to this discourse that could not entirely hide American insecurities about the international competitive-ness of homegrown performers. The Met had been particularly infamous for its preferential hiring of European singers, but the war made these in short supply after the 1941–42 season. Music critics and producers alike turned this absence into a patriotic virtue, echoing a debate favoring homegrown artists over foreign ones that went back at least to the bill sponsored by the New York Democratic Congressman Samuel Dickstein, nicknamed the Alien Actors Bill, considered in Congress in early 1935 and revived periodically thereafter. This protectionist bill aimed at excluding foreign artists from performing in the United States. Downes described the change in November 1942 as highly beneficial: "Wartime has brought its trials, but also, on the long view, certain blessings in disguise to the Metropolitan and to American opera....Up to the present time the Metropolitan has imported its principal stars from overseas. This season there has not been a single importation from Europe" (Figure 3.5).[162] The Metropolitan's manager, Edward Johnson, hit a similarly nationalist note when he announced in 1944 that "we think that

FIGURE 3.5 "Metropolitan Opera Acquires New American Singers." *Musical America* 62 (October 1942): 3. The caption of the photo reads: "Native Artists Who Will Make Their Debuts at the Opera House This Season Are Shown with General Manager Edward Johnson. Left to Right: James Melton, Tenor; Doris Doree, Soprano; Margaret Harshaw, Contralto; Mr. Johnson; Lillian Raymondi, Soprano; Walter Cassel, Baritone; Frances Greer, Soprano; Osie Hawkins, Baritone; and Jacques Gerard, Tenor."

we have proved that, given the proper opportunity, we can develop first-class performers of virtually all categories in this country. Certainly our audience has proved that it has an open mind toward our American artists and will accept them as equals of any when their merits justify."[163] This nativist emphasis on American performers was a central tenet of the New York City Opera (from which the Met tended to poach singers after a successful season) and also in companies from Philadelphia to San Francisco: the Philadelphia Opera Company prided itself, for example, for employing only Americans.[164] The advantage of this casting strategy was the creation of productions that—so the press proclaimed—offered well-rehearsed theater by youthful "singing actors."[165]

Making a virtue of wartime necessities—opera in modernized English with American singing actors—also provided a handy justification for nativist endeavors in Broadway musicals that, rightly or wrongly, claimed higher artistic merit. Rodgers and Hammerstein's *Oklahoma!* became a classic case in point: Olin Downes situated it clearly on a potential path to "American opera," citing specifically such singpiels as *The Magic Flute* and *Fidelio* as models to which it might aspire, while Oscar Hammerstein II made a distinct virtue of the homegrown talents of its cast of unknowns. Rodgers had turned down the option for his "musical play" of using specific cowboy songs—of which *Oklahoma!*'s model, Lynn Riggs's *Green Grow the Lilacs* (1931), had plenty—in part because he wanted to avoid bucolic fakery. However, the subject matter, and its associations with an American heartland owned by right of Manifest Destiny, played squarely into the themes established by works such as *Rodeo* (the two productions shared the same choreographer, Agnes de Mille), and the show's much-lauded union of all the theatrical arts was proclaimed by such critics as George Beiswanger in 1944–45 as reaching near-Wagnerian intensity. However absurd that argument might seem, it reveals just how high the stakes for American musical theater were during the war period. Likewise, the demolishing of Beiswanger's claims by the leftist critic Eric Bentley immediately (and perhaps significantly) after the war ended—he saw in them the seeds of American Fascism—suggests how dangerous was the game being played.[166]

Translated and American-produced operas from Europe served the purpose of visibly and audibly democratizing an elite art, but it left unanswered the Whitmanesque question as to whether operagoers in New York, Chicago, and San Francisco did in fact "hear America singing." Whereas the transfer of European works into an (ostensibly) democratic and national performance context solved one key aspect of opera production in the United States, it kept open the issue of American opera as its own creative category.[167] Opera performance in the United States, wrote the critic Keith Thompson in late 1943, was flourishing, and "the demand is growing." Now it was time to create American operas, for "if among composers we can find men 'of the theatre,' and among writers men not too aloof to give us a libretto of emotional appeal, we will have the prerequisites of American opera."[168] Clearly, Thompson's masculinist rhetoric formed part of his quest for a new American opera. Clifford Bair, the chairman for the National Committee for Opera in America, opened his plea for the composition of American opera in August 1944 with the sentence: "The time is now ripe to stress opera in English." As he continued his argument for the composition of American operas, he increased the rhetorical pathos of his appeal: "An American School of opera is terribly important as regards our destiny in the overall music field, for 'no nation has achieved leadership in the world of music which has not been able to dramatize its music.'" Only two sentences later, he reiterated that it was crucial to point out "how terribly important opera is to our destiny as a musical nation."[169] Bair's call for the composition of American operas formed part of a broader quest for native forms of art, modeled on the pursuit of the "great American novel." During the war, especially, new compositions for the stage were examined almost neurotically for whether they could be said to meet this national artistic goal, since the international cultural competition had made this a particularly sore failing of artistic achievement.

For a new work to count as an "American" opera, it was not enough that it be created by native librettists, composers, and producers. It also needed to be considered both formally and thematically American. Native authorship was easily clarified, although one sticking point was an author's place of birth: Weill, for example, remained in U.S. eyes a "formerly German" composer. The formal and thematic aspects of opera, however, became principal terrains of dispute. For one thing, discussions about native theatrical and musical forms focused on the purportedly American character of specific idioms and styles; for another, critics identified rural (rather than urban) topics as the key to expressing national identity. One particularly successful production in this vein was Douglas Moore's *The Devil and Daniel Webster*, a folk opera written in 1938 in collaboration with Stephen Vincent Benét and premièred in New York in May 1939. This focus on American folklore and folk music was one reason that, for example, Marc Blitzstein's opera *No For an Answer* (1937–40)—featuring Greek Americans and their complex relationship to the contemporary United States—had little chance, by 1941, of being staged at a major theater, let alone a house like the Met. As happened with so many other cultural developments, the war years intensified the trends of the 1930s, when folk theater came increasingly to be equated with an American national stage.[170] George and Ira Gershwin's *Porgy and Bess* was regarded—especially after Cheryl Crawford's 1941–42 revival—as the most serious contender for the position of "the great American opera."[171] Nonetheless, its exceptionality also kept *Porgy and Bess* from being considered the primary model for shaping American opera as a national art form. Critics looked to other works as possible realizations of the concept, even when a specific work was not necessarily expected to measure up to the ideal.[172]

Two stage works, both located in the American southwest and performed in New York in the spring of 1943, contributed to this discussion. One was Paul Horgan and Ernst Bacon's "folk opera" *A Tree on the Plains* (1942); and the other, we have seen, was Oscar Hammerstein II and Richard Rodgers's "musical play" *Oklahoma!* (1943). The critic for the *New York Times*, Howard Taubman, linked the works as two examples of an emerging indigenous operatic style: "The importance of works like *A Tree on the Plains* is that they show the way to a fresh and imaginative American style of opera, just as Broadway's *Oklahoma* does in its fashion."[173] Taubman and several other critics who had attended the New York performances of *A Tree on the Plains* attempted to identify the specific nature of this indigenous operatic style—trying to distill the positive in a work whose libretto was considered weak and antidramatic. Taubman pointed to the "simplicity and integrity" in Bacon's musical handling "of a modest American scene and of average American people."[174] Oscar Thompson lauded the "engaging lyricism" of the score and the composer's success in creating musical melodrama in the vein of Jules Massenet's blockbuster *Manon*, though Bacon himself cited underscored film dialog as his inspiration.[175] The *New York Times'* Olin Downes devoted three extensive articles to the opera in May 1943. Given that his opinion of the work was rather negative overall, especially with respect to the libretto, this cluster of reviews is rather significant and clearly motivated by the critic's decision to explore in detail which aspects of Bacon's score could in fact lead "in the right direction" toward American opera.[176] Downes approved of *A Tree on the Plains* as a "drama of the soil," and he praised "the lively and idiomatic character of the folksongs and dances, or songs and dances in the folksong manner that do cohere with the plot and the scene," comparing the choral "Hymn to Evening" in act 2 to Grant Wood's iconic painting *American Gothic* (1930).[177] This chorus opens with an a cappella section in archaic four-part harmony whose deliberate simplicity evokes the idiom of American hymnody. By singling out this number as appealing, Downes's sensibilities jibed with the contemporaneous turn to hymnodists and Yankee Tunesmiths by Bacon's fellow composers, including Copland, Cowell, and Siegmeister. In his review of the opera, Elliott Carter identified these vernacular musical styles as "derived from various kinds of Americana that Americans can sing in without seeming to carry on like opera stars."[178] Bacon's score allowed for a more democratic, more "American" form of opera.

The promise of a new national style of opera emerging from such homespun productions was also woven through the critical debate regarding *Oklahoma!* (which premièred barely six weeks before the New York performance of Bacon's opera).[179] The well-publicized rhetoric of the "integrated" musical made the show's potential for operatic impact tantalizing.[180] In early June 1943 Downes penned a programmatic article titled "Broadway's Gift to Opera," in which he promoted the folkloric narrative for the creation of "an integrated and indigenous form of American lyric theater"—a view that would remain influential well into the 1950s.[181] He declared that "American composers today have repeatedly essayed grand opera without a single significant success." Instead, "real national opera has always begun" with the more popular forms of musical theater, whether in Italy, with such works as Pergolesi's *La serva padrona*, or in Germany, with Mozart's *Magic Flute*. Moreover, *Oklahoma!* contained within it "an ancestral memory...of the adventure that has made us ourselves."[182]

It is indicative of the state of affairs during the war that neither work saw its première on a major operatic stage: Rodgers and Hammerstein's musical play was produced on Broadway, whereas *A Tree on the Plains* was commissioned by the League of Composers for its new program called the Composers' Theater, developed in collaboration with universities and colleges. It aimed at fostering "a new type of American lyric theater for small operas with modest orchestras" and at creating a parallel distribution network for contemporary opera that bypassed professional commercial houses such as the Metropolitan.[183] Ernst Bacon clearly agreed with this assessment when he wrote "that an indigenous opera had the best chance of development for the time being, at least, in college and university circles."[184] Premièred at Converse College in Spartanburg, South Carolina, in May 1942, the work toured various North Carolina locales, including the University of North Carolina at Chapel Hill, before it was staged at Columbia University's Brander Matthews Hall on May 4, 1943 (Figure 3.6). It was Columbia's second contemporary-opera production after the première in May 1941 of W. H. Auden and Benjamin Britten's "American" operetta *Paul Bunyan* (also cosponsored by the League of Composers). The Bacon production was followed by the première of Bernard Wagenaar's new two-act opera *Pieces of Eight* in May 1944.

FIGURE 3.6 "The Setting for Ernst Bacon's *A Tree on the Plains*, Showing Henry Blanchard as Pop (Center) and Herbert Norville as Jeremiah (Bearded Figure, Left Center)." *Musical America* 63 (May 1943): 21.

Whereas the large professional opera houses—especially the Met during the directorship of Giulio Gatti-Casazza—had extended their hand in the 1920s and early '30s to such contemporary American composers as Deems Taylor, Louis Gruenberg, and Howard Hansen, with World War II they took a step backward: the Met honored just one prewar commitment, the première of Gian-Carlo Menotti's *Island God* on February 20, 1942. Otherwise the seasons consisted predominantly of standard operatic repertoire—Verdi, Puccini, Mozart, and Wagner.[185] Only one repertoire staple disappeared from the American opera stage during the year: after the Japanese attack on Pearl Harbor, the Met canceled further performances of Puccini's *Madama Butterfly* (a work that had just been reprised on November 29, 1941). After all, as one journalist wrote rather glibly, a work "composed by an Italian" that "extols a Japanese dancing girl at the expense of an American—and a naval officer at that" was clearly unsuitable to an American opera stage.[186] The irony that the cancellation of *Madama Butterfly* removed the one operatic standard that problematized the consequences of American imperialism was entirely lost in the discussion. Instead, Cecil Smith judged it "wise" to ban *Madama Butterfly*, "since the libretto reflects discredit on our navy."[187] And a columnist for the *Washington Post* mused about the opera's unintended propagandistic potential during the war: "We suspect poor Cio Cio San's confidence that one fine day an American warship with her lieutenant aboard would steam into the harbor of Nagasaki, Japan, would now be the signal not for a gentle rhythmic sobbing in six flats but for a tempest of whistles, cheers, footstamping and handclapping."[188] The opera stayed off U.S. stages until April 1945, when the Connecticut Opera Association presented the work "for the first time since 1941."[189] It was back at the Met in the 1945–46 season.

Madama Butterfly shared this fate with one other, somewhat more lowbrow audience favorite, W. S. Gilbert and Arthur Sullivan's *The Mikado*. Yet before that work disappeared from American stages for the next two seasons, one last production of it was presented at Broadway's St. James Theatre in early 1942, though in the opening chorus the singers now introduced themselves as not as "gentlemen" but "gangsters from Japan."[190] The drama critic Brooks Atkinson noted rather sarcastically that nothing about this revival "was more diverting than the management's attempt to fit Gilbert and Sullivan's venerable classic into the current war program." The production was accompanied by a spurious program note "which seems to prove that W. S. Gilbert anticipated war with Japan in 1885 and wrote the *Mikado* as propaganda: 'Almost three score years have passed since William S. Gilbert wrote *The Mikado*, depicting the Japanese in the light that history now records—sly, wily, and deceitful, unconsciously corrupt, and treacherous.'"[191]

American producers and audiences were clearly more concerned about the yellow peril than they were about invasion from Europe, no doubt because the war in the Pacific came closer to U.S. shores than the one across the Atlantic—although one suspects that the interests and artistic allegiances of prominent immigrant communities from "old" Europe now on the East Coast and in the Midwest also played a part. European repertoire of both Axis and Allied origin dominated the operatic stage in the United States. More operas by Wagner, for example, were performed at the Met than by any other composer, even Verdi.[192] Only the revival of *Die Meistersinger* was delayed until the 1944–45 season, since, remarked Olin Downes in March 1942, "as is well known, the opera has passages which could be construed as more than a touch of German propaganda."[193] However, Downes rejoiced in the fact "that, as regards operas of the German repertory, we have escaped war hysteria entirely."[194] As in the case of European concert music—and as we have seen already in the case of the Erika Mann dispute—American critics celebrated the presence of universal art on the nation's opera stages not only as a gesture of cultural appropriation, but also as a response to Axis propaganda. Howard Taubman reported "that the Metropolitan Opera played a part in the propaganda battle" and shared the hope that "Axis propagandists would take note that the new season will last sixteen weeks."[195] Oscar Thompson had already written in 1940 that Wagner's "music has won and held its place purely as music, and today it is fantastic to think of regarding *Die Meistersinger* as subversive merely because Herr Hitler may happen to have a personal obsession for it."[196] He claimed that America, as a nation of immigrants, had appreciated Wagner since 1853, long before Germany accepted him. Downes joined the debate that same year with the assertion that "the musico-dramatic creations of Richard Wagner are the antithesis of Hitler, and crushing condemnation of all that Hitlerism implies."[197] This rhetorical strategy, which separated the enemy's national identity from Wagner's music in favor of a universalist humanism congruent with American values, remained the dominant strand of discourse in the United States. The few dissenting voices came largely from European immigrants such as Paul Henry Lang, who, as noted in chapter 1, published a scathing denunciation of Wagner's music dramas and theories under the title "Background Music for 'Mein Kampf'" (1945).[198]

American critics tended overall to defend the inclusion of Wagner and other operas from enemy nations, making it a point of pride that, contrary to Axis powers, the United States could rise above the pettiness of nationalist politics in music. The result, of course, was curiously nationalist, if couched in the language of the American melting pot. In the words of Eleanor

Roosevelt, written soon after Pearl Harbor (see Figure 1.8), "Music is one of the finest flowerings of that free civilization which has come down to us from our liberty loving forefathers, and we have come to regard it as an essential of the heritage of a country that has cherished the genius of the great composers and the musical artists of all lands and peoples."[199] Two years later Arthur Berger reflected that "this spectacle of extraordinary tolerance, because of its very assertion of the freedom for which the war is fought, has been comforting to a nation which idealizes music for the sake of exalted liberal principles." Yet while Berger felt that this "admission of Wagner, Verdi and Strauss may set us apart from a Germany which bans music of Allied composers, living or dead," he also worried that such "intelligent avoidance of chauvinism" might have been based less on high-minded political idealism than on aesthetic complacency and a need to justify what was a musical habit as the moral high ground.[200] Berger may have been right: the rhetoric of melting-pot inclusivity was to some extent just a mask for complacency. But other issues were also in play. Opera is by definition a conservative institution: the financial stakes are high, its production mechanisms are inflexible, and the works that emerge are neither portable nor adaptable. It was much easier to fit a new American work into the concert repertoire—or even a single program—than to stage it. It was no coincidence that traditional European operas continued to reign supreme.

On March 27, 1942, Gertrude Stein expressed to her erstwhile collaborator Virgil Thomson her wish "that we could write an opera that would be as popular as *Carmen*, it would be nice for the money but it also would be nice for satisfaction, an opera anybody would like including the farm hands and the elite."[201] When Oscar Hammerstein II tried to create a vernacular form of opera in the United States during the war, he too turned to Bizet; the result was *Carmen Jones* (1943), a self-conscious adaptation of the European "masterwork" for a specifically American wartime audience.[202] Driven both by his desire to Americanize opera and by his commitment to civil rights, Hammerstein considered Bizet's opera an ideal vehicle with which to achieve both goals. Set in the segregated south of the war years, and more appropriately in a factory where not cigarettes but parachutes were made, *Carmen Jones* was received by audiences and press alike as a powerful contribution to current debates on war, ethnicity, class, and national identity. That *Carmen Jones* kept Bizet's score intact (rather than swinging it, as *Hot Mikado* had done) counted as a significant musical statement in this context. *Carmen Jones* proved—so the African American press in particular noted—that African American musicians were on par with anyone in the business. At a time when most U.S. opera stages, including the Metropolitan Opera House, were closed to black performers, this was considered a major step toward better professional opportunities: Dan Burley reported in the *New York Amsterdam News* about one of the singers in the title role that "veteran critics . . . said Miss Muriel Smith is almost sure to sing the role in the Metropolitan 'Carmen' next season."[203]

During the war years, the use of opera as a means of "racial uplift" had other proponents as well, most prominently the National Negro Opera Company, founded in 1941 by Mary Cardwell Dawson.[204] The impulse came from a successful performance of Verdi's *Aida* in October 1941 in Pittsburgh that Dawson had produced for the National Association of Negro Musicians. The program book for this production emphasized that it had strategic import in the fight for broader recognition of African American musical achievement: "It is our hope that this performance will convince members of our racial group, and our friends among other races, many of whom are already well initiated in operatic culture, of the possibilities of our efforts in this field."[205] For Dawson, opera was a genre that could be instrumentalized in the long march toward racial equality because it offered two potential paths of African American advancement: as she wrote to potential sponsors of a performance in 1944 of Verdi's *La traviata*, "The object of the movement is two-fold: To encourage the Negro Opera Singer and to contribute something to racial pride."[206] Dawson secured patronage from such distinguished African American artists as Marian Anderson and Paul Robeson, and the 1944 souvenir program carried a message from Franklin D. Roosevelt wishing the company "continued success in your brilliant effort."[207]

Among the goals of the NNOC was to give African American singers an opportunity to gain experience and shine on the operatic stage. Whereas Marian Anderson, Roland Hayes, Dorothy Maynor, and Paul Robeson had distinguished careers on the concert stage, they remained locked out from most American opera houses in the segregated United States. It was not until 1955 that Marian Anderson and Robert McFarrin performed on the stage of the Metropolitan Opera—the first African Americans to do so. Before then, a mainstream operatic career for African Americans required them to leave the United States for the racially unsegregated theaters in Europe and South America. Lillian Evanti, who starred with great success in the NNOC's production of *La traviata*, started her operatic career in 1925 with a performance of *Lakmé* in Nîmes, then went on to perform in Paris, Genoa, Naples, Milan, and numerous other European opera houses in the later 1920s and early '30s (Figure 3.7). Giulio Gatti-Casazza, the general manager of the Met, heard her in Italy and tried to hire her in 1932, but racial discrimination made even an audition, let alone a contract, impossible.[208] Until the formation

FIGURE 3.7 "Lillian Evanti, coloratura soprano, is singing Violetta in the English version of La Traviata on tour with the National Negro Opera Company, which has appeared in New York, Chicago, Pittsburgh, Washington and other cities." *Musical Courier* (May 5, 1944): 22.

of the NNOC, Evanti could only perform in concert venues in her native country. Even an appearance at the White House in 1934 (documented in a Pathé newsreel) made no difference.[209] In 1944, at the height of her success with the NNOC, Evanti "deplored the evils of racial prejudices" with respect to opera when she explained to young African American singers that "on the European continent the color of your skin is not a handicap to your career but Americans carry prejudices wherever they go."[210]

The NNOC's decision to start with Verdi's *Aida* made programmatic sense because it featured an Ethiopian princess as its protagonist and thus allowed African American singers to claim performative authority: "After all, in writing 'Aida,' Verdi provided operatically trained Negro singers with a natural, and it has been seldom enough in the past that they have availed themselves of it."[211] C. J. Bulliet, writing for the *Chicago Daily News*, saw *Aida* as an opera with "native motifs" that offered an alternative to the "African elements in our modern Negro music[, which] are generally cited as coming from the Congo." Instead, Verdi's opera revealed that "Ethiopia and ancient Egypt had their Negro culture, too."[212] First in Pittsburgh and then in Chicago, the African American *Aida* was celebrated in the press as a production that could rival any other professional performance—and "professional" in this context means "white"—in the United States and abroad.

After *Aida*, the company tackled two audience favorites for the 1943 season, *La traviata* and *Carmen. La traviata* was an astute move, for it was one of the best-known operas of the repertoire, and the producers knew well the symbolic capital associated with such a mainstream choice. The company took the opera to several cities in 1943 and 1944, two of which witnessed particularly prominent performances: in Washington, D.C., on August 28, 1943, an audience of almost 15,000 heard the opera at the Watergate, then a popular open-air venue, and on March 29, 1944, a similar crowd saw it at Madison Square Garden. These productions aimed to show the largest possible audience the musical quality of African American–produced opera, and the press was enthusiastic about the NNOC's ambition. One critic rejoiced that "so impressed were Washington's seasoned critics with the rendition of this difficult opera by an all-Negro cast that the daily papers for the first time shelved their racial bias and gave an enthusiastic, inspiring account of the presentation of this Verdi score."[213] The violinist Louia Vaughn Jones concluded his review for the *Afro American* by stating that "this stellar performance definitely proved the race's ability to do Grand Opera."[214] The NNOC's strategy for countering what Lawrence Schenbeck described as "white America's pervasive minstrelsy-based construction of blackness" was clearly successful.[215]

By 1944 the NNOC was merging the idea of racial uplift with the broader artistic quest of an American opera. The newsletter for the Harlem branch of the YMCA reported that the NNOC's *Traviata* was hailed as "the first time that a Negro opera company has ever staged a legitimate performance in the English language with appropriate scenery, lighting, costumes and opera symphony orchestra in New York City."[216] What is unspoken but clear in such praise is the preference for a straight-down-the-line version of a canonic opera—just as would be done at the Met (save for the English translation)— over a jazzed-up and hence less "legitimate" Broadway production (hence also the NNOC's choice of Bizet's *Carmen* rather than Hammerstein's *Carmen Jones*). A year earlier, the music critic of the *Washington Evening Star* found the company's *La traviata* to have contributed to Americanizing the genre: "It has been our habit to regard opera as an alien art. For years it was exclusively an importation, performed by European artists, sung in strange tongues. Last night's performance must have done much to explode this tradition. It was done in the language of this country."[217] Furthermore, Mary Dawson also appropriated the concept of new folk-based works that writers from Thompson to Downes had hailed as one pathway to an American opera, when she claimed the NNOC's goal was "to inspire composers of all races, particularly the Negro composer, to create more interest in composition in the Operatic field using the background of Negro folk tunes," all this with the added hope that "these performances will strengthen Morale of our People at Home and Abroad."[218] Only in 1946, however, did the NNOC stage a work by an African American composer, R. Nathaniel Dett's *The Ordering of Moses*. This production began a postwar shift to increased African American programming, culminating in the 1956 performance of Clemence Cameron White's opera *Ouanga* at the Met.[219]

Although many of the NNOC's strategies were defined by its unique position as an African American enterprise in a segregated society, its artistic strategies were consonant with the broader operatic reliance on a core of European nineteenth-century opera and its translation into English as a strategy of appropriation. In concert music, institutional support in the form of commissions and distribution, on the one hand, and aesthetic debates about tradition and innovation, on the other, led to creative appropriations of both universal historic models and homegrown musical idioms in a significant body of new compositions; but the war seemed to have had the opposite effect on American opera. Relegated to the periphery of mainstream opera houses, new operas written in the United States during these years were few and far between. Instead, the war solidified a mostly nineteenth-century core repertoire in the name of American civic ideology.

CHAPTER FOUR | "The Great Invasion"

A ND THE TIME is come, O Poet, to declare your name, your birth and your race.[1] Thus ends *Exile*, a poem written in 1941 by the French diplomat and Nobel Prize–winning poet Saint-John Perse after he had taken refuge on Long Beach Island, New Jersey, from the Nazi invasion of his homeland. This naming of oneself and one's origins was a powerful antidote to the loss of an identity often taken for granted before exile had destroyed its unselfconscious character. And so, when the exiled composer Darius Milhaud started to write his autobiography on August 25, 1944, the day Paris was liberated, he opened his account with the words: "I am a Frenchman from Provence and of Israelite religion."[2] Titled "Origins," this first chapter claims an ancestry entrenched in the history of the French Mediterranean, where Jews had established their businesses "six hundred years before Jesus Christ" and "as traders, not as emigrants."[3] Milhaud's proud and poignant statement about a lineage embedded profoundly in the history of France and her soil—setting up chronological primacy over any of the nation's Catholic inhabitants— made it clear from the outset that his current exile in the United States had ruptured for but a moment that continuum of two and a half millennia of deep Gallic, and Jewish, rootedness. Indeed, the book closes with the announcement that on August 13, 1947, after the end of the summer session at Mills College, the family was to embark on their journey back to the "shores of the recovered fatherland."[4]

Like Milhaud, the numerous musicians who had fled Fascist and war-torn Europe since the mid-1930s faced complex challenges in their new home that struck to the very core of their personal and professional selves. In contrast to such American composers as Copland and Cowell, whose quest for a native identity was justified as an integral, and on the whole unquestioned, part of the American war effort, musicians in U.S. exile saw themselves confronted with multiple interplays of cultural expectations—and as much on their side as on their hosts'. A distinguished European pedigree continued to serve as a strong asset not only for famous composers, such as Stravinsky, but also for rank-and-file performers who often found work in American orchestras and similar institutions.[5] Yet this difference could prove a handicap in the context of an increasingly chauvinist public discourse, especially if the musicians in question were refugees from an Axis nation. Here it became vitally important for them to prove allegiance to the United States lest they share the destiny of such refugees as the Jewish passengers on the *M.S. St. Louis*, who were returned posthaste to Europe by the Roosevelt administration in 1939. Yet whether grounded in anxiety about the precariousness of one's welcome, as in the case of Ernst Krenek, or born of an artistic curiosity that usually predated exile, for example with Weill and Stefan Wolpe, such self-conscious engagement with the host nation and her culture often led to significant stylistic and topical developments inspired by or made in response to contemporary American music.[6]

This cosmopolitan side of wartime music in the United States spans a wide range of artistic responses that intersected not only with American musicians and their output, but also with those musical nomads and expatriates who, like Edgard Varèse and Serge Koussevitzky, had moved there well before Europe was covered by the cloud of Fascism and war.[7] Yet even these earlier visitors from Europe, who in the past could—for the most part—return to their native countries, were now stranded in the United States, where they were joined by many "a passenger on Noah's Ark" in exile.[8] The various strata of foreign musicians in American exile thus formed a complex and multidimensional matrix of personal relationships, professional rivalries, and support networks. Weill was a linchpin in facilitating entry into the United States for several fellow European musicians—for example, the Milhaud family—but he famously distanced himself from the Eurocentric nostalgia of the *Mumienkeller* on the West Coast.[9] Yet these "mummies" were the main group of artists sustaining Weill's friend Milhaud during his rare visits to Los Angeles in the years of his otherwise utterly isolated situation at Mills College in Oakland, California.[10] The West Coast contingent of exiled luminaries had its own internal fault lines, however, including the famous one between Schoenberg and Stravinsky, who lived quite close to each other but—as Madeleine Milhaud remarked rather caustically—"had no contact at all. They were like African kings, each waiting for the other, but nobody came."[11] While some groups formed along language lines—around the German Mann brothers or the French movie star Charles Boyer—others reconstituted European artistic neighborhoods, especially those of cosmo-politan Paris. These circles remained fluid and often overlapped.

Living in Exile

One key distinction among exile musicians was their nation of origin: it shaped not only their day-to-day experience of life in the United States but also their musical choices, in particular as composers.[12] The differ-ence between musicians from Axis powers, such as Germany and Italy, and those who had fled from invaded Allied countries, such as Czechoslovakia, France, and the Soviet Union, had a significant impact on what kind of music foreign-born composers now living in America could and did write during the war, not least in terms of musical and extramusical references to their country of origin. The ability to identify publicly with one's national and cultural roots was by no means trivial in a nation whose composers were busy trying to develop a national idiom themselves. A Frenchman such as Milhaud could choose to play into such essentializing identity politics (as dis-cussed in the previous chapter) in the form of, for example, his *Suite française* (1944), a work based on folk songs from Normandy, Brittany, Île-de-France, Alsace-Lorraine, and Provence and intended as a musical travel guide for his American audience.[13] One would be hard-pressed, on the other hand, to find any wartime composition citing German folk songs by Krenek, Schoenberg, or Weill.[14] Exiled German composers in particular clearly could not draw on their own folk music to represent national identity; they may even have taken some pride in their forced appeal to a universalist aesthetic or in their adoption of American musical idioms.[15]

This complex engagement with cultural origins meshed with the expec-tations of their host country. Even in the months before the United States entered the war, Deems Taylor used music as a means of celebrating a foreign musician's Allied identity in his radio program *America Preferred*. Ostensibly intended to boost the sale of Defense (later War) Bonds, the radio show was "a tribute to those musical artists of foreign birth who have elected America their homeland—America Preferred; people who are Americans *by choice*, because here that most precious gift, human freedom, still survives."[16] When interviewing musicians from countries under attack from the Axis powers, Taylor welcomed them with "music that would remind our guest...of the land of [their] birth."[17] Efrem Zimbalist was greeted with a performance of Mikhail Ippolitov-Ivanov's *Caucasian Sketches*, Jascha Heifetz with one of the dances from Mikhail Glinka's *A Life for the Tsar*, and Robert Casadesus with music by "his great compatriot, Claude Debussy."[18] Scandinavians— whether the Swedish mezzo-soprano Kerstin Thorborg or the Danish tenor Lauritz Melchior—invariably found themselves represented by the Norwegian Edvard Grieg.[19] In contrast, Taylor's scripts for the appearance of German-born musicians such as Lotte Lehmann disavowed national specificity and emphasized instead the musical universality and transcendental greatness of such composers as Beethoven and Brahms.[20] As we have seen before, this widespread U.S. strategy of appropriating music that originated in Axis countries intensified dramatically during the war years. Besides sustaining and morally justifying the maintenance of a traditional concert repertoire in the United States, it also enabled those composers and performers exiled from German-speaking countries to develop a culturally mixed form of musical identity in their new homeland.[21]

At first glance, this form of national effacement was considerably less prominent in the case of musicians from Allied nations, such as Milhaud, Stravinsky, Jaromír Weinberger, and Bohuslav Martinů, who publicly emphasized their national roots, whether by championing Czech folk music for American audiences (as did Weinberger and Martinů) or by composing Russian-themed works for high-profile radio commissions, as Stravinsky did with his *Scherzo à la russe*.[22] Milhaud's playful private letter to "Kurtschen Weilschen" (using an approximate version of the German affectionate diminutive) was signed as "Darius—musicien français," a signature made famous by Claude Debussy during World War I.[23] Milhaud emphasized repeatedly that his prime concern as a musician was the "maintenance of French culture."[24] Indeed, for Milhaud and his fellow French nationals—from Lily Pons to Nadia Boulanger—France and her current plight were the cause around which they rallied independently of their political alignment: charity projects for the French war relief, for example, brought together both officials from the Vichy Government and followers of Charles de Gaulle (Figure 4.1).[25]

Milhaud considered the promotion of French culture in the United States an important contribution to the Allied war effort in the face of American indifference, especially prior to Pearl Harbor. In his memoirs, the French composer asked diplomatically whether one could really criticize a farmer from Iowa or Texas for not understanding the threat of Hitler. Madeleine Milhaud was more outspoken: "We felt very clearly that the USA was a neutral country. Without wanting to upset anyone, we wanted to do what we could for our own. As far as Milhaud was concerned, his presence at Mills was prestigious enough to represent France. ... Until Pearl Harbor, the Californians were unaware of the war, unlike the New Yorkers."[26] However,

FIGURE 4.1 Lily Pons was often photographed with military personnel or Gaullist leaders. In this OWI promotion still, "Lily Pons, French-born star of the Metropolitan Opera Company of New York City, meets two French sailors, Jean Pons (right) and Paul Boue... the sailors were on leave from the French warship Montcalm." National Archives (208-PU-1576–1).

Milhaud considered the Japanese attack a welcome moment in the war: "The Mikado's plane attack precipitated the events; may they be thanked for it!"[27] In a letter written two months after Pearl Harbor to his benefactor, Elizabeth Sprague Coolidge, he expressed his gratitude about the U.S. entry into the war: "All our thoughts are devoted to the War and to America. America has the mission to save the world, and I know already since a long time that the only hope for my poor country, France, to live again, depends on the American Victory, and we pray for it."[28]

For refugees from Allied countries, Pearl Harbor was indeed a vital turning point. Up to that point, isolationism dominated the public discourse, and the Roosevelt administration's hostility to refugees from Europe extended into larger spheres, even including musicians.[29] A series of columns and letters in the New York Times in January and February 1941 addressed "the problem of the refugee from overseas and the place that he takes among his colleagues in the land of his adoption."[30] The rather sensationalist headlines identified the "Refugee Problem" as an "Invasion of Ideas" that threatened American cultural identity.[31] Even a writer as sympathetic to his European colleagues as Howard Hanson warned that one should not be "providing opportunities for our foreign guests by curtailing the already meager opportunities for the young American."[32] The thread of the ensuing discussion ran the gamut from Roger Sessions's sharp rejection of chauvinism as unbecoming to this nation to a Norwegian immigrant carpenter's assessment that, should America hope for an indigenous art, "this art must not get into the hands of newly arrived refugees."[33] Indeed, as Olin Downes put it, the question was whether "foreign artistic ideas" would now be "weakening to creative development" in the United States.[34] In a private note, Ernst Bacon similarly wondered whether transplanted and therefore shallow-rooted foreign composers would cast such shade on native developments as to stifle them: "The émigré must either maintain his old roots abroad or set forth new ones in another land. More than one such alien tree over here shuts out the sunlight from the younger vegetation, supported by no deep roots, but remaining erect by a system of hidden wires and supports enthusiastically supplied by his new environment."[35] Even as pro-European a critic as David Ewen found it appropriate to title his chapter on exile musicians "The Great Invasion" and used language that—for all his praise of the contribution that the "wealth of their genius" would bring to "our culture"—evoked frightening connotations when he pointed out that "composers, performers, scholars, teachers, critics escaped from their native land in hordes" and that "musicians from every part of Europe—some of them leaders in their respective field—poured into this country in ever-increasing numbers." Ewen not only used biblical metaphors when he characterized the arrival of Austrian musicians as "a great exodus of musical genius," but also military ones: "this recent infiltration of foreign genius has been felt in every phase of our musical existence."[36]

Such ambivalence, sometimes extending to outright hostility, was not lost on foreign musicians. Benjamin Britten (who lived in the United States between 1939 and 1942) chronicled these developments in letters to friends and family, where he could express his misgivings openly while also, it should be noted, emphasizing the problems rather than the joys of life in the United States, given the ravages of the war in Britain. Just after the outbreak of war, in November 1939, he wrote of his homesickness, well aware that "it is easy to get snarly about Americans—& one mustn't do it, because they have been terribly kind to us, & they *are* a vital, go-ahead race." He then reported that "the present chauvinism in their arts is horrifying," and he was put off by the United States' patronizing attitude toward France and Great Britain.[37] By April 1940 Britten was more outspoken in his criticism, citing among the negatives the Ku Klux Klan's "negro-lynchings & burnings" and the Dies Committee's investigations into "anyone vaguely liberal." For all their marked regional differences, Britten concluded, "there is only one thing in common with them at the moment—that is they are all *American*—& chauvanistically so, I'm afraid. They're fed up with Europe—they didn't like it's peace—and they're suspicious of it's war. They're full of advice as how to run the rest of the world—& refuse to take any of the consequences."[38] Britten and Pears spent the summer of 1941 in California and—like the Milhauds—remarked on the difference in political awareness between the East and West Coasts. In California, he explained to Wulff Scherchen in September 1941, "Europe seems very remote—the only thing occasionally that reminds one of the state of things to-day is the threat of Japan. . . . What I mean is, the luxury & self-ishness of so many of the people, makes one feel slightly hopeless. . . . All the weaknesses of the civilised world, all the lack of direction, find their epitome in California."[39] Though he did not have much positive to say about New York either, he longed for his return to a city that, at least, felt real.

After Pearl Harbor, Britten and Pears tried to return to Great Britain as quickly as possible but found themselves stranded in New York while waiting for "exit permits, priorities, sailing permits etc. etc. etc."[40] In March 1942 Britten painted a particularly cynical picture of the American response to the war:

> America has been strange since the actually [*sic*] entry into the war. At first there was terrific excitement, "unity" (how often have we heard that word!), and flag waving. Now most of the first two have disap-peared—after all the Pacific is a mighty long way away, and bad news (vide, China, Spain, Poland, London, Coventry ad infinitum) grows boring after a time . . . The flag waving remains, because so many people like doing it, and adore wearing uniforms (without exception hideous) . . . There has been a certain effort to ban German & Italian music, which hasn't luckily succeeded, & apart from some ludicrous restrictions on enemy aliens (99 percent refugees of course—everyone knows that most of the fifth columnists are settled citizens of, maybe, German extraction) people have kept their heads. Of course, everyone is numbered, docketed, finger printed, photographed, registered—but one gets used to that.[41]

Private utterances such as Britten's about national chauvinism and American apathy about to the war—both before and after Pearl Harbor—were not unusual among exiles who had fled war and persecution in Europe and now had to become accustomed again, in Milhaud's words, to "the kindness of peace."[42] In her diary, Hélène Hoppenot, a friend of the Milhauds, com-mented in March 1944—like Britten in his letters two years earlier—on the "indifference of the American people about the war" and worried about the "lack of understanding for the suffering others were subjected to."[43] This pronounced disparity of experience became an often unbridgeable gap between those who had lived through trauma in their homelands before fleeing for their lives and those who remained safe throughout the entire conflict in a nation whose borders were protected from either invasion or any major attack by the Atlantic on the east and the Pacific on the west, and with Allied countries as buffers to both the north (Canada) and the south (Mexico). This experiential chasm was one factor contributing to the isolation that many musicians in exile experienced, in particular those who fled Europe later in the process, after the war had already started.[44] As Hoppenot observed: "Two days at Mills were enough to realize the complete isolation of the Milhauds: no true friend, only acquaintances, professors, students and the 'wrecks,' that they call 'leeches.'"[45] Their only friends—as Madeleine Milhaud explained—were the other exiled artists, but they lived either in Los Angeles or New York.[46]

Solitude and isolation were the companions not only of the Milhauds in California but also of other recent émigrés from France such as Nadia Boulanger, whose despair over her exile was coupled with a deep longing for the home she had left behind: "I didn't know how much I loved France, how much I need her," she wrote to Stravinsky in March 1941.[47] Music remained Boulanger's sole consolation in the loss of her beloved homeland to the Nazi invasion. As she wrote to Koussevitzky about listening to music: "for us- and perhaps for the world, salvation and truth lie in art."[48] While Boulanger considered music as a means of transcendental solace shared by the world, the actual experience of exile created a distressing gulf between her and her American environment, even with such a beloved student and colleague as Copland. As she wrote to him in March 1945 about her feeling of alienation and survivor's guilt with respect to those who had remained behind in Europe: "I hope that you will never feel what we do feel after such terrible events—the torture, moral and physical, they have gone through, and we had gone! We, and especially I, found here the most faithful and wonderful friends—but . . . these years during which we have not shared their unspeakable suffering. Forgive me—but I am so profoundly sorrowful about it."[49]

Yet, almost paradoxically, this painful dimension of loss and alienation also formed an empowering foundation that enabled composers at least from Allied countries to explore in their music "what Edward W. Said has called the contrapuntal dimension of exile: the way in which experiences of loss cause exiles to become inventive, creative, mobile, and resourceful, to negotiate a plurality of competing visions, experiences, and memories rather than merely to cling to static recollections of the past."[50] Indeed, the pluralities that grew out of engagement with a new environment could develop into an artistic opportunity precisely because Allied composers could claim unequivocally, in Milhaud's words, the endurance of the "profound impulses of race."[51]

These fiercely claimed national roots allowed for artistic risk taking, exchange, appropriation, and self-invention. Channeling Martinů's opinions in an authorized account published in 1944, Miloš Šafránek credited the composer's American exile as a positive transformative force: "America gave him greater freedom and authority, and an increased craftsmanship in his work. Consequently his compositions are not attached exclusively to local soil, but contribute, rather, as a Czech component, to world culture."[52] Martinů remains Czech in essence—in a different portrait that same year, the composer was characterized as feeling "his nationalism keenly"—but fashions himself, by means of his experience of exile, into a transnational musical force to be reckoned with, whose cultural capital rested equally in his national origins and his transformed, cosmopolitan self.[53] The result might be described as music with an accent—a distinguishing marker of identity for both its author and its audience.[54] Moreover, the concept of the U.S. exile as a crucible in which musical genius was forged from a battle with alienation served both to validate and to enable the creative freedom gained in a new and liberating context. In turn, this plot of identity formation in the face of adversity—even if that adversity might consist, ironically, of the American Dream—meshed well with American tropes of the frontier mentality and individualist self-realization. The narrative thus served double duty: it became a signifier for Allied composers' acculturation within American society, and it allowed their hosts to embrace them as adhering to the American way of life.

The transition from war-torn Europe to the United States brought a range of musical responses from those composers who had fled the Nazi invasion. Some—such as the previously prolific Germaine Tailleferre—stopped composing altogether. After a short sojourn in New York in 1942, during which she wrote an article for *Modern Music*, "From the South of France," she settled in Philadelphia with her daughter, while her husband, a lawyer, found work in the diplomatic circles of Washington, D.C.[55] Her article tells of the Nazi occupation of France and its effect on music, from daily deprivation and political oppression to the threat of anti-Semitism. "The immediate problem," she pointed out, was "to preserve human beings, as well as their cultural patrimony." Though France had remained "proud and great," she saw the nation's future as depending on being liberated by "her true Allies."[56] During her years in Philadelphia, Tailleferre had some private music students, but save for some local performers, her contacts with musicians were few and far between: a single meeting with her old friend Milhaud, in New York; a handful of encounters with Stravinsky; and the odd dinner with Marcelle de Manziarly, Pierre Monteux, or Vittorio Rieti. Tailleferre felt that as a French citizen she was unwelcome in the United States.[57] Furthermore, she lived in "perpetual anguish" for the lives of her family back home.[58] Not until after she returned to France in 1946 did Tailleferre started composing again.

Other exiled composers, however, wrote almost feverishly during the war years, completing symphonies, operas, concertos, chamber music, and works in numerous other genres, from song to band music. Among the most prolific on the Allied side were Milhaud and Martinů; Stravinsky and Aleksander Tansman, too, were fairly productive and versatile. Many of the best-known Allied composers in exile had made their mark in the inter-war years in Paris or in such new-music festivals as Donaueschingen, and some careers had started even earlier, before World War I. But although they brought the prestige of distinguished international reputations and a portfolio of world-famous works from *Petroushka* to *La création du monde* (the latter had just been given as *Black Ritual* in New York in 1940 with an all–African American cast), any work they composed now for their new, American audiences would be set against a different horizon of expectation—not only in terms of the prevalent local culture, but also with respect to their own image, developed over the previous decades by way of the press, the concert hall, and in many cases, their previous visits to the United States. Well past the earlier, more experimental stages of their careers at this point, Milhaud and Stravinsky, among others, found themselves in a more conservative artistic milieu that may well have contributed to the consolidation of their styles and harmonic idioms and perhaps even accelerated it.[59] Rather than just dismissing these shifts, however, as evidence for the Adornian axiom of an aesthetic sellout to the lowest common denominator of American mass culture and millionaires, it might prove far more productive to contextualize these developments in the more complex constellation of personal and artistic identities in exile, transnational trends of musical populism, and wartime exigencies.[60] These intersections formed the parameters within which exile could indeed function as a transformative crucible for musical responses to the war as dialectic mediation between loss and opportunity.

French Connections, Czech Identities

When Darius Milhaud arrived in New York on July 15, 1940, he carried with him the first pages of his String Quartet no. 10, commissioned by

Elizabeth Sprague Coolidge and begun "on the Atlantic ocean" on board the *S.S. Excambion*; it was completed in New York on August 9, 1940. The work was the first of his to carry two opus numbers: op. 218 in terms of Milhaud's total compositional output, and *opus americanum* 1.[61] By the time the war was over in 1945, Milhaud had completed his *opus americanum* 42, a duo for two violins. In the intervening years he taught composition at Mills College, first sponsored by his faithful patron, Elizabeth Sprague Coolidge, then as a regular salaried faculty member. Teaching summer school helped him pick up additional income. Within the first year, the college built a bungalow specifically for the Milhaud family, "an enchanting oasis" with a view of San Francisco Bay.[62] Yet living at Mills College brought changes to the Milhauds' life style: with no servants available, "Madeleine wears herself out with the household" (Figure 4.2).[63] At first concert tours helped supplement the family's income, but with Milhaud's advancing arthritis, travel became more difficult. Life at Mills College for the Milhauds—famous for their sociability in interwar Paris—turned out to be "far away" from everything and "terribly isolated"—a material condition conducive, however, "to work and reflection."[64]

Work, for Milhaud, meant first and foremost composition, though he contributed to journalism (both French and American) and organized workshops and concerts at Mills College, most famously a visit of Stravinsky and Boulanger in October 1944, an occasion Milhaud described as a "great event" that had brought "a great excitement this week."[65] In her recollections, Madeleine was somewhat less discreet: "Nadia Boulanger decided to come as well, and suggested she play some piano duets with Igor. I attended the rehearsal. She was very severe and at one point slapped Igor's hand saying 'No, Igor, it isn't right. Count!' He always had a tendency to be a bit bent, but at that moment, I can tell you, his head was lower than his chest."[66] Milhaud's dealings with Stravinsky went beyond the artistic, however, for—in a complicated scheme of barely legal money transfer—Milhaud's mother, who still lived in Aix-en-Provence, sent money from her son's French bank accounts to Stravinsky's son, Theodore, for which Stravinsky then reimbursed Milhaud in dollars (though, as Stephen Walsh put it, "in terms somewhat generous to himself").[67] This matter-of-fact mixing of mundane dealings with musical concerns and familiar interactions was typical, both a sign of ongoing normalcy between colleagues and friends of long standing, and a marker of the extraordinary situation of exile, which demanded unusual maneuvers.

During his American wartime sojourn Milhaud presented himself self-consciously as a Frenchman in exile. His letters speak of the condition, and in his *Notes sans musique* he comments repeatedly on the family's

FIGURE 4.2 Madeleine and Darius Milhaud at Mills College, 1945.
Photograph by Dean Stone and Hugo Steccati. Courtesy of Daniel Milhaud.

situation. A New Year's letter in 1944 to Henri and Hélène Hoppenot—
Henri was Milhaud's erstwhile librettist and a French diplomat stationed
in Montevideo—carried the header "Year IV of the Exile" and ended with
the statement that the "faithfulness of your friendship provides comfort in
exile."[68] The Milhauds were glued to the radio, following events unfold-
ing in France, and when Paris was liberated, Milhaud recalled, the shad-
ows of exile began to dissipate.[69] How to contribute to the French cause
became one of Milhaud's greatest concerns—especially since the French exile

community was split between followers of de Gaulle and those loyal to the Vichy government. Another letter to Henri Hoppenot provides insight in Milhaud's reasoning once the United States entered the war: "The situation for a Frenchman *living here* is very simple. *Following America* until the deliverance of France." After explaining that the United States mobilized not only American citizens but also foreigners for the armed forces, he declared that he had signed up for the "draft of the grandfathers" (noncombatants aged forty-five to sixty-five).

For Milhaud, whose sympathies lay fully with the Free French and de Gaulle, this was a better way to serve France, for supporting de Gaulle meant military service, Milhaud argued, which—given the state of his health—was out of the question. He was reluctant, however, to get involved in political dissidence with Vichy, given the fact that the "Franco-American situation is so complex. . . . The average Frenchman is lost there. This is the reason why I prefer to stay outside of all 'cliques.'" Instead he proposed "to serve *on the American level*," especially in order "*to maintain* French culture" (Milhaud's emphasis).[70] But if that side of the political equation was complex, the other was not. Among Milhaud's many articles and lectures on French music was one text published in the French exile journal *Pour la victoire!* in July 1942, where he explained that "I love Gounod and Verdi" because of their Latin qualities in the face of "the most implacable assault from Germany by Richard Wagner."[71] After quoting Max d'Ollone's claim that Wagner was "sent to the earth so as to destroy French music, French art, French thought," Milhaud falls back on the old standbys of clarity, measure, and simplicity as aesthetic embodiments of true Frenchness.[72]

Here Milhaud fell into step with other French artists in American exile. In January 1943, for example, *Pour la victoire!* announced a concert series of "French Music by French Artists," with musicians ranging from Lily Pons to Robert Casadesus performing for the benefit of the Coordinating Council of French Relief Societies.[73] That same month the Parisian opera singer Marcelle Denya told the story of the overwhelming success of a concert tour in 1939 of more than thirty American colleges and universities in which she introduced students and local audiences with great success to the "intrinsic beauty, originality, subtlety of expression, harmonic invention" of French song to combat the nefarious influence of the German Lied.[74] An interview with Wanda Landowska not only drew significant attention to "the genius of a Couperin or a Rameau" but also cast the great Johann Sebastian Bach as a follower of the dominant French style.[75] Landowska's appropriation of Bach for a French musical tradition had, of course, a longer history. In this context, however, it took on new meaning.[76] After the end of the war, the journal's music critic, Edgar Feder, took stock of the contribution French musicians made to the fatherland's war effort by keeping the flame alive. He pointed out that there was "nothing chauvinist in proclaiming that the French musical school—together with her younger Russian sister—occupied the first place in the world."[77] Feder's praise of French music targeted not only his American hosts, but, more important, its Germanic rivals in the United States. One of his columns contrasted Milhaud's truly French and nature-based counterpoint, which resulted "in a more direct and accessible" polytonality, with the "arbitrarily chosen system" of Schoenberg.[78]

Milhaud and his critics foregrounded his Frenchness during the war years by characterizing him with such epithets as "France's No. 1 Composer," "the leading spirit in French music," and the "composer of France."[79] Yet at the same time U.S. critics—in contrast to such French writers as Feder— considered Milhaud's music as being shaped by a strong dose of American influence, not only his recent works but also his earlier ones. What made Milhaud modern in addition to being Gallic, Taubman implied in a 1943 review, was his American side.[80] When Alfred Frankenstein, the art and music critic of the *San Francisco Chronicle*, assessed Milhaud's wartime compositions in a 1946 article, he found few "direct or obvious reflections of the American environment" in the composer's recent output because his "style was very well formed by the time he came here." Other musicians might have been influenced by their exposure to "the folk music of the new country," but Milhaud had already engaged extensively with music of the Americas during the 1920s and '30s. "To be sure," Frankenstein pointed out, "he wrote a clarinet Concerto for Benny Goodman in 1941, and shortly after that a Suite for Larry Adler's harmonica, but neither of these things is extraordinary for the composer of *Le Bœuf sur le Toit*, the *Ragtime Caprices*, or the suite for Martenot's electrical wave instrument."[81] In short, Frankenstein painted Milhaud as a composer who was already Americanized well before his exile. For Copland, on the other hand, this mediation between modernism and French national identity was a result less of Milhaud's interwar Americanism than of his Jewish heritage. Copland asserted that Milhaud's "subjectivism, his violence, and his strong sense of logic (as displayed in his strict sense of polytonality) are indications that the Jewish spirit is still alive in him. His music can be quite French when it is gay and alert. In this mood his love for simple folklike tunes and clear-cut rhythms is apparent."[82]

Yet whether these U.S. commentators attributed Milhaud's modernity to his Americanism or to his Jewish background, his French side was consistently seen as the traditional part of the equation. Frankenstein thus explained that Milhaud's "continued interest in French traditions" was "illustrated by his orchestration of fragments from Couperin's suite, *La Sultane*; his *Chansons de Ronsard*, written for Lily Pons; and his viola sonata on eighteenth-century themes."[83] His 1936 *Suite provençale*, Taubman explained, blended "folk airs of the eighteenth century" with a musical approach characterizing Milhaud as "a man of the twentieth century. The result is a work of distinction and individual quality."[84] What made Milhaud recognizably French in the eyes of his American critics was, in the end, his use of traditional French material, whether folk song (as in his *Suite française*) or early music, and as either quotation or stylistic marker. It comes as little surprise, therefore, that Copland's *Appalachian Spring* and Milhaud's nostalgic dance suite *Jeux de printemps* were premièred on the same program by Martha Graham's ballet company in October 1944.[85] Just as the neoclassicism of Copland and Cowell took on a nationalist quest for musical roots when drawing on the style of American hymnody, so Milhaud's allusion to French early and folk musics was judged an expression of his national identity. Through such nationalist infusion of an international musical style, compositions (and composers) could be both mobile on a transnational level and specific in their symbolic creation of identity.

In *Jeux de printemps* the composer deliberately sought to write a "work clear and gay. Perhaps do I need this contrast with all our sorrows as a rest and relaxation."[86] In a letter to Copland, Milhaud used similar words—"gay" had already been cued as French by Copland—but in a manner even more evocative of the concepts of clarity and simplicity he so strongly associated with French music: "I have written a suite called *Jeux de Printemps*, trying to be clear, gay, and spring-like."[87] Scored for nine instruments—flute, clarinet, bassoon, trumpet, and string quintet—this neoclassical six-movement dance suite weaves a rich musical fabric that plays with allusions to dances from across history and cultures, evokes a number of works famous in Paris, and even echoes somewhat fleetingly such American compositions as Copland's *Rodeo*.[88] From Luigi Boccherini's famous String Quintet in E Major, op. 11, no. 5 (alluded to in the second movement) and Gabriel Fauré's *Sicilienne*, op. 78, for flute and piano (hinted at in the third) to Milhaud's own *Le bœuf sur le toit* (in the fourth) and Erik Satie (in the fifth), Milhaud's ingenious *jeux d'esprit* creates a form of referential network that is itself part of a French tradition of artistic intertextuality.[89] For the uninitiated listener, *Jeux de printemps* is simply a delightful set of elegantly crafted dances; those familiar with the intertexts, however, can hear how Milhaud wove numerous musical threads into a fabric of quite astonishing referential complexity. The fifth movement, aptly titled "Nonchalant" and fusing echoes of Satie, Copland, and Milhaud's own music (the slow movement of *Scaramouche*), can be read not only as affirmation of a deep French heritage but even as a claim—not without reason—that even the best of American music had its roots in France.

The condition of exile left other traces in Milhaud's wartime compositions. As "a Frenchman from Provence and of Israelite religion," Milhaud turned to three major liturgical texts: *Borechu* and *Shema Ysroel* in 1944, and *Kaddisch (Prière pour les morts)* the following year. These choral works were not Milhaud's first engagement with Hebrew texts in his compositional career, but they were the first since he fled France in 1940. *Borechu* ("Barekhu et Adonai ha-mevorakh") opens all morning and evening services in the synagogue, and Milhaud's setting for cantor, mixed chorus, and organ reflects the ceremonial exchange between the cantor's opening "Bless the Lord who is blessed" and the congregation's response (set homophonically), "Blessed be the Lord who is blessed for all eternity."[90] Milhaud's colleague and friend, Mario Castelnuovo-Tedesco, explained that this kind of setting reflected the practice in American Reformed synagogues, where, "in the two most important parts, the 'Shema Israel' and the 'Borechu,' the cantor and the choir sing only the first verses in Hebrew, while the remainder of this most beautiful text is recited by the Rabbi in English, generally without musical accompaniment."[91] Setting aside the possible practical reasons behind their composition, both *Borechu* and *Shema Ysroel* (the profession of faith) may be read as an affirmation of Milhaud's Jewish identity at this crucial historic moment of French liberation. Equally, over the centuries "Shema Yisrael" were also the last words on the lips of Jewish martyrs (Schoenberg's *A Survivor from Warsaw* ends with them), and the mourner's Kaddish is recited at the end of the morning prayer service for eleven months and one day by male Jews over the death of a family member. They may well have been Milhaud's own prayer in response to the terrible news that started to fly across the Atlantic after the liberation of France, when he learned that his nephew, Jean Milhaud, and more than twenty other family members had perished in German concentration camps.[92]

Echoes of Milhaud's exile pervaded numerous other wartime compositions. One work in particular encapsulated his concerns and priorities during those years: *Bolivar*, his three-act opera and *opus americanum* 20 (1943) based on Jules Supervielle's eponymous play.[93] In the spring of 1942 Milhaud started to look for a topical opera libretto,[94] one that was "action-laden...with a central male character." *Bolivar* "was dominated by a sense of liberation and freedom, which—in 1943—matched all my thoughts."[95] The plot presented the life of the Latin American freedom fighter Simón Bolívar (1783–1830) throughout his campaign for liberation from Spanish imperialism until his death in exile. Superficially, the theme corresponded to the numerous works that celebrated American "good neighbor" ideologies, from Copland's *Danzón Cubano* (1942) to Cowell's *Fanfare to the Forces of Our Latin-American Allies* (1942). Milhaud himself acknowledged this aspect in a letter to Copland with the comment that the plot was set "in South America, which should be well received here."[96] The libretto held further appeal for him because it engaged with the condition of exile. Milhaud had known Supervielle's play from the 1930s, when he wrote the incidental music for its first performance at the Comédie Française in March 1936. With the permission of the author, Madeleine Milhaud fashioned the opera's libretto in 1942 in a manner faithful overall to the original, but—Milhaud insisted—they introduced one significant change. The play ended with Bolívar's death in exile—a private moment in which he reunites with the spirit of his beloved first wife. For the opera, however, Milhaud wanted something different. He explained to Claude Rostand in 1952: "That fact that Bolivar died alone, in exile, had to determine the ending."[97] And so Madeleine created the text of a final grand aria for the dying hero, "writing his testament, in exile, and she used the authentic text of the testament."[98]

Milhaud clearly identified his work on the opera with the wartime context: he annotated a page of the full-score manuscript "September 8, 1943. Capitulation of Italy, Thank God."[99] The music was splendid and colorful, and according to Jeremy Drake, it was built more along the structure of the operas Milhaud composed in the 1920s, especially when compared to the later, "more through-composed scores of *Maximilien* and *Médée*. Not only do the songs and dances, and the hymns and military marches, add great atmospheric colour to the opera—most are strophic and in typical Latin-American rhythms, but, as sizeable set pieces they provide the architectural pillars around which Milhaud worked, and with the choruses add a distinct celebratory element to the opera."[100] Milhaud's return in *Bolivar* to the compositional idiom he was using in the 1920s, with its discrete formal elements and more tonal language, may be attributed to a number of reasons: it evoked his own, successful past; it fit the conservative tastes of his intended American audience better than his later style; and it also anchored the new score in a French operatic tradition whose clear-cut organization he valued over a Wagnerian dissolution of formal convention. Milhaud's celebration of Gounod's essential Frenchness in *Pour la victoire!* can be heard echoed, for example, in the traditionally shaped final duet of the opera, which "relentlessly invokes the shades of Gounod and Massenet in an orgy of rich, full chords."[101]

Bolivar would not be premièred in the United States, however, even though Milhaud worked hard to convince American opera houses to take it on. At one point a staged performance seemed within his grasp. He wrote to Harold Spivacke in April 1944: "I played my opera *Bolivar* to the Metropolitan. They seemed (as Lily Pons told me) very interested, but they do not have the money to produce it. Actually the Civic Center and Leopold Stokowski would like to play it. Let us hope!"[102] A newspaper report in the *Atlanta Constitution* six months later even named *Bolivar* as one of two planned premières for the newly instituted New York City Center Opera, which was intent on "furthering modern opera" in the civic opera house founded by Mayor Fiorello LaGuardia in 1943 (see chapter 3); the other work was to be William Grant Still's *Troubled Island*.[103] But in the end Milhaud shared the destiny of all other modern composers during World War II, whether American or exiled: neither the Metropolitan nor any other major opera house would première a new opera in those years. Frankenstein was blunt in his 1946 assessment: "*Bolivar* has no chance of being produced in America, thanks to the outmoded, reactionary attitude of the Metropolitan, which governs opera in this country."[104]

Instead, Milhaud relied on the concert hall and on classical-music programs on the radio to make his mark in concertos written for well-known virtuosos who would champion them in their concerts and broadcasts; string quartets and other chamber music that were either commissioned by the Coolidge Foundation or—again—created for individual performers; symphonies for major orchestras or conductors such as Serge Koussevitzky; and topical works for wartime-related series such as the League of Composers' commission, in 1943, of "eighteen short pieces, each work to be written on a war-associated theme," to which Milhaud contributed his *Introduction et Marche funèbre*.[105] Not only did such concert works dominate Milhaud's compositional output in the exile years, but they also led to his renewed engagement with traditional concert genres and idioms, most prominently in his symphonies.

Milhaud's wartime blend of traditional forms, a somewhat more tonal idiom, and noticeable markers of (in his case French) national identity was of course not unique to certain composers exiled in America. Rather, it needs to be understood in a transnational context, especially of concert composition within non-Germanic traditions such as those of France, the Soviet Union, and Latin America (Shostakovich and Heitor Villa-Lobos come to mind). It also reflects the close ties between American composers themselves and European cosmopolitanism of a particularly French variety, given the well-known preference for Paris as a place to study in the 1920s and early 1930s. Yet composers from Allied countries living in exile in the United States were well positioned to take advantage of these trends, which indeed may have provided them their only hope for negotiating fundamental questions of musical identity.[106] Milhaud was no exception in this light, but the parallel (yet also different) case of Bohuslav Martinů makes the point clearer still.

When Martinů arrived with his wife in the United States on March 31, 1941—ill, exhausted, homesick, and deeply dejected—there was little to suggest that he would have one of the most successful careers among exile composers in the United States.[107] Barely able to speak English, he relied on Czech officials and fellow émigrés as well as Francophile Americans for help in his early days in New York.[108] Yet "we had no financial worries," Martinů's wife Charlotte recalled, "as the Czech consulate in New York gave us 300 dollars a month."[109] Indeed, Martinů's annual stipend of $3,600 corresponded roughly to the pay of an American army captain, and may have been even more generous if he did not pay any taxes on it, as it seems he did not.[110] But although he was "welcomed like a great composer," as he wrote to his friends Marcel Mihalovici and Monique Haas in April 1941, the "abundance of everything here makes me depressed. The orchestras are of a perfection that one cannot even imagine, music is in abundance, too, but not modern music."[111] For all the musical riches, material support, and friendship he encountered in New York, he found life "very difficult here.... I had the firm intention of writing but did not expect such a big change or such a reaction."[112] He seemed slated to share Tailleferre's fate of losing his compositional voice in the United States, especially in the hated hustle and bustle of New York.

Eventually the Martinůs moved to the New York suburb of Jamaica, on Long Island, and the composer began to regain his musical footing (Figure 4.3). It helped that Koussevitzky's performance with the Boston Symphony Orchestra on November 14, 1941, of the *Concerto grosso*, op. 263 (1937), was an unmitigated success and led to the conductor's commission of "a symphony for which you will have at your disposal $500.00," to be dedicated (like the other Koussevitzky commissions of that time) to the memory of Nathalie Koussevitzky, who had recently died.[113] This was to be Martinů's first foray into the genre, and it set him a dual challenge, given both the role of the symphony in the United States in the 1930s and the genre's Germanic associations. Yet by then the composer was well aware—as he wrote in a letter home—that "conductors are even bigger stars here than over there.... Chamber music is practically non-existent."[114] And so Martinů adjusted, composing large-scale concert works for such star conductors as Koussevitzky, Erich Leinsdorf, and Eugene Ormandy while wresting the symphony away from what he considered that "messianism"

FIGURE 4.3 "'A Composer Should Compose,' Insists Martinů, and He Spends Many Hours Every Day with His Scores." *Musical America* 64 (January 10, 1944): 11.

and "egotism" of German romanticism, which "can lead all the way to Hitler, who actually does think of himself as a benefactor of humanity."[115] Instead, Martinů delved into the vocabularies of modernism and neoclassicism by emphasizing "objectivity" and abstraction as deliberate rejections of what he considered the "overemphasis" of the late nineteenth-century symphonic repertoire.[116]

Few works exemplify the aesthetic multivalence and polydirectional referentiality of wartime compositions by exile composers more powerfully than Martinů's First Symphony. Premièred on November 13, 1942, by the Boston Symphony Orchestra under Koussevitzky, the work cemented Martinů's place, for his American audience, as the premier contemporary Czech composer—as Virgil Thomson said, a worthy successor to "his predecessor Dvořák" and equal to "Smetana, greatest of all those symphonic composers in whose work patriotism is of the essence."[117] The Czech layer of this and other Martinů compositions resides in a musical idiom whose folklike quality echoes—though it seldom directly cites—Bohemian and Moravian music. Whether or not it is a direct quotation, the melodic proximity of the first movement's theme to the twelfth-century Bohemian chorale *Svatý Václav* could be read as a marker of national identity. This thematic material was one of the most ardently national Bohemian melodies and had served as an expression of Czech protest since the Hussite Wars of the early fifteenth century.[118] Martinů had invoked the famous hymn in his 1918 cantata *Czech Rhapsody*, and he continued alluding to it in other wartime works, including his 1943 *Memorial to Lidice*. Symphonic form and folk song, for Martinů, were not mutually exclusive: rather, as he wrote in 1944, he understood folk song as one of the key influences on sonata form.[119] Furthermore, as he put the finishing touches on his First Symphony, the composer explained in a radio interview from August 1942 that sometimes he used "Czech folk songs as themes, but more often I create thematic material coloured by the style and spirit of the Czech idiom."[120]

The use of a mediated rather than literal form of national material, especially in a symphony, corresponded to Martinů's programmatic statement about the genre that was published in the program booklet for the première.[121] This text takes on the burden of that genre for contemporary composers, and its opening statement is unequivocal: "The form of the symphony is one of the great problems of contemporary composers."[122] As Martinů's argument unfolds, the symphonic challenge is identified as a twofold historical issue: there is the genre's inherent nobility, culminating in Beethoven's Ninth Symphony, and there is its abuse at the hands of romantic and postromantic composers who trivialized the symphony's expressive power through "false magnitude" and an "overemphasis" on the extramusical. For Martinů, the solution lay not with contemporary composers' attempts at changing the genre's structure (here he clearly takes aim at both American and European composers), but with an act of modernist reinterpretation. In a personal note from 1944 he made a self-serving distinction between the "pseudo-moderns" who rejected tradition and the "really modern man" who was—so Martinů said—"often found among those who call themselves old-fashioned."[123] In a final rhetorical flourish, Martinů's program note then pulled the rug out from under the German symphonic tradition after Beethoven: a truly modern engagement with tradition meant that "a work of art must not transcend the limits of its possibility in expression," an aesthetic approach identified in the subsequent sentence as French.

Martinů's clever reconfiguration of symphonic history both as universal in its formal structure and as ideally mediated through French aesthetics leaves room for two key ideological slippages that were crucial in wartime America. Martinů's immanent aesthetic still allows for the individualized expression of "human feeling," especially since musicians at this point in time felt "obligated to espouse sentiments of grandeur and tragedy." Therefore the musical expression of wartime sentiment was ennobled by the genre rather than running the danger of vulgar Germanic propaganda.[124] But this aesthetic also merged seamlessly with the notions of such dominant American modernists as Copland and Thomson—both, of course, schooled in the French neoclassicist ideology of Nadia Boulanger. In *Our New Music* (1941), Copland emphasized the primacy of compositional craft and made the point that "the typical contemporary composer prefers an objective, impersonal approach" so as to avoid (among other things) the "melodramatic nature" of "German romanticism."[125]

These arguments will also be familiar from Stravinsky's *Poetics of Music*, his Harvard lectures from 1939–40, and his own wartime works written in the United States, not least the Symphony in C (1940), the Symphony in Three Movements (1942–45), and the *Ode for Orchestra* (1943), which have often been viewed as the epitome of this aesthetic position, now considered less "French" than international (albeit an international that excludes the Germanic). Martinů added an extra layer to the mix, however. Certainly, his recourse to neoclassicist arguments—which at this point were so well established in the United States as to be a commonplace—inserted his own transatlantic trajectory of exile into a broader and specifically American plotline of musical modernism. Heard in this framework, Martinů's First Symphony—with its shimmering orchestration, contrapuntal texture, clear formal organization, and folk-based motivic material—sits squarely within the developments of the American symphony, albeit with a slightly (and perhaps welcome) exotic tinge. One might also plausibly argue that the conditions of symphonic modernism in the United States provided the aesthetic impetus and practical conditions for Martinů's exploration of the genre from the compound position of a Czech, European, and American composer.[126] But Edward Said's metaphor of the exile's artistic accent as a distinctive creative marker may be the key to reading this composition and its reception: in the end, American audiences heard first and foremost the Czech-sounding elements of the work, whereas Martinů himself emphasized their shared language, both familiar and foreign.[127]

In contrast to Martinů's more overtly political Second Symphony from 1943—with its relatively obvious quotations of Czech folk material and a prominent reference to the passage from the "Marseillaise" that calls its citizens to arms—the composer's first foray in the genre resists such easy translation between war and music.[128] The fact that several commentators have interpreted the symphony's third movement, Largo, as a response to the 1942 massacre of Czech civilians in Lidice, about which Martinů had just heard at the time of its composition (and which he did indeed commemorate in a later work), may well reflect pious expectations of what a foreign exile in America should do—that is, experience and express the survivor guilt that was so poignant a feature of Boulanger's recounting of her own experience (see above).[129] Yet Martinů's own interpretation of the work in a letter to his patron, Koussevitzky, as well as some cryptic notations in the sketches, hint at a different reading.[130] Responding to Koussevitzky's request to compose this symphony in memory of the conductor's late wife—whom Martinů had known personally—the composer explained that he dealt with the heartbreak of her death not through the expression of mourning and tragedy, but with the nostalgic evocation of sweet memories.[131] For Koussevitzky, the Largo was not only beautiful but also "the expression of all the sentiments that I experience in my great sadness."[132] Moreover, annotations in the sketches add a further layer, relating the first names of "Bohuslav" and "CHarlotte" (Martinů's wife) to the two key pitches of the symphony: B-flat and B (expressed in European nomenclature as B and H, respectively).[133] Combined with Martinů's quotation of an early song (dated 1910)—as he pointed out to Šafránek in their conversations in 1943—these traces indicate that the musical evocation of memories also applied to the composer himself.[134] Indeed, Martinů's admonition to Koussevitzky that his music was not intended "to remind him of those tragic moments" of loss but rather "to console, rest, give the joy to live, to look around us, where each moment brings us something new and also a bit of oblivion" might well have been spoken about his own experience in exile.[135] This, Martinů wrote, was his "artistic ideal."

Whereas in their restrained musical language Martinů's symphonies and concertos of this period reflect their historical context—necessitating the avoidance of any unseemly Germanic display of the overtly extramusical— the composer did write a work that foregrounded, at least in its title, the cruelty of the current conflict as it played out in Europe: his *Memorial to Lidice* (1943). It was commissioned for the League of Composers' series of wartime pieces and first performed in a concert of the New York Philharmonic Orchestra on October 28, 1943, on the occasion of the twenty-fifth anniversary Czechoslovakia's independence.[136] About nine minutes long, the compact work is structured along the lines of a concerto grosso, drawing on one of the preclassical forms that Martinů had long favored during his career and which he considered fitting to resisting individualized emotion. For all its restraint, however, *Memorial to Lidice* encapsulated a dense cluster of musical signifiers that embody a powerful response to the tragic events which precipitated it.[137] From its opening C minor chord—the somber tone of which is colored by the use of the tam-tam, an instrument associated with the expression of horror since Gossec and Berlioz—Martinů draws on well-known and semantically overlaid musical configurations, including the "Dies irae," the Bohemian chorale *Svatý Václav* (again), and—toward the end of the piece—the opening motive of Beethoven's Fifth Symphony, rendered in a distorted but recognizable manner, as if wartime (ab)use of the motive had tainted even the music of the universal master.

As in Milhaud's *Jeux de printemps*, these musical intertexts are integrated into the structure of the music, rather than standing out by their difference. By effacing instead of foregrounding the programmatic, Martinů was able to make even his most explicit war composition resistant to the aesthetic of "messianism" that he associated with "German metaphysics and bad interpretations of Beethoven."[138] Not Germanic excess—that which led to massacre and murder—but reason and rationality, even in the face of such horror, were the key approaches in such a moment. Martinů strongly resisted the intemperate adaptation of musical form to the idea "of victory over 'fate' so that a 'climax,' [or] 'catharsis' can be reached at the end of the composition . . . forcing it [to a close] by means of an apotheosis, an allegory with great commotion." Martinů rephrased this even more explicitly in his sarcastic assessment that "the desire to 'suffer' has become a certain 'cliché.'" He contrasted this excessive and "messianic" mode of musical expression with the "closed whole of the other epochs," singling out "the epoch of the *concerto grosso* with its calm, musical development of relations."[139] Taking into account Martinů's politicized reading of musical form and language, the message—so to speak—of *Memorial to Lidice* lay in its resistance to a musical idiom associated with the unfiltered expressivity so often connected with German romanticism and its deliberate use instead of beautifully proportioned and well-crafted restraint. So subtle a shift as the invocation of C major in the concluding *pp* chords (mm. 130–35) is hardly a reference to the Beethovenian *per aspera ad astra*—a reading that would sneak the apotheosizing conclusion in through the back door—but might better be understood as a dismissal of the Germanic cliché and instead as a claim for human dignity, especially in the face of unspeakable brutality.[140] One reviewer of the première clearly picked up on this when he wrote that the work was "a chant and prayer, somber but not depressed in mood, aglow with restrained feeling, steady and strong in spirit."[141] Clearly the identity of Czech nobility that Martinů constructed in the work fit with the concepts of his artistic persona formed by his American critics.

Martinů maintained a strong presence in U.S. concert music for the remainder of the war, with concertos, symphonies, and chamber music commissioned in significant numbers. Though most carried generic titles, one—his *Czech Rhapsody*, op. 305, written in 1945 for Fritz Kreisler—foregrounded the otherwise implied national identity of his music. Based on folk songs, the rhapsody played to the identification—so prevalent in the United States—of the composer as first and foremost Czech. Fellow exiles from Allied nations also composed works that carried their national affiliation programmatically in their titles, from Weinberger's own *Czech Rhapsody* (1941) to Tansman's *Polish Rhapsody* (1940) and Stravinsky's *Scherzo à la russe* (1944). Even when performing, musicians from Allied nations proudly presented the music of their nation—as was the case with Edgard Varèse, who in February 1945 conducted his Greater New York Chorus during a "French American Pageant of Liberation" in what was touted as the first U.S. performance of Berlioz's famous arrangement of "La Marseillaise."[142] Just like Martinů and Milhaud, these musicians fervently held on to their national identities and musical accents in exile, often to the great acclaim of their American audiences. In a nation whose rhetoric of the melting pot was if anything strengthened during the war years, this emphasis on national origins from Allied nations by composers themselves was not only welcome but also made complete sense. The agendas worked in tandem: if Milhaud and Martinů toiled to preserve their national culture in the transnational environment of exile, so did their audiences still expect distinguishing markers of ethnic and national identity to be reflected in the compositions of those who were not American-born. To compose a "French" or "Czech" work in the United States was simply one more facet of the "great appropriation" of world culture during the war.

Refugees from Axis Nations

This easy transfer of cultural practice at work in the American reception of musicians exiled from Allied countries was much more complicated when it came to composers who hailed from the nations that were at war with the United States. The transition was, and remains, particularly problematic in the case of Béla Bartók, who has been identified for decades as a quintessentially Hungarian voice through his compositions, folklore research, and theoretical writings. The first country to sign the Tripartite Pact forged by Germany, Italy, and Japan, Hungary had entered the Axis in November 1940, less than two months after the Axis powers themselves had officially united. Soon thereafter Hungarian troops joined the German army in the attack on the Soviet Union. Bartók's position was somewhat ambivalent.

Although he was increasingly anti-Fascist, he had sought concert opportunities in Germany until 1937, and he performed in Italy even after the outbreak of World War II. However, in February 1939 he wrote to his former piano student Dorothy Parrish that "the fatal influence of the Germans is steadily growing in Hungary, the time seems not to be far, when we shall become quite a German colony."[143] He wondered then whether it would not be best to turn his back on all of Europe, and so he did in October 1940 (the month before Hungary joined the Axis), ostensibly to catalogue the Parry collection of Croatian and Serbian folk song at Columbia University.[144] He arrived with his wife, Ditta Pásztory, in New York on October 29, 1940, entering the country on a visitor's visa.[145] (Figure 4.4). In the later war years, Bartók described himself as a "voluntary refugee"; his American hosts, however, declared him—like all other Axis nationals—an "enemy alien" in December 1941, a status he retained until July 1945.[146] This status affected his employment contracts, such as when he was invited to be a visiting lecturer at Harvard University in the spring of 1943. The chair of Harvard's music

FIGURE 4.4 "Béla Bartók with Ditta Pasztory, his pianist wife, discusses music with a compatriot, Erno Rapee, conductor of the Radio City Symphony Orchestra." *Musical Courier* (February 5, 1942): 17.

department made clear to Douglas Moore (Bartók's employer at Columbia University at the time) that before the composer's name could be "placed before the Corporation for appointment they would like to have a statement about his political loyalties, since I presume he is still a Hungarian. Would you be willing to send me a statement to the effect that he is not pro-Axis-minded[?]"[147]

Bartók's first year in the United States was taken up with his ethnomusicological work at Columbia University and his concert performances, either as a soloist or with his wife, like him a pianist; he barely interacted with other Hungarian political émigrés. This changed in the fall of 1941.[148] The Hungarian politician Tibor Eckhart had come to the United States to set up a voice for Hungary in exile. He was, however, politically close to the current Hungarian government of Pál Teleki, which would prove problematic and eventually untenable in the United States. Named the Movement for an Independent Hungary, the newly formed exile group denounced Nazi Germany and urged Hungarians to rally to the Allies. Bartók joined the Movement as soon as it was founded in October 1941, first as a member of its Scientific and Artistic Committee and then as that committee's chair. But because the Movement and especially its leader were too close to the compromised Hungarian Axis government, it drew significant criticism, both from leftist Hungarians exiled in the United States and from Czech and Yugoslav refugees. Eckhart resigned his presidency in July 1942 in an effort to salvage the Movement. Bartók was promptly appointed the new president in the hope that the composer would prove "a sort of Paderewski" and rally his Hungarian countrymen. For Bartók, the task lay in proving that Hungarians in exile were loyal to the Allied cause, because—as he wrote in 1942—"many of our enemies try to convince people that Hungary...joined the Nazi camp of its free will."[149] Bartók's efforts on behalf of the Movement had almost no wider impact, however, and American officials considered him little more than "a front man for Eckhart."[150]

It is not surprising, then, that during the war years Bartók's views on Hungarian folk music took a new direction. He published several texts that celebrated, in deliberate contradiction of Nazi rhetoric, the lack of racial purity in his nation's folk idiom. Thus he compared the "crossing and recrossing" of materials across the Balkans with the benefits to art music of musical migration, for "every musician knows what far-reaching and fortunate consequences have resulted from the transplantation of the fifteenth century musical style of the Netherlands to Italy, and, later, from the spread of various influences from Italy to the Northern countries."[151] In another article, written during his presidency of the Movement for an

Independent Hungary, Bartók emphasized these political aspects even more strongly by distinguishing between, on the one hand, an "unspoiled treasure of folk music" that lay at the heart also of "a new musical spirit" in Hungarian art music, "rooted in the elements of music springing from the soil," and, on the other, the corruption of these idioms by "higher circles" in urban centers. The evident paradox of pairing the benefits of musical migration with elements "springing from the soil" seems to have escaped him, as did the Fascist overtones of the latter. Instead, Bartók rhapsodized that in Eastern Europe, peasants of different nationalities "live peacefully side by side, each speaking his own language, following his own customs, taking it for granted that his neighbor, speaking another language, does the same.... There is peace among the peasants; hatred against their brothers is fostered only by the higher circles!"[152] Bartók thus stylized an "authentic" and pastoral Hungary, embodied and expressed in her folk music, that was noble and genuinely peaceful. Hungarians, Bartók argued, were at war solely "at the command of their leaders," who were tainted by their "urbanized culture" and "mechanized civilization." For the composer, the proof of honesty and peacefulness in music lay not in cosmopolitanism or urban idioms, with their implicit dependence on Austro-German romanticism, but in the "Autochthon [sic] Hungarian Musical Art, inspired and influenced by this unparalleled and invaluable back ground of folk music." This rhetorical sleight of hand was perfectly appropriate in the United States during wartime because it allowed Bartók to separate both an idealized version of his homeland and his own musical past and present from what he identified as modern urban corruption, a rhetoric familiar from the likes of Roy Harris and—as we saw in chapter 3—Elie Siegmeister. It also allowed Bartók to position himself as something other than what his documentation declared him to be: an "enemy alien."

That Bartók found life in the United States challenging is well-known; his letters speak about financial worries and lack of recognition, and the "specter of depression" loomed heavily over his American years.[153] At one point he wrote, "I cannot live in this country. In this country—*lasciate ogni speranza*."[154] But although, in letters to friends and family, he repeatedly described his financial situation as desperate,[155] his annual after-tax income never fell below $3,000 per year; in 1943, for example, it was just below $4,300—equivalent to the purchasing power, in 2009, of $53,000: this was modest, certainly, but nowhere near poverty.[156] It would seem that exiles often found it necessary for psychological or other reasons to accentuate the hardships of living in a new world while still expressing gratitude for its opportunities, as we saw earlier in the case of Benjamin Britten. Unlike other composers such as Schoenberg and Stravinsky, by 1944 and 1945 Bartók was able to live almost entirely off royalties and publishers' advances.[157] In addition, as his health declined from late 1942 onward, ASCAP covered his medical costs, which ran to some $16,000.[158] Yet Bartók dwelled on the difference between his comfortable economic situation in Hungary and life in exile. In a letter dated March 2, 1942, for example, he wrote that his position kept worsening, for never since he started earning his living "have I been in such a dreadful situation as I will be probably very soon."[159] The lack of economic security came through in another letter in which he described his family as "living from half-year to half-year."[160] With ever worsening health issues because of leukemia, with his two sons fighting on opposite sides of the war (Béla in the Hungarian armed forces, Peter in the American), and with strains in his marriage, the composer returned to what he called "the eternal refrain—how I wish this exile would end at last!"[161] Worse still, by December 1942 he saw himself mainly as a scholar, his career as a composer "as much as finished: the quasi boycott of my works by the leading orchestras continues, no performances either of old work[s] or of new ones. It is a shame—not for me of course."[162]

Even though his piano music and string quartets were often and widely performed on concert programs across the United States, it never seems to have crossed Bartók's mind that—especially in the early war years and during his open involvement in the Movement for an Independent Hungary—his music might have been perceived as less suitable for American orchestra concerts than, for example, the "heroic" works of Shostakovich, especially the latter's Seventh Symphony. Yet after Bartók retired from pro-Hungarian politics at the end of 1942, and following appeals from such friends as József Szigeti, it was a committed supporter of the Soviet Union, Koussevitzky, who provided Bartók with his first major American commission for an orchestral composition in May 1943. Bartók was still convalescing in Lake Saranac in the Adirondack Mountains when Koussevitzky visited him to discuss the new work. Bartók's wife reported back to Szigeti that "Koussevitzky visited B. in the sanatorium, and I know that B. was very pleased about it.... I am so glad that plans, musical ambitions, compositions are stirred in Béla's mind—a new hope, discovered in this way quite by chance, as it were incidentally. One thing is sure: Béla's 'under no circumstances will I ever write a new work...' attitude has gone. It's more than three years now."[163] The result was one of Bartók's most popular works, the Concerto for Orchestra, completed in October 1943 and premièred on December 1, 1944, by the Boston Symphony Orchestra.[164] Though not an unmitigated success—in contrast to, for example, the première of Martinů's First Symphony—American audiences and critics heard in the work a new and appealing direction in Bartók's music.[165]

The Concerto for Orchestra has since become a *cause célèbre* in the discussion of exile composition in the United States during World War II. Spurred by René Leibowitz's well-known negative article (1947) on Bartók and the possibility of compromise in contemporary music—Leibowitz was, of course, one of the leading Schoenbergians and a member of the French resistance; he was also of Polish extraction and therefore unlikely to favor a Hungarian—the Concerto for Orchestra has been relentlessly charged with the Adornian crime of "compromise" with respect to audience taste and mediocrity.[166] Whether citing the work's comparatively rich orchestration, its noticeable thematic symmetry, or its latent functional harmony, postwar critics interpreted Bartók's first American composition as pandering to American taste. Olin Downes—the *New York Times* critic who disliked most of Bartók's music—saw it differently, however, when he addressed the issue head-on, describing the work as "a wide departure from the author's harsher and more cerebral style. There might even be the suspicion with an artist of less sincerity than this one, that he had adopted a simpler and more melodic manner with the intention of an appeal to a wider public. But that would not be Mr. Bartók's motive." Instead, Downes saw the change in direction as proof that Bartók had the courage to strike out in new directions.[167]

For Downes and Koussevitzky, the Concerto for Orchestra denoted true progress in modern music. For Bartók, it was clearly a work that laid claim to the exalted greatness of the symphony; but like Martinů before him, he tried to avoid any open association with Austro-German romanticism even while he used sonata form for the first and last movements. His program notes were a study in formalist restraint, tempered only by the final sentence, where he explained that the "general mood of the work represents—apart from the jesting second movement—a gradual transition from the sternness of the first movement and the lugubrious death-song of the third, to the life-assertion of the last one."[168] In stark contrast to Martinů—and in ways that perhaps reflect the more complex position of an "enemy alien"— Bartók instrumentalized the classic Beethovenian *per aspera ad astra* for a narrative program appropriate for his wartime audience: the final apotheosis after somber reality and commemoration of death were standard plots in war compositions, whether in the Soviet Union or the United States.[169] Bartók's own rhetoric in the program note for the première downplayed his use of folk idioms in this work, even though recent analyses have shown in great ___ folk elements than the composer's earlier works, ___ Hungarian and other Eastern European folk materials.[170]

His audience and critics followed suit. Furthermore, instead of evoking the clichés of fiery Hungarianism and barbaric rhythms (as was done in Bartók's prewar years), critics now wrote about the "typical Bartókian austerity and severity," with its "arresting archaic quality," thus grounding any Hungarian connotation of the material in a premodern and hence (following Bartók) uncorrupted utopia.[171] Contemporary critical and popular reception also submerged any unfortunate connotations of music stemming from "enemy" soil and placed the composer in a relatively safe position of transcendence.

Yet for Bartók the Concerto for Orchestra also dealt with more immediate concerns. The well-known allusion to Shostakovich's Seventh Symphony in the fourth movement (Intermezzo interrotto) has usually been read as Bartók's rather negative comment on an annoying rival composer. Commentators have also remarked on the double voicing of the reference: the melodic contour also corresponds to the opening line of "Heut geh' ich ins Maxim," perhaps the most famous aria from Franz Lehár's operetta *The Merry Widow*. That the Lehár allusion may by a sly reference to the first name of Shostakovich's son, Maxim (born in 1938), is doubtful, but the Shostakovich/Lehár quotation does stand out as a "seemingly incongruous" interpolation in a movement that also refers to Hungary's own urban, popular music by paraphrasing the aria "You are lovely, you are beautiful, Hungary," from Zsigmond Vincze's 1926 operetta *A hamburgi menyasszony* (The Bride from Hamburg).[172] In the universe of Bartók's folk-song ideology, however, the quotation might also be interpreted in a more pointed way. Early in his career, Bartók wrote about Hungary's bourgeoisie: "From now on I won't bother with them. Let asses be asses. Let them drown in their *Merry Widow*, and let us take all culture out of this country."[173] In January 1943 the Soviets destroyed the Hungarian Second Army in the Battle of Voronezh. As the year went on, Hungarians were drowning no longer in Lehár but in war. By the time the Concerto for Orchestra was premièred, Hungary itself was a major battlefield of the eastern front. For the fiercely patriotic Bartók, this double-voiced Shostakovich/Lehár quotation might well have carried an accusation against the corrupt urban middle class that had brought the fight between the Soviets and the Axis powers into his homeland—whose culture he had taken with him. The quotation was not, after all, enfolded in the moments of mourning—what he called the "lugubrious death-song" of the third movement (Elegia)—but placed as an interruption in the subsequent intermezzo. Furthermore, the fourth movement's main theme paraphrased urban music as well: it is tempting to focus on the name of the operetta—*The Bride from Hamburg*—as an admonition that even a melody that celebrates Hungary's beauty might be corrupted by Germanic associations. Yet this would be, Bartók implied, just an intermezzo in the passage of time—deeply painful, but to be superseded by something better. Not for nothing does the "life-affirming" fifth (last) movement contain quotations from several Romanian folk dances and even Colin McPhee's arrangements of Balinese music. Indeed, what does affirm life in Bartók's universe is the culture of the peasants: those who truly love peace. Whether intentional or not, Bartók's Concerto for Orchestra works with allusions and quotations in such a way as to make plausible a musical indictment of the Hungarian pro-Axis regime and support of its possible punishment at the hands of the anti-Fascist Soviets.[174]

Following the Concerto for Orchestra, Bartók continued his work as a composer and—to a lesser degree—an ethnomusicologist, although his health grew more and more precarious; he wrote the Sonata for Solo Violin for Yehudi Menuhin and during the last year of the war worked on both the Third Piano Concerto and the never-to-be-finished Viola Concerto. In these later compositions he maintained the tendency toward foregrounding the universalist formalism present in his Concerto for Orchestra, even though the idioms of these two works were still suffused with elements of Hungarian and Eastern European folk music. The fact that the Third Piano Concerto continues the Beethovenian references both for broad aesthetic reasons and, it seems, for personal ones—the famous reference to Beethoven's "Heiliger Dankgesang" in the slow movement presumably refers to Bartók's brief recuperation from his illness in Asheville, North Carolina—also reveals the pivotal role still played by German masterworks in the wartime rhetoric of American and exile composers alike. Given that Americans themselves often made the case that these works transcended their roots in the cause of musical universalism, it was plausible and perhaps even necessary for enemy aliens to follow suit.

Although Bartók could still claim the cachet of the folkloric, and therefore an idealized uncorrupted authenticity, the same was not true of other refugees from the Axis, many of whom were left only with a rhetoric of universalism grounded in both past and present. The compositional idioms of Paul Hindemith, Arnold Schoenberg, Ernst Krenek, Hanns Eisler, and Kurt Weill were not at all associated with folklore-based nationalism before they moved into U.S. exile. Rather, those idioms were linked with European modernism writ large when the composers suddenly found themselves needing to distinguish themselves from their Nazi countrymen, who had claimed Germany's heritage as their own while denouncing artistic "internationalism" as a signifier of cultural "degeneration." Austro-German composers in exile thus faced conundrums different from Bartók's, for their identities were caught in this realignment between nationalist and universalist ideologies.

As each of these musicians fled Hitler, they responded individually to the vicious Fascist attack on their artistic identities and physical safety.[175] In each case, however, the points of reference lay with the two incongruous Germanies they fled—that of the old and that of the present—and the shifting perceptions of their new home. The dialectical relationship between what was foreign and what was familiar became a central and dynamic foundation of artistic identity in exile.[176] But this same field of tension—between an idealized Germany of the past with its universalist appeal, its current disfigurement at the hands of the Nazis, and American concerns about cultural identity—also played into their reception in the United States.

This triangulation was made explicit with respect to Hindemith in a concert announcement in the *Washington Post* in March 1943. The cellist Gregor Piatigorski was to perform "a concerto written for him by Hindemith, distinguished German composer now on the staff of Yale University. Before Hitler's rise to power, Hindemith was hailed as 'the messiah of German music and the symbol of German youth in foreign lands.' Later the Nazi regime denounced his works as 'the vilest perversion of German music and of no value to our movement.'"[177] Clearly, the reviewer implies, the American Ivy League university knew musical quality better than the uncultured Nazi regime. A few other reviews over the years addressed Hindemith's nationality in the context of his American exile, as when Irwin Edman declared that—because only "democratic civilization" and political freedom provided the "conditions for creative liberty"—"creative talents like Hindemith and [Thomas] Mann could not live in the Germany of Hitler."[178] Instead, they found their intellectual home in the political freedom of the United States. One critic contrasted the experimentalism of Hindemith's European (not German!) days, when he could reach only "little cult groups," with the composer's greater fortune on crossing the Atlantic: "Now that the composer himself has become a part of the American cultural scene, even to the point of accepting an appointment at so understandable an institution as Yale University, audiences across the country have become more eager to listen to his compositions."[179] By late 1943 journalists had stopped mentioning Hindemith's nationality: instead, he was celebrated simply as "a great master," "a contemporary genius," or "one of the big names in music, contemporary or otherwise."[180] When Roger Sessions presented the address for Hindemith's honorary doctorate at the University of Pennsylvania on June 4, 1945, he lauded him as a composer, theorist, performer, and teacher, without any reference to his national origin. Even when, in his peroration, Sessions addressed the issue of why Hindemith had moved, he spoke only of the United States, making Hindemith part of the national community by virtue of a shared destiny: "Finally, as a fugitive from tyranny, as were our fore-fathers from the earliest days of our country, he has come to our shores, and by his very presence has contributed inestimable riches to our musical life."[181]

This transformation of Hindemith from "the renowned German expatriate composer" (as he was characterized in 1941) to an integral part of contemporary American concert life was the result of a number of interrelated circumstances.[182] On the one hand, Hindemith himself contributed by down-playing his national identity during the war years—he quietly accepted his "enemy alien" status—and by foregrounding those aspects of his compositional craft that related to his American audiences; on the other, Hindemith's compositional style, educational activities, and musical theories reverberated with key contemporary concerns of American composers and critics. Most important for these concerns—besides Hindemith's overall turn toward neoclassicism in the 1930s—was his interest in premodern idioms. Whereas for Martinů the archaic signified anti-Germanic resistance and for Bartók true Hungarianness, in Hindemith's case it became a marker of a musical craft that was universalist in terms less of message than of technique. Copland, for example, characterized the neoclassical Hindemith as a "forthright" musician "without the slightest trace of affectation." His was "the craftsmanlike attitude of the eighteenth century composer, with the honest desire to do a job simply and well."[183] This was high praise indeed in Copland's objectivist neoclassical universe. For Copland, Hindemith's theories may have borne the danger of underestimating "the unconscious part of creation," which was probably a response to his experiencing Hindemith as a fellow teacher who used methods wholly contrary to his own at Tanglewood in 1940. However, "in works like the opera *Mathis der Maler*, the four-hand piano *Sonata*, or the *Saint Francis* ballet, we know we are listening to a creative mind that transcends mere methodic formulas."

References to Hindemith's craft as a composer served also to denationalize him by distancing him from the (Germanic) romantic genius and instead aligning him with the rhetoric of musical modernism in its American neoclassical vein.[184] The pivotal composition in this realignment was his symphony *Mathis der Maler*, which—not entirely ironically—had lain at the heart of the storm over Hindemith in Nazi Germany after its première in March 1934. Originally championed by Koussevitzky and the Boston Symphony Orchestra, the work was finding its way "frequently on orchestra programs these days," and the first U.S. recording of the work was released in January 1942 by the Philadelphia Orchestra under Eugene Ormandy.[185] In a long review of the recording in the *New York Times*, Howard Taubman rhapsodized about Hindemith's musical portrayal of *Matthias the Painter* (as he translated the title), that "painter-warrior" of the Reformation "who fought on the side of the peasantry during the Peasants' War." Besides its appealing subject (one that was clearly suited to wartime), what made this work "stand high among the works produced in our generation" was that the composer "has woven into his score old folksongs, Gregorian chants and Reformation tunes, but he has fused these elements in a strongly personal way. The flavor is not merely antique; it is strong and modern, intense and full blooded."[186] Taubman described Hindemith's symphony as a form of medievalism in Technicolor, as if Matthias Grünewald had morphed into a symphonic version of Errol Flynn's 1938 Robin Hood. The symphony's splendidly modern medievalism became an *idée fixe* of wartime music criticism that shaped the reception of this and other orchestral works by Hindemith. Later that year Olin Downes lauded the "vigor and almost symbolic austerity" of the score as having "intrigued the ears of this generation, what with the ruggedness and authority of the counterpoint, the combination of archaic chords and tonalities, the modernity of key relations and an almost Gothic stress and significance of detail."[187] In the summer of 1944 Claudia Cassidy reported that "4,000 were mesmerized" by "Hindemith's superb symphony, a strong, singularly pure score touched with wonder and with splendor wrought by a master craftsman."[188]

While numerous American critics in the early 1940s celebrated Hindemith's symphonic idiom as a model of modern music forged by a pre-modern master craftsman, one musician wondered whether this turn toward "what we might call a medievalizing mood—the mood of resignation, of the elegiac tableau—and a corresponding absence of that robust and aggressive manner that was once so typical of Hindemith's work" might not be the composer's musical response to "the cruel years through which Germany and all the world have passed."[189] Copland, who published these words in 1941, was again serving Hindemith's purpose—this German composer was responding sensitively to the harshness of the "new" Germany—but he may well have been on to something. There is no doubt that Hindemith retreated into the world of early music during the war years in America, both as a teacher and as a composer. Whether explicitly (in his *Ludus tonalis* of 1942) or implicitly (as can be seen from the isorhythms in the Sonata for Alto Horn and Piano of 1943), Hindemith's tendency of the 1930s to draw on earlier forms and idioms intensified during the war years. In contrast to the blatantly obvious and German-national medievalism of, say, Carl Orff's *Carmina burana*, however, Hindemith's turn to early music can be seen as part of a broader transnational trend shared by composers from Michael Tippett to Copland and Cowell, whose search for the archaic was inextricably tied to modernist concerns.

These uses of early music were both structural and referential: Hindemith's *Ludus tonalis* and Cowell's *Hymns and Fuguing Tunes* are closely related.

By the time Hindemith arrived in the United States on February 15, 1940, he had already spent several months on concert tours there in the late 1930s. In 1938 he wrote to his wife, "I suddenly felt what great possibilities an indigenous American composer must be having here and started to identify myself with him. And all of the sudden I was inspired and had so many ideas."[190] Yet for all his positive views of the United States, Hindemith, like Martinů, had to deal with a compositionally fallow period for some months after his move. In March 1940 he lamented: "For the time being, I still feel as if I had never thought nor written a single note in my life."[191] The realities of émigré life and the scramble for material security took their toll. Within months of his arrival, however, Hindemith was offered first a visiting position, then a full-time one, at Yale University, with the generous salary of $6,500 per year.[192] America did indeed offer great advantages, and he started to get used to what would be their new home (Figure 4.5).[193] Once Gertrud joined the composer in September 1940, the couple lived a quiet life in

FIGURE 4.5 Paul and Gertrud Hindemith in their garden in New Haven, ca. 1945. Courtesy of the Fondation Hindemith, Blonay (Switzerland).

Connecticut. A second summer spent teaching in Tanglewood proved the main event of 1941. After Pearl Harbor, the Hindemiths lived as registered enemy aliens. "We had to stand in a long line and to fill out [forms] about relatives and get our fingerprints taken. Now we have little books to carry around, and we cannot leave New Haven without permission!"[194] The couple took these restrictions in their stride and focused on supporting their students and colleagues in military service by sending letters and packages. In the spring of 1946 Hindemith recalled that, for all their inner tension about the war, their existence had been calm and peaceful: at Yale—which had become "completely militarized" by late 1943[195]—even the music school had been put into wartime service, but "personally," he continued, "we never had any difficulties. We were neither put into concentration camps nor were we made to feel that we were, after all, the enemy aliens."[196]

Much of Hindemith's output in the war years displays the introspective qualities that Copland had identified before 1941 as a response to the political situation in Europe. Hindemith would have agreed with his American colleague that music carried, in effect, the influence of its creative environment. "We are not asked," Hindemith declared in 1940, "whether we consider these influences good or bad, whether we recognize or reject them, whether we believe that we conquer them or whether we submit to them, they are there, and we have to reckon with them."[197] For Hindemith, the wartime context spelled first and foremost retreat into what he considered essential and timeless musical qualities. In teaching, this inclination led to his emphasizing musical and historical fundamentals, as in his *Concentrated Course in Traditional Harmony*, published in New York in 1943, and his tireless efforts promoting early-music performance and study at Tanglewood in 1941 and Yale. In terms of composition, after a brief excursion into orchestral brilliance in his Symphony in E-flat (1940) Hindemith took a stance against what he considered superficial expressivity.[198] *Ludus tonalis* was the work that truly offered the "moral conquest" that Hindemith claimed was needed, rather than Shostakovich's "symphonic description of the siege of Leningrad":[199] "it is precisely today—when every sniveling juvenile has a symphony in his head, when every orchestral conductor performs the most impossible crap because it is either American or Russian and otherwise has no interest in anything but orchestral music, when music is rated only by how it works on the sex glands—it is precisely today that something must appear which shows what music and composition really are."[200] Songs—created for performance at home with his wife, an amateur soprano—made up a large part of his composing in 1942, and chamber works dominated his output until the end of the war.[201]

Yet even in wartime, Hindemith was not entirely immune to orchestral brilliance. His *Symphonic Metamorphosis on Themes of Carl Maria von Weber*, composed in the summer of 1943, can be characterized as a cultural translation project in which an enemy alien recasts and transforms music by an unquestionably German composer for an American wartime context. Written in four movements—whose sequence (like Copland's *Rodeo* Suite) flirts with the outline of a symphony—the work seems carefree, at least on the surface.[202] Each movement works its way through a composition by Weber, though Hindemith revealed only one of those sources at the première (Weber's 1809 overture *Turandot*) and left the music critics guessing as to the others. The remaining three movements were based on little-known four-hand piano pieces by Weber that Hindemith had begun to adapt for a ballet score in 1940.[203] The relative obscurity of the originals gave the composer the freedom—as Downes paraphrased the program notes of the première—"to treat them as he pleases!"[204] Yet, as the Ovidian roots of the title suggest, "metamorphosis" refers not just to transformation—whether of the symphony or of Weber's themes remains ambiguous—but also to some kind of artistic transcendence for a greater purpose that becomes manifest in Hindemith's treatment of his material.

Although each movement plays with musical signifiers of Americana—for example the fleeting references to "The Star-Spangled Banner" and barn-dance figures in the middle of the first movement—the most obvious echo of contemporary events and idioms can be found in the *Turandot* Scherzo (the second movement), which fuses Chinese and American musical idioms with European-style counterpoint in a virtuosic showpiece. Written during the height of American pro-Chinese sentiment in the summer of 1943—fuelled by Madame Chiang Kai-shek's high-profile visit to the United States—Hindemith's choice of Weber's *Turandot* Overture as the basis of the movement was highly topical. Furthermore, early in 1943 Yale's drama department had presented the Chinese play *The Circle of Chalk* (also the basis for Bertolt Brecht's play *The Caucasian Chalk Circle* of 1944). As Gertrud Hindemith reported in a letter to William Theo Brown, "one of Mr. Hindemith's students, the Chinese Tam, made the music. Very good. Did you ever hear a Chinese flute? Sounds magically attractive."[205] The sound world of that magically attractive Chinese flute—floating over bells and string harmonics—opens the Scherzo in a moderato introduction before the motive begins to bounce through various instruments and orchestra sections in an increasingly frenetic intensification, the tempo now marked "lively." With the interpolation of a thrilling jazz fugue in the middle of the Scherzo, Hindemith pushes the envelope of musical representation and transformation: instead of the irony associated with a Mahlerian synchronicity of heterogeneous elements, Hindemith's homogeneous fusion in this fugue of idioms associated with Asia, the United States, and a preclassical (and thus untainted) Europe not only forms a coherent symbolic portrayal of an Allied identity but inscribes the "good German" into this new harmonious world order. In the context of exile and war, Hindemith's transnational metamorphosis of the nineteenth-century German Weber can be read, in effect, as a political statement—discreet, perhaps, under the veneer of an orchestral showpiece, but nevertheless audible to a careful listener.

Hindemith's self-representation as a "good German"—and one willing to put up with the inconveniences of "enemy alien" status while keeping his head beneath the ivory-tower parapet—was in part inevitable because he could not claim the moral high ground available to many of his compatriots: the flight from racist genocide. Exiles such as Schoenberg and Weill were politically far more outspoken in their compositions and public statements alike.[206] Both had moved to the United States in the mid-1930s, fleeing for their lives after Hitler came to power, and by the time war reached the United States both had become established as significant, though not wholeheartedly accepted, fixtures in contemporary American music. Often they were asked by the press to address topics that ranged from current events to musical aesthetics.[207] Schoenberg had the added advantage of regularly being called "the Einstein of music": the fact that he was the doyen of European musical modernism—alongside Stravinsky (who also received the same Einsteinian label)—meant that however little his works might be understood, any *ex cathedra* pronouncements were usually treated seriously.[208] By the time Pearl Harbor was attacked, Schoenberg had become an American citizen (in April 1941), and he had been firmly ensconced since 1936 as a professor of composition at the University of California at Los Angeles. After the outbreak of war Schoenberg commented on a range of war-related topics, from military music to the suggested postwar treatment of Nazi collaborators.[209] As a composer, he produced works that were either almost hermetic (such as a four-part mirror canon in 1943) or notable for their expressive directness, most famously in his *Ode to Napoleon Buonaparte*, op. 41 (1942), heralded in the American press as Schoenberg's "first specifically political gesture."[210] According to Leonard Stein, the Japanese attack and the subsequent declarations of war had prompted Schoenberg to reflect on the role of art in the current conflict.[211] Barely a month later, the League of Composers approached Schoenberg with a request for a chamber work in honor of the League's twentieth anniversary (it was founded in 1923). The result was the *Ode*, written relatively quickly between March and June 1942. As letters and other documents reveal, Schoenberg configured the work self-consciously as a political composition, and it was received as such when it was finally premièred in late 1944.

Schoenberg's first order of business for the new work was finding a suitable text—for, as Stein tells the story, "Schoenberg definitely wanted to use an English text" for this topical work.[212] In contrast to other exiles (for example, Weill and Hindemith) who turned to such American stalwarts as Walt Whitman in the early war years, Schoenberg found his poet in Lord Byron, whose death during the Greek War of Independence made him a perfect symbol for a war entered into by the United States expressly to fight Axis aggression.[213] Byron's ironic *Ode to Napoleon Buonaparte* (1814) was a passionate attack on despotic oppression; at the same time, it related the cause of freedom unequivocally to American democracy through the triumphant final call on George Washington as the heroic "Cincinnatus of the West" (though Washington was long dead by the time Byron wrote his text).[214] Schoenberg patently ignored the poem's resonance of exile as ignominy: it is prefaced by an epigraph from Edward Gibbon's account of the Emperor Nepos ("By this shameful abdication, he protracted his life a few years, in a very ambiguous state, between an Emperor and an Exile, till—"). However, the *Ode* suited the composer's anti-Fascist stance, and his new search for political relevance, perfectly: as Schoenberg wrote in 1943, "I remembered Mozart's *Marriage of Figaro*, supporting repeal of the *jus primae noctis*, Schiller's *Wilhelm Tell*, Goethe's *Egmont*, Beethoven's *Eroica* and *Wellington's Victory*, and I knew it was the moral duty of the intelligentsia to take a stand against tyranny."[215] His choice of German models is revealing indeed.

Setting the text for reciter, string quartet, and piano, Schoenberg wrote a passionate melodrama that fit into the landscape of contemporary political compositions in the United States, including such works as Earl Robinson's famous and frequently performed *Ballad for Americans* (1939) and Copland's contemporaneous *Lincoln Portrait* (1942). In the *Ode* Schoenberg, like Robinson and Copland, fused his own compositional idiom with the dramatic-recitation style of the 1930s left-wing stage that characterized this type of melodramatic composition.[216] From the way in which Schoenberg foregrounded key verses—for example, the unaccompanied exclamation "Fair Freedom! we may hold thee dear"—to the driving, sometimes syncopated rhythms and the final E-flat major chord reached after a crescendo (so similar in gesture to Copland's C major ending of *Lincoln Portrait*, but also, presumably, a reference to Beethoven's "Eroica" Symphony), the *Ode* is in fact more closely related to its musical context in wartime American than to Schoenberg's earlier *Pierrot lunaire*, the work with which scholars usually tend to compare it.[217]

Yet for all its fleeting echoes of tonality and its musical references to such works as Beethoven's Third and Fifth Symphonies—the latter's famous opening theme is cited in mm. 63–64 to the words "voice of Victory"—the *Ode* remains firmly in the realm of dodecaphony.[218] This compositional choice made double sense in the context of the work's creation. Schoenberg's decision to retain his twelve-tone technique in a political work affirmed his own compositional freedom in the face of a tyrant who had declared his idiom "degenerate," while the combination of what was considered a musical avant-garde technique with accessible dramatic recitation fit the ideological parameters of American populism—if not closely, then closely enough to be received as such. Schoenberg himself repeatedly pitched the work along those lines. In June 1942 he thought that "this piece will be very attractive during this war time already," for the text was "full of allusions to Hitler and our current events."[219] In 1943 he described the work as suitable "for political propaganda" and expected it to be understood as "a satire on Mussolini and Hitler."[220] By 1944 he discussed possible uses of the *Ode* by the OWI.[221] In all that time, however, the *Ode* had not yet been performed.

Its première finally took place on November 23, 1944, with the New York Philharmonic Orchestra, conducted by Artur Rodzinski. By now, however, the political climate had changed from the heightened patriotism of the war's early days to the self-assured certainty of a nation on the brink of victory. What was conceived as a timely composition that would rally American compatriots against tyranny in 1942 was now—at least politically—somewhat behind the curve. This affected the work's reception. In the summer of 1943, when Rodzinski announced the new season, the parallel between Hitler and Napoleon was still newsworthy: in Julia Spiegelman's article for the *New York Sun*, a subheading announced that the *Ode* was "applicable to Hitler."[222] Closer to the concert, the *New York Times* critic Noel Straus pointed to the "climactic moment in the final stanza...where Washington is lauded as the ideal conqueror."[223] Yet when the performance took place, critics pushed the discussion from the topical to the musical. Downes and others still reiterated the parallel between Hitler and Napoleon (*Newsweek* even felt the need to use the pun of "Arnold Schoenberg Scores Off Tyrants" as a headline), but they were now more concerned with such questions as whether the genre of melodrama actually worked (or whether the music would be more efficient without recitation) and with an assessment of Schoenberg's stylistic development. Predictably, traditionalists bemoaned the difficulties of the score, but a number of critics saw the work as heading toward a more accessible idiom, mentioning "swinging" rhythms and a "Hollywood finish"—code for the new, American qualities of Schoenberg's music that were considered a positive improvement.[224] With both his piano concerto and the *Ode to Napoleon* recorded by the OWI for international distribution (see chapter 2), the new "American" Schoenberg also could be appropriated for U.S. propaganda by highlighting the continued modernism of the "Einstein of music" in the land of the free.

Schoenberg was not the only Austro-German composer to turn to American themes and English texts. Ernst Krenek composed a set of variations on the balladeer John Jacob Niles's Christmas carol "I Wonder as I Wander," based on a folk-song fragment he encountered in the southern Appalachian town of Murphy, North Carolina, in his *Symphonic Movement*, op. 94, in 1942. The next year he turned to Civil War poems by the American novelist Herman Melville for his *Cantata for Wartime*, op. 95. The variations on "I Wonder as I Wander" were commissioned by Dimitri Mitropoulos for the Minneapolis Symphony Orchestra, with whom Krenek collaborated closely during his tenure at Hamline University in St. Paul, Minnesota.[225] The composer tried to integrate what he thought was a southern folk song with twelve-tone techniques, bringing together the two idioms he associated with America and Europe, respectively. "The problem is," he wrote in his diary, "how to contrive thematic material of monumental simplicity in the new complex idiom. Now, in this case I derive the material from the folk song, so the simplicity is secured, and complexity comes in through development."[226] Premièred not in Minneapolis but during Mitropoulos's first appearance as a guest conductor with the New York Philharmonic on December 20, 1942, the work received a relatively positive reception. Mitropoulos announced that he considered it to be "the beginning of a new period in the composer's creative career, the work being less aggressive and more mellow than his earlier endeavors."[227]

As with Schoenberg, the emphasis lay on the possible shift—forged through American exile—from a radical modernism perceived as alienating to a tempered and hence acceptable form of new music that combined the best of both worlds. Even though Krenek privately despised (at least if one is to trust his diary) the Americanism "now identified with the return to the soil, romanticism, [and] irrationalism," his public statements about the *Symphonic Movement* talked about the inspiration he found in the song recording and the "very unusual modal pattern of the simple and moving tune."[228] Noel Straus lauded the promising opening but was less impressed with the rest of the work. He found it "hard to reconcile the quasi-Schoenbergian and thoroughly European treatment of the dissonant music with the inherent nature of the theme which inspired it." While Straus recognized the attempted fusion in this work, he found that it lacked "a compelling sense of unity."[229] For Krenek, the perceived American rejection of dodecaphony (and modernism more generally) was hard to accept. He was distressed by what he considered an inescapable "wave of fascism," paradoxically present in the arguments made by some Americans against twelve-tone composition that drew on anti-Fascist rhetoric by characterizing dodecaphony as "a symbol and parallel of totalitarianism."[230] As an antidote to the twelve-tone technique, one American commentator suggested "relaxing" that infamous "international style"; Krenek wondered "whether my attempts to modify the twelve-tone technique are to be interpreted as such relaxing measures."[231]

The fact that "international" here becomes almost a code word for "un-American"—a parallel too close for comfort to the use of the word in Nazi Germany as a negative signifier for Jewish music—exposes one of the many fault lines in the musical universalism claimed by and for the United States during the war years, as many exiled composers must have realized given their various attempts to negotiate the issues. Austro-German composers such as Hindemith, Schoenberg, Krenek, and many others faced particular complexities in terms of identity politics in exile, especially after the United States entered the war. The proud proclamation of one's name, birth, and race that the French poet Saint-John Perse had called for at the culmination of his poem *Exile* was not an option for them—at least not publicly. It was no accident that both Schoenberg and Weill celebrated their American citizenship as a milestone in their new life, and works such as the *Ode to Napoleon Buonaparte* and Weill's *Mine Eyes Have Seen the Glory* (see chapter 1) made a public and easily discernible statement on their composers' pro-American loyalties. Yet both Schoenberg and Krenek held on to their dodecaphonic foundation in these overtly American works as a way of preserving key aspects of their pre-exile identity even in their adaptation to their new home.[232] The stronger the retention of that identity, the more problems these composers faced, even in a public discourse that was willing at least in some cases to camouflage rather than emphasize issues of nationality. It is probably no coincidence that the exiled German composer who was most successful in the United States—at least in terms of making a living outside of a secure university or similar position—was the one most willing and able to adapt to new circumstances: Kurt Weill. But of course, Weill paid the price in terms of his subsequent critical reception.

The Axis exiles perhaps best able to negotiate these thickets of identity politics were, in fact, the Italians. There are a number of reasons: Italy's own relatively recent record in fighting for liberation; a long history of

Italian–American association (and emigration); and even, perhaps, the feeling that the country mattered less in the new geopolitical world order. Nor
did the Italians, at least, play for high stakes in the game of musical modernism. Neither Mario Castelnuovo-Tedesco nor Arturo Toscanini, for example,
hid their nationality; rather, they stood as figureheads in the U.S. contingent
of Italian anti-Fascist resistance.[233] For his American audiences, Toscanini
remained the great Italian conductor who had spurned both Mussolini's
Milan and Hitler's Bayreuth to come to the United States. In the OWI propaganda film featuring Verdi's *Hymn of Nations* (see chapter 2), Toscanini is
portrayed as "the son of a soldier of Garibaldi," refusing "to allow his music
to become the servant of tyrants." But for all Toscanini's championship
of democracy, the film's narrator insisted that Toscanini's "thoughts have
never been far from his beloved Italy."[234] In June 1942 he had called on his
anti-Fascist credentials to claim the American première of Shostakovich's
Seventh Symphony when he wrote to Stokowski how he was taken by the
work's "antifascist meaning," asking whether it would not be "very interesting for every body and yourself too, to hear the old Italian conductor (one
of the first artist, who strenuously fought against fascism) to play this work
of a young Russian antinazi composer?"[235] Given Toscanini's own commitment both to the American war effort and to the fight against Fascism—
which entailed a continued and prominent form of public testimony and
private engagement—it was galling to see his British conducting colleague
Sir Thomas Beecham being received in the United States without question
as a musician faithful to the Allied cause when—at least so far as Toscanini
was concerned—Beecham's close involvement with Hitler's Germany before
1938 cast strong doubts on his political allegiances. In a furious letter to Olin
Downes, Toscanini complained that music lovers in war-torn Great Britain
toiled "with joy, faith, love and hope in their own fatherland," while "that
nazi-sympathizer man...lives here, in America protected, adulated and hon-
oured by critics and american public."[236] Downes ignored the letter—as was
his wont when art collided with politics (witness the Erika Mann debate)—
and continued to praise Beecham as a conductor. But Toscanini remained in
the public eye a staunch anti-Fascist in defense of "democratic Italy," happy
to receive the cheers of his American audiences.[237]

Whereas Toscanini had left Fascist Italy early on, Castelnuovo-Tedesco
remained in his beloved Florence until the 1938 anti-Semitic racial laws made
it impossible to stay. He decided—for the good of his family, he wrote—to
emigrate to the United States; but, as he explained in 1956, this was a "*huge
rupture*...a near-physical rupture from which I have struggled to recover,
and from which (I confess) I have not entirely healed." He described his new

life as that of a nomad "suspended between two worlds."[238] In the United States he first presented himself as an Italian composer and pianist, whether on the concert stage or in newspapers such as the *New York Times*.[239] After he moved from New York to Los Angeles to work for Metro-Goldwyn-Mayer in the fall of 1940, his main musical activities were those of a sought-after film composer, although many of his contributions (especially in the war years) remained uncredited.[240] Besides his film work, he continued to write for the concert hall, including a set titled *Indian Songs and Dances*, op. 116 (1942), and *An American Rhapsody*, premièred by Alexander Smallens on August 11, 1943.[241] His new musical allegiances were obvious.

He recast his Italian identity in those years as Jewish in the music he wrote for the local synagogue in Westwood, California. The *Sacred Service (for Sabbath Eve)*, op. 122, was composed in December 1943 at the request of the synagogue's rabbi. "Because it was intended for a reform Synagogue," the composer explained, "the work had to be for a 'Cantorial' soloist (in this case a baritone, though afterwards, other synagogues wanted it for a tenor), mixed chorus, and organ." This composition brought Castelnuovo-Tedesco back to his musical, cultural, and religious roots: "At any rate (because I was born in Italy), I decided to follow the Italian polyphonic tradition. The choral education I received from Pizzetti was more 'Monteverdian' than 'Palestrinian' and besides, I remembered a humorous thing that Pizzetti once said to me with reference to some choruses that I wrote in school—'You write like a Jewish Monteverdi.' Therefore, I decided to write precisely like the 'Jewish Monteverdi,' but intentionally this time."[242] For Castelnuovo-Tedesco, his nationality had become inextricably intertwined with the religious identity that had forced his exile. Here his path was similar to that of Milhaud, Schoenberg, Weill, and other Jewish refugees who reaffirmed their religious identity in the wake of anti-Semitic persecution.

Similar thoughts about cultural identity returned in a speech that Castelnuovo-Tedesco delivered during the Musicians Congress in 1944 in a panel on music under Fascism that included Theodor W. Adorno, Hanns Eisler, and Paul Nettl. In this speech Castelnuovo-Tedesco insisted that Fascism was, and remained, the enemy, but he made a clear distinction between Nazi ideology and Italian Fascism. Before Italian cultural politics was contaminated by Nazi Germans, Castelnuovo-Tedesco claimed, Italy maintained a pluralist culture in which he himself could continue to flourish, even though he never was an "accomplice" of the Fascists: "While German Nazism came up with a very precise ideological program, with very definite prejudices and all sort of limitations, Italian Fascism, at least at its start, had none of them; they came much later, in its final phase, and were mostly accepted from the Nazis, as one of the conditions to their 'alliance'; they were not only 'foreign' to the spirit of the Italian people but even to the initial apparition of their government."[243] Here Castelnuovo-Tedesco's more accommodating reasoning diverged sharply from Toscanini's uncompromising anti-Fascism, yet both musicians could maintain their pride in Italian culture. Just as French exiles were split into those who sympathized with Vichy and those who supported de Gaulle, so Italian ones covered a range of responses to Mussolini. Once Italy was under the direct influence of Nazi Germany, however, Italian exiles in the United States rallied in their denunciation of totalitarianism, both in such speeches as Castelnuovo-Tedesco's and in such performances as Toscanini's OWI film.

Indeed, whether in the case of Allied exiles such as Milhaud or Martinů or in that of musicians who had fled from Axis countries, musical composition and performance were powerful means of negotiating the complex and competing demands of exile—between past and present, between the lost home and the new one, between the composers and their audiences. While music's oft-evoked quality as an expressive medium unbound by semantic specificity made processes of adaptation and translation both more fluid and less obvious than those of language, the strategies of cultural transfer at work during the war were nevertheless shaped by the specific situation of the United States as a host country. It is precisely because the musical landscape in America before the war—with its transnational repertoire and national compositional concerns—had already put into place a system of cultural transfer that such a wide range of composers could shape their individual responses to their new environment. A neoclassicist like Martinů and a dodecaphonist like Schoenberg could each find points of access into the culture of their new home because of its unique configuration. On the one hand, the celebration of national identities had long been a part of musical practice in the United States, and exiled musicians were thus able to find myriad ways in which to engage with national identity, both their own (witness the different strategies of Milhaud and Hindemith) and that of their host (as in the case of Schoenberg and Krenek). On the other, the long American history of cultural appropriation—the ardor of which was renewed during the war—created a construct of musical universality that allowed musicians from either Allied or Axis cultures to immerse their own compositional concerns into the musical practices of their new home. The same composer—and Hindemith is the perfect example—could thus be both foreign and American in his musical production, and at times even in the same work.

CHAPTER FIVE | "Hail Muse Americana!"

To celebrate July 4, 1944, New York radio station WQXR broadcast solely works by American composers all day long. The American philosopher and poet Irwin Edman wrote a somewhat cheeky poem in response to this patriotic zeal. Titled "Muse Americana," it opens:

Oh, splendid isolation this,
Today no transatlantic muses!
Today for strictly homemade bliss,
For local lyres one enthuses.[1]

Edman's poem poked gentle fun at the "blessed patriotic mood" and "chauvinistic fervor" that replaced the works of Bach, Beethoven, and Brahms with compositions by "home-grown talent." Whereas tomorrow, he ended his poem, the musical world would, once again, be "wide and vast—/ Today, hail Muse Americana!"

Though treated here with a light hand, the themes in Edman's poem touched on several key issues in U.S. musical culture during World War II: an unapologetic nationalist chauvinism, its associated anxieties about provincialism, and the cultural need for fervent expressions of patriotism during wartime. At the heart of the debate were the long-standing quest for an American identity in art music and the issue of how native composers might someday prevail in the nation's musical life. Similar discussions had taken place in the United States as early as the nineteenth century and regained currency in the 1930s, but with the outbreak of the war, patriotic dedication risked being conflated with blinkered jingoism in a binary world of enemies and allies.[2] In this respect Pearl Harbor became a watershed event in the United States. Even though musical Americanism in and of itself was not a new phenomenon—on the contrary, its history reaches back into the eighteenth century—its wartime incarnation was unusually pronounced. Blatant Americanism was nothing more than the U.S. brand of the nationalist posturing that was rampant among both Axis and Allied nations; it was tempered, however, by the openly critical responses of musicians and critics alike and by a cultural practice that—because of its cosmopolitan concert repertoire—remained unabashedly universalist at its core.

Composers put pro-American sentiment during World War II to good use in support of their works. William Grant Still, for example, declared in an article published in the *Chicago Defender* in 1942 that "we, as Americans, need to become proud of our own achievements in this field and learn more about them. We should adopt our own culture in preference to the culture of any other nation or nations on earth. Now is the time to make a complete swing in that direction. Since it is patriotic to be American, we should let our Americanism extend to every field of endeavor....It is worth just as much to our future as carrying a gun against the enemy." His concluding sentence drove the point home: "Music for morale? Certainly. But let it be AMERICAN music!"[3] Still's was one of the crasser comments about the need for a compositional Americanism that could be justified by the exigencies of the time, though others shared his sentiment. William Schuman made it clear that "the most important music of the day...is being written in America by Americans."[4] For Morton Gould, composing American music was a fact of life: "I am an American, so I write American music....I am influenced, consciously and unconsciously, by the musical currency of my place." But for all his musical Americanism, there was "no reason for packaging and labeling my music 'Made in the U.S.A.' and then making a fetish of it." Clearly, for Gould there was a line between nationalism and chauvinism that he did not wish to cross, for music was always in danger of being "singled out for repression in reactionary periods."[5]

Whereas Gould expressed reservations about openly fetishistic Americanism, few musicians were as stridently and deliberately nationalist as Roy Harris, whose persona as a "ruggedly" American composer "of the soil and of the people" was bolstered by the war. His task as a wartime composer, Harris claimed, was to capture "the emotional characteristics and qualities of America in this period of its people."[6] As the "great white hope" of American music, the composer had acquired a loyal following among U.S. concert and radio audiences, who considered his works to be music "that expresses us Americans, and today more than ever we need the strength that comes through this expression."[7] One radio listener responded to the announcement that the Boston Symphony Orchestra would broadcast the première of Harris's Fifth Symphony with unbridled enthusiasm, claiming that "Americans want American music."[8] Although Harris spent most of the war as a college educator, once he clinched a senior government position by taking over as the OWI's music director in the spring of 1945 (see chapter 2), the unrestrained promotion of American music became his chief purpose. His predecessor's wife, Sidney Robertson Cowell, recalled in rather sharp tones that "American programs not only multiplied in number," but also for the most part "leaned heavily on the music of Harris (played by his wife Johana), on the sincere ground that no other American composer was as completely American."[9]

It was precisely this kind of hooray-patriotism and nationalist mobilization of the arts that led the more cautious Roger Sessions to warn his fellow composers quite explicitly that using art for political ends was a kind of quasi-Fascism.[10] He identified the threat as "the present trend towards nationalism and cultural isolationism among American musicians" and made clear its affinities when he pointed out that "a certain number of our musicians, together with a not negligible part of our musical press, is demanding with a voice quite reminiscent of various totalitarian phrases which we have heard, that music which shall express 'the national feeling,' 'reflect the American scene,' 'establish an American style.'"[11] For Sessions, this pernicious trend was embodied in the kind of antiformalist musical aesthetic that put accessibility before artistic integrity. The composer feared that "the reactionary coalition in the U.S." was well on its way to destroying civilization, and in a letter to John Duke he again evoked the specter of Fascism, fearing that in the current political context art would simply be one half of a bread-and-circuses formula.[12]

Harris and Sessions could be seen as representing the two outermost boundaries of American discourse about national and political identity in music in and around the war years, but other musicians placed themselves somewhere along this continuum in their comments and compositions. If Earl Robinson and Virgil Thomson leaned more toward Harris's nationalist position, for example, John Cage was clearly closer to Sessions's transnationalist views. In some form or other, however, the vast majority of American composers engaged musically with the war and with their national identity, often by highlighting American-themed compositions, which increased exponentially in number. Purely abstract music carried the suspicion of avoiding the issues, as Blitzstein warned Copland: "What are your plans, after *North Star*? The Violin Sonata? Why not? It takes all kinds of pieces to make a culture. What one has to be sure of is that the work comes out of no escapism."[13] A composer—so this line of thought went—might choose to write in a more formalist vein so long as that choice did not indicate a lack of patriotic engagement. The resulting works ranged from simple songs to symphonic frescoes and were often cast as musical commemorations or patriotic celebrations. Typically, such pieces would engage with specific aspects of American identity by way of musical references or through a programmatic title, and very often both. By thus providing an interpretive frame for contemporary audiences and critics, composers shaped the reception of these works within the parameters of musical Americana during the war.

Commemoration and Patriotic Celebration

One significant cluster of patriotic and commemorative wartime compositions was made up of the seventeen works commissioned by the League of Composers in 1943 and intended to be premièred during the 1943–44 season of the New York Philharmonic Orchestra.[14] Among the composers who contributed were John Alden Carpenter, Henry Cowell, Norman Dello Joio, Roy Harris, Bernard Herrmann, Quincy Porter, Roger Sessions, and William Grant Still, each of whom wrote a short orchestral work "commemorative of the present war."[15] Artur Rodzinski claimed in the concert programs that he considered the commissions to serve "three excellent purposes": the preservation of culture in the United States, the creation of "a living musical record of various aspects of this war," and the encouragement of contemporary composers in this country.[16] For all the rhetoric about a musical contribution to the war effort, however, Rodzinski and his orchestra performed only half of the commissioned works: seven in the 1943–44 season, and one straggler in 1944–45 (Walter Piston's *Fugue on a Victory Tune*). By the summer of 1944 the war had turned in favor of the Allies, and victory music was now more appropriate; such melancholy or even grim pieces as Norman Dello Joio's *To a Lone Sentry* or Roger Sessions's *Dirge*—dropped by Rodzinski—no longer fit the bill.

The seven works that Rodzinski chose to première during the 1943–44 season were all specifically tied to the events of the war. Three of them were memorials to the dead: Herrmann's *For the Fallen*, Martinů's *Memorial to Lidice*, and Still's *In Memoriam*. The other four dealt with American warfare and military life: Nicolai Berezowsky's *Soldier on the Town*, Carpenter's *The Anxious Bugler*, Harris's *March in Time of War*, and Bernard Rogers's *Invasion*. By balancing commemoration and patriotic engagement in his selection for the season, Rodzinski's approach reflected broader trends in musical and cultural responses to the war in the United States, where public coping with the tremendous loss of life called both for acknowledgment of heroic deaths in memorials and for ennobling these sacrifices by celebrating their patriotic meaning.

The public commemoration of the dead, with the dual goal of providing solace and forging a national consensus, has a long history in the post-Enlightenment West—witness the cult of the revolutionary martyrs in France after 1789, which translated monarchic and religious rites into civic rituals that could be either performative or frozen in time and space by way of monuments.[17] Whereas France, Britain, and other European nations developed a national (if sometimes contested) repertoire of public tribute to wartime sacrifice during the nineteenth and early twentieth centuries, the United States was divided, after 1865, along the Mason-Dixon Line in its commemorative responses to the Civil War. It took World War I and its "accumulated presence of death" to unite the nation in the remembrance of countrymen who perished in combat.[18] In the U.S. capital, servicemen killed in action were commemorated and symbolically laid to rest in the Tomb of the Unknowns in Arlington National Cemetery in November 1921. Memorials of the Great War in the United States and elsewhere enshrined the myth of the fallen as the heroic embodiment of sacrifice, and they often represented the soldiers as "sleeping dead," resting in peace.[19] As President Warren G. Harding proclaimed at the inauguration of the tomb on Armistice Day, 1921, the "unknown soldier" and his brethren were now "sleeping in these hallowed grounds." He had "died for his country," Harding reminded his audience, "and greater devotion hath no man than this. He died unquestioning, uncomplaining, with faith in his heart and hope on his lips, that his country should triumph and its civilization survive."[20] This form of remembrance turned the fallen into patriotic saints, a sacralization that would dominate military commemoration through the interwar years and into World War II.[21] But it also led to a second strand of memorial culture in the United States, that of the living memorial: a contribution to the democratic community in the form of, for example, a public space and its associated activities dedicated to the memory of those who died, as if they could thus share in the living community of Americans and serve as an inspiration to their fellow citizens.[22]

When the United States entered the war after Pearl Harbor, memorials for those who died in battle were once again needed to provide public recognition of loss, a site for grief, and a justification of sacrifice. Music provided an ideal form of commemoration in this context, for it combined aspects of the monument (as a fixed compositional text) and the living memorial (as a shared experience). "Instead of statues as war memorials," Isabel Morse Jones claimed, "this new war-generation intends to bring music and other arts closer to the life of all."[23] Thus, when Herrmann and Still wrote their musical war memorials in 1943, they drew on the tropes of the fallen hero and the sleeping dead. Herrmann's short orchestral work *For the Fallen* was, in the composer's words, "a tribute to the war's dead. It is a berceuse for those who lie asleep on the many alien battlefields of this war."[24] Written in a post-Mahlerian idiom, the work opens with a 6/8 undulation in the strings, outlining a descending tetrachord (a typical sign of lament) in the first note of each measure (mm. 1–4). This then provides the melodic contour for the headmotive of the first theme (mm. 5–8) in the high register of the bassoon. A second theme, presented by the horns (starting in m. 16), emphasizes the lullaby gesture in a descending three-note motive on which that theme is built. As the work unfolds and the various motives begin to be superimposed and symphonically developed, the texture evolves from the undulation of a berceuse into a heavily accented climactic section with the full orchestra. The piece winds down with the successive statement of three themes: the second in the oboe and English horn, then the first, again in the bassoons, and finally a quotation of a well-known melody from Handel's *Messiah*, "He shall feed His flock like a shepherd," here a flute duo in parallel thirds. The quotation stands out both harmonically and instrumentally, a deliberate anachronism in the chromatic dissonance of the work. Yet it is not unrelated to the sonic world of the piece, for Herrmann's first and second themes are both distorted derivations from Handel's famous melody that only at that moment appears fleetingly restored, a beautiful moment in a world of death that carries both nostalgic and utopian traits.[25] This melody brings not the consolation and finality of Bach's chorale "Es ist genug" in Alban Berg's 1935 Violin Concerto, but a view through a glass, darkly, of a different world at peace.

Still's *In Memoriam*, on the other hand, paid tribute to the figure of the "fallen soldier" as the embodiment of the greater struggle between good and evil in an archetypal construct of heroic sacrifice. His hero was not the symbolic unknown soldier, but the first American serviceman killed in action—who, as the composer pointed out, "was a Negro soldier."[26] Written to commemorate "The Colored Soldiers Who Died for Democracy" (the work's subtitle), *In Memoriam* combined the heroic gesture of a military fanfare with a lyrical theme drawing deliberately on the gesture of a spiritual.[27] Developing its themes both contrapuntally and in several call-and-response sequences, the score culminates in two expansive climactic segments. The first is interrupted in m. 49 by a *ffff* cymbal beat; the second concludes the work in an orchestral apotheosis, based on the fanfare motive and once more pushed to the dynamic level of *ffff* supported by timpani, snare drums, and cymbal. The masculinist, monumental affirmation leaves no doubt: the fallen African American soldier was a true hero.[28] Though short—in keeping with the limits set by the League of Composers—Still's work carries traits of emphatic symphonic aspirations through its complex thematic development and contrapuntal texture, and not the least in the unmistakable allusion to Dvořák's "New World" Symphony (the second-movement Largo) when—in the opening sequence of *In Memoriam*—the spiritual-like theme is presented in the English horn over low strings after a short mournful fanfare by the muted trumpets and winds. While Still's spiritual-inflected melody starts in B-flat minor (the relative minor to Dvořák's D-flat major), it winds its way to D-flat major by the cadence in mm. 14–15. These are not Still's first intertextual references to Dvořák's symphony, though they are more prominent and transparent here than in the *Afro-American Symphony*.[29] By relating this musical war memorial back to the "foundational" work of the "Great American Symphony"—and Dvořák was seen as honoring African American music through the great European concert tradition—Still asserted an aesthetic claim not only for his composition, but also for his program. Audiences of the New York première would have been able to make this sonic connection immediately, since Dvořák's symphony followed Still's *In Memoriam* on the program (Figure 5.1).

Both white and black critics acknowledged the music's African American character and discussed its message. The *Pittsburgh Courier* lauded the "noted composer" for capturing "the feeling of the brave Yankee Doodle Tans fighting all over the world" and "paying special tribute to the first American soldier to give his life for democracy who was colored."[30] Nora Holt, whose highly informed criticism appeared regularly in the columns of the *New York Amsterdam News*, discussed the work in great detail, pointing out that "the idiom of the spiritual was employed rather than facsimile motifs." Her description of the first climax hedged that it was "not program music" even as she heard "the tramp of feet, the humming from weary throats, sending up a prayer in the moment of death and destruction, when the crash of a cymbal portends oblivion." The final apotheosis, for Holt, was "a resplendent closing...presaging undying hope for the future."[31] W. E. B. Du Bois not only rejoiced in the performance of *In Memoriam* but also found it "fitting that this work should have been bracketed with Dvorak's New World Symphony."[32]

For white critics, Still's musical reference to African American idioms gave the work its attractiveness but marginalized it into a special-interest composition. Downes thought that Still had produced a work about "the

THE PHILHARMONIC-SYMPHONY SOCIETY
1842 OF NEW YORK 1878
CONSOLIDATED 1928
ARTUR RODZINSKI, Musical Director

1943	ONE HUNDRED SECOND SEASON	1944

CARNEGIE HALL

*WEDNESDAY EVENING, JANUARY 5, 1944, AT 8:45
FRIDAY AFTERNOON, JANUARY 7, 1944, AT 2:30
4055th and 4056th Concerts

Under the Direction of
ARTUR RODZINSKI

Assisting Artist:
RUTH POSSELT, Violinist

PROGRAM

WILLIAM GRANT STILL   "In Memoriam: The Colored
                     Soldiers Who Died for Democracy"
                     (First performance)

DVORAK   Symphony in E minor, No. 5, "From the
                     New World," Opus 95

       I. Adagio; Allegro molto
      II. Largo
    III. Scherzo
    IV. Allegro con fuoco

INTERMISSION

DUKELSKY   Concerto for Violin and Orchestra
       I. Allegro molto   in G minor
     II. Valse
   III. Tema con variazioni e coda
       (First performance in New York)
RUTH POSSELT

STRAVINSKY   Suite from the Ballet, "The Fire Bird"

---

* Instead of Thursday Evening.

ARTHUR JUDSON, Manager   BRUNO ZIRATO, Associate Manager
    THE STEINWAY is the Official Piano of The Philharmonic-Symphony Society
COLUMBIA AND VICTOR RECORDS
ORCHESTRA PENSION FUND—*It is requested that subscribers who are unable to use their tickets kindly return them to the Philharmonic-Symphony Offices, 113 W. 57th St., or to the Box Office, Carnegie Hall, at their choice either to be sold for the benefit of the Orchestra Pension Fund, or given to the uniformed men through the local organizations instituted for this purpose. All tickets received will be acknowledged*
"Buy War Bonds and Stamps"

C# 1435

FIGURE 5.1 Program for the concert of the New York Philharmonic Orchestra on January 5 and 7, 1944, under the direction of Artur Rodzinski. Courtesy of the New York Philharmonic Archives.

heroes of his own race."[33] Though Downes found it among the best of the series of League commissions, his description focused on what marked the work racially: the "semi-barbaric chant" at the beginning of the work and "a second lyrical melody of the 'spiritual' type."[34] Felix Borowski found the work "moving," and "not the less so because its material, much of it in the nature of the Negro spiritual, was definitely racial."[35] Claudia Cassidy was among the few who did not emphasize the African American character of the work, describing it instead as "a harsh requiem" and "terse music, rejecting mourning," yet "deeply felt and quickly effective."[36] She was the exception among reviewers in assessing the work predominantly for its potential as a musical memorial for all.

Still's was, indeed, a political work, and in his commentary on *In Memoriam* he emphasized the point: "Our civilization has known no greater patriotism, no greater loyalty than that shown by the colored men who fight and die for democracy. Those who return will, I hope, come back to a better world. I also hope that our tribute to those who died will be to make the democracy for which they fought greater and broader than it has ever been before."[37] Still was all too aware of the bitter irony that African Americans were fighting abroad for freedom and equality that eluded them at home.[38] In expressing the hope that African Americans returning from the battlefield might find better conditions, Still aligned himself with the rhetoric of the Double V Campaign, started by the *Pittsburgh Courier* in 1942, which linked the battle against Fascism abroad to the internal struggle for civil rights.[39] At the same time, by celebrating African American contributions to the armed conflict (in 1945 Still wrote a *Fanfare for the 99th Fighter Squadron* honoring the Tuskegee Airmen), Still joined other leading intellectuals tied to the Harlem Renaissance in encouraging black enlistment as a strategy for equality. Langston Hughes, for example, directly addressed Jim Crow laws in *Brothers*, a radio play "written in an attempt to face and resolve some of the problems troubling the minds of some American Negro citizens today in regard to our war effort and their own unresolved problems of democracy at home."[40] In it, an enlisted seaman confronts his younger brother, who refuses to enlist "as long as old Jim Crow's a captain in the army." Fighting Hitler in Europe, the older brother points out, meant fighting the "little Hitlers" and fifth columnists in the United States, for Hitler would support them, making "a double-barreled padlocked ghetto out of Harlem" should he win the war and bringing over "the Gestapo to back up the Ku Klux Klan."[41] Service in the armed forces, in the eyes of Hughes and other African American leaders such as the union boss Philip Randolph, combined patriotic duty with commitment to civil rights. In this context, Still's *In Memoriam* could only be the kind of "harsh requiem" Cassidy had identified, and it needed a final triumphant apotheosis as a musical expression of African American pride. A lullaby like Herrmann's would not do as a memorial when so much was at stake.

The third of the musical memorials of the New York Philharmonic series, Martinů's *Memorial to Lidice*, focused on those Nazi atrocities that had shaken the Western world in June 1942. "According to the composer," Robert Bagar wrote in the program note for the work's première, "the work is in the nature of a religious chant, constructed along the lines of a prayer and response based on a theme which resembles in style the ancient Czech church melodies."[42] As we saw in chapter 4, Martinů chose a restrained idiom closer to Herrmann's concept of a musical memorial, though like Still he relied on motivic material deeply associated with his cause. But Martinů's was not the only musical work in the United States shaped by the events at Lidice. Two earlier compositions responded to this massacre at least to some extent, though neither was shaped specifically as a musical memorial in the way Martinů's was. One was George Antheil's Symphony no. 4, "1942," written that year and "deeply influenced"—so the composer said—by the war. He described the second movement as "tragic—news of Lidice and the horrors in Poland had just come in."[43] Lidice also played a role in Paul Creston's *Chant of 1942*, which, according to the composer, echoed the war events of that year, including "the acts of barbarism in the degradation of Poland and Greece, and the murder of Lidice."[44] The episodic and fragmented quality, of Creston's work captures the roller coaster of American response to the war in the first year of U.S. involvement, from anguish to chauvinist triumphalism. Drawing on such familiar musical devices as sighing violin figures and dramatic percussion eruptions, *Chant of 1942* moves from the continuously changing character of the first part into a frantic middle section before the final part builds up over a timpani ostinato—with the relentless drive and sonorities familiar from Maurice Ravel's *Boléro*—to end in a triumphalist fanfare. The contrast with Martinů's taut, poignantly reflective score could hardly be greater.

Though Creston's work clearly responded to the death and suffering caused by the war, its compositional and ideological approaches were in fact more closely related to the patriotic and militaristic compositions that made up the second group of the series commissioned by the League of Composers and premièred by the New York Philharmonic in the 1943–44 season. These four works focused on soldiers in action (or during recreation) and on military campaigns. The piece that opened the series was Rogers's *Invasion*. Written around the time of the Allied landing on Sicily, the composition followed the same trajectory from darkness to triumph as Creston's *Chant of 1942*: "Its intention is to evoke an atmosphere and mood of anxious tension and foreboding. Its introduction is of dark character, followed by episodes of nervous and, finally, vigorous nature."[45] The familiar symphonic plot of struggle and resolution is here applied to the American war experience: the symbolic transformation of musical materials is a metaphor for military developments and the turn to victory.

The compositional strategy of symbolic transformation as musical allegory is most obvious in those wartime works that—like Harris's *March in Time of War*—rely on a variation form for their organizational structure. Based on the American folk song "True Love, Don't Weep," Harris's march was a tribute "to the American composers in the armed services."[46] Though not unsuccessful in the concert hall, it did not match the popularity of one of Harris's earlier patriotic works, an overture based on the Civil War tune "When Johnny Comes Marching Home" (1935). Nor did it come close to the broad appeal of Morton Gould's widely performed *American Salute* (1943), a piece of Americana in which the composer created a set of variations on the same song. *American Salute* has an easily followed musical narrative leading from national tribute through commemoration to victorious triumphalism: a fanfarelike opening; the dramatic buildup from the low woodwinds to the full orchestra, with its prominent percussion section and (from m. 78) jazzy syncopations; the work's subsequent shift (in m. 116) to a slower-moving minor section, bell references included; and a triumphant tutti ending (mm. 157–81).[47] The *Los Angeles Times* music critic praised the "rollicking number" as a composition "as American as *The Stars and Stripes Forever*, and that personifies Uncle Sam."[48] Few melodies were deemed as well suited to represent "Uncle Sam" at this time as "When Johnny Comes Marching Home"— Gould himself pointed out that "for an American representation I can think of no better song for this purpose than 'Johnny.'"[49] Not only had the song been appropriated by both sides in the Civil War (and in subsequent U.S. military engagements), but its eponymous hero also had the name often associated with American GIs. What makes *American Salute* so successful a piece of wartime Americana, however, is the complete unselfconsciousness with which Gould drew on a smorgasbord of musical signifiers and stylistic elements—from Tin Pan Alley rhythms to the sonorities of Hector Berlioz's *Symphonie fantastique*—in creating his Americanist narrative.

Herein lies the key difference between the kind of propagandist surface Americana employed in *American Salute* and the compositional concerns with a national musical idiom that guided composers such as Cowell and Copland in their quest for an American musical vernacular (see chapter 3), even though both approaches reflected similar nationalist impulses that were amplified by the heightened wartime patriotism. If anything, this type of musical Americana pushed composers toward greater musical conventionalism. Marion Bauer's *American Youth Concerto* for piano and orchestra (1943), for example, is infused with the sonorities of Rachmaninoff, especially in the first movement's opening minor theme and its presentation in a combination of lush strings and piano arpeggios in the lower register that mimics the opening of the all-time-favorite Second Piano Concerto by the Russian composer.[50] Although Bauer shapes the second theme as a somewhat perky march, the movement is dominated by the sumptuous romanticism of the first. For all its nods to blue notes, the sentimental lyricism of the second movement remains no less mired in the sonic universe of Rachmaninoff. Only the third movement seems to shift into unabashed Americana, with a lively hoedown and cakewalk framing a slower blues section. Here Bauer's instrumentation draws on popular American sound worlds, from woodblocks to saxophones. Even in this movement, however, Bauer retains the heightened lyricism of the earlier two when the violins take over the blues in a luxuriantly soaring passage. This play with late-romantic sonorities was rather unusual for Bauer, but it is not at all untypical for Americana composed during the war years. Nor was it too far from the nostalgic sound world of another wartime piano concerto, Richard Adinsell's *Warsaw Concerto* (1941), which featured prominently in the British war film *Dangerous Moonlight* (released in the United States in 1942). Indeed, by integrating American vernacular styles into lyrical symphonism, Bauer's *American Youth Concerto*, with its unrestrained pathos, embodied an expressive register similar to those found in wartime dramas from *Sergeant York* (1941) and *So Proudly We Hail* (1942) to *Happy Land* (1943) and *Since You Went Away* (1944).[51] These cultural artifacts carried an emphatic nationalist message of which conventionalism was, in effect, an essential component.

Another quality that the two remaining League of Composers commissions from the 1943–44 season share with Hollywood and Broadway was the focus on military life from the perspective of the soldier. Nicolai Berezowsky's *Soldier on the Town* was the sole lighthearted piece in the series—"an attempt to portray soldiers on leave on a week-end pass anywhere, any town."[52] The antics of soldiers and sailors on leave and their interactions with American civilians (especially women) were a standard trope in Hollywood movies and Broadway shows even before the war, as in the film musical *Born to Dance* (1936), but they became prominent in movies and musicals after Pearl Harbor, whether set in Los Angeles as in *Anchors Aweigh* (1945) or in the New York of *On the Town* (1944), a musical by Leonard Bernstein inspired by Jerome Robbins's ballet *Fancy Free* (also 1944). These were soldiers who were young and alive and enjoying their well-deserved R & R on native soil. The danger and destruction of war is far away, so their music cannot be but cheerful or (once the love interest enters the plot) romantic.

However, the other League commissions representing soldiers in combat reached for the musical idioms discussed earlier in the context of commemorative and patriotic works such as *For the Fallen*, *In Memoriam*, *Chant of 1942*, and *American Salute*. Carpenter's *The Anxious Bugler* veers between fear and nostalgia, and Dello Joio's *To a Lone Sentry* (1943)—one of the works eventually performed elsewhere—draws on nostalgic memories and solitary danger: "Sentries walk their posts at night. The man alone has only thoughts for company. Great distance makes these thoughts vivid. The strong ties of friends and loves become painfully real to the man alone. Recapturing both the sad and happy memories of a once peaceful life helps to pass the time of the sentinel's solitary vigil."[53] These two are among only a few concert works that attempted to take the listener into the emotional realm of American servicemen in the war theater. Fewer still took for their program major battles, though in his symphonic movement, *Bataan* (1942), Harl McDonald tried his hand at a dramatic battle piece, heavy on brass and percussion.[54] But for most, musical portrayals of soldiers in combat were limited to the myriad of wartime film scores, in both motion pictures and documentaries. Music for combat documentaries, such as Gail Kubik's score for *Memphis Belle* (1944), served different functions, however, from patriotic concert pieces.[55] Because the visual and verbal narratives of the documentary carried the semantic burden, the composer was free to leave the conventionality of musical Americana behind for extended periods to write, instead, a score that integrated modernist features only rarely found in wartime concert music.

Not all Americana composed during World War II was instrumental music, however. Composers from Elliott Carter to Roger Sessions also turned to texts by iconic American writers, from Emily Dickinson and Walt Whitman to Robert Frost and Stephen Vincent Benét, for their choral works and song compositions. Not surprisingly, Walt Whitman was the favorite choice during these years.[56] As the quintessential poetic embodiment of Americanism—"He *is* America," Ezra Pound famously wrote in 1909—Whitman was all the more attractive because so much of his poetry dealt either with war or with democratic liberty, the two key concerns of U.S. public discourse in World War II.[57] Thus, when Sessions searched for a poem in 1944 to use as the text for a short chorus with two pianos for the New York Temple Emanu-El's "Concert Salutes" to the Allies, he chose Whitman's "Turn O Libertad" from *Leaves of Grass*.[58] Sessions commented later that it was "not one of Whitman's very good poems; it just has an irreproachable sentiment to it," meaning that "Liberty wins out in the end always."[59] But the composer actually changed the opening of the poem, for Whitman's opening lines—"Turn O Libertad, for the war is over/From it and all henceforth expanding, doubting no more, resolute, sweeping the world"[60]—were not yet appropriate for the times. Instead, Sessions condensed the lines to "Turn O Libertad, no more doubting."[61]

The composer divided Whitman's poem in two halves (reflecting the text's conceit of turning from the past to the future) separated by a brief interlude for the two pianos alone. The text is set for the most part homophonically, which allows the rhythm and cadence of the poetry to come through. Each vocal section is each accompanied by a nearly relentless *perpetuum mobile*: for example, in mm. 5–34 there is hardly a measure without continuous running sixteenth notes in the pianos (the break at "slave" is an exception for obvious reasons). The technique has echoes of Stravinsky—for example the first movement of the *Symphony of Psalms*—from whom Sessions also probably took the ostinato patterns and the tendency to build up motives from interlocking fifths and fourths. Less Stravinskian, however, is the harmonic language. Session gives the work a key signature of one sharp. Although it is tempting to analyze the opening as some kind of mixed-mode G major, this reading soon founders in a welter of what one might call free atonality, wherein only motivic manipulation provides some kind of anchor. Like the sixteenth notes, this kind of free dissonance suits the text, whether to represent endless turning or, more likely, the fruitlessness of the exercise: the text is strikingly ambivalent about what the present might be able to learn, and reject, from the past. But Sessions, like his fellow wartime composers, seems to have felt the need to come up with a more apotheosizing conclusion, and as we reach the final measures, the purpose of that key signature becomes blindingly clear. At "The future, greater than all the past, is swiftly, surely, preparing for you," tonality returns in all its glory: the key signature indicated actually E minor, and the Picardy ending in the pianos (a *fff* E major chord) is magnified by the preceding A major chord in the voices, producing a rock-solid plagal cadence, like a triumphant "Amen." Indeed, for all his misgivings about the dangers of quasi-Fascist attitudes in American wartime music, even Sessions could not escape the prevailing aesthetic and political currents of his time, with their heroic triumphalism and sacralized patriotism.

William Schuman, too, chose poems from Whitman's *Leaves of Grass* for what would become his Pulitzer Prize–winning cantata *A Free Song*, completed in October 1942.[62] Amalgamating three poems (two as extracts) from this collection, Schuman created a narrative fitting for the early war years. Starting with the evocation of a peaceful nation thrown into the anguish of war ("Long, too long America"), the work moves into a commemorative middle section in E minor ("Look down, fair moon") that speaks of the "sacred moon" pouring down over the dead, who were disfigured in combat. After a long contrapuntal interlude, the composition shifts into a triumphal second choral section, titled "Song of the Banner," that celebrates the sonorous manifestations of a victorious army from the drums and trumpets to the "jubilant shouts of millions of men," ending in the full-voiced exclamation of the chorus: "We hear Liberty!"[63] Schuman made no secret of the composition's patriotic intention as a wartime contribution when he wrote to Harold Spivacke in October 1942 after having been rejected for armed service: "Since I cannot serve in the Specialist Corps I am trying to do what I can with my pen. The first work is a Cantata for Chorus and Orchestra which Koussevitzky will perform. It has wonderful words by Walt Whitman. If I've done my job well it can't help but be a moving patriotic affair."[64] But although the audience of the 1943 première responded enthusiastically to Schuman's work as a war composition, his fellow composers were somewhat caustic in their reaction. Elliot Carter found it "well-intentioned enough but not convincingly realized," Virgil Thomson insisted that it was only "superficially warlike," and Arthur Berger considered it "a real low" and contrasted it with one of Schuman's models for *A Free Song*, Beethoven's Ninth Symphony.[65] It speaks to the concerns of the time that it was Schuman's emphatically monumental Whitman setting, rather than either an abstract symphonic composition or a more mundane piece of Americana such as Copland's *Rodeo*, that in 1943 won the newly introduced Pulitzer Prize in composition.[66] When Copland did win the Pulitzer Prize two years later, the jury's report mixed up his earlier Whitmanesque composition, *Lincoln Portrait* (1942), with the prize-winning *Appalachian Spring* (1944): according to that report, *Appalachian Spring* was "very simple, using fragments of Springfield Mountain and other American folk tunes interwoven and developed with great elegance and deftness"[67] ("Springfield Mountain" does not appear in *Appalachian Spring*). *Lincoln Portrait* was furthermore on the same program as Schuman's *A Free Song* when the latter was premièred in Boston in 1943.[68]

Composers turned to Whitman not only for war poetry but also for the evocation of American nature and pastoral bliss—whether in Otto Luening's miniature *A Farm Picture* (1944) or Elliott Carter's more expansive song for soprano and chamber orchestra, *Warble for Lilac Time* (1943). For Carter, the choice of poetry was serious business—and his turn to Whitman's poem about nature and birdsong was clearly motivated by a pastoral mode of

Americana that he explored in other works of the time, such as his Symphony no. 1 (1942).[69] In the latter, Carter tried to suggest Cape Cod's "characteristic beauties and something of the extraordinary cultural background of New England."[70] When he then turned "to some Whitman songs" (of which only *Warble for Lilac Time* has survived), he stayed with the pastoral mode and the sonic evocation of place that had characterized so many Americana compositions since the nineteenth century.[71] But *Warble for Lilac Time*, while ending on a nostalgic note ("returning in reminiscence"), emphasizes music itself as the natural expression of the American soundscape in the extended *ff* melisma at the height of the soprano's range in the penultimate line, "to sing with the birds."[72] Carter's E-flat major setting—with its play on birdsong in the accompaniment—thus inscribes the composer's voice into the American landscape itself through the words of "America's Bard."

Celebrating the American Way

These various strands of commemorative and patriotic music during World War II—somber, triumphal, and pastoral—came together in a group of works that featured the founding fathers of U.S. national identity, most prominently Abraham Lincoln. Such political evocations had been molded into populist art forms during the New Deal, permeating not only the visual arts, as in the murals of the Federal Arts Project, but also the theater (including the Living Newspapers) and music in the form of such political cantatas as Earl Robinson and John Latouche's *Ballad for Americans* (1939).[73] That work forms a bridge between the 1930s and the war years thanks to its strong and continued presence in concerts, radio, and recordings in the early 1940s.[74] Not only did the work's famous champion, Paul Robeson, perform it before and during the war years, but so too did numerous other musicians (both white and African American), from Bing Crosby, Lansing Hatfield, Kenneth Spencer, and Lawrence Tibbett to high school choruses across the United States.[75] Eleanor Roosevelt repeatedly commented on the *Ballad for Americans* in her newspaper column "My Day"—for example, on April 22, 1942, after hearing Robeson and the Fisk Jubilee Singers perform it in Nashville, Tennessee, at an award ceremony for the Thomas Jefferson Prize. "It always stirs me as a ballad," Roosevelt wrote, "but last night there was something peculiarly significant about it. It was very beautifully done."[76] In October 1943 the work was presented by African American soldiers (led by Private James McDaniel) in two concerts in the Royal Albert Hall in London, where "two nights running, 5000 Britons and the members of the London Symphony Orchestra stood up, cheered, stamped, clapped, laughed and cried."[77] *Ballad for Americans* was performed in military camps such as Fort Bragg in North Carolina, school festivals, and war-bond drives. Indeed, during the war it turned into a patriotic work that could be coopted for any patriotic occasion, whether as a symbol of national identity or as a tool in the Double V campaign.

Robinson and Latouche had—in their own words—created a "musical history of the United States."[78] The work starts with the Revolutionary War, touches on the westward expansion and frontier (with the inevitable banjo in the accompaniment), crests with the Civil War and Lincoln's Gettysburg Address, moves into industrialization and urbanization, and ends with a rousing finale about a melting-pot present (or perhaps a future) that ends with a full-throated climactic exclamation in chorus and solo voice on the thrice-repeated word "America!"[79] The soloist, chorus, and orchestra present a multitude of American voices in dialogue with each other throughout this historical timeline. Even the two foundational quotations embedded in the cantata—the preamble to the Declaration of Independence and the conclusion of the Gettysburg Address—are shared between soloist and chorus, or (to follow the work's final words) America and her people. This people is characterized by the work's creators as ethnically mixed—they are named as Irish, Negro, Jewish, Italian, French and English, Spanish, Russian, Chinese, Polish, Scotch, Hungarian, Litvak, Swedish, Finnish, Canadian, Greek and Turk, and Czech and double Czech American (though neither German nor Japanese, one might note)—and practicing a multitude of faiths, from Orthodox Judaism to Roman Catholicism. For all this diversity in the text, however, the ballad form, with its recurring strophes in a generic American folk tone, serves to homogenize this ethnic patchwork musically into a unified nation. Although—especially in recent scholarship—the *Ballad for Americans* has become conflated with Robeson's performance in the painful context of U.S. racism, its performative reach during the early 1940s tells a more complex story about the uses of history during the war that instrumentalized the pan-ethnic Americanism at the heart of the work for a propagandistic celebration of American exceptionalism.[80]

Indeed, *Ballad for Americans* touches on the key tenets of U.S. exceptionalist ideology, including the nation's foundation in the American Revolution, the frontier spirit, Manifest Destiny, liberty and equality for a multiplicity of immigrants, and the universalist claim of American nationalism.[81] The bloody sacrifice of two wars fought over the principles of liberty and equality imbued American exceptionalism with an aura of existential validity— not for nothing did Robinson and Latouche link Patrick Henry's "Give me Liberty, or give me Death!" to Lincoln's Gettysburg Address. U.S. imperial wars arising from the ideology of American exceptionalism—for example, the Mexican–American War (1846–48)—were, of course, conveniently excluded from any such narrative, as was any reference to the social injustices and racial inequality of the time. The historical plot of American exceptionalism presented the nation as a shining city on the hill whose hard-fought progress now served as a beacon for the rest of the world. This plot became a standard trope in wartime musical representations of a melting-pot America, whether in such apotheosizing nationalist movie finales as *The Bells of Capistrano* (1942) and *Star-Spangled Rhythm* (1942), or—as we saw in chapter 3—Kerr and Siegmeister's *Sing Out, Sweet Land!* (1944).

World War II brought a milestone Revolutionary-era commemoration: the bicentenary of Thomas Jefferson's birth (1743). As the principal drafter of the Declaration of Independence and the only revolutionary with a significant anniversary during the war, Jefferson could be coopted particularly well for the wartime consecration of U.S. political ideologies.[82] As we saw in chapter 3, the bicentenary was marked by the dedication of the Jefferson Memorial in Washington, D.C., a major national event accompanied by exhibitions, celebrations, and a nationally broadcast speech by President Roosevelt that anointed the founding father as an "apostle of freedom."[83] But the Jefferson bicentenary also inspired reflections on the foundational values of American democracy and the role of history in the formation of U.S. identity. This was the brainchild of the *New York Times*, which sponsored an essay contest for schoolchildren of all ages on the general topic of "what the people of a great democracy owe to Thomas Jefferson, particularly in these challenging days."[84] This seemed all the more urgent because a survey sponsored by the same newspaper of seven thousand college freshmen revealed "striking ignorance of even the most elementary aspects of United States history."[85] The Jefferson bicentenary was thus turned into a national history lesson, taught in newspapers from the *New York Times* and the *Chicago Tribune* to the *New York Amsterdam News*. A newspaper article by Carl Sandburg, author of a famed Lincoln biography (for which he won a Pulitzer Prize in 1940), not only called for a better biographical study of Jefferson but also made explicit the link between the two iconic figures, pointing out that "the younger Abraham Lincoln studied his Jefferson," absorbing "some parts of Jefferson's thoughts ... so completely that they became part of him."[86]

A Broadway costume drama by the Pulitzer Prize–winning playwright (and now army sergeant) Sidney Kingsley emphasized the ten years between Jefferson's return from Europe and his presidency. *The Patriots* set Jefferson, as the true voice of democratic freedom, in a sharp conflict with an elitist Alexander Hamilton. "Starring Jefferson," the *New York Times* exclaimed in a headline for a photo spread about the work's première on January 29, 1943. *The Patriots* was produced by the Playwrights Company with incidental music by Stanley Bates, who included such well-known eighteenth-century melodies as "Yankee Doodle," "Lovely Peggy," and "Liberty Tree" to add an authentic touch.[87] Critics lauded the play's presentation of the "foundations of the republic our men in service are fighting these days to preserve" by giving "a lesson on American tradition—and making a stirring and moving play besides."[88] The idea for the play, said Kingsley, came on a trip to Europe in 1939: "It seemed to me that Americans, myself included, didn't understand what Democracy meant...and it was for my own enlightenment as much as for anything else that I began a study of American democracy."[89] Significantly, however, Kingsley could not bring this study to fruition until after Pearl Harbor. In the midst of the play's successful Broadway run of 173 performances, the cast and crew came to Washington, D.C., to perform the play in the Coolidge Auditorium of the Library of Congress for "members of Congress, the Cabinet and the Supreme Court" to launch the official celebrations for the Jefferson bicentenary in April 1943.[90] They joined numerous other artistic commemorations, including a concert by the Budapest String Quartet, broadcast nationwide by NBC, of music from Jefferson's library.[91]

Indeed, "Jefferson and His Music" formed part of the Jefferson Exhibition presented at the Library of Congress during the bicentenary celebrations, which aimed to show the statesman as a "multi-sided" American: scientist, farmer, and even musician. That Jefferson played the violin was a well-known biographical detail; the exhibition exemplified, however, the fact that Jefferson called music "the favorite passion of my soul"—a comment that served as the motto for the Budapest String Quartet concert.[92] According to the press release, by Harold Spivacke, the exhibition included "manuscript letters from and to Jefferson evincing his interest in music, music items formerly in Jefferson's personal library and American musical imprints reflecting Jefferson's national and political importance....No American statesman has ever shown a greater interest or love for music than he. The current exhibit, therefore, will bring closer to the American people Jefferson's incalculable importance as a patron of the arts, a practitioner of music, and a man of genuinely wide culture."[93] This exhibition portrayed Jefferson as, among other things, an ardent and educated music lover who exchanged letters about the art with another founding father, Francis Hopkinson, whom the press release dubbed "the eminent American statesman now recognized as the first native born American composer."[94] By characterizing the writer of the Declaration of Independence and third U.S. president as a musical figure, Spivacke and other musicians inscribed music into the very fabric of the nation.

One bicentenary concert in New York brought musical past and present together and even managed to relate the event to musical representations of war. In the first half of the program the School for Democracy presented the baritone Kenneth Spencer, the pianist Judith Sidorsky, and the American People's Chorus performing "music of Jefferson's time," including James Hewitt's piano sonata *The Battle of Trenton*—listed in the program somewhat approximately as "a favorite historical military piece of 1797."[95] Sidorsky played the work and recited the commentary printed in the score—which explains the score's various extramusical references, from the "Crossing of the Delaware" to the "General Rejoice" after victory. This historical part was then followed by the first performance of *That Freedom Plow*, a musical play by Louis Lerman and Earl Robinson that presented Jefferson as not only a champion of freedom, but also "an ardent musician" (violin performance included).[96] Just like Albert Einstein—whose violin playing was among his best-known public traits—Jefferson was humanized through his musical instrument.[97]

For all this public emphasis on Jeffersonian ideas of democracy in the context of the current war, however, only one other large-scale musical work emerged from this nexus relating Jefferson's writings to the current political debates in the United States: Randall Thompson's *Testament of Freedom*. Setting "four passages from the writings of Thomas Jefferson," Thompson wrote the work for the University of Virginia Glee Club. Its first performance took place at Cabell Hall "on Founder's Day, April 13, 1943," with the composer at the piano (Figure 5.2).[98] It was broadcast by CBS and recorded by the OWI for overseas shortwave distribution to the armed forces. "No doubt," Howard Taubman speculated, "it was also heard by some people in the occupied countries and perhaps they drew some small measure of courage from it."[99] Serge Koussevitzky premièred the orchestral version two years later (in April 1945) in Boston with the Boston Symphony Orchestra and the Harvard Glee Club.[100]

In contrast to Latouche, who had turned to the preamble of the Declaration of Independence in *Ballad for Americans*, Thompson chose lesser-known texts, including the *Declaration of Causes and Necessity of Taking Up Arms* (1775) and a letter to John Adams from 1821. The work consists of four movements with the titles:

1. The God who gave us life
2. We have counted the cost
3. We fight not for glory
4. I shall not die without a hope

FIGURE 5.2 Randall Thompson in *Musical America* 64 (November 10, 1944): 8.

Thompson's choice of texts was clearly made in response to the war. The third movement, for example, opens with: "We fight not for glory and conquest. We exhibit to mankind the remarkable spectacle of a people attacked by unprovoked enemies, without any imputation or even suspicion of offense. They boast of their privileges and civilization, and yet proffer no milder conditions than servitude or death." Jefferson's words barely needed any translation into the ubiquitous rhetoric of the period, which presented the U.S. entry into World War II as a defensive act, fought after the unprovoked attack on Pearl Harbor and against the Nazis and Fascists who boasted of their cultural superiority yet brought nothing but servitude or death. That Thompson set this movement in C minor, with a motive of three accented eighth notes followed by a half note tied to the next measure placed prominently and repeatedly in the introduction, makes the reference to Beethoven's Fifth, with its so-called V for victory motive, glaringly obvious. In contrast to that in the other movements, however, Thomspon's choral writing and harmonic language here also plays on Soviet idioms familiar from Shostakovich and the marches of the Red Army. Add the fanfares and snare drums, and this third movement can be read as the epitome of an Allied anthem.

The final movement—"I shall not die without a hope that light and liberty are on steady advance"—with its contrapuntal opening, slowly expands the sacred hymnody of the beginning into the monumental *ff* evocation of "Liberty" in the apotheosizing F major conclusion. Here, too, German music offers an intertext through the rather strong echoes of—though no direct quotation from—the first movement of Brahms's *Ein deutsches Requiem* ("Selig sind, die da Leid tragen"), especially its ending and the shared key of F major. Though to our eyes this allusion might seem ironic, during World War II Brahms's Requiem was often performed in the United States as a commemoration of those who perished in the war. Ray C. B. Brown, the music critic for the *Washington Post*, made it clear in a column published in 1942 that the work's universalist appeal to an American audience had nothing in common with its origin in enemy territory: "Brahms named his great choral work 'A German Requiem' not as a tribute to Deutschland or as a glorification of an 'Aryan' superiority unclaimed in his day, but as an indication of his purpose to express the faith of the common man in the immortality of the soul."[101] Here again the great appropriation of world culture (discussed in chapter 3) served as a powerful justification for the continued performance in the United States of standard concert repertoire. By drawing on Brahms's well-known work, Thompson could tap into a commemorative idiom then perceived as universalist, which connected closely to the contemporary appeal of Jefferson's words, including those specifically relating to Europe: "And even should the cloud of barbarism and despotism again obscure the science and liberties of Europe, this country remains to preserve and restore light and liberty to them." One might read the allusion as meaning that Brahms and other German markers of civilization were to be preserved and restored to their rightful place in American culture when the conflict was over.

After the 1945 Boston performance Leslie A. Sloper, the critic for the *Christian Science Monitor*, pointed to the contemporary relevance of *Testament of Freedom* when he explained that "the text evidently was chosen for its timeliness when considered in connection with the present war. Jefferson's eloquent words are stirring today, when victory seems near; no doubt they were even more so two years ago, when the future was less clear."[102] For the composer, the clarity of Jefferson's words and his creation of "a democratic government for all the people" demanded a musical equivalent in a compositional "simplicity of design and structure" that could be "enjoyed the length and breadth of the land."[103] Olin Downes considered the *Testament of Freedom* "an expression of our national traditions and spirit," rendered through "simple and excellent music," with "the pomp of ceremonial in the proper places and almost the flavor of ritual in the others."[104] It helped his assessment that the performance he attended took place on the day Roosevelt was buried, for the president, wrote Downes, "had lived and died for the ideals that Jefferson and his nation have cherished. The atmosphere was that almost of a religious observance."[105] A work whose musical language did not challenge its listeners but, rather, fit with prevalent musical taste was particularly suitable for such an occasion. Indeed, as with the commemorative works and Americana discussed earlier—whether by Herrmann, Gould, or Bauer—Thompson's recourse to musical conventionalism and familiar idioms in his Jefferson setting was par for the course and created a comfortable musical memorial.

If the turn to Jefferson as a historical guarantor of Americanism was spurred by the bicentenary celebrations, the appeal of Abraham Lincoln as a consecrated embodiment of the American way reached its apex during World War II, though it had a significantly longer history in the validation of American exceptionalism.[106] Never more than during World War II was Lincoln evoked so unanimously as a rallying figure, and the increasingly widespread references to Lincoln and the Civil War in American public discourse helped cast current events as part of an ethical narrative in defense of global freedom.[107] Whether in OWI posters or newspaper articles, Lincoln was ever-present as the nation's symbolic leader during this new crisis (Figure 5.3). We have already seen the slippage between the Civil War Lincoln and the political propaganda of World War II in Gould's *American Salute*, where a potentially divisive (between North and South) song is read, instead, as a force for national unification. Several wartime works, however, referred to Lincoln specifically, including Jaromír Weinberger's *Lincoln Symphony* (1940), Gould's *A Lincoln Legend* (1941–42), Copland's *Lincoln Portrait* (1942), and Harris's Symphony no. 6, "Gettysburg" (1944).

Weinberger's *Lincoln Symphony* was the work of a Czech exile—famous especially for his opera *Schwanda the Bagpiper*—who had fled war and persecution in Europe. This was his first large-scale composition in the United States, and he must have felt that there was none better than Lincoln to express his new American identity while simultaneously reminding noninterventionist Americans of a glorious past when liberty for all was worth dying for.[108] As Weinberger had explained to Howard Taubman in 1939, right after his arrival in New York, it was to be "a symphony on the life of a hero...who lived and died for a great idea."[109] The allusion here to Beethoven's "Eroica" Symphony was deliberate and later carried through in the four programmatic movements: "The Hand on the Plough," "Scherzo Héroïque," "O Captain! My Captain!—Recitative and Marcia Funebre," and "Deep River."[110] The work's narrative trajectory, from Lincoln's close ties to the land through his heroic sacrifice, a nation's mourning, and the conflict's

FIGURE 5.3 Cartoon relating Lincoln's Gettysburg Address to the war dead in World War II, *Dziennik dla Wszystkich* (Journal for All), 1944. Image courtesy of the Abraham Lincoln Library and Museum, Lincoln Memorial University, Harrogate, Tennessee.

justification, is born out in both the program and its musical realization. To heighten the work's message (and to emphasize his American credentials) Weinberger, like many of his contemporaries, used poetry by Whitman—in this case through his programmatic use of "O Captain! My Captain!" (the poem Whitman wrote following Lincoln's assassination) as the title of the third movement. The movement's opening orchestral Recitativo, carried by the first violins, is followed by a Marcia Funebre whose Beethovenian inter-text is particularly noticeable in the timpani's muffled triplets. The symphony closes with an orchestral rondo based on the spiritual "Deep River," whose connotations—as Downes pointed out—were "intended to be obvious."[111]

If Weinberger's *Lincoln Symphony* could be read as a composition mediating between Europe at war and a United States still dominated by isolationist rhetoric, Gould's *A Lincoln Legend* was a work that straddled the official entry of the United States into World War II: composed just before the attack on Pearl Harbor, it was premièred the year after in Arturo Toscanini's first all-American concert, conducted on November 1, 1942 (see chapter 1). *A Lincoln Legend* was clearly written in the left-wing tradition of the 1930s of adopting Lincoln for anti-Fascist causes, as when the American volunteers during the Spanish Civil War named themselves the Abraham Lincoln Brigade.[112] During the Spanish Civil War, Gould was "active on the Loyalist Committee," though he did not go as far as Conlon Nancarrow, who joined the brigade in the battle against General Francisco Franco. As Gould recalled in 1943, these activities "earned me the reputation of being a Communist."[113] His anti-Fascist stance shines through in a letter to Toscanini in which he lauded the conductor for his performance of Shostakovich's Seventh Symphony: "This work, its attending circumstances, and your conducting, signified to me the essence of Anti-Fascism." In the same letter Gould explained the program of *A Lincoln Legend* in relative detail, tying the prairie nationalism of the 1930s to the war.

> I have attempted to express some of the things that Abraham Lincoln symbolizes, and to bring out musically some of the qualities that Carl Sandburg has so magnificently expressed in his book on Lincoln. The subtitle of this composition might almost be Carl Sandburg's title "The Prairie Years—The War Years." The first part of the work is warmly lyrical—nostalgic and simple, a sort of American idyll. Thru here, as in the rest of the composition, there runs a sense of forebody [*sic*] and of the stark tragedy that was hovering continually in Lincoln's background. There occurs a group of dances and village band marches, based on tunes that were popular during Lincoln's day—and used politically for him. Then the grim war and funeral music—in which I make use of the "Battle Hymn of the Republic" which I think is one of the great songs of a free people. The work closes on a return to the opening tender and lyrical mood, but with the feeling of tragedy and emotion ever present.[114]

Toscanini responded that he was "much taken and fascinated with the incisive and penetrating musical strokes of your Lincoln's Legend" and programmed it for his "first concert at the N.B.C. on November the first."[115]

Like many other left-leaning musicians, Gould turned hawkish after the German attack on the USSR in June 1941. This tendency became even more pronounced after Pearl Harbor and was part of the massive political shift that took place for the American Left once the United States entered the war. Lincoln, as a president who embodied the move from social to military battles, was ideally suited to mediate such a change. The shift was made possible also because of the role that Sandburg, as a modern biographer of the sixteenth president, played. His weighty tomes—*Abraham Lincoln: The*

Prairie Years was published in 1926, and *Abraham Lincoln: The War Years* came out in 1939—were not only the most renowned texts on Lincoln to come out in the interwar years, but were also firmly rooted in pro-labor sentiment and Roosevelt's New Deal ideology: in 1934, Sandburg famously linked the National Industrial Recovery Act to Lincoln's Emancipation Proclamation.[116] It was thus no surprise that a left-leaning musician such as Gould should draw on Sandburg's biographies. The author and poet also inspired the next major composition about Lincoln by a populist American icon, Copland's *Lincoln Portrait*, written in early 1942 in response to a commission by the conductor Andre Kostelanetz.

Eleven days after Pearl Harbor, on December 18, 1941, Kostelanetz had commissioned Copland, together with Jerome Kern and Virgil Thomson, to write musical portraits "of some outstanding Americans."[117] In January 1942 Copland settled on Lincoln as an alternative to Walt Whitman (his original idea), after having been convinced by Kostelanetz to focus on the Civil War president as a more appropriate choice: "From that moment on, the choice of Lincoln as my subject seemed inevitable."[118] Rather than composing a purely instrumental portrait, Copland wrote the work for speaker and orchestra—he felt any attempt at portraying Lincoln musically was doomed to failure: "I think, that no composer can hope to match in purely musical terms the impressive stature of Abraham Lincoln. When Andre asked me to attempt a Lincoln portrait, I hesitated, but agreed to try only when it occurred to me that I might use Lincoln's own *words* in my design. The words I have chosen are not the most familiar Lincoln quotations, and yet I think you will agree that they contain a meaning for our own times."[119] Copland selected extracts from a range of lesser-known texts when creating his libretto, including "On Slavery in a Democracy" (1858) and the Annual Message to Congress of December 1, 1862.[120] He framed the quotations in a quasi-biblical tone by introducing each fragment with the words, "This is what he said."

Yet even though Copland deliberately stayed away from the best-known Lincoln texts for most of his composition, his work nevertheless reveals to what extent the Gettysburg Address had, by the early 1940s, become inseparable from any reference to his subject.[121] He addressed this in the 1942 program notes for the first performance of *Lincoln Portrait*: "I avoided the temptation of quoting only well-known passages, permitting myself the luxury of only one from a world-famous speech."[122] Furthermore, this one famous segment—the peroration of the Gettysburg Address—was selected for the culmination of the work. And it is exactly the appearance of the Gettysburg Address that changes the work's music from melancholy to triumphalism, leading to a C major symphonic apotheosis that would have done Shostakovich proud and that echoes a Beethovenian *per aspera ad astra*. Copland himself admitted that in trying to portray Lincoln he seemed to return almost inexorably to the C major triad, especially when, at the end, "the orchestra blazes out in triple forte with a strong and positive C-major statement of the first theme."[123] This shift to apotheosizing monumentality concluded a score infused throughout with signifiers of American military music familiar from other commemorative compositions, from fanfarelike renderings of the motivic material to evocations of "Taps"—the bugle call used in military funerals in the United States.[124]

What situated *Lincoln Portrait* as an early wartime composition was not only Copland's reliance on the musical idiom of commemorative music, but also the integration of two American songs—the folk tune "Springfield Mountain" and Stephen Foster's "Camptown Races" (itself a song that had entered the popular repertoire)—as signifiers of national identity. In 1942 the composer himself drew attention to the folk-song quotations: "I worked with musical material of my own, with the exception of two songs of the period: Foster's 'Camptown Races' and a ballad published in 1840 under the title of 'The Pesky Serpent,' but better known today as 'Springfield Mountain.' In neither case is the treatment literal. The tunes are used freely, in the manner of the cowboy songs in 'Billy the Kid.'"[125] Just as Gould relied on "The Battle Hymn of the Republic" and Weinberger quoted "Deep River" for historical and local color in their Lincoln works, so Copland turned to folk songs associated specifically with the American Civil War and its connection to the end of slavery to sound the work's message.[126]

Through the fanfarelike motives, the recourse to Civil War folk song, the pathos of the finale, and the solemn quasi-biblical presentation of the text, *Lincoln Portrait* presented itself a work aimed at stirring patriotic fervor—Kostelanetz, after receiving the score, characterized it as a "magnificent work which I believe, aside from its wonderful musical value, will convey a great message to the American public."[127] Copland's friend and former teacher Nadia Boulanger was deeply moved by the emotional appeal of the work. After hearing the radio broadcast, she wrote: "You have succeeded in something indefinable and of great significance. And your sensibility—your understanding touch so deeply. Love—there is always real love in your music—human, broad and destroying the walls which so easily separate us all."[128] Koussevitzky, with customary ardor, described it as a "stirring work...of patriotic and national significance at this time."[129] For Sandburg, this message consisted in the obvious parallel to contemporary events, as he explained in August 1942, just before performing the speaker's part in the radio première: "Most of us, I find, are surprised when we notice how closely Lincoln's words sometimes fit our own needs today. We should not be surprised. Lincoln spoke for the people. There are always those who do not believe in the people, those who are ready to oppose the march of mankind toward new freedom. Today the unbelievers, the enemies of man, are called Fascist and Nazi. Today cynicism battles faith in the man, the ideas of Lincoln fight the ideas of Hitler, all through the world."[130] Indeed, the equation of Hitler with American slaveholders was ubiquitous in American wartime propaganda, especially in the posters created under the auspices of the OWI.

This conflation of Lincoln's ideas and current U.S. politics lay also at the heart of another wartime composition, Harris's Symphony no. 6, "Gettysburg." The work was commissioned in May 1943 by the Blue Network, a major radio station (which would be renamed ABC in 1945) that broadcast—among others—performances of the Metropolitan Opera and the Boston Symphony Orchestra. The network's president, Mark Woods, chose Harris for this significant commission because he believed that "Roy Harris and his works have helped to create the pattern of the American scene. That there is an undeniable need for his music today has been proved by the praise and appreciation received from service men all over the world, our fighting men and those of our allies."[131] The work was to be dedicated to the U.S. armed forces, and its theme was to be related to the current war. As Woods explained in a press conference: "I made no demands or even suggestions...other than to hope that since he is essentially a man of the soil and one of our own, the Sixth symphony will be dedicated to the American fighting forces, and that it will be a symbol of the struggle which our nation is making and has made throughout its eventful history for the freedom of mankind." The composer added that he would compose "a 'major moral symphony' that would dwell on the Lincoln era."[132] (Figure 5.4)

The moral exhortation would come in the symphony's program, which was none other than the Gettysburg Address, with each movement corresponding to a segment of Lincoln's speech.[133] Harris informed his close friend Nicolas Slonimsky that this choice was inspired by a dream: "One morning I woke up at 3:00 A.M....and I saw the Gettysburg Address divided into four logical parts, four movements of a symphony. They seemed exceedingly right. I heard bell-like harmonies suggesting the shout: Let Freedom Ring!"[134] For Harris, Lincoln's famous speech was a historical blueprint for the current war. Once he had decided on the program, he tried to convince another collaborator, Archibald MacLeish, to write an introduction for the work's radio première: "What I had in mind was a short, incisive statement from your powerful pen to the effect that the world today, as a global unit, faces a position similar to which America faced during the Civil War. We

FIGURE 5.4 "Harris Looks Over the Score of His Sixth Symphony with Serge Koussevitzky and Mark Woods, Blue Network President." *Musical America* 64 (March 25, 1944): 7.

are fighting for world freedom and world suffrage, for a world Bill of Rights. Collective mankind is a house divided, and out of this great civil war of the world an ideal will be born into the blood of man; that social and economic injustice is no longer acceptable to mankind."[135] Harris made the comparison even more obvious to Koussevitzky, who was to conduct the work's première: "Archibald MacLeish . . . is going to write a beautiful introduction for the symphony, showing how today the world is facing the same problems of liberty which America faced during Lincoln's time and about which the Gettysburg speech was made."[136]

With Harris then employed as a composer-in-residence at Colorado College and most of his interlocutors on the East Coast, his letters during the gestation of the symphony chronicle three interwoven concerns— the patriotic content of the symphony, the relationship between content and musical means of expression, and the work's contribution to American music. A fourth thread—the biographical connection between Harris and Lincoln through their shared birthday on February 12—became increasingly important when it emerged that the composer would be able to time the work's completion for this symbolic date. In a letter to Koussevitzky dated

February 7, 1944, he announced, "I will send you a telegram on Lincoln's Birthday, which will be the 12th. If I remember rightly, you are playing in Carnegie Hall on the 12th, and I will send it to you to tell you the work is completed."[137] The composer wrote to Slonimsky that this completion date had been planned long before: "This is to tell you that the Sixth Symphony will be finished as planned last fall—on the 12th day of February."[138] Similar symbolism characterized the date of the first performance in Boston: April 14 and 15, 1944, spanning the seventy-ninth anniversary of Lincoln's assassination (John Wilkes Booth shot the president on April 14, and Lincoln died the following morning)—with the radio première on April 15 publicized as taking place "exactly 79 years after the death of Lincoln."[139]

The use of the Gettysburg Address was, in Harris's opinion, "absolutely pertinent to world conditions today."[140] Yet such heightened patriotic content had consequences for the composer's structuring of the score. In contrast to folk-based music—such as his 1935 overture *When Johnny Comes Marching Home*—the score needed to inscribe nationalist sentiment into the fabric of the music itself. Harris reminded Koussevitzky that when they settled on Lincoln as the subject of the work, they had concluded that "it must be simple, simple, simple—something so direct that everybody could understand it, and yet it must have the grandeur and depth worth of such as subject." Such grandeur called for heroic gestures, masculinist rhetoric, and large-scale developments. The third movement, titled "Dedication," for example, reflected the sadness that, in Harris's opinion, most people associated with the Gettysburg Address. However, for all its "elegiac character," the composer said, the movement needed to exude "manly and very firm spiritual strength." Harris also felt that he needed to include, in addition to the overall emotional appeal required of a work intended for a mass radio audience, specific musical structures in the service of his program, especially in the last movement, "a strong, surging song of faith and hope and courage."[141] There Harris chose a contrapuntal texture as the musical equivalent of democratic structure. For all its learnedness, however, the musical texture had to appeal to the man on the street in order to serve the composer's Americanist cause. He explained to Koussevitzky that this movement "is a double fugue but it is so simple and so direct that I feel that the man on the street can understand it at the first hearing. . . . I believe that I have captured the faith of people towards a noble ideal of justice and peace and understanding. . . . I am sure you will understand because you know how deeply this democratic ideal is a part of my blood."[142] Whether or not the man (or woman) on the street could understand the double fugue at first hearing was irrelevant in and of itself. What was essential for Harris was that his musical means of expression be tailored to, and emerge from, the work's patriotic program and intended function.

This intrinsic fusion of musical means and message meant, to Harris's mind, that he was going "to ring the bell with this work."[143] He wrote to MacLeish, "I have a hunch that this Sixth Symphony may be the peak of my life work. Certainly as music I will never do anything better than I am doing now."[144] Composing this symphony, he confided in Koussevitzky, brought on an "an enthusiasm which has led me further and further and deeper and deeper into the profound and inner secrets of symphonic writing." Indeed, this work was channeling the important development "of a new dynamic form which must be America's contribution to the symphonic world."[145] It was normal for Harris to be excited about whichever major work he was composing at the time, but this fervent belief of having reached a pinnacle of symphonic achievement—inspired by Lincoln's Gettysburg Address—was unusual even for him. The way in which Harris's letters intermingle references to Lincoln's famous speech with commentaries about his own musical choices hints at a quest for validation though a compelling symbol of both American greatness and U.S. exceptionalism. His symphony was to be a true musical embodiment of the American way because, Harris intimates, Lincoln himself guided his hand.

By April 1944, when the symphony was premièred, however, this kind of propagandistic approach to American music in wartime—which had been highly successful in 1942—no longer appealed to either audiences or critics. The Boston critic Rudolph Elie was "unmoved by Mr. Harris's latest determined go at creating the Great American Symphony." Warren Storey Smith, in the *Boston Post*, was tired of the fact that "of late our American composers have been endeavoring to ride to fame on the shoulders of Abraham Lincoln." Harris had to face the criticism that the work was too conventional and overly mired in his "ideological concepts." Even a sympathetic critic like Moses Smith writing in *Modern Music* found the symphony lacking. He claimed that the work did contain "beautiful things, including the entire slow movement," but he also revealed those elements he found wanting, such as the third movement, which he described as "quite naïve," reminding him "of an accompaniment for an Indian war dance in an old-fashioned Western."[146] Sloper put his finger on the crucial issue when he compared Harris's symphony with Copland's *Lincoln Portrait*. In Sloper's view, Copland "was wise in making no attempt to compete with or elaborate upon the words of the Emancipator." Harris, in contrast, had overstepped this boundary. "The Gettysburg Address," so Sloper wrote, "has long been accepted as one of the masterpieces of oratory. To attempt to say it over again in music is like Massine trying to tell us by means of choreography what Brahms meant to say in the Fourth Symphony. It is an undertaking not likely to succeed."[147]

Indeed, the difference between the reception of Copland's *Lincoln Portrait* and that of Harris's "Gettysburg" Symphony tells an important story about music, propaganda, and nationalism in the United States. The presence or absence of words became a matter of some importance in the eyes and ears of American critics and audience members. That both Copland and Thompson—in his setting of Jefferson—chose to efface themselves (at least in their public statements) gave the impression that the message of the great national heroes could be mediated through music but must not be appropriated for personal, nonpatriotic goals. In contrast, the use of Lincoln in a work such as Harris's (or, earlier, Weinberger's) symphony led to resistance against possibly self-serving preening on the part of the composers: in these works Lincoln was perceived as being the means to specifically musical ends—even if, as with Harris, the patriotic fervor of the composer was not in question. This debate was also bound up with questions of genre: a work such as Copland's *Lincoln Portrait* harked back to familiar presentations of heightened speech, whether religious or political; a symphonic composition, especially in wartime, prompted the question of whether a symphony—considered the epitome of abstract music—could really be, as Harris claimed, "worthy of our great national crisis."[148]

New World Symphonies

Yet the crowning genre of musical Americana during World War II was, ironically, the symphony, and that because—rather than in spite—of its universalist pedigree. For over a century now, the genre had embodied the pinnacle of classical music in the United States, whether as imported concert repertoire or as native products. Discussions about native symphonic compositions in the United States raged—mostly on the East Coast—during most of the nineteenth century, and after Dvořák's "New World" Symphony blew the dying embers of the debate back into a flame in 1893, American composers and critics across the nation went on a quest for the "Great American Symphony."[149] Their search was characterized by an aesthetic framework shaped simultaneously by reference to folklore and by universalist tendencies, appropriating—especially during the 1930s—the genre for the artistic validation of nationalist populism: a striking example is Still's *Afro-American Symphony* (1930), which fused local and transnational symphonic idioms in an endeavor to create, in the composer's words, "an *American* work."[150] One might add that this dual reference to local particularity and universalist form was a central strategy employed by American critics to cast individual symphonies composed between 1893 and 1950 as the musical equivalent of the "great American novel," a term that had gained new currency in the 1920s and whose conceptual matrix focused on realist storytelling, especially—as Lawrence Buell has pointed out—because of "related phenomena of multiple ethno-literary renaissances starting in the 1920s."[151]

As a genre, the symphony after Beethoven had accumulated significant symbolic capital as a privileged locus of cultural expression. Imbued with status as the capstone of concert music, the symphony after Mahler gained new currency even before the war as a form in which to express musically one's *Weltanschauung* on a grand scale.[152] But the symphony in America carried even greater weight. In Europe music lovers go to the concert, *au concert*, *ins Konzert, al concerto, na kontsert*—but in America we go to the symphony. The linguistic slippage that overlies the name of an ideologically conspicuous musical genre with the entire ritual and institution of classical music making opened a creative space for composers within which to explore this double meaning: the genre with its complex musical, aesthetic, and political connotations on the one hand, and the full experience of a concert on the other. Thus the composition of a symphony as an ideological marker in both musical and social terms was particularly suited to the cultural war that the United States fought against not only her enemies but even, at least to some extent, her allies.

War symphonies abounded in the United States: even a cursory overview of the output of American composers shows a noticeable increase in their production, whether by young composers such as David Diamond, who wrote his first four symphonies between 1941 and 1945, or by seasoned composers such as Sessions and Copland, who returned to the genre in the last war years after a break of more than a decade. As with most other developments during the war, this spike in the United States was no different from parallel compositional trends in Europe, not only with Shostakovich's Seventh and Eighth Symphonies, but also with numerous works by both Axis and Allied composers, including Benjamin Britten, Johann Nepomuk David, Karl Amadeus Hartmann (his *Sinfonia tragica* of 1940 was a well-known document of inner exile), Aram Khachaturian, Gian Francesco Malipiero, Hans Pfitzner, Sergey Prokofiev, Edmund Rubbra, and Ralph Vaughan Williams. For some—Roberto Gerhard, André Jolivet, Michael Tippett, and Grace Williams—it was their first foray into symphonic composition.

Both aesthetic and performing conditions during the war favored the genre as a form of heightened expression. Opera, of course, suffered from the deteriorating material conditions, especially in Europe, but symphony orchestras were strongly supported across the warring parties as morale-boosting carriers of culture, and while concertos and other orchestral genres were certainly excellent "entertainment," they did not carry the weight of musical monumentality associated first and foremost with the symphony.[153] But although the classic symphonic repertoire fulfilled its role as a harbinger of cultural greatness through performance and reception, new symphonies cemented each nation's claim to cultural ownership through creation. Whereas symphonic composition in the 1930s could be characterized (roughly speaking) by the turn to classical forms as a populist strategy in the context of the "Great Appropriation" (see chapter 3), the sustained engagement with the genre during World War II was based on a centuries-old concept of it as an all-embracing expression of a collective, whether national or even that of humanity as a whole.[154]

Before American composers started writing their own war symphonies, however, one work by an Allied composer established a reference point that could not be ignored. Shostakovich's Symphony no. 7, "Leningrad," was written in the months before Pearl Harbor, completed exactly twenty days after the Japanese attack, and premièred during the first year of U.S. involvement in the war. It swept into American concert life as the essence of a war symphony, "solemn and majestic," yet also "a symphony to kill Hitler" through its rallying power.[155] The famed and much-publicized story of the work's journey, on microfilm, from Kuybyshev, in the Soviet Union, to the United States via Tehran, Cairo, and South America added cloak-and-dagger romance to its mystique. Such was the anticipation raised before the American première by the NBC Symphony Orchestra, conducted by Toscanini, that whole families—even those who did not normally listen to classical music—huddled around the radio on the afternoon of Sunday July 19, 1942, to witness this extraordinary event.[156]

The Soviet composer and his "Leningrad" Symphony became the touchstone for the concept of a war symphony in the United States, not only because of the romanticized circumstances of the work's genesis but also because—despite its length—it conformed to the classical mold of the genre, with its pedigree unequivocally rooted in Beethoven and mediated through another American favorite, Tchaikovsky.[157] Slonimsky explained that the "Soviet line of symphonic succession has thus become crystallized: from Beethoven to Tchaikovsky to Shostakovitch."[158] Even though composers from Copland to Arthur Berger sniffed at the work's conventionality, its accessibility and clearly shaped program appealed to the American audiences, who responded to it enthusiastically and with rapt attention.[159] Critics and composers explained this popular success as a result of what they considered Shostakovich's pandering to the masses. "It is apparently designed for easy listening," Thomson concluded, and Berger found that it avoided "almost anything that requires the listener's effort, while at the same time audiences have the illusion of being confronted with grand, difficult and important symphonic proportions."[160]

That the hyperbole and propaganda surrounding Shostakovich's Seventh Symphony in the United States, and the work's numerous and well-publicized performances across the nation, was a thorn in the side of American composers was not surprising. Copland's cousin, the playwright Harold Clurman, asked pointedly: "And what do *you* think about Shostakovich's 'Seventh'?!" and continued rather sarcastically, "It doesn't matter what you think about anything else in music these days. You've *got to* have an opinion on the 7th of Sho. Nothing else really matters!"[161] Although Harris was careful in his correspondence with known supporters of Shostakovich, he let loose in letters to like-minded correspondents such as Thomson and MacLeish. He wrote to Thomson that it seemed "a strange situation when we in America have space for every slightest movement of Shostakovich here—and find difficulty for space in our own papers when our native composers are recognized abroad. It seems like a form of inverted chauvinism to me."[162] He told MacLeish that he hoped that the Blue Network would promote him in the context of the "Gettysburg" Symphony: "I think they are somewhat provoked by the amount of publicity Shostakovich has been having by American organizations at the expense of our own people, and they are going to make an issue of it. At least that seems to be the tacitly understood idea. I, for one, know that certainly no American composer has had a hundredth part of the promotion that Shostakovich has had right under our own noses, and I do not think it is intrinsic. I think it is a ph-o-n-e-y."[163]

Harris was quite possibly the most vocal American composer in denouncing what he saw as the unwarrantedly preferential reception of the Soviet composer by the American performers and audiences. And yet, his compositional response was his Fifth Symphony (1943), commissioned by the renowned Shostakovich supporter Koussevitzky and dedicated to "to the heroic and freedom-loving people of our great ally, the Union of Soviet Socialist Republics, as a tribute to their strength in war, their staunch idealism for world peace, their ability to cope with stark materialist problems of world order without losing a passionate belief in the fundamental importance of the arts" (Figure 5.5).[164] This dedication was clearly an important part of Harris's ploy to gain public exposure for the new symphony. In a letter to

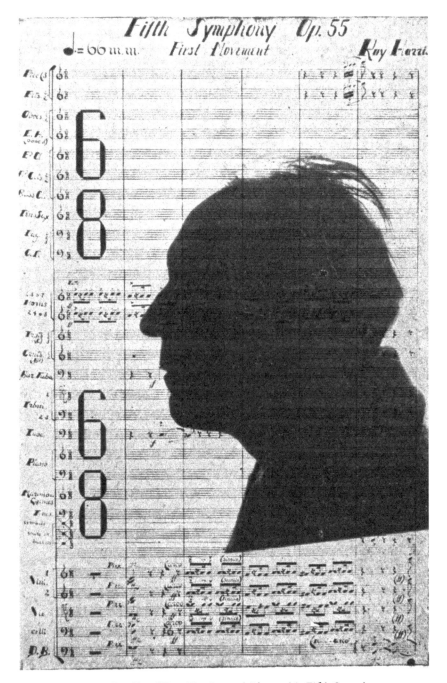

FIGURE 5.5 "Profile of Roy Harris overlaid over his Fifth Symphony Dedicated to the Soviet People." *Musical Courier* (April 5, 1943): 7.

Koussevitzky, he wrote that "the dedication of the work to the Russian people must be done with the proper respect, and I feel that since this means so much to you and me, the dedication should be made when the work receives its broadcast premiere, and acknowledged by the Soviet Embassy at the same time." With a recording by the OWI lined up for worldwide distribution, Harris emphasized the parallel with Shostakovich even more strongly when he announced that "they plan to microfilm the score and send it to England and Russia with the records."[165] The Boston concert that included the work's première, on February 26, 1943, paid tribute to the twenty-fifth anniversary of the Soviet armed forces and opened with an arrangement of the "Internationale"—perhaps the one that Koussevitzky had commissioned from Copland the previous year.[166] The OWI did, in the end, broadcast the Boston performance, including a relay to the Soviet Union. In response, nine leading Soviet composers (including Prokofiev and Shostakovich) sent Harris a message: "Greetings to Roy Harris from the composers of the USSR. We salute in your person young music of American people. Across seas and oceans we extend to your [sic] our hand in sincere fraternal handshake. Long live our victory!"[167]

Harris's Fifth Symphony had much in common with his *bête noire*, Shostakovich's Seventh. Both written in C major, they are characterized by their intentionally simple harmonic language, their use of contrapuntal techniques, and their embrace of monumentality as nationalist musical device. Rudolph Elie related the two works (and he was one of the few critics who liked both) in his review of the première of Harris's work: "As to the Fifth Symphony, it reveals time and again the aspects of the self-conscious prophet of Americana, and in that regard it has much in common with Shostakovitch's Seventh Symphony, as both Shostakovitch and Harris were motivated by much the same impulse to apotheosize the homeland. Yet, like those who self-consciously sit down to write the great American novel or the great American play, it isn't that easy, for the truly monumental work springs into being without premeditation." Yet even through Harris might have failed—as he would again—at writing the "Great American Symphony," Elie allowed for the possibility that his work was "the first truly indigenous composition of any lasting significance."[168] This is where the significance of Harris's musical choices in a self-consciously American work resided, for the Fifth was very ambitious in its compositional program, which fused complex contrapuntal techniques with thematic material that Harris declared as being steeped in the character of the American people, even though he did not quote any identifiable folk songs. In particular, the final movement—its barn-dance idiom combined with a triple fugue and an ending dominated by fanfares and percussion—claimed the symphonic high ground from the jingoist perspective of a "prophet of indigenous American music."[169]

In contrast to Harris's unapologetic nationalism, Marc Blitzstein's musical response to Shostakovich's "Leningrad" Symphony was tempered by his position as an active serviceman stationed abroad, his Americanist credentials already affirmed simply by virtue of his being a member of the army air forces. In that respect (and unlike Harris, who, as head of a family, was not drafted) he had nothing to prove. Yet Blitzstein too saw the propaganda effort swirling around the Soviet war symphony as a major point of reference in the context of what would become his *Airborne Symphony*. Blitzstein had enlisted on August 29, 1942, as an entertainment specialist. He was stationed in London from October 8, 1942, to May 22, 1945, where he served in a number of positions.[170] He wrote to his sister that he started thinking about the composition of "a big concert work on the subject of the air force" soon after his arrival in England.[171] In December 1942 Blitzstein recorded in his notebook: "Thinking now—and seriously—about outlining a project which would concern only myself—adopted to propaganda purposes for the Air Force...a big work, which, sufficiently publicized in advance, would be scheduled for performance before completion."[172] His next entry concerning the project, on December 23, 1942, described it as "the 'lyric symphony'— 'We are Airborne'—The Airborne."[173] Two weeks later, he explored other genre labels, such as drama-symphony, dramatic cantata or oratorio, lyric symphony, and dramatic suite.[174]

When he proposed the work on January 25, 1943, to his unit commander, Colonel Beirne Lay, it was simply called a "symphony," the subject of which was "The U.S. Army Air Force—in peace, in war, in victory," and consisted of four movements plus a prelude.[175] To make his case to headquarters, Blitzstein drew on the precedent set by the Soviet Union with Shostakovich's Seventh Symphony: "Last summer, in the midst of battle, the Soviet Union took time off to introduce Shostakovich's Seventh ('Leningrad') Symphony to a world waiting and prepared for the event by a record-breaking barrage of publicity."[176] After reiterating the familiar story of the work's composition during the siege of Leningrad and international distribution via microfilm carried on bomber planes, Blitzstein concluded that "the symphony, symbolizing, even representing courage in the face of withering fire and destruction, was responsible for an immense worldwide wave of enthusiasm and admiration for the people of the USSR and their fighting forces. Music was on the map as a positive weapon in winning the war."[177] The implication that Blitzstein's own symphony would have a similar impact on behalf of

American warfare is obvious. As he wrote to David Diamond about wartime composition: "Of course symphonies must be written now."[178] And so far as Blitzstein was concerned, his was a symphony in the tradition established by Liszt with his *Faust Symphony* and carried on by Stravinsky in his *Symphony of Psalms*.[179]

Blitzstein's special assignment of composing a symphony had a precedent in Samuel Barber's release to write his Second Symphony (see chapter 1). Once his leave was approved, Blitzstein started work officially in mid-February 1943.[180] He still was clearly thrilled that his "lyric-and-dramatic symphony" was going "to be exploited in a big way (translations in Russian for Moscow performance, Spanish for Mexico and S. America, French for the underground movt.), with initial London performance radiating repeats everywhere else."[181] The symphony itself was not to be an Americanist work in the way Harris had framed his ideological take on the crisis, but an American-centered perspective on a global war—for, as Blitzstein wrote in an early draft, while the work concerned "the *American* Air force . . . it might equally apply to the British or Chinese or Russian. . . . But it is the Air Force in the hands of the Democracy-lovers; the Winged Victory; it gives Liberty wings."[182] In his early notes Blitzstein quoted Roosevelt's exhortation to "bomb them constantly from the air."[183] He wondered about representing the enemy as a *"mystic-barbaric* cult . . . a composite picture of the Jap-fascist-nazi in his most typical ritual."[184] In rhetoric worthy of Shostakovich, the composer returned to identifying heroes and villains in yet another note from January by defining the theme of the symphony as "the sacred struggle of airborne free men of the world, but particularly of the USA and in the US Army Air Forces—to crush the monstrous fascist obstructionist in their path."[185]

Blitzstein's notes about the music reveal that Shostakovich was never far from his mind, as when he described the musical style as "symphonic— but don't be thrown by the implications—remember the implications of Prok., . . . Shost," thus positioning the Soviets as a countermodel to the then problematic Austro-German mold.[186] An outline of March 17 proposes a classical four-movement work with a prelude dedicated to the air.[187] But as Blitzstein developed his ideas, the formal structure became increasingly episodic. In March he found that the "idea of subdivision may become a curse or disease, but there are some developing notions: The whole thing can be a checkerboard-mosaic."[188] The final work—which Blitzstein described in a letter to Copland as a "ballad-symphony"—was structured in three large-scale movements, each with four subsections and each containing a "ballad."[189]

First Movement

Second Movement

Third Movement

Blitzstein's musical language in *The Airborne Symphony* is deliberately heterogeneous, in tune with the multiplicity of threads running through the work and reflecting an epic concept of the genre famously explained by Mahler: "to me, 'symphony' means constructing a world with all the technical means at one's disposal."[190] Blitzstein references a wide range of styles, from barbershop quartet to Stravinskian octatonicism and neoclassical fugues. In the opening, for example, the narrator alternates with a neoclassical orchestral texture and a mostly homophonic chorus. Dissonance and distortion are used in the middle movement—whether in the portrayal of "The Enemy" or in the section called "Threat and Approach." Here Blitzstein remains purposely in a Stravinskian idiom steeped more in the sound world of *The Rite of Spring* than in that of *Symphony of Psalms*, although Blitzstein did more to acknowledge the latter's influence on the *Airborne Symphony*, perhaps because it was a safer modernist work as well as one famously dedicated to the glory of God and the Boston Symphony Orchestra. After the dirgelike "Ballad of the Cities," with its implacable list of places destroyed by enemy air strikes from London to Rotterdam and Warsaw, we shift into a more upbeat context in the third movement. Its sassy "Ballad of Hurry-Up" introduces the plucky U.S. airmen through the narrator's description, in response to which Blitzstein's orchestra seems to transform into an increasingly American idiom. The narration is followed by a barbershop-style chorus, a moment of tongue-in-cheek lightness and innocence. The American tone is carried through in the near-Broadway style of "Night Music." Blitzstein ends his work in affirmation, with a celebration of victory, whose opening gesture conforms to a familiar socialist realist and Americanist trope of a final apotheosis. Yet in this last movement, the work shows its roots in the universe of a prominent popular-front pacifist who had been turned into a soldier by the attack on Leningrad. "Warning, warning, warning," the narrator intones over the victory chimes, setting a limit on the unabashed celebration of chorus and orchestra.

Even though the narrative trajectory of the *Airborne Symphony* followed the familiar plot of wartime symphonies from innocence through struggle to victory, it differed not only in the somewhat incongruous note of the ending but also through the inclusion of such Allied heroes as the British bombardier in "Morning Poem" and of the innumerable victims across the Allied world from Malta to Manila. Blitzstein's war was universal in its perspective, even if, in the end, the American Air Force won the day. For all its U.S. propagandist credentials, this transnational representation distinguished Blitzstein from his more blatantly nationalist colleagues Harris and Barber. His war symphony was about modern war itself: "The threat is airborne; the fight is airborne; and victory will be airborne."[191] That the victory would be American was less important than that it would be the victory of "free men." Ironically, then, the war symphony that seems at first glance the most topical (especially when compared to more abstract works such as Harris's Fifth Symphony or, as we will see, Copland's Third) is in fact the least nationalist of the group. Yet by integrating musical elements that are clearly identified with American popular and concert culture, Blitzstein's work remains grounded in his own national context, if in a less strident way. Circumstances delayed the work's première until 1946, a year after the end of the war, when Leonard Bernstein and the New York Philharmonic gave it a brilliant and highly successful launch.[192]

Blitzstein's close friend Copland found a different solution to the juggling act between national(ist) credentials and universalist appeal in his Third Symphony (Figure 5.6). Premièred in 1946, this work perches intriguingly on the cusp between the wartime symphony and the postwar one. Unlike Blitzstein, who composed a symphonic ode to air combat, Copland was much more traditional and abstract. He produced a four-movement symphony that he characterized as "in the grand manner." It follows the genre's traditional mold, including the final movement: in sonata form, with a "massive restatement of the opening phrase" at the end, it creates not only a monumental closure but also thematic unity.[193] According to the program note from the première, the Third Symphony was "intended to reflect the euphoric spirit of the country at the time."[194] Although earlier he had publicly embraced

FIGURE 5.6 This group portrait shows several of the composers discussed in this chapter, together with the conductor Leopold Stokowski. *Left to right:* Leopold Stokowski, Deems Taylor, Paul Creston, Aaron Copland, and William Schuman. *Musical Courier* (January 5, 1944): 8.

the use of nationalist content in his wartime music, however, Copland was rather cagey about these issues when it came to this work. A program, he claimed, would create an ideological context ex post facto. He insisted on the work's abstract nature—in his note he described the symphony as "absolute music"—and claimed that there were neither folk nor popular materials used in it. His sole concession was the adoption of his *Fanfare for the Common Man*, because, after all, the symphony "was a wartime piece—or more accurately, an end-of-war piece." Other than that, Copland's comments focused on the abstract formal structure of his "longest orchestral work."[195] Greatness was clearly what Copland aimed for, and his friends confirmed that he had succeeded. Irving Fine told him that the work, while too popularist for his liking, contained "some of the noblest music you have ever written," and Koussevitzky (who generally showered the works he premièred with extravagant praise) went all out, compounding the trope of the "Great American Symphony" when he exclaimed to the reporter from *Time*: "There is no doubt about it—this is the greatest American symphony. It goes from the heart to the heart."[196]

Yet for all his claims of absolutist abstraction, Copland's Third Symphony carried far more war-related programmatic elements than he let on, which tied the work tightly to the wartime context of its genesis. Although the United States was involved in World War II for barely four years, it had transformed the public understanding of American musical populism from one tied to the ideals of the popular front (and therefore politically suspect in many quarters) to one equated with musical wartime Americana (and therefore a universal, accepted universally). Copland's choice of a tonal idiom, a classical musical form, and a deliberately monumental finale for his Third Symphony located the work smack in the center of this reinterpretation of nationalist populism as wartime music. Copland made the link blindingly obvious in the quotation, in the fourth movement, of the *Fanfare for the Common Man* (whose origins in 1942 as one for the "series of wartime fanfares" commissioned by Eugene Goossens he acknowledged in the program note).[197] But it was not only the well-known theme from *Common Man* that made it into the symphony; he also used an alternative motive that he had considered for the Goossens commission at the beginning of the second movement, an *allegro molto* scherzo.[198] In this passage Thomson heard the "use of brass instruments and drums to express a frankly military thesis," which he compared to Shostakovich, linking Copland's Third to the (in)famous "Leningrad" Symphony.[199] But the quotation of the fanfare has additional overtones, for its iteration at the beginning of the fourth movement evokes Copland's instrumentation of "Simple Gifts" when the Shaker hymn is first introduced in *Appalachian Spring*. While the lesson might seem an obvious one of turning swords into plowshares, there is also a more subliminal one at its heart: wartime Americana would retain its populist uses even during times of peace. Whereas the *Fanfare for the Common Man* carried both patriotic and populist references—the "common man" in the fanfare's title evokes Henry Wallace's dictum that his was the century of the common man—its pastoral recasting in the symphony through the sonorities of *Appalachian Spring* allows for a more equivocal reading that ties left-wing populism to wartime nationalism.

This referentiality, together with the work's classical form and tonal character, situate the Third Symphony in precisely the context that Copland tried to deny in his program notes. Such authorial rejections seem more in tune with postwar reactions against the openly political character of wartime works and point to the major shift in U.S. music in the later 1940s and early '50s. But in 1946, when the work was premiered, Copland's listeners were clearly still attuned to wartime musical rhetoric. Whether they enjoyed the Americanist quality of the work or found it suspicious—one of the most famous quips about the work described it as "Shostakovich in the Appalachians"[200]—Copland's Third was situated somewhat ambiguously between waning notions of the wartime symphony and uncertainties over what might follow. In either case, however, even somewhat abstract signifiers could carry clear referential signification for an interpretive community.[201] Thomson's reviews of the work, in particular, created a discursive matrix that position the symphony somewhere between the positive quality of a transparent simplicity inspired by man's "common humanity" and the dangerous proximity to the "patriotic-versus-pastoral formula" associated with Soviet wartime compositions.[202]

In this respect, Copland's Third Symphony had much more in common with a work like Harris's Fifth, which similarly claimed the symphonic high ground and rejected quotations of the vernacular, only to be accused of bombast. Yet in the competitive writing of symphonies during World War II—both among American composers and between them and Allied (especially Soviet) ones—the more abstract form of musical Americanism carried far greater appeal, and greater aesthetic weight, than folkloric quotations on the one hand, or even the vocal symphonism of Blitzstein on the other. One could choose any number of other wartime symphonies to illustrate the point: deliberately neutral compositions such as Piston's Symphony no. 2 (1943) and Moore's Symphony no. 5 (1945); works that understood themselves as representative of Americana to some degree, such as Carter's Symphony no. 1 (1942) and George Antheil's Symphony no. 4, "1942" (1943); symphonies with explicit programs, including Robert Russell Bennett's *Four Freedoms Symphony* (1943) and Still's Symphony no. 5, "Western Hemisphere" (1945); and vocal symphonies such as Leonard Bernstein's Symphony no. 1, "Jeremiah" (1942) and Dello Joio's Symphony for Voices and Orchestra after Stephen Vincent Benét's *Western Star* (1945). One should add to these the symphonies written by European composers in U.S. exile who turned to the genre because of the nature of American musical life: Stravinsky, Martinů, and Milhaud spring to mind, for all of whom (even Stravinsky) their American symphonies were their first mature compositions in the genre.[203] As we saw in chapter 4, the symphony's universalism allowed exiled composers either to fuse their own nationalist particularities with Americanist elements into hybrid realizations or to pursue a transnational universalism in works that were often highly successful both during the war and after. Clearly the symphony held an important, if not the most important, position in the output of both native and foreign composers in

U.S. exile during the war, and also, of course, in the programming strategies of the country's orchestras and broadcast networks.

Yet Americanism during the war years was not characterized solely by the discovery or reinvention of conventional forms and idioms. Another, fledgling side was the deliberate experimentalism and iconoclasm championed by the group of artists that included, among others, John Cage, Merce Cunningham, Lou Harrison, and Harry Partch. The latter's topical *Y.D. Fantasy: On the Words of an Early American Tune* (1944) and *U.S. Highball: A Musical Account of a Transcontinental Hobo Trip* (1943) offered a quizzical approach to American themes, although these two pieces were as grounded in U.S. culture as the more conservative works usually associated with Americana.[204] For his part, Cage was highly productive in the war years, with works that focused on percussion ensembles and prepared piano and included such electronic media as the radio and phonograph. His was the ultramodernist ideology of an Americanism steeped in the rhetoric of difference—and therefore exceptionalism—characterized by the well-known trope of noise as an acoustic signifier of modernity. In the late 1930s Cage claimed that "wherever we are, what we hear is mostly noise. When we ignore it, it disturbs us. When we listen to it, we find it fascinating. The sound of a truck at fifty miles per hour. Static between the stations. Rain."[205] Modernity and nature thus merged into a sonic landscape worthy of auditory contemplation and compositional engagement. The role of the musician was to integrate this contemporary soundscape into modern music through recourse to the most "primitive" (as the critics called them) sonorities, those of percussion. In an article accompanying a photo spread about a percussion concert held at the Metropolitan Museum of Art on February 7, 1943, the writer paraphrased Cage as saying that "when people today get to understand and like this music, which is produced by banging one object with another, they will find new beauty in everyday modern life, which is made by objects banging against each other."[206]

But whereas Cage grounded his aesthetic justification in a populist interwar rhetoric that aimed at revealing beauty in everyday life—including (in a 1942 article) the technologies of cinema—Thomson, in a 1945 concert review, put Cage squarely into the modernist endeavors of Italian futurists while declaring him the logical consequence of Schoenberg's emancipation of dissonance. The tracing of this lineage might seem a conventional theme of current textbooks, but for its time it cut an edge. Perhaps more surprising, however, is that Thomson felt himself able to praise Cage: "the novelty of his timbres, the logic of his discourse, are used to intensify communication, not as ends in themselves."[207] Here, then, was another form of populist art, one that sought to communicate to a broader audience even as it lay out on the ultramodernist fringe. We might associate Cage's experimentalism with wartime technological innovation, and even his noise with contemporary soundscapes, but his would-be populism sits squarely in the American context of its time.

Cage's works during the war years rarely respond directly to world events: once he achieved his goal of being exempted from the draft in December 1942, he ignored them almost entirely, at least in his music.[208] But two of these works—each written to be choreographed by Merce Cunningham and Jean Erdman—bear titles referring to the conflict. *Credo in US* and *In the Name of the Holocaust* both stem from 1942, when the war was uppermost in everyone's mind. And for all its purported irony (which Cage later claimed), *Credo in US*, composed in July, engages with issues of U.S. cultural identity that were much discussed that year. This work for four players—two percussionists, one pianist, and one performer using a radio or phonograph—was Cage's first to require the haphazard insertion of music by other composers, and his preferred repertoire came straight from the symphonic classics of the American concert hall: "If Radio is used, avoid News programs during national or international emergencies. If Phonograph, use some classic: e.g. Dvorak, Beethoven, Sibelius or Shostakovich."[209] His choice of composers—especially the reference to Shostakovich in July 1942, the month of the U.S. première of the Seventh Symphony—embraces the musical universe of American middlebrow culture.

In a conversation with Richard Kostelanetz in 1970, Cage talked about *Credo in US* as a work of its time, characterizing it as "a kind of satire on America." Kostelanetz sought clarification: "So the irony is also romantic, classical music bursting out of the speakers, and that was America's idea of culture." In response, Cage added, "And the cowboy solo, and the jazz solo, and so forth."[210] Besides the music and dance, Erdman and Cunningham also included dialogue (now lost) in a work that was a commentary on American taste. It consists of four sections titled "Façade" and three interpolated "Progressions," and their stylistic heterogeneity allows play on musical identity markers. As well as the modernist sonorities associated with Cowell and Stravinsky (including polytonal writing for the piano), the score draws, for example, on diatonic, folk song–inspired passages in the "First Progression" (what Cage called a "cowboy solo") and blues and jazz in the "Third Progression" (the "jazz solo").[211] Whether ironic or not, the work's conclusion, with its repeated loud closing gestures (gong, cans, piano, and phonograph/radio) resonates with the monumental endings of wartime compositions, including the one that rang in so many American ears in July 1942: the finale of Shostakovich's Seventh.[212] Nor did Cage appear ironic in his "Lecture on Nothing" (1959) when he wrote: "Half intellectually and half sentimentally, when the war came along, I decided to use only quiet sounds. There seemed to be no truth, no good, in anything big in society."[213] The retrospective statement that war should need a counterpoint in quiet sounds seems more an acknowledgment of Cage's reflective mindset at the time than a description of his compositional output.

Reading *Credo in US* as a work about the United States and its musical culture reveals the familiar sonic representation of nation based on vernacular (folk and blues) and symphonic musics. What Cage satirized (or claimed in 1970 to have satirized) in *Credo in US* a music lover would have found in abundance in New York's major performing spaces in 1942: Copland's *Rodeo* on the stage of the Metropolitan Opera House, the Gershwins' *Porgy and Bess* in Cheryl Crawford's famous revival at the Majestic Theater, Beethoven performed by the New York Philharmonic, and Shostakovich's "Leningrad" Symphony on the radio at home. Indeed, from its stylistic heterogeneity to its overall classical construction (borrowed from the symphonic rondo-finale), with its reliance on imported music, its use of vernacular signifiers as markers of national identity, and its integration of such mass media as phonograph and radio, *Credo in US* amalgamates key elements of the American soundscape during World War II. It refracts the image of an American musical identity constructed at the crossroads of the vernacular and the universal, both appropriated for a usable past, on the one hand, and for contemporary musical practice, on the other. In that respect, *Credo in US* might well be viewed as one of the more emblematic pieces of Americana emerging from World War II.

Neither Cage nor his fellow composers forgot the lessons in Americana learned in the crucible of this last "good" war. Cage, for example, would return to nativist sources in such later works as *The Harmony of Maine* (1978) and *Hymns and Variations* (1979), the latter a composition based on William Billings's "Old North" and "Heath." Other composers reconfigured their war compositions by integrating them into new works, as in the case of William Schuman, whose 1956 *New England Triptych* incorporated his 1943 *William Billings Overture*.[214] Others still—like Copland—distanced themselves from the topical implications of their compositions. For them, the postwar musical landscape changed quickly, especially as a disenchanted avant-garde, particularly in Europe, questioned the legitimacy of any musical reference to national identities or other ideological tenets in music composed after a world war rooted in a poisoned ideology. With the end of the war, the desirability of creating a national musical language disappeared not only in Europe but soon in the United States as well. Yet the musical idioms of

World War II have maintained such a strong presence in American life as the archetypal national sound such that they served a presidential inauguration almost seventy years later. How they did so is a topic for another book. Why they did, however, should now be clear. The soldiers cheering Lily Pons in an Asian jungle, the sailors listening to string quartets on the afterdeck, the flyers thrilling to the sounds of airborne symphonies—they may or may not have known what they were hearing, but they understood what it represented. Music mattered.

Introduction

1. John Burlingame, "Williams' Music to Obama's Ears," *Variety*, January 15, 2009, http://www.variety.com/article/VR1117998645?refCatId=16 (accessed July 30, 2011). Tim Smith refers to Copland as one of the president's favorite composers in "Inaugural Premiere Resonates with Copland," *Baltimore Sun*, January 20, 2009.

2. This was not the first time that Copland's wartime music played a role in this president's political career. When he was the junior senator for the state of Illinois, Barack Obama himself performed the narration of Copland's *Lincoln Portrait* with the Chicago Symphony Orchestra in 2005, on the fourth anniversary of the 9/11 attacks; for a short video clip, see http://www.therestisnoise.com/2009/01/lincoln-copland-obama.html (accessed July 30, 2011). For recollections of the rehearsal and performance, see the blog of Bill Eddins, who conducted the concert, at http://www.insidethearts.com/sticksanddrones/2008/02/02/billeddins/82/ (accessed July 30, 2011).

3. Pullen, *Patriotism in America*, 104–5.

4. Tucker, *Swing Shift*.

5. Samuel Barber, letter to Aaron Copland, September 16, 1944, *ACC*, Box 246.

6. Tucker, *Swing Shift*; Smith, *God Bless America*; Jones, *Songs That Fought the War*; Young and Young, *Music of the World War II Era*.

7. Gaines, "Duke Ellington"; Barg, "National Voices/Modernist Histories"; Carter, *"Oklahoma!" The Making of an American Musical*.

8. Kowalke, "'I'm an American!'"; Walsh, *Stravinsky: The Second Exile*; Feisst, *Schoenberg's New World*.

9. Crist, *Music for the Common Man*; Swayne, "William Schuman"; Swayne, *Orpheus in Manhattan*; Wright, "The Enlisted Composer."

10. Zuck, *History of Musical Americanism*. With respect to the symphony, World War II is addressed in a section of Tawa, *Great American Symphony*. Studies on composers and performers that discuss the war include Gordon, *Mark the Music*; Pollack, *Marc Blitzstein*; Crist, *Music for the Common Man*; Swayne, *Orpheus in Manhattan*; Horowitz, *Understanding Toscanini*.

11. Potter, "What Is 'Nazi Music'?," especially 444.

12. This issue is addressed critically in Denning, *Cultural Front.*

13. Some recent examples include Riethmüller, ed., *Geschichte der Musik im 20. Jahrhundert,* vol. 2, *1925–1945,* 243–315; Huener and Nicosia, eds., *Arts in Nazi Germany;* Grochulski, Kautny, and Keden, eds., *Musik in Diktaturen des 20. Jahrhunderts;* Levi, *Mozart and the Nazis.*

14. Tomoff, *Creative Union,* 63–94; Frolova-Walker, *Russian Music and Nationalism,* 344–46.

15. For France, see in particular Schwartz, "Die Musikpolitik der Nationalsozialisten"; Sprout, "Music for a 'New Era'"; Chimènes, ed., *La vie musicale sous Vichy;* Simon, *Composer sous Vichy.* For Italy, see Stenzl, *Von Giacomo Puccini zu Luigi Nono;* Nicolodi, *Musica e musicisti;* Sachs, *Music in Fascist Italy;* Illiano, ed., *Italian Music during the Fascist Period.* For a broader geographical scope, see Illiano and Sala, eds., *Music and Dictatorship.* See also Bianchi, "Musica e Guerra."

16. Young and Young, *Music of the Great Depression,* 172.

17. This section draws on Fauser, "Cultural Musicology."

18. Steven Spielberg, dir., *Saving Private Ryan* (1998); DVD released by Dreamworks Video, 2004.

19. Lowens, *Music in America.* For a recent assessment of the U.S. appropriation of German music and aesthetics, see Gienow-Hecht, *Sound Diplomacy.*

20. See, for example, DeLapp, "Copland in the Fifties"; Murchison, "Nationalism in William Grant Still and Aaron Copland"; Oja, *Making Music Modern;* Levy, "Frontier Figures"; Beal, *New Music, New Allies;* Fosler-Lussier, *Music Divided;* Ansari, "'Masters of the President's Music.'"

21. For example, see my "Gendering the Nations"; *Musical Encounters at the 1889 Paris World's Fair;* "Aaron Copland, Nadia Boulanger, and the Making of an 'American' Composer,"; "'Dixie *Carmen.'"*

22. Lerner, "Aaron Copland, Norman Rockwell, and the 'Four Freedoms.'"

23. "Roland Hayes, Famed Tenor, Wife Beaten by Georgia Cops," *New York Amsterdam News,* July 25, 1942. According to the *New York Times,* Mrs. Hayes said: "This is no time to talk about racial prejudice and segregation. Hitler ought to have you." See "Beaten in Georgia, Says Roland Hayes," *New York Times,* July 17, 1942.

24. Alex Ross, *Listen to This* (New York: Farrar, Straus, & Giroux, 2010), 242.

25. Tick, *Ruth Crawford Seeger,* 280–90.

26. Cusick, "'You Are in a Place That Is Out of the World.'"

27. Wolfe and Akenson, eds., *Country Music Goes to War;* Martus, Münkler, and Röcke, eds., *Schlachtfelder;* Firme and Hocker, eds., *Von Schlachthymnen und Protestsongs;* Hanheide, *Pace: Musik zwischen Krieg und Frieden.*

28. Watkins, *Proof through the Night;* Kelley and Snell, eds., *Bugle Resounding.*

Chapter 1

1. Harold Clurman, letter to Aaron Copland dated (by Copland) December 8, 1941, *ACC,* Box 250.

2. Serge Koussevitzky, "Musicians as Soldiers," typescript, *SKC,* Box 127.

3. Ross Lee Finney, undated questionnaires, late January 1943; responses collected in Ross Lee Finney, Correspondence, *WcM*, ML94.F55, Boxes 1 and 2. Finney published a digest of the answers in "The American Composer and the War," *Proceedings of the Music Teachers National Association*, ed. Theodore M. Finney (Pittsburgh: M.T.N.A., 1943): 31–51.

4. Finney, "The American Composer and the War," 36 (Robinson) and 40 (Donovan).

5. Marion Bauer, undated response to questionnaire, in Ross Lee Finney, Correspondence, *WcM*, ML94.F55, Box 1; Freed, in Finney, "The American Composer and the War," 37. Bauer's is the only response by a woman composer and one of the very few questionnaires *not* incorporated into Finney's article.

6. Barber, in Finney, "The American Composer and the War," 33.

7. Claire Reis, letter to Harold Spivacke, January 28, 1942, *JANCSM*, Box 15. Reis eventually sent the responses to the questionnaires to the Subcommittee on Music of the Joint Army and Navy Committee on Welfare and Recreation (*WcM*, ML390.L37).

8. In a letter to Spivacke dated March 4, 1942, Reis referred to an article published in the *New York Times* that same day in which Arthur Krock reported on the proposed creation of a national talent pool; see *JANCSM*, Box 15.

9. Statistics from the website of the Selective Services System: History and Records, http://www.sss.gov/induct.htm (accessed December 1, 2009). Ten million is the cumulative number of people inducted into the military by the end of the war.

10. Typescript "Musicians in the Army," *JANCSM*, Box 11.

11. Christy Fox, "20 Wacs from Varied Walks Rank as Majors," *Los Angeles Times*, September 22, 1943.

12. For a short history of the band, see http://www.nps.gov/archive/wapa/indepth/extcontent/usmc/pcn-190-003129-00/sec16.htm (accessed November 30, 2009).

13. Stone and Medin, *Musical Women Marines*. Copy available at the Research Center of the Wisconsin Veterans Museum, Madison.

14. Engel, *This Bright Day*, 141.

15. Robert Ward opened his 1943 "Letter from the Army" (*Modern Music* 20/3 [1943]: 170–74) with this question. On musicians as chaplain's assistants, see 172.

16. Harold Spivacke, letter to Sydney Beck, May 11, 1942, *JANCSM*, Box 2.

17. Ulysses Simpson Kay, letter to Aaron Copland, October 8, 1942, *ACC*, Box 257.

18. Ulysses Simpson Kay, letter to Aaron Copland, April 8, 1943, *ACC*, Box 257; see also his letter to Virgil Thomson, October 14, 1943, which complains about the "routine and dull work" (*VTP*, Box 56).

19. Program in Lehman Engel's 1943–45 scrapbook, *LEC*.

20. Reis, *Composers, Conductors and Critics*, 157.

21. "In the World of Music: Service Men Are the Soloists in a Program Dedicated to Men in the Armed Forces," *New York Times*, July 23, 1943; R. L., "Stars in Service Excel at Stadium," *New York Times*, July 30, 1944. The work was commissioned by the conductor Thor Johnson, a warrant officer and bandleader in the U.S. Army Signal Corps; see Hobson and Richardson, *Ulysses Kay*, 34.

22. Aaron Copland, letter to William Schuman, September 3, 1942, in Crist and Shirley, eds., *Selected Correspondence of Aaron Copland*, 146.

23. Aaron Copland, letter to Harold Spivacke, August 3, 1942 (carbon copy), *ACC*, Box 346. An extract is published in Crist and Shirley, eds., *Selected Correspondence of Aaron Copland*, 145–46.

24. Harold Spivacke, letter to Aaron Copland, August 28, 1942 (carbon copy), *JANCSM*, Box 4. An extract is published in Crist and Shirley, eds., *Selected Correspondence of Aaron Copland*, 146.

25. Aaron Copland, letter to Harold Spivacke, September 3, 1942, in Crist and Shirley, eds., *Selected Correspondence of Aaron Copland*, 145.

26. Harold Spivacke, letter to Aaron Copland, September 19, 1942 (carbon copy), *JANCSM*, Box 4.

27. For the lost paperwork, see the folder on Copland, in *JANCSM*, Box 4.

28. Heyman, *Samuel Barber*, 212. Data about Barber's wartime service come from Heyman's biography. See also Wright, "The Enlisted Composer."

29. Claude Debussy (1913), cited in Watkins, *Proof through the Night*, 170.

30. Heyman, *Samuel Barber*, 216.

31. Ibid., 223, 225.

32. Ibid., 236.

33. Samuel Barber, letter to Aaron Copland, September 16, 1944, *ACC*, Box 246.

34. Pollack, *Marc Blitzstein*, 261.

35. Gordon, *Mark the Music*, 223–25.

36. Ibid., 224.

37. Army Separation Qualification record for Marc Blitzstein, June 26, 1945, *MBA*.

38. Lehman Engel, letter to Harold Spivacke, September 7, 1942, *JANCSM*, Box 5.

39. Engel, *This Bright Day*, 133.

40. Concert programs in Lehman Engel's scrapbooks for 1942–45, *LEC*.

41. Engel, *This Bright Day*, 143.

42. "Shumski to Play Solo at Watergate Concert," *Washington Post*, June 6, 1943.

43. Ray C. B. Brown, "Navy Band Orchestra Gives Better, Varied Performance," *Washington Post*, January 30, 1943.

44. Programs of the U.S. Navy Band Symphony Orchestra, *JANCSM*, Box 12.

45. Programs of the U.S. Navy Band Symphony Orchestra, May 12, 1944, January 12, 1945, *JANCSM*, Box 12.

46. "Marine Orchestra to Give Concert Wednesday Night," *Washington Post*, January 18, 1942.

47. Ray C. B. Brown, "Music of Latin Neighbors Is Thrilling," *Washington Post*, April 15, 1942.

48. "This Week's Radio Concerts," *New York Times*, February 14, 1943; Audrey Walz, "National Gallery Sponsors Events," *Musical America* 63 (June 1943): 32.

49. Isabel Morse Jones, "Concert Series Arranged for Service String Quartet," *Los Angeles Times*, August 20, 1944.

50. "They Shall Have Music in War as in Peace," *Musical America* 63 (February 10, 1943): 7.

51. Nathan Gottschalk, undated letter to Harold Spivacke (late November 1943), *JANCSM*, Box 6.

52. "Back from Hell of Dunkirk, He's Set to Battle Nazis," *Chicago Defender*, February 20, 1943.

53. La Roe, *Woman Surgeon*, 366. Ish-ti-Opi performed in June 1939 for the Roosevelts and the British royal couple during the latter's visit to the United States. See Eleanor Roosevelt, "My Day," June 13, 1939, http://www.gwu.edu/~erpapers/myday/displaydoc

.cfm?_y=1939&_f=mdo55291 (accessed January 2, 2010). This performance is recreated in Roger Michell, dir., *Hyde Park on Hudson* (2012).

54. Conrad, *Dodascalies*, 226–81.

55. Ross Lee Finney Papers, *NYpM*, JPB 04–15, Box 2; see also Finney, *Profile of a Lifetime*, 114–45.

56. "Opera and Concert Asides," *New York Times*, April 12, 1942; "Musicians Serving with Armed Forces," *Musical America* 62 (February 25, 1942): 4.

57. "Carroll Glenn Wed to Sgt. Eugene List," *New York Times*, August 17, 1943.

58. See the articles in the *New York Times* on June 2, 1943 (Olin Downes, "Concert in Honor of Rachmaninoff"), June 20, 1942 ("Concert Tribute to Soviet Union"), and March 1, 1943 (R. L., "Sgt. Eugene List Soloist").

59. "Music: Court Pianist," *Time*, April 22, 1946, http://www.time.com/time/magazine/article/0,9171,792804,00.html (accessed January 2, 2010).

60. For female jazz players, see Tucker, *Swing Shift*.

61. Olin Downes, "Opera Opening," *New York Times*, November 22, 1942.

62. *Newsweek*, October 2, 1939, in clippings file "World War II," *NYpM*.

63. "U.S. Attorneys Give Rules for Aliens," *New York Times*, January 9, 1942.

64. Gertrud Hindemith, letter to William Theo Brown, March 29, 1942, *PHC*, Box 21.

65. Krenek, *Die amerikanischen Tagebücher*, 240.

66. Kurt Weill, letter to Erika Mann, June 17, 1940, cited in Kowalke, "'I'm an American!,'" 112.

67. Pinza, *Ezio Pinza*, 205, 209. With his FBI file no longer available (as the FBI informed me), Pinza's suspicion that his arrest was the result of having been denounced by an opportunistic fellow singer cannot be verified.

68. Pinza, *Ezio Pinza*, 208.

69. "Ezio Pinza Freed after 11 Weeks on Ellis Island as Enemy Alien," *New York Times*, June 5, 1942; see also Pinza, *Ezio Pinza*, 223–24.

70. Françoise Dony, "Belgian Artists Filtering into Brussels; Musical Life Reported Slowly Reviving," *Musical America* 60 (October 10, 1940): 15.

71. "Concert Opens National Series for Polish Aid," *New York Herald Tribune*, November 15, 1939.

72. Gordon, *Mark the Music*, 211. A copy of the concert program can be found in *ACC*, Box 246.

73. Olin Downes, "Wartime Weapon: Music Swings Its Weight in the Battle between Nations and Systems," *New York Times*, October 26, 1941.

74. Eleanor Roosevelt, "Music Should Go On! A Message from the First Lady," *Musical America* 62 (February 10, 1942): [3].

75. "Music Goes to War," *Musical Courier* 125 (February 5, 1942): 5–7, 116, at 7.

76. "'Victory Concert' Held: Ernest Hutcheson Plays for Men in Armed Services," *New York Times*, February 8, 1942.

77. Irving Kolodin, "Victory Concerts Pass a Milestone," *New York Sun*, January 8, 1943.

78. "Allied Nations' Concert Will Be Heard March 18," *New York Herald Tribune*, March 4, 1942.

79. Howard Taubman, "Grieg Centenary Is Observed Here," *New York Times*, June 16, 1943.

80. "Two Significant Appeals: For Music and to Our Musicians," *Musical America* 62 (January 25, 1942): 16.

81. Ibid.

82. Koussevitzky, in ibid.; Heifetz's remark is quoted in a letter by the husband of Blanche Siegelbaum, transcribed in a folder of press releases from 1943–45, USO Papers, *NYpT*, *T=Mss 1991–007, Box 3.

83. Chester I. Barnard, "USO Yesterday, Today, and Tomorrow: Annual Report of the President," self-published USO pamphlet dated February 4, 1945; copy in *WcM*, Old Correspondence.

84. USO publicity materials in the folder "USO Camp Shows," *JANCSM*, Box 20.

85. Lawrence Phillips, letter to Harold Spivacke, December 3, 1942, *JANCSM*, Box 20, folder "USO Camp Shows."

86. Chester I. Barnard, "USO Yesterday, Today, and Tomorrow: Annual Report of the President," self-published USO pamphlet dated February 4, 1945; copy in *WcM*, Old Correspondence.

87. Frances Quaintance Eaton, "Keep 'Em Listening," *Musical America* 63 (February 10, 1943): 5, 14, 18, at 18.

88. "USO Concert Unit No. 275 Reports 'Successful Mission Accomplished!'" *Musical America* 65 (February 10, 1945): 280–81.

89. Ibid., 280.

90. Chaplain Theodore B. Mitzner, letter to USO Concert Division, August 2, 1944, USO Papers, *NYpT*, *T=Mss 1991–007, Box 2, Folder 3.

91. Tucker, *Swing Shift*, 277.

92. Letter by an anonymous seaman, January 5, 1945, quoted in Clayton Hamilton, *Keep 'Em Laughing: A Commentary on the Contribution of USO–Camp Shows, Inc. to the Winning of the War*, typescript, p. 15. USO Papers, *NYpT*, *T=Mss 1991–007, Box 1, Folder 5.

93. Hamilton, *Keep 'Em Laughing*, 214.

94. Handwritten memo (signature illegible) to Colonel Marvin Young, May 10, 1943, General Records (1941–45) of the Special Services Division, Office of the Director of Personnel, *NARA*, RG 160, Box 249. Young's response is attached to the memo.

95. Gino Bandini, memo to Lawrence Phillips, September 25, 1943, General Records (1941–45) of the Special Services Division, Office of the Director of Personnel, *NARA*, RG 160, Box 249.

96. Francis Keppel, memo dated July 21, 1942, *JANC-NARA*, Box 45.

97. "Menuhin Plays at Aleutian Bases," *Musical America* 64 (August 1944): 9, 22, at 22.

98. "Best Music Urged for Troops Abroad," *New York Times*, April 18, 1943.

99. Elmer A. Carter, "Plain Talk: Morale Equals Victory," *New York Amsterdam News*, May 1, 1943.

100. Alfred E. Smith, "Dett Sees Music as Potent Weapon against Race Hate," *Chicago Defender*, July 3, 1943.

101. This and the following citations are from ibid.

102. Chester I. Barnard, "USO Yesterday, Today, and Tomorrow: Annual Report of the President," self-published USO pamphlet dated February 4, 1945, copy in *WcM*, Old Correspondence.

103. Menuhin, *Unfinished Journey*, 157.

104. http://www.uso.org/whatwedo/entertainment/historicalusocampshows (accessed February 12, 2010).

105. Press releases can be found, for example, in the papers of the *JANCSM* and those of the USO at *NYpT*.

106. Lieutenant Colonel Frederick M. Warburg, memo to Colonel Kerr, August 20, 1944, General Records (1941–45) of the Special Services Division, Office of the Director of Personnel, *NARA*, RG 160, Box 396.

107. Stern, *My First 79 Years*, 42.

108. Compare, for example the reports on Unit #264 (with Isaac Stern as the lead artists) as published in *Musical America* 64 (August 1944): 9, 22, and the so-called "Interview Notes" in the USO press release of July 13, 1944, in the USO Papers, *NYpT*, *T=Mss 1991–007, Box 3, Folder 3.

109. "Menuhin Plays at Aleutian Bases," 9. For the dates and unit assignation, see Abe Lastfogel, "USO Camp Shows, Inc. (Stage, Radio, and Screen): Report on Year of 1944 (January 1, 1944, to December 31, 1944)," typescript, USO Papers, *NYpT*, *T=Mss 1991–007, Box 2, Folder 3.

110. Cited in Burton, *Yehudi Menuhin*, 225.

111. Menuhin, *Unfinished Journey*, 154, 156.

112. Frances Quaintance Eaton, "Musical Mission to the Southwest Pacific," *Musical America* 64 (January 10, 1944): 5, 13, 18, at 18.

113. The 1944 radio broadcast has been released online at http://www.youtube.com/watch?v=SHawNTX7Ntc (accessed February 14, 2010).

114. Publicity Department, USO Camp Shows Inc., press release, April 11, 1945, *NYpT*, *T=Mss 1991–007, Box 3.

115. Entry of January 13, 1945, in: Andre Kostelanetz and Lily Pons, Travel Diary (typescript), p. 7; *NYpT*, *T=Mss 1991–007, Box 3.

116. Andre Kostelanetz, letter to Ethel and Boris Kostelanetz, January 12, 1945, *AKC*.

117. Andre Kostelanetz, letter to Ruth Prynne, March 8, 1945, *AKC*.

118. Andre Kostelanetz, letter to Ethel and Boris Kostelanetz, March 15, 1945, *AKC*.

119. Ibid.

120. Andre Kostelanetz, letter to Ruth Prynne, March 15, 1945, *AKC*.

121. Andre Kostelanetz, letter to his CBS Orchestra, June 1, 1944, *AKC*.

122. Kostelanetz and Pons, Travel Diary, entry for January 13, 1945.

123. Andre Kostelanetz, letter to Ethel and Boris Kostelanetz, January 12, 1945, *AKC*.

124. Andre Kostelanetz, green-bound, handwritten diary of the USO tour to India, Burma, and China, *AKC*.

125. Andre Kostelanetz, letter to Ethel and Boris Kostelanetz, January 3, 1945, *AKC*.

126. Harry Marlatt, "Pons and Kostelanetz Win G.I. Ovations in Persian Gulf Command Tour," *Musical America* 64 (September 1944): 5, 22.

127. Telegrams in the correspondence files of the General Records (1941–45) of the Special Services Division, Office of the Director of Personnel, *NARA*, RG 160, Box 284.

128. Report sheet for the concert of Vladimir Horowitz, May 25, 1943, General Records (1941–45) of the Special Services Division, Office of the Director of Personnel, *NARA*, RG 160, Box 284.

129. See General Records (1941–45) of the Special Services Division, Office of the Director of Personnel, *NARA*, RG 160, Box 284.

130. See report sheets in General Records (1941–45) of the Special Services Division, Office of the Director of Personnel, *NARA*, RG 160, Box 284. The program for the Ballet Russe is given in "Ballet Season Opening," *New York Times*, March 28, 1943.

131. "Festival of Allied Music Held to Aid Detroit Players," *Musical America* 62 (March 10, 1942): 3, 6.

132. See, for example, the list in "Kindler Names Native Works to Be Played," *Washington Post*, September 17, 1944.

133. Olin Downes, "Toscanini Gives All-U.S. Program," *New York Times*, November 2, 1942.

134. However recent scholarship might rethink the level of Toscanini's anti-Fascism, at the time the conductor was portrayed as a stalwart on the Allied side. For a critical evaluation of Toscanini, see Taruskin, "The Darker Side of Modern Music."

135. Olin Downes, "Toscanini Gives All-U.S. Program," *New York Times*, November 2, 1942.

136. John Selby, "'Hepcat' Toscanini, Goodman Do Things to *Rhapsody in Blue*," *Atlanta Constitution*, November 2, 1942; John Selby, "Symphonic 'Jivesters' Let Go Under 'Hepcat' Toscanini," *The Sun*, November 2, 1942.

137. Adams, "Martinů and the American Critics," 81.

138. Leopold Stokowski, letter to Goddard Lieberman, May 27, 1942, Lieberson Papers, Yale University, Irving S. Gilmore Music Library, Correspondence, Box 4.

139. For the U.S. reception of Shostakovich's Seventh Symphony, see chapter 4.

140. Private Bernard B. Ross, letter to Serge Koussevitzky (April 1942), *SKC*.

141. Goossens's letter to Copland is quoted in Crist, *Music for the Common Man*, 180; for the complete list of fanfares premièred by the Cincinnati Symphony Orchestra, see ibid., 239n97. Ten were published as *Ten Fanfares by Ten Composers for Brass and Percussion* (New York: Boosey & Hawkes, 1944).

142. Copland and Perlis, *Copland: 1900 through 1942*, 341. The letter is in *ACC*, Box 257.

143. Andre Kostelanetz, letter to Fiorello LaGuardia, December 30, 1941, *AKC*.

144. Alan Keyes, letter to Lela Mae Stiles, January 6, 1942, *AKC*.

145. Fiorello LaGuardia, letter to Andre Kostelanetz, January 8, 1942, *AKC*.

146. Andre Kostelanetz, program notes for the concert on May 14, 1942, with the Cincinnati Symphony Orchestra, *AKC*.

147. See the letters to Andre Kostelanetz by Aaron Copland (January 30, 1942) and Virgil Thomson (February 1, 1942), *AKC*.

148. Jerome Kern, letter to Andre Kostelanetz, January 23, 1942, *AKC*.

149. "Program Notes on 'A Lincoln Portrait' by Aaron Copland," first discarded draft, ca. April 1942, *AKC*. See also Copland and Perlis, *Copland: 1900 through 1942*, 341–42.

150. "Composers Doing. Their Stuff," *New York Times*, May 3, 1942.

151. Arthur Berger, "Music in Wartime," *The New Republic*, February 7, 1944, 175.

152. Finney, "The American Composer and the War," 39.

153. See, for example, Berger, "Music in Wartime," *The New Republic*, February 7, 1944, 175–78; Henry Cowell, "In Time of Bitter War," *Modern Music* 20 (1942): 82–83; and the numerous articles on Shostakovich's Seventh Symphony cited in Gibbs, "'The Phenomenon of the Seventh.'"

154. Sergei Prokofiev, "Prokofieff, Soviet Composer, Sends Greetings to U.S. for Colleagues," *New York Times*, January 2, 1943.

155. Roger Sessions, "On the American Future" (1940), in Cone, ed., *Roger Sessions on Music*, 288–94, especially 290.

156. Arthur Berger, "Music in Wartime," *The New Republic*, February 7, 1944, 178.

157. Finney, "The American Composer and the War," 35.

158. Warren Dwight Allen, "Music in Wartime," *Music Educators Journal* 30/2 (November–December 1943): 14.

159. Wendy L. Wall explores the shifting roles of "freedom" in the solidifying of the concept of the "American Way" between the 1930s and 1960s, identifying the war years as the key turning point; see her *Inventing the "American Way."*

160. Arthur Berger, "Music in Wartime," *The New Republic*, February 7, 1944, 178.

161. Ibid.

162. Marc Blitzstein, "Composers Doing Their Stuff," *New York Times*, May 3, 1942.

163. Olin Downes, "Composers on War," *New York Times*, October 10, 1943.

164. Arthur Berger, "Music in Wartime," *The New Republic*, February 7, 1944, 177.

165. Shirley, "Aaron Copland and Arthur Berger," 200.

166. Milton Babbitt, letter to Harold Spivacke, October 25, 1942, *JANCSM*, Box 2.

167. In an email to the author of April 21, 2010, Milton Babbitt explained that he could not comment further on the nature of the Washington assignment.

168. Meyer and Shreffler, *Elliott Carter*, 51.

169. Ibid.

170. Ibid., 67.

171. A copy of Weill's petition in which he declared his nationality as "none, formerly German," is in *WLP*, Box 47, Folder 15. I have received copies of this and numerous other documents courtesy of Dave Stein of the Weill-Lenya Research Center, New York—an invaluable resource for my discussion of Weill's wartime activities. Weill's Certificate of Naturalization (dated August 27, 1943) is reproduced in Farneth, Juchem, and Stein, *Kurt Weill*, 222.

172. Adorno's formulation is cited in Kowalke, "Formerly German,'" 37.

173. Kurt Weill, letter to Erika Mann, June 17, 1940, *WLP*, Box 47, Folder 11. Jürgen Schebera cites most of this letter in "Der 'alien American' Kurt Weill," 269; but he leaves out Weill's sentence about the fifth column. I strongly disagree with his assessment that this letter proves that Weill was thinking and acting like an American. Likewise, Weill's agonizing over proving his American loyalties tends to be overlooked in the essays by Werner Grünzweig, Kim H. Kowalke, Joachim Lucchesi, Jürgen Scherbera, and Jürgen Thym in Kowalke and Edler, eds., *A Stranger Here Myself*.

174. Interview published on January 16, 1942, in *Aufbau*; quoted in English translation in Thym, "The Enigma of Kurt Weill's Whitman Songs," 291.

175. Mukherjee, "Imagining Homelands," 73. On Adorno's criticism of Weill, see Kowalke, "Kurt Weill, Moderne und populäre Kultur."

176. David W. Stowe's account of religious music in the United States doubles also as an excellent introduction in the role of religion in American identity formation; see *How Sweet the Sound*.

177. Kowalke, "Formerly German," 53.

178. Although Lydia Goehr's model of dualism allows the capture of the interstitial identities of such composers as Schoenberg, it is too binary to do full justice to the more fluid identities of either Weill or exiles from Allied nations such as France; see Goehr, "Music and Musicians in Exile." For a discussion of exile identities from the perspective of cosmopolitanism, see Cohen, "Migrant Cosmopolitan Modern," 18–22.

179. Thym, "The Enigma of Kurt Weill's Whitman Songs," 291.

180. For pertinent interpretations of Weill's Whitman songs, see Grünzweig, "Propaganda der Trauer"; Kowalke, "'I'm an American!'"

181. Kurt Weill, letter to Herbert Wechsler, February 9, 1943, *WLP*, Box 50, Folder 71. For an overview of Weill's wartime work, see Schebera, "Der 'alien American' Kurt Weill," especially 272–75. The most extensive study on the *Lunchtime Follies* is Roarty, "The *Lunchtime Follies.*"

182. Stewart Asher, "Lunchtime Follies for Workers in War Production," *Philadelphia Inquirer*, clippings file, "*Lunchtime Follies,*" *WLRC*, Ser. 52A.

183. "News of the Stage," *New York Times*, September 25, 1942.

184. Carly Warton, letter to Oscar Hammerstein II, August 12, 1942, *OHC*.

185. Oscar Hammerstein II, letter to Carly Warton, August 27, 1942, *OHC*.

186. Lewis Nichols, "*Lunchtime Follies*: The American Theatre Wing Sends Out Entertainment to War Workers," *New York Times*, June 13, 1943; Arlene Wolf, "*Lunchtime Follies*, S.R.O.*" New York Times Magazine*, July 11, 1943.

187. Kurt Weill, letter to Archibald MacLeish, June 9, 1942, *WLRC*, Ser. 40. The beginning of the letter (just before this quotation) is cited in Scherbera, "Der 'alien American' Kurt Weill," 274.

188. Samuel Grafton, "I'd Rather Be Right," *New York Post*, June 10, 1942.

189. Kurt Weill, letters to Ruth Page, April 24 and June 6, 1943, and letter to Ira Gershwin, April 5, 1943, *WLRC*, Ser. 40.

190. William S. Cunningham, letter to Colonel Jason Joy, September 11, 1944, *OWI-NARA*, Box 3529.

191. Drew, *Kurt Weill*, 340.

192. An extract of the interview is published in Scherbera, "Der 'alien American' Kurt Weill," 280.

193. Kurt Weill, letter to Ira Gershwin, February 27, 1944, *WLRC*, Ser. 40.

194. *Tuesday in November* has been made available at http://www.archive.org/details/Tuesdayi1945 (accessed April 12, 2010); on Copland's score for *The Cummington Story*, see Lerner, "Aaron Copland, Norman Rockwell, and the 'Four Freedoms.'"

195. Kurt Weill, liner notes, http://www.kwf.org/kwf/liner-notes-for-qmine-eyes-have-seen-the-gloryq (accessed October 14, 2008).

196. William Grant Still, untitled typescript, early 1930s, cited in Murchison, "Nationalism in William Grant Still and Aaron Copland," 297.

197. Weill, *Johnny Johnson (1936)*.

198. These (and three more) attendees are listed in Edwin Hughes, letter to Harold Spivacke, January 11, 1942, *JANCSM*, Box 12.

199. Ibid.

200. Howard Taubman, "The Arts United: Musicians Join Artists and Writers to Take Place in Nation's War Effort," *New York Times*, January 11, 1942.

201. Edwin Hughes, letter to Harold Spivacke, January 11, 1942, *JANCSM*, Box 12.

202. Edwin Hughes, letter to Harold Spivacke, January 24, 1942, *JANCSM*, Box 12.

203. Edwin Hughes, letter to Harold Spivacke, January 31, 1942, *JANCSM*, Box 12.

204. Harry Futterman, letter to Harold Spivacke, January 4, 1943, *JANCSM*, Box 6; Harry Futterman, letter to the President's War Relief Control Board, August 25, 1943, *JANCSM*, Box 1.

205. Harold Taubman, "Record for the Camps," *New York Times*, June 14, 1942.

206. "Letter from Harry Futterman of the Armed Forces Master Records, Inc.," *Notes*, 2nd ser. 1–2 (March 1944): 3–9, at 4. Futterman, letter to Harold Spivacke, May 2, 1943, *JANCSM*, Box 6.

207. Philip L. Miller, "Harry Futterman," *Notes*, 2nd ser. 3/2 (March 1946): 131–34, at 132.

208. Captain Edward Davens (Medical Corps), letter to Armed Forces Master Records, January 25, 1945, copy in *JANCSM*, Box 6.

209. Harry Futterman, undated report, typescript, *JANCSM*, Box 23.

210. Paul Lewinson, undated donor solicitation for the Armed Forces Master Records, *JANCSM*, Box 1.

211. "'Times' Backs Concerts to Help Servicemen," *Los Angeles Times*, January 16, 1944.

212. Correspondence relating to the record library destined for the *USS Wisconsin* in *JANCSM*, Boxes 6 and 16.

213. Harry Futterman, letter to Commander Norvelle W. Sharpe, August 10, 1944; Harry Futterman, letter to Harold Spivacke, May 19, 1944; both in *JANCSM*, Box 6.

214. Armed Forces Master Records, Inc., unsigned report sent to JANCSM (stamped as received on December 22, 1943), *JANCSM*, Box 1.

215. Harry Futterman, letter to his clients, copied to Harold Spivacke; Oscar Hammerstein II, letter to Harold Spivacke, February 16, 1944; both in *JANCSM*, Box 6.

216. Numerous articles about the concert were published in the *Los Angeles Times* between January 16 and April 27, 1944.

217. Philip L. Miller, "Harry Futterman," *Notes*, 2nd ser. 3/2 (March 1946): 131–34, at 131.

218. Harry Futterman, "Purposes—Program Summary," enclosed in Harry Futterman, letter to Harold Spivacke, January 4, 1943, *JANCSM*, Box 6.

219. Philip L. Miller, "Harry Futterman," *Notes*, 2nd ser. 3/2 (March 1946): 131–34, at 131; Gladys E. Chamberlain, "He Got Disks to G.I.s," letter to the music editor, *New York Times*, January 6, 1946.

220. Pegolotti, *Deems Taylor*, 254–55.

221. Deems Taylor, radio script for *America Preferred*, September 6, 1941, *DTP*, series V, "Scripts."

222. Deems Taylor, radio script for *America Preferred*, February 14, 1942, *DTP*, series V, "Scripts."

223. Deems Taylor, radio script for *America Preferred*, September 6, 1941, *DTP*, series V, "Scripts."

224. Deems Taylor, radio script, "Intermission Talks, New York Philharmonic," December 14, 1941, *DTP*, series V, "Scripts."

225. Nicolas Slonimsky, radio scripts, 1944–46, *NSC*, Box 22.

226. Deems Taylor, radio script, "Intermission Talks, New York Philharmonic," February 22, 1942, *DTP*, series V, "Scripts."

227. Deems Taylor, radio script, "Intermission Talks, New York Philharmonic," April 20, 1941, *DTP*, series V, "Scripts."

228. Mann's approving response to Weill is given in Scherbera, "Der 'alien American' Kurt Weill," 269.

229. "Erika Mann Protests," *New York Times*, February 15, 1942. For the presentation of the conflict from the perspective of Erika Mann, see Von der Lühe, *Erika Mann*, 196–98. For a discussion of the issue in the context of Deems Taylor's career, see Pegolotti, *Deems Taylor*, 260–61.

230. Samuel F. Pogue, "By Way of Reply," *New York Times*, February 22, 1942.

231. Deems Taylor, radio script, "Intermission Talks, New York Philharmonic," February 22, 1942, *DTP*, series V, "Scripts."

232. Deems Taylor, radio script, "Intermission Talks, New York Philharmonic," March 1, 1942, *DTP*, series V, "Scripts."

233. Von der Lühe, *Erika Mann*, 197. Mann's radio script is published in German translation in Mann, *Blitze überm Ozean*, 255–61.

234. Lowens, *Music in America*.

235. Paul Nettl, "Wandering National Anthems," *Musical America* 63 (February 10, 1943): 114, 171.

236. Paul Nettl, "Music and the Hands of Politics," *Musical America* 63 (July 1943): 12, 26, at 26.

237. Paul Henry Lang, "Our Musical Life: A Discussion by a Historian of the Forces at Work in Our Time," *New York Times*, January 25, 1942.

238. Lang, *Music in Western Civilization*.

239. Bennett, "The Anxiety of Appreciation."

240. Paul Henry Lang, "Musical Scholarship at the Crossroads," *Musical Quarterly* 31 (1945): 371–80.

241. Paul Henry Lang, "Background Music to 'Mein Kampf,'" *Saturday Review of Literature* (January 20, 1945): 5–9. I am grateful to William Boone for drawing this essay to my attention.

242. Program for Dwight D. Allen's lecture recital, "Our Marching Civilization," May 26, 1942, *JANCSM*, Box 1.

243. Warren Dwight Allen, undated letter to Harold Spivacke, *JANCSM*, Box 1.

244. Allen, *Our Marching Civilization*, 14.

245. Ibid., 16 (Japanese), 18 (Germans).

Chapter 2

1. Henry Cowell, "Shaping Music for Total War," in Higgins, ed., *Essential Cowell*, 304–7.

2. Cowell, "Shaping Music for Total War," 307.

3. Commander Harry S. Etter (Medical Corps), in the radio script for a United Nations Club Broadcast, July 24, 1945, Victor Babin Collection, *WcM*, ML94.B2.

4. Charles Seeger, transcript of interview with Andrea Olmstead, July 7, 1977, p. 40, *HCC*, Box 9.

5. Cowell, "Shaping Music for Total War," 304.

6. Roosevelt's Executive Order 9182 is reproduced in the online document collection of the American Presidency Project by John Woolley and Gerhard Peters, University of California at Santa Barbara. See http://www.presidency.ucsb.edu/ws/print.php?pid=16273 (accessed January 27, 2008). On the history of the OWI, see Winkler, *Politics of Propaganda*; Laurie, *Propaganda Warriors*.

7. F. R. Dolbears, secret memorandum to Hugh Wilson, dated October 13, 1942, Archives of the Office of Strategic Services, *NARA*, RG 226, Box 136.

8. "Union to Ban Recordings," *New York Times*, June 9, 1942. For discussions of the recording ban, see Seltzer, *Music Matters*, 39–45; Kraft, *Stage to Studio*, 130–61; Anderson, "'Buried under the Fecundity of His Own Creations.'"

9. "Petrillo Told: Lift Music Ban as 'Duty' to U.S." *Chicago Daily Tribune*, July 29, 1942.

10. All three quotations in "Elmer Davis Asks Petrillo to Yield," *New York Times*, July 29, 1942.

11. "Petrillo Rejects Davis Plea to End Ban on Recordings," *New York Times*, August 1, 1942.

12. *Use of Mechanical Reproduction of Music. Hearings before a Subcommittee of the Committee on Interstate Commerce, United State Senate. Second Session Pursuant To S. Res. 286 . . . September 17, 18, and 21, 1942* (Washington: United States Government Printing Office, 1943), 5. The quoted testimony was given on September 17.

13. See in particular the materials from the office of William B. Lewis, assistant director in charge of planning and programs, *OWI-NARA*, Box 603.

14. Both telegrams in *OWI-NARA*, Box 603.

15. Henry McLemore, "The Lighter Side," *Los Angeles Times*, August 3, 1942.

16. Szwed, *Alan Lomax*, 197.

17. List of Personnel, Bureau of Special Operations, February 22, 1943, Records of Interdepartmental and Intradepartmental Committees (State Department), *NARA*, RG 353.3, Box 30.

18. Alan Lomax, letter to Harold Spivacke, March 6, 1943, *JANCSM*, Box 9.

19. William B. Lewis, memorandum to Alan Lomax, Records of Interdepartmental and Intradepartmental Committees (State Department), *NARA*, RG 353.3, Box 30.

20. See the undated memorandum from Macklin Marrow to Louis G. Cowan (ca. March 22, 1943), *OWI-NARA*, Box 34.

21. Both quotations from Alfred Frankenstein, "The OWI Employs Music in a War Message," *San Francisco Chronicle*, March 28, 1943.

22. Ibid.

23. Andrea Olmstead, interview with Bess Lomax Hawes (transcript), November 18, 1977, *HCC*, Box 81.

24. Bess Lomax Hawes, letter to Harold Spivacke, May 31, 1944, *WcM*, Old Correspondence.

25. Cowell, "Shaping Music for Total War," 307.

26. These numbers are based on an internal memorandum (dated April 16, 1945), from Harold Spivacke to the Acquisitions Department, related to the transfer of the OWI recordings to the Library of Congress in 1945 (see subject file "OWI," *WcM*).

27. Hawes, *Sing It Pretty*, 50.

28. Henry Cowell, "The Use of Music by the OWI," *Proceedings of the Music Teachers National Association* 7 (1946): 61–65, at 63.

29. Hawes, *Sing It Pretty*, 48.

30. Sidney Robertson Cowell, letter to Rose Mary Spivacke, August 1, 1977, Harold Spivacke Collection, *WcM*, Box 7. After his earlier release from prison, Cowell was pardoned by the California governor only on December 29, 1942. Date given by Sidney Robertson Cowell, transcript of reminiscences on Henry Cowell's U.S. government employment, *HCC*, Box 92.

31. Henry Cowell, letters to Olive and Harry Cowell, January 31 and March 23, 1943 (quotation from the latter), *HCC*, Box 21.

32. Henry Cowell, letters to Olive and Harry Cowell, June 18, 1943, and April 9, 1945, *HCC*, Box 21.

33. Olmstead, interview with Bess Lomax Hawes (transcript).

34. Henry Cowell, letter to Olive Cowell, May 12, 1944, *HCC*, Box 21. Some of the material in this paragraph is also presented in Sachs, *Henry Cowell*, 389–94.

35. "Government Musical Activities," *National Music Council Bulletin* 5/1 (August 1944): 21.

36. Henry Cowell, "Music as Propaganda," *Bulletin of the American Musicological Society* 11–13 (September 1948): 9–11, at 11.

37. Martin Gansberg, "OWI's Cultural Formula," *New York Times*, April 1, 1945.

38. Hawes, *Sing It Pretty*, 46–47. According to Laurie (*Propaganda Warriors*, 123), by the end of the war the OWI controlled "thirty-six shortwave transmitters in the continental United States and fourteen overseas."

39. Macklin Marrow, cited in R.F.E., "Music Programs of Armed Forces Subject of Forum," *Musical America* 63 (January 25, 1943): 6.

40. For a detailed discussion of the OWI's propaganda politics as reflected in the Voice of America (which, however, does not mention music at all), see Shulman, *The Voice of America*.

41. Cowell, "Shaping Music for Total War," 307; Colin McPhee, letter to Harold Spivacke, August 23, 1945, *WcM*, Old Correspondence.

42. Cowell, "The Use of Music by the OWI," 65.

43. Cowell, "Shaping Music for Total War," 306.

44. Howard Taubman, "Songs That Chinese People Are Singing These Days—Other Releases," *New York Times*, November 30, 1941. A year later Robeson's interpretation was included in the 1942 record *For Free Men*. A recording of "Chee Lai" by Mark Warnow and His Orchestra was released on V-Disc no. 5.

45. Sidney Robertson Cowell, transcript of reminiscences on Henry Cowell's U.S. government employment, *HCC*, Box 92.

46. "Draft Outline of a Directive for Projection of America," November 30, 1944, p. 2, *OWI-NARA*, Box 13.

47. See, for example, Goebbels's anti-American and anti-Semitic diatribe of August 9, 1942, "Aus Gottes eigenem Land," reprinted in his collected essays, *Das eherne Herz*, 420–26. On Goebbels's music-focused anti-American propaganda, see Lepenies, *Kultur und Politik*, 135–41.

48. "Program Guide for France/Office of War Information, United States of America/ Compiled April 1, 1945/Management Planning Office," *OWI-NARA*, Box 13.

49. "Examples of Records for Information Centers," undated memorandum, *OWI-NARA*, Box 13.

50. Minutes of the OWI National Wartime Music Committee, March 19, 1943, *OWI-NARA*, Box 34.

51. Meyer and Shreffler, *Elliott Carter*, 51.

52. Cowell, "Music as Propaganda," 10.

53. Feisst, *Schoenberg's New World*, 165.

54. All of these recorded programs are among the records transferred to the Library of Congress and can be consulted in the Performing Arts Reading Room there.

55. Radio Symphonies was shorthand for Radio Symphony Orchestras; see "Government Musical Activities," 21.

56. Recordings preserved in *WcM*. See also "Program Guide for France."

57. Henry Cowell, letter to Charles Ives, September 21, 1944, *HCC*, Box 21.

58. Henry Cowell, letter to Charles Ives, December 4, 1943, *HCC*, Box 21. A short extract of this letter is cited in Paul, "From American Ethnographer to Cold War Icon," 429.

59. See Schnepel, "Critical Pursuit of the Great American Symphony," 25.

60. Harold Taubman, "Music Speaks for America," *New York Times Magazine*, January 23, 1944, 12, 31, at 12.

61. The OWI film is added as bonus material to the DVD release of the documentary *The Internationale* (produced and directed by Peter Miller), First Run/Icarus Film Release (NTSC FRF921357D), 2000.

62. OWI Motion Pictures Bureau, Production Schedule, May 18, 1944, *OWI-NARA*, Box 1715. I am grateful to Dave Stein of the *WLRC* for sharing this document with me.

63. On OWI documentaries, especially those of the Overseas Branch, see Scott, "From Toscanini to Tennessee."

64. Lyall, "The Piano Music of Gail Kubik," 5–6.

65. "Music Serves in the O.W.I. Films," *Musical Digest* 25/8 (Spring 1943): 17, 38–40, at 17. See also Cochran, "The Documentary Film Scores of Gail Kubik," 120.

66. "Music Serves in the O.W.I. Films," 39.

67. Ibid., 40.

68. Gail Kubik, "Music in Documentary Film," *Music Publishers Journal* 3 (September–October 1945): 13, 54–56, at 13.

69. Marc Blitzstein, confidential memorandum to Lewis Galantière, dated November 29, 1944, *ACC*, Box 355. Miller's plane went missing on December 15, 1944, on a flight from England to France.

70. Conway Bruner, confidential memorandum to Daniel Saidenberg, dated December 29, 1944, *ACC*, Box 355: "Ellington is being contacted by Blitzstein."

71. Mark A. Schubart, "U.S. Music Festival Planned in Paris," *New York Times*, March 1, 1945.

72. Aaron Copland, letter to Nadia Boulanger, March 1, 1945, *ACC*, Box 248.

73. Aaron Copland, letter to Nadia Boulanger, April 14, 1945, *ACC*, Box 248.

74. "Paris Hears Concert of American Music," *New York Times*, October 14, 1945.

75. President Truman terminated the OWI by executive order on August 31, 1945, effective September 15, 1945; see Winkler, *Politics of Propaganda*, 149.

76. Carter sent a carbon copy of his outline to Copland; it is reproduced in Meyer and Shreffler, *Elliott Carter*, 67–70 (quotations at 68).

77. Meyer and Shreffler, *Elliott Carter*, 69–70.

78. Roy Harris, form letter dated May 2, 1945, to Aaron Copland, *ACC*, Box 56; form letter dated April 19, 1945, to Virgil Thomson, *VTP*, Box 47. See also Beal, *New Music, New Allies*, chapter 1.

79. Virgil Thomson, letter to Roy Harris, April 26, 1945, *VTP*, Box 47; Aaron Copland, letter to Roy Harris, May 10, 1945, *ACC*, Box 56.

80. Cowell, "Music as Propaganda," 9.

81. Kubik, cited in "Music Serves in the O.W.I. Films," 40.

82. Doherty, *Projections of War*, 24–26.

83. Beal, "The Army, the Airwaves, and the Avant-Garde."

84. Haldore Hanson, *The Cultural-Cooperation Program, 1938–1943*, printed brochure from the Department of State, copy in *WcM*, Old Correspondence.

85. Charles A. Thomson, memorandum of conversation, March 19, 1943, State Department Decimal Files (1940–44), *NARA*, RG 59, 111.46 Music.

86. Ansari, "'Masters of the President's Music,'" 17, 23–24.

87. Ninkovich, *Diplomacy of Ideas*, 35–36. On the OCIAA and musical diplomacy, see Campbell, "Creating Something Out of Nothing."

88. Thomson and Laves, *Cultural Relations*, 27. The Division's operating budget in 1938–39 was $28,000.

89. Ninkovich, *Diplomacy of Ideas*, 35–36.

90. Carleton Sprague Smith (1940), cited in Shepard, "The Legacy of Carleton Sprague Smith," 640–41.

91. Minutes of the Meeting on June 24, 1943, of the Advisory Committee on Music, Division of Cultural Relations, Department of State, p. 8, Records of Interdepartmental and Intradepartmental Committees (State Department), *NARA*, RG 353.3, Box 30. This box contains a complete set of minutes from 1941 to 1944, and hereafter I will refer to any minutes by the date only.

92. Minutes, June 13, 1941 (p. 8), and October 1–2, 1941 (p. 3).

93. Thomson and Laves, *Cultural Relations*, 49.

94. Minutes, June 13, 1941, p. 7. The other committee members were Marshall Bartholomew, William Berrien, Evans Clark, and Aaron Copland; see Ansari, "'Masters of the President's Music,'" 129–30. See also Leila Fern, "Origin and Functions of the Inter-American Music Center," *Notes* 1 (December 1943): 14–22.

95. Both the OCIAA's contributions and some private sponsorship are detailed in the minutes from 1941 to 1944.

96. Ninkovich, *Diplomacy of Ideas*, 38.

97. Minutes, October 1–2, 1941, p. 2.

98. Minutes, June 13, 1941, p. 15.

99. Sumner Welles, letter to Alain Locke, November 24, 1942, State Department Decimal Files (1940–44), *NARA*, RG 59, 111.46 Music.

100. Ninkovich, *Diplomacy of Ideas*, 48. The reorientation after December 7, 1941, is discussed in the minutes of the meeting of January 16, 1942, p. 4.

101. Minutes, June 24, 1943, p. 4.

102. Lasswell (1935), cited in Schivelbusch, *Entfernte Verwandtschaft*, 72.

103. Department of State, Press Release no. 222, June 1, 1943, *WcM*, Old Correspondence.

104. Copland kept a travel diary and wrote a detailed report; some of this material is reproduced in Copland and Perlis, *Copland: 1900 through 1942*, 320–29.

105. For a detailed exploration of the role of folk music in inter-American cultural diplomacy, see Pernet, "'For the Genuine Culture of the Americas.'"

106. "General Statement on the Music Program of the Department," May 1944, State Department Decimal Files (1940–44), *NARA*, RG 59, 111.46 Music.

107. Minutes, June 24, 1943, p. 8. Seeger's comments on this issue are consistent with his earlier remarks in "Inter-American Relations in the Field of Music," *Music Educators Journal* 27/5 (March–April 1941): 17–18, 64–65.

108. "General Statement on the Music Program of the Department," May 1944.

109. Minutes, June 24, 1943, p. 5.

110. Melville J. Herskovits, letter to Charles A. Thomson, May 10, 1943, State Department Decimal Files (1940–44), *NARA*, RG 59, 111.46 Music.

111. Charles Seeger, letter to William Berrien, June 3, 1942; William Berrien, letter to Charles A. Thomson, June 9, 1942; both in State Department Decimal Files (1940–44), *NARA*, RG 59, 111.46 Music.

112. Olin Downes, letter to Charles A. Thomson, April 26, 1943, State Department Decimal Files (1940–44), *NARA*, RG 59, 111.46 Music.

113. Charles A. Thomson, memorandum to the members of the Advisory Committee (State Department), October 9, 1943; and Warner Lawson, letter to Charles A. Thomson, June 28, 1943; both in State Department Decimal Files (1940–44), *NARA*, RG 59, 111.46 Music.

114. Charles A. Thomson, memorandum of conversation, March 19, 1943, State Department Decimal Files (1940–44), *NARA*, RG 59, 111.46 Music.

115. Minutes, June 24, 1943, p. 2. On the "near craze for Pan Americanism" in the fall of 1941, see Ninkovich, *Diplomacy of Ideas*, 41.

116. Minutes, June 24, 1943, p. 5.

117. Ibid., pp. 22–23.

118. Wong, "From Pariah to Paragon."

119. Eleanor Roosevelt, *My Day*, February 19, 1943, online edition, *The Eleanor Roosevelt Paper Project*, http://www.gwu.edu/~erpapers/myday/displaydoc.cfm?_y=1943&_f=md056426 (accessed May 14, 2010).

120. "Felicitations and Felicities," *Musical America* 63 (March 25, 1943): 35.

121. Thomson and Laves, *Cultural Relations*, 54.

122. Ninkovich, *Diplomacy of Ideas*, 55.

123. Report by Fanny Pomeroy Brown and Bliss Wyant, reproduced in the minutes of the June 24, 1943, meeting of the Music Advisory Committee (State Department), pp. 25–28.

124. Adler and Paterson, "Red Fascism," especially 1048–50; Bennett: "Culture, Power, and *Mission to Moscow*," 493.

125. Ninkovich, *Diplomacy of Ideas*, 107–8.

126. Minutes, June 24, 1943, p. 5.

127. Charles A. Thomson, letter to Loy W. Henderson, July 7, 1943, State Department Decimal Files (1940–44), *NARA*, RG 59, 111.46 Music.

128. Olin Downes, letter to Charles A. Thomson, August 13, 1943, State Department Decimal Files (1940–44), *NARA*, RG 59, 111.46 Music.

129. Olin Downes, letter to Charles A. Thomson, October 7, 1943, State Department Decimal Files (1940–44), *NARA*, RG 59, 111.46 Music. For Downes's enthusiasm for *Oklahoma!*, see Carter, *"Oklahoma!" The Making of an American Musical*, 206–7.

130. Minutes, May 12–13 and June 9, 1944, pp. 12–14.

131. Elizabeth Bergman notes the overlapping membership between the two committees of Copland and Koussevitzky; see Crist, *Music for the Common Man*, 178.

132. "Music Interchange Plan: Koussevitzky Speaks Here in Aid of U.S.–Soviet Proposal," *New York Times*, May 16, 1944; Crist, *Music for the Common Man*, 238n85.

133. "U.S.–Soviet Friendship Marked at Concert," *New York Times*, November 8, 1943.

134. "U.S. Honored in Moscow," *New York Times*, May 24, 1944.

135. See, for example, Daniel Saidenberg, letter to Charles J. Child, July 11, 1944, State Department Decimal Files (1940–44), *NARA*, RG 59, 111.46 Music.

136. Minutes, May 12–13 and June 9, 1944, p. 7. On the State Department's postwar efforts in Europe, see in particular Beal, *New Music, New Allies*; Ansari, "'Masters of the President's Music.'"

137. Correspondence between the State Department, the American Embassy in Mexico, and the Treasury Department between February 19 and March 2, 1943, State Department Decimal Files (1940–44), *NARA*, RG 59, 811.4038/49–52.

138. Captain Joe Jordan, "A Singing Army Is a Winning Army," *Local 802*, September 1943, 12; Raymond Kendall is quoted in Isabel Morse Jones, "Place of Music in Global War Conditions Defined," *Los Angeles Times*, October 3, 1943.

139. Howard C. Bronson, cited in R.F.E., "Music Programs of Armed Forces Subject of Forum," *Musical America* 63 (January 25, 1943): 3.

140. Minutes of the Subcommittee on Music, February 27 and 28, 1942, Appendix, *JANCSM*, Box 23.

141. On the introduction of homophobic regulations and screening procedures into the American military in 1941, see Bérubé, *Coming Out under Fire*, 11–13.

142. Minutes of the Subcommittee on Music, February 27 and 28, 1942, Appendix, *JANCSM*, Box 23.

143. Howard C. Bronson, "Music, a Factor in Morale," typescript of a presentation given to a Morale Officers Conference, January 22, 1942, *JANCSM*, Box 3.

144. After intensive lobbying, the Burke–Wadsworth Draft Bill (1940) led to the inclusion of a mandatory 10 percent quota of African American inductees in what was otherwise an almost all-white military; Booker, *African Americans in the United States Army*, 53.

145. On the draft legislation and its application, see Kennedy, *Freedom from Fear*, 631–37.

146. Minutes of the Subcommittee on Music, July 29, 1942, *JANCSM*, Box 23.

147. Minutes of the Joint Army and Navy Committee on Welfare and Recreation, December 5, 1941, *JANCSM*, Box 23.

148. Fairfax Downey, "Strike Up the Bands!," *Los Angeles Times*, September 21, 1941; Lawrence Tibbett, "Tibbett Sees Flaws in Music for Forces," *Musical America* 63 (January 25, 1943): 7, 17, at 17.

149. Minutes of the Joint Army and Navy Committee on Welfare and Recreation, December 5, 1941, *JANCSM*, Box 23.

150. Minutes of the Subcommittee on Music, September 24–25, 1941, *JANCSM*, Box 23.

151. Harold Spivacke, letter to Francis Keppel, October 22, 1943, *JANCSM*, Box 23.

152. "Enlisted Men's Preferences in Music," Report by the Research Branch, Special Service Division, Army Service Forces, War Department, May 20, 1943, *JANCSM*, Box 15.

153. "Compendium of Soldiers' Attitudes toward Music and Singing," Report by the Research Branch, Special Service Division, Army Service Forces, War Department, January 17, 1944, *JANCSM*, Box 15.

154. Sergei Radamsky, "Music in the Camps," *New York Times*, May 30, 1943.

155. "History, in Brief, of the Music Section, Athletic and Recreation Branch, Special Services Division, Army Service Forces," October 1943, p. 3, *JANCSM*, Box 24.

156. Captain M. Claude Rosenberry, "The Army Music Program," *Music Educators Journal* 30 (April 1944): 18–19, 48–49, at 18.

157. Rosenberry, "The Army Music Program," 18.

158. The Subcommittee on Music of the Joint Army and Navy Committee on Welfare and Recreation was instrumental in the often complicated process of copyright clearance, starting with the *Army Song Book*. Correspondence can be found in numerous folders in *JANCSM*, especially Box 5.

159. Rosenberry, "The Army Music Program," 18. By the summer of 1945, the numbers of *Hit Kits* had changed: whereas the word editions dropped to less than half, with 925,000 copies per month, the piano-vocal editions doubled to 145,000; see Florence Taaffe, "Music Activities, Special Services Division, Army Service Forces," August 3, 1945, p. 2, *JANC-NARA*, Box 33.

160. Rosenberry, "The Army Music Program," 18.

161. Florence Taaffe, "Music Activities, Special Services Division, Army Service Forces," August 3, 1945, pp. 2–3, *JANC-NARA*, Box 33.

162. Ibid., p. 5.

163. "V-Disc Records to Supply Wide Variety of Music to U.S. Soldiers Everywhere," press release, Joint Army and Navy Committee on Welfare and Recreation, December 8, 1942, *JANC-NARA*, Box 9.

164. Doris Goss, Memorandum to Harold Spivacke, January 1, 1944, *JANC-NARA*, Box 33.

165. The development of a U.S. cultural canon is discussed in Levine, *Highbrow/Lowbrow*. Especially in the 1990s, the critique of a masculinist and hegemonical musical canon was at the forefront of significant scholarly discussion. Citron, *Gender and the Musical Canon*, explores the formation of musical canons in Europe and the United States in the nineteenth and twentieth centuries.

166. "Conference Re Kinds of Records to Be Included in Lists for Records for Our Fighting Men, Inc.," September 17, 1942, *JANCSM*, Box 23.

167. "'Times' Backs Concerts to Help Servicemen," *Los Angeles Times*, January 16, 1944.

168. Harold Spivacke, letter to S. L. Drumm, January 13, 1945, *JANCSM*, Box 4.

169. Yehudi Menuhin, quoted in Julius Haber (RCA Victor), undated press release, clippings file "World War II," *NYpM*.

170. R.F.E., "Music Programs of Armed Forces Subject of Forum," *Musical America* 63 (January 25, 1943): 32.

171. Memorandum of Projected Initial Program Schedule, Radio Division, Information Branch, Special Services [early 1943], Papers of Jerome Lawrence and Robert E. Lee, *NYpT*, *T-Mss 1967–00, Box 5.

172. William Hammerstein, letter to Oscar Hammerstein II, December 16, 1944, *OHC*, Box A.

173. Frances C. Gewehr, letter to Harry Futterman, October 25, 1943 (carbon copy), *JANCSM*, Box 6.

174. Frances C. Gewehr, letter to Harry Futterman, April 4, 1944 (carbon copy), *JANCSM*, Box 6.

175. Mrs. Barton K. (Mildred) Yount, letter to Harold Spivacke, October 12, 1943, *JANCSM*, Box 21.

176. Hunt's report of September 16, 1944, quoted in Helbig, *History of Music*, 122.

177. "Program Notes to Be Used in Presenting Record Programs," A & R Branch, Special Services Division, Army Services Forces, *JANCSM*, Box 25.

178. "Program Notes to Be Used in Presenting Record Programs," pp. 1–2.

179. Chauncey G. Lee, "Brahms's Second Symphony in D Major." Script for Music Appreciation Hour 1, June 20, 1943, p. 1, *JANCSM*, Box 8.

180. Ibid., pp. 2–3, *JANCSM*, Box 8.

181. Ibid., pp. 7–8, *JANCSM*, Box 8.

182. Chauncey G. Lee, "Beethoven's Third Symphony in E Flat, 'Eroica,'" Script for Music Appreciation Hour 2, June 27, 1943, p. 2, *JANCSM*, Box 8.

183. Chauncey G. Lee, "Beethoven's Influence on Symphonic Form; Musical Experimenters, Beethoven's Fifth Symphony in C minor," Script for Music Appreciation Hour 3, July 4, 1943, p. 1, *JANCSM*, Box 8.

184. The story and the quotations are from "Records and Gun Crews, Tankers and Tin Fish," undated press release, Julius Haber (RCA Victor), clippings file "World War II," *NYpM*.

185. Alvin Josephy, letter to Harold Spivacke, April 18, 1944, *JANCSM*, Box 8.

186. Letter (signed "Ray") to Harold Spivacke, March 20, 1944, *JANC-NARA*, Box 33.

187. This and subsequent quotations from Charles Bacharach's letter to Edward Waters, April 15, 1944, *WcM*, Old Correspondence.

188. "Chanute Field Soldiers Produce Leoncavallo's *Pagliacci*," *Musical America* 65 (April 25, 1945): 34

189. Florence Taaffe, "Music Activities, Special Services Division, Army Service Forces," August 3, 1945, p. 4, *JANC-NARA*, Box 33.

190. Raymond Kendall, "Ensemble Music for the Armed Forces," *Notes*, 2nd ser. 1 (March 1944): 27–28, at 28.

191. A photograph of the orchestra is published in Helbig, *History of Music*, 244.

192. George Hoyen, letter to Harold Spivacke, January 4, 1944, *JANCSM*, Box 3.

193. George Hoyen, letter to Harold Spivacke, December 30, 1943, *JANCSM*, Box 3.

194. Camp Lee Symphony Orchestra, Concert Program, December 21, 1943, *JANCSM*, Box 3. Martinů's *Memorial to Lidice* was premièred by the New York Philharmonic on October 28, 1943.

195. For correspondence about the Illinois WPA Music Library, see *JANCSM*, Box 3; this library was eventually housed in the Newberry Library, Chicago. The New York WPA collection was handed over to the USO in 1943, and that of the Far West went to UCLA; see Kendall, "Ensemble Music for the Armed Forces."

196. Florence Taaffe, "Music Activities, Special Services Division, Army Service Forces," August 3, 1945, p. 8, *JANC-NARA*, Box 33.

197. Leslie Bunt, "Music Therapy," in *Grove Music Online. Oxford Music Online*, http://www.oxfordmusiconline.com.libproxy.lib.unc.edu/subscriber/article/grove/music/19453 (accessed April 28, 2010).

198. Davis, "Music Therapy in 19th Century America"; Holden, ed., *Music as Medicine*, 321–25.

199. Emotion as a historical agent and a historiographic category is discussed in Frevert, "Was haben Gefühle in der Geschichte zu suchen."

200. John Warren Erb, "Music, Great Spiritual Force," *Musical Digest* 25 (Fall 1943): 14–15, 18, at 14.

201. "'Healing' by Music Tried in Hospitals," *New York Times*, March 20, 1938.

202. For an overview of these issues across multiple disciplines, see Juslin and Sloboda, eds., *Music and Emotion*. Lydia Goehr draws a direct line from Plato to Nietzsche and Adorno in *Elective Affinities*, 177. For a historical perspective on this topic, see Gouk and Hill, eds., *Representing Emotions*. With respect to the therapeutic aspect of music through history, see Holden, ed., *Music as Medicine*.

203. Doron K. Antrim, "Music Therapy," *Musical Quarterly* 30 (1944): 409–20.

204. Langer, *Philosophy in a New Key*, 243. This edition is a reprint of the original 1942 text.

205. Howard Hanson, "A Musician's Point of View toward Emotional Expression," *American Journal of Psychiatry* 99 (1942): 317–25, at 325.

206. On laboratory-based experimental research on emotions since the late nineteenth century, see Drot, "Dangerous Liaisons."

207. The following summary is based on Davis, "Keeping the Dream Alive."

208. All quotations in this paragraph come from Harriet Ayer Seymour, *How to Use Music for Health* (1939), self-published pamphlet (unpaginated), *JANCSM*, Box 8.

209. Davis, "Keeping the Dream Alive," 42.

210. Harold Spivacke, letter to Raymond B. Fosdick, June 21, 1943, *JANCSM*, Box 5.

211. Harold Spivacke, letter to Cliff V. Buttleman, June 5, 1945, *WcM*, Old Correspondence.

212. Esther Goetz Gilliland, "Music for the War Wounded," *Music Educators Journal* 31 (April 1945): 24–25, 51.

213. Willem van de Wall, letter to Earl Moore, August 12, 1943, *JANCSM*, Box 10.

214. Raymond Kendall, letter to Harold Spivacke, February 26, 1945, *JANCSM*, Box 8.

215. Both quotations from Raymond Kendall, letter to Harold Spivacke, April 11, 1945, *JANCSM*, Box 8.

216. McKay, "Music as a Group Therapeutic Agent," 235.

217. Guy V. R. Marriner, "Music in Reconditioning in Army Service Forces Hospitals," *Notes*, 2nd ser. 2 (1945): 161–63. The research program is outlined in a memo by Willem van de Wall, "Prospectus for a Program of Rehabilitation Activities," February 26, 1943, *JANCSM*, Box 10.

218. Willem van de Wall, letter to Earl Moore, August 12, 1943, *JANCSM*, Box 10.

219. "Music Program for Hospital Ships," reproduced in Helbig, *History of Music*, 114–17.

220. Commander Harry S. Etter (Medical Corps), in the radio script for a United Nations Club Broadcast, July 24, 1945, Victor Babin Collection, *WcM*, ML94.B2.

221. Ira Altshuler, cited in Ronald F. Eyer, "New Science of Music Therapy Develops," *Musical America* 63 (January 25, 1943): 8, 26, at 8.

222. Unsigned memo, October 23, 1944, "Music in Reconditioning in Army General Hospitals," *JANC-NARA*, Box 33.

223. War Department Technical Bulletin MED 187 (1945): "Music in Reconditioning in ASF Convalescent and General Hospitals," 7, *JANCSM*, Box 17.

224. Ibid., 1, 3.

225. Marriner, "Music in Reconditioning in Army Service Forces Hospitals," 162.

Chapter 3

1. Isabel Morse Jones, "City College Choir Heard in Interesting Program," *Los Angeles Times*, May 28, 1942.

2. "Sans égard à la nation, la race, les opinions politiques ou la religion du compositeur." This formulation comes from the ISCM Statutes of 1937, codifying the more loosely formulated objectives of 1922. See Haefeli, *Die internationale Gesellschaft für Neue Musik (IGNM)*, 623.

3. I have discussed the question of musical identity in the transatlantic context during the 1920s with respect to Aaron Copland in my "Aaron Copland, Nadia Boulanger, and the Making of an 'American' Composer." For the United States, see in particular Oja, *Making Music Modern*, where Oja traces the various nationalist and internationalist trends in American music during the 1920s.

4. The political intersections between Germany, Italy, and the United States are discussed in Schivelbusch, *Entfernte Verwandtschaft*.

5. One example presenting the variety of craft revivals in the United States is Kardon, ed., *Revivals! Diverse Traditions, 1920–1945*.

6. I borrow this term from Clark, *Moscow, the Fourth Rome*, 8.

7. I am grateful to Galin Tihanov for sharing this information with me.

8. Rubin, *Making of Middlebrow Culture*, 188–90.

9. Herbert Hoover (February 22, 1933), cited in Carter, "Celebrating the Nation," 329.

10. Rubin, *Making of Middlebrow Culture*, xii–xiii. On the FMP and its influence on new music in the U.S., see also Ross, *The Rest Is Noise*, 277–84.

11. On the role of the phonograph in this process, see Katz, "Making America More Musical." On music appreciation in 1930s America, see Bennett, "The Anxiety of Appreciation." See also the overview on music criticism's take on music appreciation in Grant, *Maestros of the Pen*, 195–225.

12. Horowitz, *Understanding Toscanini*, 196–98.

13. FMP program (1935), cited in Horowitz, *Understanding Toscanini*, 200.

14. Engel, *This Bright Day*, 73; Carter, "Schoenberg, Weill, and the Federal Arts Projects."

15. Olga Samaroff (1935), cited in Horowitz, *Understanding Toscanini*, 212.

16. This term was coined with respect to the Federal Art Program, though it also represents the ethos behind the FMP's program; see Saab, *For the Millions*, 65.

17. Filene, *Romancing the Folk*, 144.

18. Cited in Conkle, "Building Our Cultural Defenses," 18.

19. John Warren Erb, "Music, Great Spiritual Force," *Musical Digest* 25 (Fall 1943): 14–15, 18, at 14.

20. Pierre V. Key, "The Music World," *Musical Digest* 25 (Fall 1943): 3–4, 22, at 3.

21. Ewen, *Music Comes to America*, 298–99.

22. Bernard B. Ross, letter to Serge Koussevitzky, [April 1942], *SKC*, Box 113.

23. Serge Koussevitzky, letter to the BSO trustees, June 4, 1942, cited in Daniel, *Tanglewood*, 49.

24. Deems Taylor, radio script, "Intermission Talks, New York Philharmonic," December 14, 1941, *DTP*, Series V, "Scripts."

25. Daniel, *Tanglewood*, 51.

26. Both quotations in Nicolas Slonimsky, radio script, May 13, 1945, *NSC*, Box 22.

27. Isabel Morse Jones, "Concert Series Arranged for Service String Quartet," *Los Angeles Times*, August 20, 1944.

28. Olin Downes, "Toscanini Directs *Missa Solemnis*," *New York Times*, April 23, 1942.

29. Olin Downes, "Toscanini Offers Beethoven Works," *New York Times*, May 2, 1942.

30. Concert Programs, Coolidge Auditorium, September 15–October 8, 1943 (Brahms), and March 9–May 26, 1944 (Beethoven), *WcM*, Concert Programs Collection.

31. Diamond acknowledged Beethoven's influence retrospectively in an interview with the cellist Steven Honigberg (January 25, 2002), published as program notes with the recording of the quartet released by Albany Records in 2002 (TROY540 Albany Records).

32. Samuel Barber, letter to Aaron Copland, September 16, 1944, *AAC*, Box 246. For an interpretation of Barber's *Capricorn Concerto* as both nostalgic and modernist, see Wright, "The Enlisted Composer," 148–62.

33. Ada Rainey, "American Art Show Opens at Library," *Washington Post*, February 15, 1942. On the "usable past" in the context of the Federal Art Project, see Grieve, *Federal Art Project*, 37–58.

34. Paul Rosenfeld, "'Americanism' in American Music," *Modern Music* 27 (1940): 226–32, at 226.

35. Shepard, "The Legacy of Carleton Sprague Smith."

36. Ibid., 623–24.

37. Oja, "Composer with a Conscience," 171; Carter, "Celebrating the Nation." See also Bentley, "Finding *The Lost Colony* (1937)."

38. "Concert and Opera Asides," *New York Times*, March 8, 1942.

39. "Early American Songs Arranged by Buchman," *Musical America* 62 (February 10, 1942): 246.

40. Lehman Engel, "Songs of the American Wars," *Modern Music* 29 (1942): 147–52, at 152.

41. Noel Straus, "3-Choir Festival Held at Emanu-El," *New York Times*, March 28, 1942; Straus, "Choral Concert Directed by Shaw," *New York Times*, April 6, 1944; Olin Downes, "Varèse Choral Program," *New York Times*, June 6, 1945.

42. "Service Flag Dedicated in D.C. Church," *Washington Post*, November 21, 1942.

43. "Weekend Program of Starlight Concerts Will Feature Many Native American Songs," *Washington Post*, July 13, 1943.

44. Oja, "Composer with a Conscience," 170.

45. "Ballad Singers Recount Tales of Adventure on Their Tours," *Washington Post*, July 18, 1943.

46. Elie Siegmeister, "Music of the People," *New York Times*, February 6, 1944.

47. Given in ibid.

48. Siegmeister, *Songs of Early America*, 3.

49. Elie Siegmeister, "Music in Early America," in Siegmeister, ed., *The Music Lover's Handbook*, 661–62, at 661.

50. Siegmeister, "Music in Early America," 661.

51. Siegmeister, *Songs of Early America*, 3.

52. Siegmeister, "Music in Early America," 662.

53. Siegmeister, *Songs of Early America*, 5.

54. Rourke, *Roots of American Culture*, 161–94.

55. Ibid., 177, 180.

56. R. L. Duffus, "Roots of American Culture," *New York Times*, August 9, 1942.

57. Elie Siegmeister, "Music of America," in Siegmeister, ed., *The Music Lover's Handbook*, 659–60, at 660.

58. Filene, *Romancing the Folk*, 154.

59. Lee Lyons Kaufman, "The True Folk Music of America," *Musical America* 65 (February 10, 1945): 13, 226, at 6.

60. Virgil Thomson, "America's Musical Autonomy," in Thomson, *A Virgil Thomson Reader*, 246–48.

61. Olin Downes, "Luening Conducts Bennington Series," *New York Times*, February 2, 1937. See also Luening, *Odyssey of an American Composer*, 393–94.

62. Olin Downes, "Rodzinski Offers Schuman's Music," *New York Times*, February 18, 1944. On the genesis of the work, see Swayne, *Orpheus in Manhattan*, 168–69.

63. "14-Year-Old Pianist in Stadium Concert," *New York Times*, August 12, 1944.

64. Finney, *Hymn, Fuguing, and Holiday*. In 1942 and 1945 Finney also based some compositions on the *Ainsworth Psalter*.

65. Thomson (1977), cited in Smolko, "Reshaping American Music," 16.

66. Thomson (1944), cited in Shirley, "The Hymns and Fuguing Tunes," 104.

67. Shirley, "The Hymns and Fuguing Tunes," 96.

68. Henry Cowell, foreword to *American Muse*, 2.

69. Rosenfeld, "'Americanism' in American Music," 226.

70. Shirley, "The Hymns and Fuguing Tunes," 99–100; Cowell, foreword to *American Muse*, 2.

71. "Critics Prize Won by *The Patriots*," *New York Times*, April 14, 1943.

72. Roosevelt's address was widely excerpted in newspaper reports of the dedication and even reproduced in its entirety (for example, in the *Washington Post* and the *New York Times*).

73. Anne O'Hare McCormick, "When Jefferson Was in Europe," *New York Times*. April 12, 1943.

74. Cowell, *American Muse*, 4.

75. Cowell, foreword to *American Muse*, 2.

76. Cited in Shirley, "Aaron Copland and Arthur Berger," 191.

77. Foreman, "Forging a Relationship and a Role," 132; Stenzl, *Von Giacomo Puccini to Luigi Nono*, 154.

78. The literature on early-music revivals has proliferated in recent years. Some key texts that explore these issues are Nicolodi, "Nationalistische Aspekte im Mythos von der 'alten Musik' in Italien und Frankreich"; Ellis, *Interpreting the Musical Past*; Applegate, *Bach in Berlin*.

79. D. F. Aitken writing in the *Radio Times* (1936), cited in Potter, *Nadia and Lili Boulanger*, 143.

80. Introduction to Kerr and Siegmeister, *Sing Out, Sweet Land!*, n.p.

81. Siegmeister (1944), cited in Oja, "Composer with a Conscience," 172; Siegmeister, "Music of America," 660.

82. The poster for *Oklahoma!* is reproduced in Carter, *"Oklahoma!" The Making of an American Musical*, 175.

83. Sam Zolotov, *"New Horizon* Role to Dudley Digges," *New York Times*, October 13, 1943.

84. Nelson B. Bell, "A Film Adaptation Is Not Always Able to Shorten Life of Its Stage Original," *Washington Post*, May 28, 1944.

85. Nelson B. Bell, "Community Theater Wisely Bides Its Time; Amusement Gossip," *Washington Post*, July 27, 1944.

86. Both quotations from Elie Siegmeister, "Probing the Treasury of Native Minstrelsy," *New York Times*, January 14, 1945.

87. Introduction to Kerr and Siegmeister, *Sing Out, Sweet Land!*

88. Olin Downes, "Folk-Tunes in the Theatre," *New York Times*, January 21, 1945.

89. *Sing Out, Sweet Land!*, Souvenir Program, p. 7. Yale University, Beinecke Library, Theatre Guild Collection.

90. *Sing Out, Sweet Land!*, Souvenir Program, p. 4.

91. *Sing Out, Sweet Land!*, Production Script, p. 2–5–2. Yale University, Beinecke Library, Theatre Guild Collection.

92. *Sing Out, Sweet Land!*, Production Script, pp. 2–5–2 and 2–5–3.

93. *Sing Out, Sweet Land!*, Production Script, p. 2–5–4.

94. *Sing Out, Sweet Land!*, Production Script, p. 2–5–6. The staging seems reminiscent of the famous "flying wedge" used for the title song of *Oklahoma!*

95. *Sing Out, Sweet Land!*, folders of music, Yale University, Beinecke Library, Theatre Guild Collection, Box 2A. In the programs, the song is titled "More than These." The title song is used, albeit with a different text, for the Theatre Guild Broadcast of *Sing Out, Sweet Land!* on October 21, 1945. See http://www.archive.org/details/TheaterGuildontheAir (accessed June 6, 2010).

96. *Sing Out, Sweet Land!*, Production Script, p. 2–6–6.

97. Richard P. Cooke, "The Theatre: Folk Music," *Wall Street Journal*, December 29, 1944.

98. All three quotations from Lewis Nichols, "The Play," *New York Times*, December 28, 1944.

99. Claudia Cassidy, "On the Aisle," *Chicago Daily Tribune*, April 2, 1945.

100. Both quotations in Nelson B. Bell, *"Sing Out, Sweet Land* Scores a Rousing Hit at the National," *Washington Post*, May 3, 1945.

101. Elie Siegmeister, "Our American Folk Music," in Siegmeister, ed., *The Music Lover's Handbook*, 671–82, at 672.

102. "Cavalcade of American Song," *New York Times*, December 24, 1944.

103. Siegmeister, "Probing the Treasury of Native Minstrelsy."

104. Filene, *Romancing the Folk*, 154.

105. Archibald MacLeish, "Introduction to the 1941 Edition," in Lomax and Lomax, *Our Singing Country*, xix–xx.

106. Horace Reynolds, "More Ballads and Folksongs Collected by the Lomaxes," *New York Times*, December 28, 1941.

107. William Schuman, "Songs America Has Sung," *New York Times*, June 13, 1943. See Downes and Siegmeister, *A Treasury of American Song*.

108. Lomax and Lomax, preface to *Our Singing Country: Folk Songs and Ballads*, xxi–xxviii, at xxviii.

109. Roy Harris, "Folk Material in Art Music," *New York Times*, December 27, 1942. For Harris's nationalist agenda, see Levy, *Musical Nationalism*, 86–104. Beth Ellen Levy discusses Harris's prewar ideology in "Frontier Figures."

110. On the role of Dvořák's symphony in U.S. concert composition, see Schnepel, "Critical Pursuit of the Great American Symphony."

111. Bartók's musical engagement with an archaic Hungarian and (more broadly conceived) Eastern idiom fluctuated during his life, but, as I will discuss in chapter 4, it was reconfigured in the intellectual context of the United States during World War II. For Bartók's shifting approach to traditional music before the war, see Schneider, *Bartók, Hungary, and the Renewal of Tradition*. I address Copland's perception of Stravinsky's folk-based idiom in my "Aaron Copland, Nadia Boulanger, and the Making of an 'American' Composer."

112. Bartók (1941), cited in Kárpáti, *Bartók's Chamber Music*, 124.

113. Tim Carter discusses the role of the American frontier as a wartime theme in *"Oklahoma!" The Making of an American Musical*.

114. Levy, "Frontier Figures," 167–68. See also Lerner, "The Classical Documentary Score," 50–153.

115. Siegmeister, *Western Suite*.

116. "Original Script Rodeo 1942—given to Copland," Agnes de Mille Correspondence, *NYpT*, (S) *MGZMD 100, Box 39.

117. Kirstein (1937), cited in Crist, *Music for the Common Man*, 124.

118. Agnes de Mille, "Handwritten Scenario of Rodeo—earliest version," Agnes de Mille Papers, *NYpT*, (S) *MGZMC-Res. 27. This extract reappeared almost verbatim in the scenario sent to Copland, which is quoted in Levy, "Frontier Figures," 335.

119. Lynn Garafola remarked first on the strong resemblance between Agnes de Mille's descriptions and Oliver Smith's stage design in "Making an American Dance," 134–35.

120. John Martin, "*Rodeo* Presented by Ballet Russe," *New York Times*, October 17, 1942.

121. The genesis of the ballet is discussed in Pollack, *Aaron Copland*, 363–74.

122. Copland and Perlis, *Copland: 1900 through 1942*, 357. The three melodies that Agnes de Mille sent to Copland are included in the sketches for *Rodeo* preserved in *ACC*.

123. Copland and Perlis, *Copland: 1900 through 1942*, 364–65.

124. "The Week's Radio Concerts," *New York Times*, October 25, 1942; Aaron Copland, telegram to Serge Koussevitzky, November 14, 1942, *ACC*.

125. On *American Legend*, see Brooks Atkinson, "The Play: American Actors Company Weaves *American Legend* into a Sunday Night Show," *New York Times*, May 12, 1941; and Garafola, "Making an American Dance," 132. On the National Folk Festival, see John Martin, "Folk Fete Draws 22,000 to Garden," *New York Times*, May 12, 1942; John Martin, "The Dance: A New Period?" *New York Times*, November 1, 1942: Carter, *"Oklahoma!" The Making of an American Musical*, 140.

126. Martin, "The Dance: A New Period?"; Claudia Cassidy, "Ballet Russe's *Rodeo* Dance Wins Acclaim," *Chicago Daily Tribune*, December 26, 1942; John Martin, "The Dance: Travel Notes," *New York Times*, January 3, 1943.

127. Alfred Frankenstein, *"Rodeo* Is Refreshing and as American as Mark Twain," *San Francisco Chronicle*, November 20, 1942.

128. Copland and Perlis, *Copland: 1900 through 1942*, 359. Copland's "American style" is characterized as "distressingly similar to German efforts to create a nationalistic musical idiom" in Kennicott, "Aaron Copland: Mythical America," 64–65.

129. Garafola, "Making an American Dance," 132.

130. For a discussion of the intersections between folk music and Copland's idiom in *Rodeo*, see Pollack, *Aaron Copland*, 367–71; Levy, "Frontier Figures," 331–33; Crist, *Music for the Common Man*, 132–45; Taruskin, *Oxford History of Western Music*, 4:663–66.

131. See Pollack, *Aaron Copland*, 373.

132. Copland, *What to Listen for in Music*, 159. For the correspondence of Nadia Boulanger and Aaron Copland, see Fauser, ed., *"Mon cher Copland."*

133. Judith Tick observes the close temporal proximity of the letter to Berger and the move into the concert hall of Copland's *Rodeo* score; see Tick, ed., *Music in the USA*, 483. Copland's letter to Berger is reproduced on p. 484.

134. For an overview, see Dizikes, *Opera in America*. Goehr discusses the concept of "American opera" in *Elective Affinities*, 257–305.

135. Elinor Wallace Shrader, letter to Virgil Thomson, April 27, 1942, *VTP*, Box 97.

136. For a survey of opera in the United States in the nineteenth and early twentieth centuries, see Levine, *Highbrow/Lowbrow*, 85–104.

137. Dizikes, *Opera in America*, 462–70.

138. For an excellent discussion of the rhetorical valuation of democratic values in wartime America, see Schwartz, "Memory as a Cultural System." I discussed the new moral imperative of cultural inclusion in my 2008 AMS–Library of Congress lecture "After Pearl Harbor: Music, War, and the Library of Congress"; see http://www.loc.gov/today/cyberlc/feature_wdesc.php?rec=4400.

139. Between 1942 and 1945 the Office of War Information would make use of these broadcasts to reach attentive American listeners during the intermissions with such prominent speakers as Archibald MacLeish and Sinclair Lewis. See subject file "Metropolitan Opera," *OWI-NARA*.

140. Olin Downes, "Rule of the Pit," *New York Times*, December 27, 1942 (on lowered ticket prices); Downes, "Concert and Opera Asides," *New York Times*, March 22, 1942: "The Metropolitan Opera gave free seats to between 170 and 200 service men every week of its recently completed season."

141. Olin Downes, "Season in Review," *New York Times*, March 21, 1943.

142. [Isabel Morse Jones], "Music and Musicians," *Los Angeles Times*, May 30, 1943.

143. H. D. C., "'The Barber' Sung in English," *Christian Science Monitor*, June 20, 1942.

144. "Plans Complete for 'American' Grand Opera," *Washington Post*, January 3, 1943.

145. According to the *Annals of the Metropolitan Opera: Performances and Artists, 1883–2000*, CD-ROM, ed. Geoffrey R. Peterson (New York: Metropolitan Opera Guild, 2002), the following works were given in English translation during World War II: Johann Sebastian Bach, *Phoebus und Pan* (1941–42); Ludwig van Beethoven, *Fidelio* (1944–45); Wolfgang Amadeus Mozart, *The Magic Flute* (1941–45); Nikolai Rimsky-Korsakov, *The Golden Cockerel* (1944–45); Bedřich Smetana, *The Bartered Bride* (1941–42); and Giuseppe Verdi, *Falstaff* (1943–44).

146. With each reprise of this production, critics unfailingly pointed to the high-quality translation. See, for example, Oliver J. Gingold, "A Magical Event at the 'Met,'" *Wall Street Journal*, December 13, 1941; Olin Downes, "Walter Conducts 'The Magic Flute,'" *New York Times*, November 28, 1942; Howard Taubman, "Ezio Pinza Sings in Mozart's Opera," *New York Times*, December 2, 1943.

147. "Vote on Language for Opera Near-Tie," *New York Times*, February 11, 1942.

148. The debate was originally scheduled as a closed event for members of the Metropolitan Opera Guild, but because of the broad general interest, it was opened to the public; see "Public to Join in Opera Debate," *New York Times*, February 7, 1942.

149. The National Committee for Opera in America was established in the spring of 1941 as part of the National Music Council in order "to promote and stimulate the production of opera in English in this country." See "Concert and Opera Asides," *New York Times*, May 31, 1942. Among its members were the composer Quincy Porter, Claire Reis (of the League of Composers), and Alfred Wallerstein (from the Metropolitan Opera).

150. "Survey Lists Translations of English Operas," *Chicago Tribune*, March 15, 1942.

151. "Opera and Concert Asides," *New York Times*, February 8, 1942: "Now a new problem arises. How are English texts to be standardized that a singer will not be forced to learn a new version of an opera whenever he sings a given role at a new locality?"

152. "Survey Lists Translations of English Operas," *Chicago Tribune*, March 15, 1942.

153. "Diamond Jubilee of Opera on Nov. 22," *New York Times*, October 5, 1943.

154. Ray C. B. Brown, "'Barber of Seville' in English Delights 5000 at Watergate," *Washington Post*, August 14, 1942.

155. Claudia Cassidy, "Opera 'Martha' Singing Good, for a Hayride!" *Chicago Tribune*, November 14, 1942.

156. This translation is also discussed in Mordden, *Beautiful Mornin'*, 80. The production folded after six performances.

157. Review of *Once Over Lightly*, reprinted in Nathan, *The Theatre Book of the Year 1942–1943*, 137. Lewis Nichols ("The Play," *New York Times*, November 20, 1943) similarly dismisses the translation with some pointed quotations from the libretto. *Once Over Lightly*'s production team included Robert H. Gordon, who had directed the famous left-wing production of *Pins and Needles* in 1937.

158. Nathan, *Theatre Book of the Year 1942–1943*, 137.

159. "News of the Stage," *New York Times*, October 16, 1942. This column also reported that the actor and director Max Reinhardt was seen to have attended rehearsals. The conductor of this production was Wolfgang Erich Korngold. One highlight of the production was the ballet that concluded act 2, which was choreographed by George Balanchine.

160. Strauß, *Rosalinda (Fledermaus)*, 61 and 135–36.

161. Olin Downes, "Music in Review," *New York Times*, October 29, 1942.

162. Olin Downes, "Opera Opening," *New York Times*, November 22, 1942. He reinforced this point in a *New York Times* column on March 21, 1943 ("Season in Review"): "For the first time in Metropolitan annals they present more Americans than Europeans, there being forty-six native-born artists to forty aliens in the personnel of the association."

163. Edward Johnson, "American Opera Comes of Age," *New York Times*, November 26, 1944. For a short assessment of this shift, see Flynn, "Americans at the Met."

164. Josephine Ripley, "Philadelphia Opera Company Starts Rehearsals in Boston," *Christian Science Monitor*, January 7, 1942; Olin Downes, "Philadelphia Opera," *New York Times*, February 14, 1943.

165. S. S., *"Pelléas et Mélisande," Christian Science Monitor*, January 10, 1942.

166. See Carter, *"Oklahoma!" The Making of an American Musical*, especially 206–11.

167. In this context, Goehr's distinction between the practice of opera in America and the concept of American opera provides a valuable differentiation; see Goehr, *Elective Affinities*, 257–305.

168. Keith Thompson, "Opera in America Today," *Modern Music* 21/1 (November–December 1943): 18–22, at 22.

169. Clifford Bair, "What's the Matter with Opera in America?," *National Music Council Bulletin* 5 (August 1944): 5–6.

170. I have traced this development in "'Dixie *Carmen*,'" 150–53.

171. Crawford's production is discussed in Alpert, *The Life and Times of "Porgy and Bess,"* 137–39; Pollack, *George Gershwin*, 609–12; and Johnson, "Gershwin's 'American Folk Opera,'" 606–11 (see p. 608 on the work's patriotic appeal during World War II).

172. Goehr, *Elective Affinities*, 279–80.

173. Howard Taubman, "Records: U.S. Operas," *New York Times*, May 23, 1943.

174. Taubman, "Records: U.S. Operas."

175. Oscar Thompson, "American 'Folk Opera' Depicts Dust Bowl," *Musical America* 63 (May 1943): 21.

176. Downes's three essays published in the *New York Times* are "American Opera" (May 2, 1943); "Ernst Bacon Work Is Presented Here" (May 6, 1943); and "Opera, Folk Style" (May 9, 1943). The quotation is from "Opera, Folk Style."

177. Downes, "American Opera," *New York Times*, May 2, 1943.

178. Elliott Carter, "Theatre and Films," *Modern Music* 20/4 (May–June 1943): 282–84, at 283.

179. Downes, "American Opera," *New York Times*, May 2, 1943.

180. On musicodramatic integration and its reception as proto-operatic in *Oklahoma!*, see Carter, *"Oklahoma!" The Making of an American Musical*, 206–11. See also the reproduced page (p. xiii) from *PM* with the title: "*Oklahoma!* New Musical Plays Up Homespun U.S.A."

181. Olin Downes, "Broadway's Gift to Opera," *New York Times*, June 6, 1943. The term "folkloric narrative" with respect to American opera in the 1940s and '50s was coined by Goehr, *Elective Affinities*, 282.

182. All quotations from Olin Downes, "Broadway's Gift to Opera."

183. Bauer and Reis, "Twenty-five Years with the League of Composers."

184. Olin Downes, "American Opera," *New York Times*, May 2, 1943.

185. I have discussed this in more detail in my article *"Carmen in Khaki."*

186. "Opera and Concert Asides," *New York Times*, December 14, 1941.

187. Cecil Smith, "Gilbert and Sullivan Operas Return after 6 Years," *Chicago Daily Tribune*, January 31, 1943.

188. "Tabu or Not Tabu?" *Washington Post*, December 2, 1942.

189. *"Butterfly* Given First Time in War," *New York Times*, April 12, 1945.

190. "Impolite *Mikado* Will Bow Tonight," *New York Times*, February 3, 1942.

191. Both quotations from Brooks Atkinson, "The Play," *New York Times*, February 4, 1942.

192. Fauser, *"Carmen in Khaki,"* 310–11.

193. Olin Downes, "Season in Review," *New York Times*, March 15, 1942.

194. Downes, "Season in Review," *New York Times*, March 21, 1943.

195. Howard Taubman, "War Fervor Keys Opening of Opera," *New York Times*, November 24, 1942.

196. Oscar Thompson, "Our 'Cultural Defenses,'" *Musical America* 60 (1940): 16.

197. Olin Downes, "On Misrepresenting Wagner," *New York Times*, March 3, 1940.

198. Paul Henry Lang, "Background Music for for 'Mein Kampf,'" *Saturday Review of Literature* (January 20, 1945): 5–8. I am grateful to William Boone for sharing this text with me.

199. Eleanor Roosevelt, "Music Should Go On! A Message from the First Lady," *Musical America* 62 (1942): [3].

200. Arthur Berger, "Music in Wartime," *The New Republic*, February 7, 1944, 175–78, at 176.

201. Gertrude Stein, letter to Virgil Thomson dated March 27, 1947, in *Letters of Gertrude Stein and Virgil Thomson*, 269.

202. On *Carmen Jones* during World War II, see my "'Dixie *Carmen*,'" which explores Hammerstein's adaptation and the work's production and reception in great detail.

203. Dan Burley, "All-Negro Opera, 'Carmen Jones,' Scores in Philly Première," *New York Amsterdam News*, October 30, 1943. Burley's article was picked up by the Associated Negro Press (ANP) and published, in abbreviated form, in the *Pittsburgh Courier*, also on October 30, 1943.

204. On the role of classical music in the context of "racial uplift," see Schenbeck, *Racial Uplift and American Music*, especially 3–14. I have discussed the National Negro Opera Company in my *"Carmen in Khaki,"* 320–24. See also Wells, "Grand Opera as Racial Uplift."

205. Program book for *Aida*, Pittsburgh, October 30, 1941, 2, *NNOCC*, Box 1.

206. Mary Cardwell Dawson, letter to potential sponsors, February 24, 1944, *NNOCC*, Box 1.

207. Souvenir Program for the 1944 Madison Square Garden performance of *La traviata*, *NNOCC*, Box 1. On Dawson's patronage network, see Wells, "Grand Opera as Racial Uplift," 11–16.

208. I could not find contemporary sources for this event, though all the obituaries mention the aborted plan. See, for example, "Mme Evanti Dies in Washington at 77," *New York Amsterdam News*, December 16, 1967; "Mrs. Roy Tibbs; Soprano Appeared as Mme. Evanti," *New York Times*, December 9, 1967.

209. Florence M. Collins, "Applause Given Evanti at the White House," *Afro-American*, February 17, 1934.

210. "'Study Hard,' Mme Evanti Tells Operatic Aspirants," *Afro-American*, July 8, 1944.

211. Remi Gassman, "Open Opera Season with All-Negro 'Aida,'" in *La Julia Rhea: America's First Black Artist to Star with a Major Opera Company* (N.p: The author, n.d.), unpaginated, *NNOCC*, Box 63.

212. Clarence Joseph Bulliet, "Negro Singers Find Native Motifs in Verdi's 'Aida,'" *Chicago Daily News,* August 28, 1944.

213. "Negro Singers Score Hit in Verdi's 'Traviata,'" unattributed press clipping, *NNOCC*, Box 17, folder 1943.

214. Louia Vaughn Jones, "15,000 See Evanti Triumph in 'La Traviata' at Watergate," *Afro-American*, September 4, 1943.

215. Schenbeck, *Racial Uplift and American Music*, 6.

216. Carl Diton, "Negro Opera Co. at Madison Square Garden," *The New Sign* 25 (February 26, 1944): 2–3, at 2.

217. Glenn Dillard Gunn, "National Negro Opera Enchants 12,000 Here," *Evening Star*, September 6, 1943.

218. Mary Cardwell Dawson, 1944 press release, *NNOCC*, Box 1. This is also printed in the Souvenir Program for the company's 1944 "Opera beneath the Stars" festival in Washington, D.C. (*NNOCC*, Box 1). Some newspapers picked this release up. See, for example, "WD Employees Take Part in Negro Opera," *War Times*, July 21, 1944.

219. Wells, "Grand Opera as Racial Uplift," 20–29.

Chapter 4

1. Perse, *Exile and Other Poems*, 95. The original French text is: "Et c'est l'heure, ô Poète, de décliner ton nom, ta naissance, et ta race...." Given that the translation was published during the poet's lifetime, I assume that he endorsed this translation of *décliner*. The word is more ambiguous in French: it can also mean "to decline" in the sense of "to refuse." After it appeared in the American review *Poetry*, Milhaud called the poem "admirable" in a 1942 letter to his librettist, the French diplomat Henri Hoppenot. See Milhaud, Milhaud, Hoppenot, and Hoppenot, *Conversation*, 216.

2. Milhaud, *Notes sans musique*, 9: "Je suis un Français de Provence et de religion israélite." Erin Maher pointed out to me that in his first draft Milhaud made the opening sentence even sharper by combining his nationality and religion: "Je suis Français et de religion israélite"; see Darius Milhaud, "Notes sans musique," manuscript draft, *WcM*, ML95.M459 (case). In his "prelude" to the book, Milhaud makes the point that he started it on August 25, 1944 (p. 7). The issue of Jewish and national identities of exile musicians has been discussed mostly with respect to Schoenberg and Weill. Klára Móricz integrates earlier Eastern-European and also Ernest Bloch's approach to Jewish identity in music in her *Jewish Identities*. See also Walden, "'An Essential Expression of the People.'"

3. Milhaud, *Notes sans musique*, 9: "Six cent ans avant Jésus-Christ... ils y installèrent donc en négociants et non en émigrants."

4. Milhaud, *Notes sans musique*, 334: "les côtes de la Patrie retrouvée."

5. See, for example, the story about the conductor Max Reiter and his founding of the Waco Symphony Orchestra in Heinsheimer, *Menagerie in F Sharp*, 22–39. See also Horowitz, *Artists in Exile*.

6. Recent work on musicians in American exile during the 1930s and '40s focuses on the cosmopolitan aspects of cultural production during that period, in marked contrast to the emphasis on loss that pervades such essay collections as Brinkmann and Wolff, eds., *Driven into Paradise*. See in particular Cohen, "Migrant Cosmopolitan Modern"; Feisst, *Schoenberg's New World*. In her discussion of Nadia Boulanger and Igor Stravinsky, Kimberly Francis explores the transnational aspect of identity in exile; see her "Mediating Modern Music."

7. For a thoughtful discussion of the concepts of nomad, migrant, exile, expatriate, refugees, and immigrant, see the fascinating collection of Aciman, ed., *Letters of Transit*. The term "nomad" in the context of artistic exile is explored by Eva Hoffman in her essay "The New Nomads" (ibid., 35–63). Horst Weber also engages with terminology in his essay "Exilforschung und Musikgeschichtsschreibung." I have chosen to use a range of terms, including "refugee," because they were used by the musicians themselves to describe their situation.

8. Heinsheimer, *Menagerie in F Sharp*, 6.

9. For Weill's support of Milhaud, see, for example, *Notes sans musique*, 306–7. Weill's caustic remarks about exile communities in Los Angeles have been discussed in numerous essays. The reference to German exiles as *Mumienkeller* (cellar of mummies) is from a letter by Kurt Weill to Lotte Lenya dated August 21, 1944, in Simonette and Kowalke, eds., *Speak Low (When You Speak Love)*, 428.

10. Milhaud, *Notes sans musique*, 319. In a letter to Hélène Hoppenet from August 1943, Madeleine Milhaud refers to a "solitude à peu près totale"; given in Milhaud, Milhaud, Hoppenot, and Hoppenot, *Conversation*, 243. In conversation with Roger Nichols, Madeleine Milhaud mentions cousins who had settled in Berkeley and, in retrospect, offers a less bleak perspective with the comment "that, although so far from France, we were not isolated"; see Nichols, *Conversations with Madeleine Milhaud*, 60.

11. Nichols, *Conversations with Madeleine Milhaud*, 27.

12. The literature on composers in American exile is prolific with respect to German and Austrian composers such as Arnold Schoenberg and Kurt Weill; literature on musicians originating from other countries is far more limited. On the issue of cultural identity and aesthetic response to exile, see Goehr, "Music and Musicians in Exile."

13. I address this work and its ramifications in "Music for the Allies." This and the next paragraph are based on this essay.

14. Feisst, *Schoenberg's New World*, 69–70, discusses Schoenberg's postwar return to German folk song in 1948 with his nostalgic but ambivalent *Three Folksong Settings*, op. 49.

15. See, for example, Kowalke, "'I'm an American!,'" 109–31; Feisst, "Arnold Schoenberg in America Reconsidered." See also the contributions by Hermann Danuser (155–71), Claudia Maurer Zenck (172–93), and Stephen Hinton (261–78) in Brinkman and Wolff, eds., *Driven into Paradise*.

16. Deems Taylor, Radio Script for *America Preferred*, September 6, 1941, *DTP*, Series V, "Scripts." *America Preferred* was aired from September 6, 1941, to May 30, 1942.

17. Ibid.

18. Taylor, Radio Scripts for *America Preferred*, September 6, October 18, November 13, 1941.

19. Taylor, Radio Scripts for *America Preferred*, October 25, December 4, 1941.

20. Taylor, Radio Scripts for *America Preferred*, September 13, 1941, March 21, 1942 (both featuring Lehmann).

21. Cohen, "Migrant Cosmopolitan Modern," 20. On the role of musical universalism as a cultural strategy for exile musicians, see Schmidt, "Kulturelle Räume und ästhetische Universalität."

22. On the *Scherzo à la russe*, see my "Music for the Allies."

23. Darius Milhaud, undated letter to Kurt Weill (sent from Mills College), copy in *WLRC*.

24. See, for example, Darius Milhaud, letters to Henri Hoppenot, May 22, 1942, and April 13, 1943, in Milhaud, Milhaud, Hoppenot, and Hoppenot, *Conversation*, 215, 231.

25. See Milhaud, Milhaud, Hoppenot, and Hoppenot, *Conversation*, 214–15. The French exile community's internal split in the United States ran deep, as the power struggle between the two factions would determine the postwar government in France; see Nettelbeck, *Forever French*.

26. Nichols, *Conversations with Madeleine Milhaud*, 61.

27. Milhaud, *Notes sans musique*, 321: "Peut-on critique un fermier de l'Iowa ou du Texas de ne pas comprendre la menace hitlérienne? . . . L'attaque des avions du Mikado précipita les événements; qu'il en soit remercié." Increasing American involvement in the war was among the priorities of a number of exiles, especially from France. According to Colin Nettelbeck (*Forever French*, 5), "If Pearl Harbor had not happened, it would have been necessary to invent it."

28. Darius Milhaud, letter to Elizabeth Sprague Coolidge, February 11, 1942, *ESCC*, Box 69.

29. On Roosevelt's notoriously negative attitude toward European refugees and on anti-immigration legislation, see Daniels, "Immigration Policy in a Time of War."

30. Olin Downes (1941), given in Josephson, "The Exile of European Music," 113.

31. Ibid., 152.

32. Howard Hanson (1941), given in Ibid., 133.

33. Ibid., 116.

34. Ibid., 117.

35. Ernst Bacon, "Notebook," 1944, Ernst Bacon Collection, *WcH* Box 37.

36. Ewen, *Music Comes to America*, 282–84.

37. Benjamin Britten, letter to Enid Slater, November 7, 1939, in Mitchell, ed., *Letters from a Life*, 725. I am preserving Britten's idiosyncratic spelling. On his complex and increasingly negative relationship with the United States, see Robinson, "'An English Composer Sees America.'"

38. Benjamin Britten, letter to Kit Welford, April 4, 1940, in ibid., 793.

39. Benjamin Britten, letter to Wulff Scherchen, September 9, 1941, in ibid., 977.

40. Benjamin Britten, letter to Albert Goldberg, January 20, 1942, in ibid., 1014.

41. Benjamin Britten, letter to Kit Welford, March 1, 1942, in ibid., 1021.

42. Milhaud, *Notes sans musique*, 308: "Nous nous adoptions lentement aux bienfaits de la paix."

43. Diary entry for March 6, 1944, in Milhaud, Milhaud, Hoppenot, and Hoppenot, *Conversation*, 266: "l'indifférence du peuple américain pour la guerre"; "son absence de compréhension des souffrances subies par les autres."

44. Several essays in *Driven into Paradise* comment in the issue of isolation; see also the introduction by Brinkmann, "Reading a Letter," 3–20, at 9.

45. Diary entry for March 6, 1944, in Milhaud, Milhaud, Hoppenot, and Hoppenot, *Conversation*, 242: "Deux jours vécu à Mills sont suffisants pour se rendre compte de l'isolement complet des Milhauds: aucun véritable ami, rien que des connaissances, professeurs, élèves et les 'épaves' qu'ils appellent 'sangsues'."

46. Nichols, *Conversations with Madeleine Milhaud*, 27.

47. Francis, "Mediating Modern Music," 162; French original on p. 376: "Mais je ne savais pas combien j'aimais la France, combien j'ai besoin d'elle."

48. Nadia Boulanger, letter to Serge Koussevitzky, November 6, 1940, *SKC*, Box 8: "entendre de la musique—pour nous—et peut-être pour le monde, le salut, et la vérité, sont dans l'art."

49. Nadia Boulanger, letter to Aaron Copland, March 6, 1945, *ACC*, Box 248. Boulanger's sense of isolation is discussed in Francis, "Mediating Modern Music," 161–63.

50. Eckmann and Koepnick, "Introduction: Caught by Politics," in Eckmann and Koepnick, eds., *Caught by Politics*, 1–13, at 4.

51. Goehr, "Music and Musicians in Exile," 77.

52. Šafránek, *Bohuslav Martinů* (1944), 110.

53. Ronald F. Eyer, "Meet the Composer: (3) Bohuslav Martinů," *Musical America* 64 (January 10, 1944): 11, 14, at 11.

54. Edward W. Said points to the accent as an important aspect of exile identity in "No Reconciliation Allowed," in Aciman, ed., *Letters of Transit*, 87–113. In her discussion of Riccardo Viñes, Catherine Hughes similarly draws on Said's notion of accent; see "Accented Cosmopolitanism: Reception of Ricardo Viñes, the Spanish Expatriate in Paris," paper read at the symposium "Music, Sound and Space in France, 1850–1914," King's College, London, May 19–21, 2011.

55. Germaine Tailleferre, "From the South of France," *Modern Music* 20/1 (November–December 1942): 13–16. A short note (p. 13) explains that "Mlle. Tailleferre left Marseilles late in September and after a thirty-three day journey arrived in New York." Shortly after her arrival in the United States in 1942, Tailleferre wrote an Ave Maria for the women's choir of Swarthmore College, near Philadelphia, but no other composition from her American exile is known. On Tailleferre's years in the United States during World War II, see her "Mémoires," 71–72; Gelfand, "Germaine Tailleferre," 78–81.

56. Tailleferre, "From the South of France," 13, 16.

57. Tailleferre, "Mémoires," 72: "L'atmosphère n'y était guère accueillante, car on n'aimait pas beaucoup les Français."

58. Gelfand, "Germaine Tailleferre," 79–80.

59. This important point was made first in Adams, "Martinů and the American Critics," 81.

60. Adorno, *Minima Moralia*, 56. These historiographic issues are addressed specifically with respect to Schoenberg in Feisst, *Schoenberg's New World*, 3–14.

61. Cherry, "The String Quartets of Darius Milhaud," 282. For a brief overview of Milhaud's years in the United States, see also Walker, "Milhaud and America."

62. Milhaud, *Notes sans musique*, 312.

63. Milhaud, letter to Hélène Hoppenot, January 13, 1942, in Milhaud, Milhaud, Hoppenot, and Hoppenot, *Conversation*, 210: "Madeleine s'éreinte au ménage." In *Notes sans musique*, p. 316, Milhaud comments that "il n'y a pas de domestiques aux Etats-Unis."

64. Darius Milhaud, letter to Paul Claudel, March 21, 1945, in Petit, ed., *Correspondance Paul Claudel—Darius Milhaud*, 250: "Nous sommes loin de tout et terriblement isolés...notre isolement est favorable au travail et à la méditation."

65. Darius Milhaud, letter to Elizabeth Sprague Coolidge, October 29, 1944, *ESCC*.

66. Nichols, *Conversations with Madeleine Milhaud*, 28.

67. Walsh, *Stravinsky: The Second Exile*, 130–31.

68. Darius Milhaud, letter to Hélène and Henri Hoppenot, January 1, 1944, in Milhaud, Milhaud, Hoppenot, and Hoppenot, *Conversation*, 262: "An IV de l'exil...La fidelité de votre amitié est le reconfort de l'exil."

69. Milhaud, *Notes sans musique*, 325. In a letter to Elizabeth Sprague Coolidge from June 7, 1944 (*ESCC*), Milhaud wrote: "Since yesterday, we are hanging to the Radio with the exciting news of the invasions in Normandy. All our hopes are in this battle, and our prayers for the allied soldiers."

70. Darius Milhaud, letter to Henri Hoppenot, May 22, 1944, in Milhaud, Milhaud, Hoppenot, and Hoppenot, *Conversation*, 214–15: "La situation pour un Français *vivant ici* est très simple. *Suivre l'Amérique* jusqu'à la délivrance de la France....Je n'ai jamais voulu être inscrit dans une organisation dissidente, car j'estime qu'il n'y a qu'un moyen de servir de Gaulle, c'est militairement et d'aller se battre, mais si c'est pour faire des banquets à San Francisco zut! Mais on peut très bien servir *sur le plan américain* sans être 'embringué' dans la dissidence. D'ailleurs la situation Franco-Américaine est si complexe....Le Français moyen s'y perd. C'est pourquoi je préfère rester en dehors de toute 'clique' étant donné que mon état de santé ne me permet pas d'envisager une vie active (militaire!)...Mais il y a beaucoup à faire pour *maintenir* la culture française."

71. Darius Milhaud, "Pourquoi j'aime Gounod et Verdi" (1942), reproduced in Milhaud, *Notes sur la musique*, 209–13, at 209: "Ils on maintenu l'idéal latin au moment où la musique a subi l'assaut le plus implacable venu d'Allemagne avec Richard Wagner."

72. Milhaud, "Pourquoi j'aime Gounod et Verdi," 210: "Il a dû être envoyé sur la terre pour détruire la musique française, l'art française, la pensée française."

73. *Pour la victoire!*, January 2, 1943.

74. Marcelle Denya, "La musique française à l'étranger," *Pour la victoire!*, January 16, 1943: "La beauté intrinsèque, l'originalité, la subtilité d'expression, les inventions harmoniques de l'école française des mélodies, depuis 1850, n'ont pas de parallèle, ni d'équivalent dans aucun pays, y compris l'Allemagne."

75. Edgar Feder, "Une heure avec Madame Wanda Landowska," *Pour la victoire!*, November 18, 1944: "l'influence prépondérante exercée par la musique française dans la période dont Bach représente l'apogée."

76. I have discussed Landowska's gallicizing of Bach in "Creating Madame Landowska."

77. Edgard Feder, "Nos musiciens en Amérique ont bien mérité de la Patrie..." *Pour la victoire!*, July 14, 1945: "Point n'est besoin d'être Chauvin pour proclamer que l'école

musicale française—avec sa sœur cadette, l'école russe—occupe la première place dans le monde."

78. Edgar Feder, "La musique," *Pour la victoire!*, July 17, 1943: "Maître contrepointiste, façonné à l'école sévère de Gédalge et de Pierné, Milhaud est un 'polytonal', moins en raison d'un système choisi arbitrairement que par nature. Sa polytonalité, plus directe et accessible que celle d'un Schoenberg, résulte d'une superposition d'harmonies diatoniques voisines."

79. Marion Bauer, "Darius Milhaud," *Musical Quarterly* 28 (1942): 139–59, at 139; Copland, *Our New Music*, 86; Isabel Morse Jones, "Sharps and Flats," *Los Angeles Times*, June 13, 1943.

80. Howard Taubman, "Records: Milhaud's Suite," *New York Times*, October 31, 1943.

81. Alfred Frankenstein, "Darius Milhaud's Recent Works," *Tempo*, n.s. 2 (December 1946): 13–15, at 13.

82. Copland, *Our New Music*, 83–84.

83. Alfred Frankenstein, "Darius Milhaud's Recent Works," *Tempo*, n.s. 2 (December 1946): 13–15, at 14.

84. Howard Taubman, "Records: Milhaud's Suite," *New York Times*, October 31, 1943.

85. Shirley, *Ballet for Martha*.

86. Darius Milhaud, letter to Elizabeth Sprague Coolidge, undated [early summer 1944], *ESCC*.

87. Darius Milhaud, letter to Aaron Copland, undated [early summer 1944], *ACC*, Box 259.

88. The autograph score was offered to the Library of Congress as part of the commission process through the Coolidge Foundation. See *WcM*, ML29c M29 (Case). On Milhaud's admiration for *Rodeo*, see his letter to Aaron Copland from probably the fall of 1942 (*ACC*, Box 259): "Votre *Rodeo* est un chef d'œuvre et votre musique m'a enthousiasmé! Monteux donne *Billy the Kid* cette semaine. Quelle joie d'entendre enfin vos œuvres. Dans *Rodeo* tout est parfait. Votre orchestre est d'une nostalgie magnifique et d'une force sobre et somptueuse à la fois."

89. On the French play with intertextual references and the Barthian "second degree," see Fauser, "Musik als 'Lesehilfe.'"

90. I am grateful to Don Harrán for his help with the three liturgical texts discussed here. I have not been able to find out whether *Borechu* and *Shema Yisroel* were commissions from an American synagogue or were Milhaud's representation of congregational singing, written as a personal response to events. *Kaddisch* was commissioned by Cantor David J. Putterman for the Park Avenue Synagogue. See "Events in the World of Music," *New York Times*, May 6, 1945. In 1947 Milhaud was commissioned by the Temple Emanu-El in San Francisco to compose a different liturgical work, the *Service sacré*, op. 279, for baritone, reciter, chorus, and orchestra (or organ).

91. Mario Castelnuovo-Tedesco, materials and scripts for *Una vita di musica*, typescript extract in English translation by James Westby, *MCTP*, Box 113.

92. Milhaud, *Notes sans musique*, 325: "Malheureusement, les premières lettres qui nous parvinrent d'Europe nous annonçaient des deuils atroces: la mort de mon jeune neveu Jean Milhaud et de plus de vingt cousins directs ou éloignés dans des camps d'extermination allemands."

93. The opera was composed at Mills College between January 21 and June 3, 1943, and orchestrated later that same year; see Drake, *The Operas of Darius Milhaud*, 294.

94. In a letter to Henri Hoppenot dated May 22, 1942, Milhaud announced that he was "commencer un opéra sur mon *Bolivar*"; in Milhaud, Milhaud, Hoppenot, and Hoppenot, *Conversation*, 216.

95. Milhaud, *Notes sans musique*, 331: "Un livret plein d'action, avec un personnage central masculin; de plus cette pièce était dominée par un sentiment de Libération et de Liberté, ce qui en 1943 correspondait à toutes mes pensées."

96. Darius Milhaud, letter to Aaron Copland, October 3 [1942], *ACC*, Box 259: " Et puis c'est l'Amérique du Sud, ce qui devait être bien vu ici."

97. Milhaud (1952), given in Drake, *The Operas of Darius Milhaud*, 292: "Bolivar étant mort seul, en exil, ce fait devait conditionner la fin de l'œuvre."

98. Milhaud, *Notes sans musique*, 331: "Un air de Bolivar écrivant son testament, en exil, et elle utilisa le texte authentique du testament."

99. Given in Drake, *The Operas of Darius Milhaud*, 291n2: "8 Sept. 1943. Capitulation de l'Italie. Deo Gratias."

100. Drake, *The Operas of Darius Milhaud*, 303.

101. Ibid., 305.

102. Darius Milhaud, letter to Harold Spivacke, April 28, 1944, *WcM*, Old Correspondence.

103. "Stokowski Program to Include Opera," *Atlanta Constitution*, October 1, 1944.

104. Alfred Frankenstein, "Darius Milhaud's Recent Works," *Tempo*, n.s. 2 (December 1946): 13–15, at 14.

105. Reis, *Composers, Conductors, and Critics*, 163. For a discussion of Milhaud's symphonies in the context of 1940s America, see Winkler, *"La mélodie essentielle."*

106. On the complex confluence of transnational and U.S. compositional concerns, see the discussion in Rathert, "Die Sinfonien von Bohuslav Martinů."

107. Adams, "Martinů and the American Critics," 82.

108. Among his fellow Czechs in the United States were, in particular, Miloš Šafránek and Frank Rybka. Aaron Copland and other members of the League of Composers supported Martinů. In a letter of October 6, 1941, to Aaron Copland, Martinů asks to see "cher Copland" for his advice "le plus tôt possible"; *ACC*, Box 259. This was Martinů's second move to a country whose language he did not speak; seventeen years earlier he had relocated from Prague to Paris, where he developed a professional network that included Koussevitzky and Copland, who helped facilitate his transition to the United States.

109. Martinů, *My Life with Bohuslav Martinů*, 72. See also Large, *Martinů*, 83.

110. By comparison, Arnold Schoenberg's annual salary at UCLA in 1944 was $5,400 per year, or $450 per month. See Feisst, *Schoenberg's New World*, 6.

111. Erismann, *Martinů*, 209–10: "J'étais accueilli ici comme un grand compositeur...il y a une telle abondance de toutes les choses que cela me donne le cafard. Les orchestres sont d'une perfection qu'on ne peut même pas imaginer, la musique en abondance aussi, mais pas la musique moderne."

112. Large, *Martinů*, 83.

113. Serge Koussevitzky, letter to Bohuslav Martinů, February 24, 1942, *SKC*, Box 42. In contrast to other commission letters from Koussevitzky, e.g., to Béla Bartók, which left the genre open, his commission to Martinů specified that he had commissioned a symphony. Šafránek (*Bohuslav Martinů* [1944], 87) wrongly indicates that "the Koussevitzky Foundation called for an orchestral composition in any form the composer

might choose. So it was Martinů who decided upon a symphony." Březina speculates that Koussevitzky's specific commission was in response to Martinů's own idea to write a symphony. See Březina, "... *the essential nobility of thoughts and things which are quiet simple.*" Březina misquotes Martinů in the title and in the transcription of the Boston program; correct would be "quite simple."

114. Erismann, *Martinů*, 214: "Les chefs d'orchestre sont encore des plus grandes vedettes ici que là-bas....La musique de chambre est presque inexistante."

115. Martinů, "Ridgefield Diary" (1944), published in English translation in Svatos, "Martinů on Music and Culture," 157–228, at 198.

116. Martinů, program notes for the first performance of his Symphony no. 1 in Boston, November 13, 1942, given in Šafránek, *Bohuslav Martinů* (1944), 88–91.

117. Virgil Thomson (1942), given in Adams, "Martinů and the American Critics," 85.

118. Large, *Martinů*, 89.

119. Martinů, "Ridgefield Diary" (1944), 161.

120. Martinů (August 1942), given in Březina, "...*the essential nobility of thoughts,*" 232.

121. Martinů's program note is cited extensively—often in its entirety—in most texts that engage with his symphonic works. It was written originally in French and published in English translation. Given the obvious typographical errors in Březina ("...*the essential nobility of thoughts,*" 240–42), I have decided to use the version published in Šafránek, *Bohuslav Martinů* (1944), 88–91. Šafránek had access to both the French and the English versions and in his 1944 edition corrected an important error in translation.

122. Unless otherwise indicated this and the following citations are from Martinů (November 1942), given in Šafránek, *Bohuslav Martinů* (1944), 88–91.

123. Martinů, "Ridgefield Diary" (1944), 159.

124. Martinů makes this point explicitly in his 1944 "Ridgefield Diary" (188–93, 198–99).

125. Copland, *Our New Music*, 12–13. I am taking this point from Rathert, "Die Sinfonien von Bohuslav Martinů," 118. The role of French music for American modernism is discussed in Oja, *Making Music Modern*, especially 231–83.

126. Compare Rathert, "Die Sinfonien von Bohuslav Martinů."

127. On the emphasis on Martinů's nationality in American reception, see Renton, "Martinů in the United States,", especially 269–70.

128. Large, *Martinů*, 89–90. The segment of the "Marseillaise" is: "Aux armes, Citoyens! Formez vos bataillons!"

129. See, for example, Erismann, *Martinů*, 226; he and others cite Harry Halbreich as the source for this reading.

130. Březina, "...*the essential nobility of thoughts,*" contains excerpted transcriptions of the Koussevitzky–Martinů correspondence as well as some reference to the sketches. The correspondence is preserved partially in *SKC*, Box 42 (Martinů's letters plus some carbon copies of Koussevitzky's responses).

131. Bohuslav Martinů, letter to Serge Koussevitzky, October 1942, given in Březina, "...*the essential nobility of thoughts,*" 238: "Et c'est ici que ma Symphonie est devenue non tragique ni triste, mais calme avec la poésie de tous ces souvenirs."

132. Serge Koussevitzky, letter to Bohuslav Martinů, October 10, 1942: "J'ai bien reçu votre partition et en suis profondément ému, surtout par l'adagio, tellement beau et exprimant si bien les sentiments que j'éprouve dans ma grande tristesse."

133. Březina, "...the essential nobility of thoughts," 239.

134. Šafránek, Bohuslav Martinů (1961), 250–51.

135. Bohuslav Martinů, letter to Serge Koussevitzky, October 1942, given in Březina, "...the essential nobility of thoughts," 238: "Et je n'ai voulais [sic] pas vous rappeler ces moments tragiques même dans ma musique. Et dans cela il y a aussi mon idéal artistique, qui ne veut pas, que la musique vous attriste, vous enquiète [sic], mais qui veut consoler, reposer, donner le plaisir de vivre, de regarder autour de nous, ou [sic] chaque moment nous apporte de nouveau et aussi un peu de l'oubli."

136. Memorial to Lidice is among Martinů's most frequently discussed compositions, especially in German musicology. See, among others, Andraschke, "Bohuslav Martinů: Musik gegen Krieg und Zerstörung"; Hanheide, Pace: Musik zwischen Krieg und Frieden, 164–68; Richter, "A Music-Political Confession"; Döge, "Das entsetzliche Grauen zum Ausdruck gebracht."

137. Döge, "Das entsetzliche Grauen zum Ausdruck gebracht." The remainder of this paragraph summarizes Döge's detailed analytical findings.

138. Martinů, "Ridgefield Diary" (1944), 192.

139. All quotations from Martinů, "Ridgefield Diary" (1944), 200.

140. Martinů, Memorial to Lidice, 20. For the reading of C major as possibly a "hoffnungsvolles Nachzeichnen des Prinzips 'per aspera ad astra,'" see Döge, "Das entsetzliche Grauen zum Ausdruck gebracht," 90. On the trope as a feature of Beethoven reception, see Bonds, After Beethoven.

141. Oscar Thompson in the Sun (October 20, 1943), given in Šafránek, Bohuslav Martinů (1944), 102.

142. The performance was advertised repeatedly in Pour la victoire!, e.g., February 3 and February 24, 1945; H. C., "Où Edgar [sic] Varèse nous parle de Berlioz," Pour la victoire!, March 10, 1945. See also Meyer and Zimmermann, eds., Edgard Varèse, 279.

143. Béla Bartók, letter to Dorothy Parrish, February 8, 1939, printed in Bartók, Letters, 276.

144. Bartók's earlier ambivalence toward Fascist nations is discussed in Gillies, "Bartók in America," 193.

145. Cooper, Bartók: Concerto for Orchestra, 16–17.

146. Gillies, "Bartók in America," 192.

147. A. Tillman Merritt, letter to Douglas Moore, September 26, 1942, given in Lampert, "Bartók at Harvard," 123.

148. The discussion of Bartók's involvement with the Movement for an Independent Hungary in this paragraph is based entirely on the excellent in-depth research published in Dreisziger, "A Hungarian Patriot in American Exile." For a short, apologetic rendering of events, see Lenoir, "Folklore et transcendance," 101–2.

149. Both quotations given in Dreisziger, "A Hungarian Patriot in American Exile," 294.

150. Memo by Allen W. Dulles (OSS), July 1942, given in Dreisziger, "A Hungarian Patriot in American Exile," 295.

151. Béla Bartók, "Race Purity in Music," Modern Music 19 (March–April 1942): 153–55.

152. These and the subsequent quotations in this paragraph are from Béla Bartók, "Bartók Views Folk Music Wealth of Hungary," Musical America 63 (January 10,

1943): 27. Leon Botstein mentions laconically that Bartók's celebration of uncorrupted Hungarian folk traditions "could easily become misunderstood—a potential that Bartók grasped all too well in the 1940s"; see Botstein, "After Fifty Years," 230.

153. Móricz, "Operating on a Fetus," 476.

154. Given in Tallián, "Bartók's Reception in America, 1940–1945," 105. Suchoff points out that for all of Bartók's own perceptions of hardship, "in the USA no-one considered it a sacrifice to emigrate to the country, whatever the purpose; ignorance of that attitude brought about another misunderstanding of American life." Suchoff, "Bartók in America," 123.

155. This view is most recently promoted in Peter Bartók, *My Father*.

156. Gillies, "Bartók in America," 199. Purchasing power calculated according to http://www.measuringworth.com/ppowerus (accessed April 12, 2011).

157. Gillies, "Bartók in America," 201.

158. Ibid., 198. Medical fees incurred during his Harvard lectures in 1943 were covered by A. Tillman Merritt, who was then the chair of the music department; see Lampert, "Bartók at Harvard," 119.

159. Béla Bartók, letter to Wilhelmine Creel, March 2, 1942, in Bartók, *Letters*, 320.

160. Béla Bartók, letter to Wilhelmine Creel, December 31, 1942, in Bartók, *Letters*, 325.

161. Béla Bartók, letter to Pál Kecskeméti, August 22, 1944, in Bartók, *Letters*, 333. For the difficult family situation, see Gillies, "Bartók in America," 197.

162. Béla Bartók, letter to Wilhelmine Creel, December 31, 1942, in Bartók, *Letters*, 325.

163. Ditta Pásztory, letter to József Szigeti, May 23, 1943, in Bartók, *Letters*, 326.

164. Cooper, *Bartók: Concerto for Orchestra*, 22–23. On the genesis of the work, see Móricz, "New Aspects of the Genesis of Béla Bartók's *Concerto for Orchestra*."

165. For a short summary of the American reception in 1944–45, see Cooper, *Bartók: Concerto for Orchestra*, 25–27.

166. Leibowitz, "Béla Bartók ou la possibilité du compromis dans la musique contemporaine." Leibowitz not only saw Bartók as compromising in exile but considered his use of folklore—for all its "authenticity"—a fundamental weakness (p. 711). He uses twice the term "médiocrité" to describe Bartók's American works (731, 733). Cooper, *Bartók: Concerto for Orchestra*, 81–84, discusses Leibowitz's charges of compromise in significant detail, though mostly in analytical terms.

167. Olin Downes (1945), given in Cooper, *Bartók: Concerto for Orchestra*, 26–27.

168. Béla Bartók, program notes for the Boston première of the *Concert for Orchestra*, given in Cooper, *Bartók: Concerto for Orchestra*, 85.

169. Móricz, "Operating on a Fetus," 476, points to the "official optimism in the United States in the middle of the Second World War" as the reason for Bartók's description of the final movement as "life-assuring."

170. Two examples include Cooper, *Bartók: Concerto for Orchestra*, and Lenoir, "Folklore et transcendance."

171. Rudolph Elie (1944), given in Cooper, *Bartók: Concerto for Orchestra*, 25; Albert Goldberg, "Menuhin Plays Bartók Sonata Superlatively," *New York Times*, February 7, 1944.

172. Cooper, *Bartók: Concerto for Orchestra*, 56–57.

173. Given in Gillies, "Redrawing Bartók's Life," 312.

174. This reading is not entirely without a basis in the sources surrounding the genesis of the work; see the report by György Sándor, given in Cooper, *Bartók: Concerto for Orchestra*, 54–55.

175. Responses related to existing aesthetic identities are categorized in Danuser, "Composers in Exile."

176. Weber makes the point that the understanding of exile necessitates the tracing of this dialectical process: "Die Heimat wird zur Fremde und die Fremde zur Heimat"; see Weber, "Exilforschung und Musikgeschichtsschreibung." Goehr describes this constantly shifting self-awareness of exile musicians as "double life"; see Goehr, "Music and Musicians in Exile," 68–71.

177. "Philadelphia Orchestra's Final Concert," *Washington Post*, March 28, 1943.

178. Irwin Edman, "No Blackout for the Arts," *New York Times*, April 19, 1942.

179. Cecil Smith, "Piatigorsky to Play Hindemith Cello Concerto," *Chicago Daily Tribune*, February 22, 1942.

180. Olin Downes, "Rodzinski Offers Hindemith Music," *New York Times*, January 21, 1944; Isabel Morse Jones, "Concert Offers Contrasts," *Los Angeles Times*, May 3, 1944; Claudia Cassidy, "Kurtz Reading of Hindemith Work Pleasing," *Chicago Daily Tribune*, July 28, 1944.

181. Roger Sessions, address on the occasion of Hindemith's being awarded an honorary doctorate, June 4, 1945, in Briner, Rexroth, and Schubert, *Paul Hindemith*, 169.

182. "Premiere for Symphony," *Chicago Daily Tribune*, December 7, 1941.

183. Copland, *Our New Music*, 111.

184. Critics were not unanimous in their praise of Hindemith as a craftsman. Some, such as Albert Goldberg (writing for the *Chicago Daily Tribune*) and Noel Straus (a contributor to the *New York Times*), saw Hindemith's craftsmanship as an indication of his lack of romantic inspiration. See also Jennert, *Paul Hindemith und die neue Welt*, 212–13. By the 1940s such references to a composer's craft in U.S. music criticism were not—as Jennert thinks—veiled allusions to Hindemith's nationality but, rather, a sign of transnational achievement.

185. Jay Walz, "Hindemith's Work Recorded by Philadelphia Orchestra," *Washington Post*, January 11, 1942.

186. Howard Taubman, "Records: Hindemith," *New York Times*, January 18, 1942.

187. Olin Downes, "Ormandy Directs at Carnegie Hall," *New York Times*, December 16, 1942.

188. Claudia Cassidy, "Monteux Baton Stirs a Glow of Old Symphony," *Chicago Daily Tribune*, July 2, 1944.

189. Copland, *Our New Music*, 115.

190. Paul Hindemith, letter to Gertrud Hindemith (1938), given in Schubert, "'Amerikanismus' und 'Americanism,'" 95: "Ich fühlte plötzlich, was für große Möglichkeiten ein eingeborener amerikanischer Komponist haben müßte und begann mich mit ihm zu identifizieren. Und da hatte ich Einfälle über Einfälle."

191. Paul Hindemith, letter to Gertrud Hindemith, dated March 3, 1940, given in Briner, Rexroth, and Schubert, *Paul Hindemith*, 170.

192. Noss, *Paul Hindemith in the United States*, 83.

193. Paul Hindemith, letter to Gertrud Hindemith, dated July 14, 1940, given in Danuser, "Paul Hindemiths amerikanische Lieder," 157: "Die Aussichten hier sind gut für mich, ich gewöhne mich langsam an Land und Leute und finde, daß beides nicht schlechter ist als anderswo auch, sondern im Gegenteil große Vorteile bietet."

194. Gertrud Hindemith, letter to William Theo Brown, March 29, 1942, *PHC*, Box 21.

195. Luther Noss, letter to Paul and Gertrud Hindemith, August 7, 1943, *PHC*, Box 21.

196. Paul Hindemith, circular to friends and family, spring 1946, given in Jennert, *Paul Hindemith und die neue Welt*, 105: "Persönlich hatten wir niemals die geringsten Schwierigkeiten. Weder hat man uns in Konzentrationslager gesteckt, noch hat man uns auch nur fühlen lassen, daß wir ja immerhin die feindlichen Ausländer waren."

197. Paul Hindemith, lecture notes, April 1940, given in Briner, Rexroth, and Schubert, *Paul Hindemith*, 166: "Wir werden gar nicht danach gefragt, ob wir diese Einflüsse für gut oder schlecht halten, ob wir sie anerkennen oder ablehnen, ob wir sie zu bezwingen glauben oder uns ihnen unterwerfen, sie sind da, und wir haben mit ihnen in irgendeiner Form zu rechnen."

198. On Hindemith's Symphony in E-flat, see in particular Schubert, "'Amerikanismus' und 'Americanism,'" 99–101, and Kirsch, "Brechungen symphonischer Tradition."

199. Paul Hindemith, letter to his publisher, November 24, 1942, given in Briner, Rexroth, and Schubert, *Paul Hindemith*, 184.

200. Paul Hindemith, letter to his publisher, November 24, 1942, given in English in Noss, *Paul Hindemith in the United States*, 117.

201. Danuser, "Paul Hindemiths amerikanische Lieder," shows through historically contextualized analysis that these songs were private in their scope and expressive quality.

202. Horowitz characterizes the *Symphonic Metamorphosis* as an "orchestral showpiece as carefree as the times were not"; see *Artists in Exile*, 121.

203. Noss, *Paul Hindemith in the United States*, 120.

204. Olin Downes, "Rodzinski Offers Hindemith Music," *New York Times*, January 21, 1944.

205. Gertrud Hindemith, letter to William Theo Brown, February 15, 1943, *PHC*, Box 21.

206. Horowitz, *Artists in Exile*, 114, describes Hindemith as "an ivory-tower exile who minded his own business."

207. On Weill in America, see the literature quoted in chapter 1, especially Kowalke, "'I'm an American!'" The most extensive discussion on Schoenberg's American identity can be found in Feisst, *Schoenberg's New World*.

208. On Schoenberg and Stravinsky as the "Einstein[s] of music," see Portnow, "Einstein, Modernism, and Musical Life in America."

209. For Schoenberg's response to Minna Lederman's talent-pool survey, see chapter 1; see also Arnold Schoenberg, "A Dangerous Game," *Modern Music* 22 (1944): 3–5. On Weill's wartime activities, see chapter 1.

210. Kurt List, "Ode to Napoleon," *Modern Music* 21 (1944): 139–45, at 139.

211. Leonard Stein, "A Note on the Genesis of the *Ode to Napoleon*" (1977), given in Auner, ed., *A Schoenberg Reader*, 337.

212. Ibid.

213. Judith Ryan discusses in detail the American reception of Lord Byron in the late 1930s; see "Schoenberg's Byron." On the choice of Whitman, see Kowalke, "Reading Whitman/Responding to America."

214. Besides Ryan, numerous other authors have discussed Schoenberg's choice of poem; see in particular Buhrmann, *Arnold Schönbergs "Ode to Napoleon Buonaparte,"* 21–33, 61–121.

215. Arnold Schoenberg, "How I Came to Compose the Ode to Napoleon," in Auner, ed., *A Schoenberg Reader*, 338.

216. On Robinson's and Copland's works and their musical and political contexts, see in particular Barg, "Paul Robeson's *Ballad for Americans*"; Crist, *Music for the Common Man*, 149–65.

217. Schoenberg, *Ode to Napoleon Buonaparte*, 38, 67. Feisst mentions the American compositional context (*Schoenberg's New World*, 149) but does not relate the compositional strategies to comparable works by U.S. composers.

218. Schoenberg, *Ode to Napoleon Buonaparte*, 16. Besides Buhrmann's extensive analysis, see also Gruber, "Ode to Napoleon Buonaparte." On Schoenberg's shift of position about the evocation of tonality in the wake of World War II, see Watkins, *The Gesualdo Hex*, 99–133.

219. Arnold Schoenberg, letters to Gertrude Greissle (May 17, 1942) and Carl Engel (June 22, 1942), both given in Buhrmann, *Arnold Schönbergs "Ode to Napoleon Buonaparte,"* 28.

220. Arnold Schoenberg, letters to Hermann Greissle (October 15, 1943) and Felix Greissle (June 28, 1943), both given in Buhrmann, *Arnold Schönbergs "Ode to Napoleon Buonaparte,"* 27.

221. Buhrmann, *Arnold Schönbergs "Ode to Napoleon Buonaparte,"* 46–47; Ryan, "Schoenberg's Byron."

222. Julia Spiegelman, "Artur Rodzinski Stirs New York Philharmonic," *New York Sun*, September 26, 1943. Olin Downes reports the information about Schoenberg's *Ode* almost identically, which usually means that the journalists were paraphrasing a press release; see "Philharmonic Season Outlook," *New York Times*, August 29, 1943.

223. Noel Straus, "Schoenberg at the Age of 70," *New York Times*, September 10, 1944.

224. For an overview of the critical reception, see Buhrmann, *Arnold Schönbergs "Ode to Napoleon Buonaparte,"* 49–59.

225. Stewart, *Ernst Krenek*, 246.

226. Krenek, *Die amerikanischen Tagebücher*, 260 (entry of June 22, 1942).

227. Noel Straus, "Beginning—Season No. 101," *New York Times*, October 4, 1942.

228. Ernst Krenek, program note for the première of *Symphonic Movement*, given in Noel Straus, "Music of Krenek in Premiere Here," *New York Times*, December 21, 1942.

229. Straus, "Music of Krenek in Premiere Here."

230. Krenek, *Die amerikanischen Tagebücher*, 188 (entry of July 3, 1941).

231. Ibid., 262 (entry of July 9, 1942). By the time Krenek's *Cantata for Wartime* was premièred in March 1944, his audiences were more comfortable with his idiom and responded enthusiastically; see Stewart, *Ernst Krenek*, 248.

232. Danuser, "Composers in Exile," 163.

233. For a critical view of Toscanini's politics, see Taruskin, "The Darker Side of Modern Music."

234. The OWI film is added as bonus material to the DVD release of the documentary *The Internationale* (produced and directed by Peter Miller), First Run/Icarus Film Release (NTSC FRF921357D), 2000.

235. Arturo Toscanini, letter draft (?), June 1942, in Sachs, ed., *The Letters of Arturo Toscanini*, 385 (original spelling retained).

236. Arturo Toscanini, letter to Olin Downes, October 15, 1941, in ibid., 382 (original spelling retained). See also Lucas, *Thomas Beecham*, 265–66. Lucas reproduces as figures 20 and 21 photographs of Beecham in Nazi Germany (figure 21 shows the conductor with a Nazi official in 1936).

237. Howard Taubman, "Toscanini, an Enemy of Fascism, Directs Radio Victory Program," *New York Times*, September 10, 1943.

238. Mario Castelnuovo-Tedesco, autobiographical notes (manuscript), dated February 18, 1956, *MCTP*, Box 109: "'il grande streppo'...: uno streppo quasi fisico dal quale ho stentato a rimettermi, e di cui (lo confesso) non sono mai completamente guarito...sono rimasto 'sospeso fra due mondi'! posizione, a volte, alquanto nomade." These notes are not included in the printed posthumous edition of the autobiography, published as Castelnuovo-Tedesco, *Una vita di musica*.

239. Mario Castelnuovo-Tedesco, "A Composer on Writing Concertos," *New York Times*, October 29, 1939; Castelnuovo-Tedesco, "The Italian Overture," *New York Times*, April 14, 1940.

240. See "Castelnuovo-Tedesco" in the Internet Movie Database, http://www.imdb.com/name/nm0005997 (accessed May 3, 2011), which lists 147 contributions to the filmic "Music Department" and 47 film scores; almost all of the former and most of the latter are uncredited.

241. R. L., "Stadium Concerts End 26th Season," *New York Times*, August 12, 1943.

242. Mario Castelnuovo-Tedesco, "Una vita di musica," chapter 87, trans. James Westby (typescript), *MCTP*, Box 113.

243. Mario Castelnuovo-Tedesco, "Music under Italian Fascism," manuscript, September 1944, *MCTP*, Box 116. Isabel Morse Jones mentions Adorno and Castelnuovo-Tedesco as the two speakers who "told of the insidious destruction of freedom in art and culture under the Fascist and Nazi state"; see "Music Forum Speakers Refute Ludwig Views," *Los Angeles Times*, September 16, 1944.

Chapter 5

1. Irwin Edman, "Muse Americana," *New Yorker*, July 22, 1944; copy in Scrapbook, *RHP*, Box 42.

2. For a discussion of musical nationalism in the United States, see the still foundational work by Zuck, *History of Musical Americanism*. American discourse in nineteenth-century music is discussed in, among others, Gienow-Hecht, *Sound Diplomacy*, 151–76; Shadle, "Music of a More Perfect Union."

3. William Grant Still, "Composer Says 'Lend Lease' in Music Extends to Our Enemies," *Chicago Defender*, October 17, 1942.

4. Ronald F. Ever, "Meet the Composer: (4) William Schuman," *Musical America* 64 (January 25, 1944): 8, 25, at 25.

5. Ronald F. Ever, "Meet the Composer: (2) Morton Gould," *Musical America* 63 (December 25, 1943): 7, 26.

6. Ronald F. Ever, "Meet the Composer: (6) Roy Harris," *Musical America* 64 (March 25, 1944): 7, 25. On Harris's "strident Americanism," see Levy, *Musical Nationalism*, 86–104. See also the discussion of Harris's 1930s Americanism and the styling of Harris as the "great white hope" of American music in Levy, "Frontier Figures," 133–45.

7. Captain Revel Lahmer, letter to Serge Koussevitzky, February 27, 1943, *SKC*, Box 27.

8. Alexander Gordon Wilcox, letter to Serge Koussevitzky, February 20, 1943, *SKC*, Box 27.

9. Sidney Robertson Cowell, transcript of reminiscences on Henry Cowell's U.S. government employment, *HCC*, Box 92.

10. Roger Sessions, "On the American Future" (1940), in Cone, ed., *Roger Sessions on Music*, 288–94, at 290: "The tendencies which I have enumerated are of course quasi-fascist attitudes—*Blut und Boden!*—but they are dangerous for other reasons as well."

11. Sessions, "On the American Future" (1940), 289. For a discussion of similarities and differences between Germany, the Soviet Union, and the United States during the 1930s, see Schivelbusch, *Entfernte Verwandtschaft*.

12. Roger Sessions, letter to Miriam Gideon, December 16, 1942, and letter to John Duke, July 30, 1944, in Olmstead, ed., *Correspondence of Roger Sessions*, 331, 335–36.

13. Marc Blitzstein, V-Mail to Aaron Copland, August 1, 1943, *ACC*, Box 246.

14. Reis, *Composers, Conductors, and Critics*, 163–66. The series was announced in Olin Downes, "Composers on War," *New York Times*, October 10, 1943. See also the list of works and discussion in Zuck, *History of Musical Americanism*, 194–96. Reis refers to "a series of eighteen short pieces" (p. 163), but the programs of the New York Philharmonic Orchestra mention only "seventeen well-known composers" as having been commissioned to write for this series (see, for example, the program of October 17, 1943, http://archives.nyphil.org, accessed June 27, 2011).

15. Concert program, New York Philharmonic Orchestra, October 17, 1943, http://archives.nyphil.org (accessed June 27, 2011).

16. Ibid.

17. Clarke, *Commemorating the Dead*. George L. Mosse traces the origin of the myth of the "fallen soldier" that dominated commemorations in and after World War I back to the Revolutionary and Napoleonic Wars; see *Fallen Soldiers*, 9–10.

18. Goebel, *The Great War and Medieval Memory*, 3.

19. Goebel, "Re-membered and Re-mobilized," 474.

20. *Address of the President of the United States at the Ceremonies Attending the Burial of an Unknown American Soldier in Arlington Cemetery, November 11, 1921* (Washington: Government Printing Office, 1921), 4, 3.

21. For discussion of the continuity in memorial culture between the two world wars in the United States, see Shanken, "Planning Memory," 142.

22. Shanken, "Planning Memory," 131–32.

23. Isabel Morse Jones, "Music Value in Wartime Recognized," *Los Angeles Times*, September 27, 1942.

24. Commentary by the composer, concert program, New York Philharmonic Orchestra, December 16, 1943, http://archives.nyphil.org (accessed June 27, 2011). The program note is also reproduced in the published score; see Herrmann, *For the Fallen*.

25. Theodor W. Adorno discussed the musical and aesthetic function of the "beautiful moment" in "Schöne Stellen," in Adorno, *Gesammelte Schriften*, ed. Tiedemann, 18:695–718, especially 700.

26. Commentary by the composer, concert program, New York Philharmonic Orchestra, January 5, 1944, http://archives.nyphil.org (accessed June 27, 2011).

27. Still, *In Memoriam*.

28. Still's and other U.S. composers' turn to monumentality in commemorative compositions can be traced back to the nineteenth-century concepts discussed in Rehding, *Music and Monumentality*.

29. On the musical characteristic of Still's *Afro-American Symphony*, see Smith, "The *Afro-American Symphony* and Its Scherzo." On the role of the symphony as a universalist genre in Still's conception of the *Afro-American Symphony*, see Moe, "A Question of Value"; Fauser, "'Presenting a Great Truth.'"

30. "Still's Concert Memorializes Negro Soldier," *Pittsburgh Courier*, January 15, 1944.

31. Nora Holt, "Still Still Impresses," *New York Amsterdam News*, January 22, 1944.

32. W. E. B. Du Bois, "As the Crow Flies," *New York Amsterdam News*, February 12, 1944.

33. Olin Downes, "Composers on War," *New York Times*, October 10, 1943.

34. Olin Downes, "Rodzinski Offers W. G. Still's Music," *New York Times*, January 6, 1944.

35. Felix Borowski, "Georg Szell at Ravinia," *Christian Science Monitor*, July 29, 1944.

36. Claudia Cassidy, "Serkin and Szell Concert Thrills Ravinia Crowd," *Chicago Daily Tribune*, July 19, 1944.

37. Commentary by the composer, concert program, New York Philharmonic Orchestra, January 5, 1944, http://archives.nyphil.org (accessed June 27, 2011).

38. For a short overview of the issues, see Kennedy, *Freedom from Fear*, 760–76. On African Americans in the armed forces, see Booker, *African Americans in the United States Army*.

39. In an article for *Musical America*, Isabel Morse Jones paraphrased Still in terms that could have come right out of the Double V campaign: "The present struggle for world democracy is closely bound, in Still's mind, with the struggle for democracy at home in which his race is engaged"; see Isabel Morse Jones, "Meet the Composer: (12) William Grant Still," *Musical America* 64 (December 25, 1944): 7, 25, at 25.

40. Langston Hughes, "Brothers," typescript, September 1942, distributed by the Writers' War Board, title page, *WcM*, Old Correspondence. In an article on the role of the boxer Joe Louis in promoting African American enlistment, Lauren Rebecca Sklaroff explores the various cultural strategies employed by the OWI and the War Department; see Sklaroff, "Constructing G.I. Joe Louis." Numerous African American leaders emphasized the commitment of black Americans to the war effort; see Wall, *Inventing the "American Way,"* 148–55.

41. Hughes, "Brothers," 6–8.

42. Robert Bagar, "Memorial to Lidice," concert program, New York Philharmonic Orchestra, October 28, 1943, http://archives.nyphil.org (accessed June 27, 2011).

43. Antheil, given in Tawa, *The Great American Symphony*, 95. I have silently omitted Tawa's parenthetical additions.

44. Paul Creston, program note, given in Naomi Freilicoff, "Young Audience Applauds James Melton and Dr. Kindler in First '15–30' Concert," *Washington Post*, November 28, 1943.

45. Commentary by the composer, concert program, New York Philharmonic Orchestra, October 17, 1943, http://archives.nyphil.org (accessed June 27, 2011).

46. Commentary by the composer, concert program, New York Philharmonic Orchestra, December 30, 1943, http://archives.nyphil.org (accessed June 27, 2011).

47. Gould, *American Salute*.

48. Isabel Morse Jones, "Operatic Farce Wins Approval," *Los Angeles Times*, February 4, 1944.

49. Gould, *American Salute*, 2. *American Salute* was one in a series of patriotic numbers that Gould wrote in these years, including *Buck Private*, *American Youth*, *American Legion Forever*, and *March of the Yanks*; see Goodman, *Morton Gould*, 137.

50. Bauer, *American Youth Concerto*.

51. On the role of *Sergeant York* in the context of World War II, see Docherty, *Projections of War*, 100–103; on "Defining America" in wartime movies, see Koppes and Black, *Hollywood Goes to War*, 142–84.

52. Commentary by the composer, concert program, New York Philharmonic Orchestra, November 25, 1943, http://archives.nyphil.org (accessed June 27, 2011).

53. Norman Dello Joio (1943), given in Reis, *Composers, Conductors, and Critics*, 164.

54. McDonald, *Bataan*. The score carries an epigraph citing General Douglas MacArthur: "No army has ever done so much with so little."

55. See Cochran, "The Documentary Film Scores of Gail Kubik."

56. For an extensive list of Whitman settings, see Wannamaker, "The Musical Settings of the Poetry of Walt Whitman," 575–606.

57. Ezra Pound, "What I Feel About Walt Whitman" (1909), in Pound, *Early Writings*, ed. Nadel, 187–89, at 187.

58. The work was premièred on April 30, 1944 at the Town Hall in New York, with Roger Sessions conducting; see "Concert in Tribute to Russia Is Heard," *New York Times*, May 1, 1944.

59. Olmstead, *Conversations with Roger Sessions*, 112.

60. Whitman, "Turn O Libertad," in *Leaves of Grass*, 254.

61. Sessions, *Turn O Libertad*.

62. My comments in this paragraph on Schumann's *A Free Song* are based on Swayne, "William Schuman." Schuman's wartime compositions are also discussed in Swayne, *Orpheus in Manhattan*, 123–76. In contrast, the war is mentioned only in passing in Polisi, *American Muse*, 69–79.

63. Swayne, "William Schuman," 297–99.

64. William Schuman, letter to Harold Spivacke, October 17, 1942, in Polisi, *American Muse*, 71.

65. Meyer and Shreffler, *Elliott Carter*, 54; Swayne, "William Schuman," 305, 310n1, 310n3.

66. The 1942 transformation of the composition scholarship into a composition prize is discussed in detail in Swayne, "William Schuman."

67. Swayne, "William Schuman," 306. The 1945 jury consisted of Chalmers Clifton, Henry Cowell, and Otto Luening.

68. The program of the première is reproduced in Fischer, ed., *Musical Composition Awards*, 4.

69. "Poetry still presents a terrible problem to me," wrote Elliott Carter in a letter to John Kirkpatrick, October 8, 1944, given in Meyer and Shreffler, *Elliott Carter*, 57.

70. Program note for the première, given in ibid., 49.

71. Elliott Carter, letter to Aaron Copland, May 10, 1943, given in ibid., 57. On the representation of landscape in American concert music, see Von Glahn, *The Sounds of Place*, especially chapters 1 and 4.

72. The piano-vocal version was published in 1956, thirteen years after the composition; see Carter, *Warble for Lilac-Time*. The long melisma spans pp. 15–16 of the piano-vocal score. Carter set the revised version of 1891–92 of the poem; those various versions can be compared in the online edition by the Walt Whitman Archive, http://www.whitmanarchive.org (accessed July 18, 2011).

73. On the aesthetic foundations of populist art during the 1930s, see Denning, *Cultural Front*, 115–59.

74. *Ballad for Americans* has been discussed extensively in recent years; see, for example, Barg, "Paul Robeson's *Ballad for Americans*" (which also engages extensively with the previous secondary literature); Wall, *Inventing the "American Way,"* 69–70.

75. Wall, *Inventing the "American Way,"* 69; Hagopian, "'You Know Who I Am!,'" 170.

76. Eleanor Roosevelt, *My Day*, April 22, 1942, in The Eleanor Roosevelt Paper Project, http://www.gwu.edu/~erpapers/myday/displaydoc.cfm?_y=1942&_f=md056166 (accessed July 19, 2011).

77. "Music: Ballad for Britons," *Time*, October 11, 1943.

78. Barg, "Paul Robeson's *Ballad for Americans*," 39.

79. Latouche and Robinson, *Ballad for Americans*. The famous 1940 recording with Paul Robeson, the American People's Chorus, and the Victor Symphony Orchestra, conducted by Nathaniel Shilkret, was reissued on CD in 1997 (*Songs for Free Men*, Pearl CD 9264).

80. Denning relates "pan-ethnic Americanism," popular-front ideologies, and contemporary notions of American exceptionalism in his discussion of *Ballad for Americans*; *Cultural Front*, 128–30. For a critical overview of American exceptionalism from early colonial settlement to the early 2000s, see Hodgson, *Myth of American Exceptionalism*. On U.S. imperialism and the ideology of exceptionalism, see Hietala, *Manifest Design*.

81. Hodgson, *Myth of American Exceptionalism*, 15.

82. The 150th anniversary of John Hancock's death in 1943 had less traction in U.S. public discourse.

83. "Address by Roosevelt," *New York Times*, April 14, 1943.

84. "Pupils to Compete in Essay Contest," *New York Times*, January 22, 1943.

85. Benjamin Fine, "Ignorance of U.S. History Shown by College Freshmen," *New York Times*, April 4, 1943.

86. Carl Sandburg, "A New Story of Jefferson Needed Now," *Washington Post*, April 25, 1943.

87. Hal Bobland, *"The Patriots*—Starring Jefferson," *New York Times*, January 31, 1943. For a short commentary on the score, see Michael Barlow and Robert Barnett, "Stanley Bate: Forgotten International Composer," Musicweb International, http://www.musicweb-international.com/bate/index.htm (accessed July 19, 2011).

88. Burns Mantle, *"The Patriots* Broadway's Newest Historical Play," *Chicago Daily Tribune*, February 7, 1943; Lewis Nichols, "Jefferson and Democracy," *New York Times*, February 7, 1943.

89. Kingsley interviewed in Peggy Preston, "Sergt. Sidney Kingsley, Soldier-Playwright, Believes That Every Man Has a Story," *Washington Post*, April 11, 1943.

90. "Congressional Audience Sees Broadway Hit in Opening of Jefferson Celebration Here," *Washington Post*, April 12, 1943.

91. "President Works on Jefferson Talk," *New York Times*, April 11, 1943; "Dedication Planned Tuesday for Jefferson Memorial," *Washington Post*, April 8, 1943.

92. "Many-Sided Jefferson," *New York Times*, April 12, 1943. On the choice of motto, see Harold Spivacke, letter to Elie Siegmeister, April 21, 1943, *WcM*, Old Correspondence, Folder "Siegmeister, Elie."

93. Harold Spivacke, press release for "Jefferson and His Music," *WcM*, Old Correspondence.

94. Ibid.

95. "Jefferson Concert Given," *New York Times*, April 26, 1943. See Hewitt, *Battle of Trenton*.

96. "Jefferson Concert Given," *New York Times*, April 26, 1943.

97. On the role of the violin in Einstein's U.S. reception, see Portnow, "Einstein, Modernism, and Musical Life in America," especially chapter 2.

98. Thompson, *Testament of Freedom*, 5.

99. Howard Taubman, "Records: In Honor of Jefferson," *New York Times*, July 21, 1946.

100. L. A. Sloper, "Randall Thompson Chorus; Shostakovitch Eighth Again," *Christian Science Monitor*, April 7, 1945.

101. Ray C. B. Brown, "2000 Thrill to Brahms Requiem," *Washington Post*, November 3, 1942.

102. L. A. Sloper, "Randall Thompson Chorus; Shostakovitch Eighth Again," *Christian Science Monitor*, April 7, 1945.

103. Jay Walz, "Meet the Composer: (11) Randall Thompson," *Musical America* 64 (November 10, 1944): 8, 25, at 8.

104. Olin Downes, "Choral Program at Carnegie Hall," *New York Times*, April 17, 1945; Downes, "New Trends in Composition," *New York Times*, April 22, 1945.

105. Olin Downes, "New Trends in Composition," *New York Times*, April 22, 1945.

106. Schwartz, *Abraham Lincoln in the Post-Heroic Era*, 59–90. See also Schwartz, "Memory as a Cultural System"; and (for the period from Lincoln's assassination through World War I) Schwartz, *Abraham Lincoln and the Forge of National Memory*. Crist discusses the Lincoln reception of the 1930s and '40s in *Music for the Common Man*, 149–55.

107. Schwartz, *Abraham Lincoln in the Post-Heroic Era*, 60.

108. David Josephson discusses Weinberger's *Lincoln Symphony* in "The Exile of European Music." Schwartz addresses the use of Lincoln in the rejection of noninterventionism; see *Abraham Lincoln in the Post-Heroic Era*, 61–63.

109. Howard Taubman, "Weinberger Seeks Time to Compose," *New York Times*, January 29, 1939. In the interview, the composer outlined the symphony as a multi-movement work with a choral finale "using the words of Longfellow's 'Excelsior'."

110. Weinberger, *Lincoln Symphony*. For a brief discussion of the symphony, see Kushner, "Jaromír Weinberger (1896–1967)," 309–10.

111. Olin Downes wrote a scathing review of the work, describing is as a "poor and meretricious symphony"; see "'Fidelio' Featured by Philharmonic," *New York Times*, February 13, 1942.

112. On the Abraham Lincoln Brigade and U.S. anti-Fascism, see Denning, *Cultural Front*, 374–75; Crist, *Music for the Common Man*, 151; Schwartz, *Abraham Lincoln in the Post-Heroic Era*, 34–35.

113. Ronald F. Ever, "Meet the Composer: (2) Morton Gould," *Musical America* 63 (December 25, 1943): 7, 26, at 26.

114. Morton Gould, letter to Arturo Toscanini, August 3, 1942, *MGP*, Box 110.

115. Arturo Toscanini, letter to Morton Gould, September 1, 1942, *MGP*, Box 110. Also given in Goodman, *Morton Gould*, 138.

116. Crist, *Music for the Common Man*, 152–54.

117. Copland and Perlis, *Copland: 1900 through 1942*, 341. The letter is in *ACC*, Box 257; see also chapter 1.

118. Aaron Copland, given in the program notes for the première by the Cincinnati Symphony Orchestra, May 14, 1942, *AKC*, Box 2.

119. Aaron Copland's contribution to the Radio Script for CBS, "Coca Cola…'The Pause That Refreshes on the Air,'" August 16, 1942, *AKC*, Box 2.

120. Crist, *Music for the Common Man*, 156.

121. Ibid., 157.

122. Given in "Kostelanetz, Lily Pons Here on Wednesday," *Washington Post*, July 12, 1942. These comments were integrated in the narrative of Copland's memoirs; see Copland and Perlis, *Copland: 1900 through 1942*, 342.

123. Copland and Perlis, *Copland: 1900 through 1942*, 343.

124. Crist, *Music for the Common Man*, 160.

125. Quoted in "Kostelanetz, Lily Pons Here on Wednesday," *Washington Post*, July 12, 1942. See also Crist, *Music for the Common Man*, 149–65; Pollack, *Aaron Copland*, 357–62.

126. Crist analyzes the folk-song quotations in detail in *Music for the Common Man*, 158–60. See also Pollack, *Aaron Copland*, 358–59.

127. Andre Kostelanetz, letter to Aaron Copland, April 19, 1942, *AKC*, Box 2.

128. Nadia Boulanger, letter to Aaron Copland, April 10, 1943, *ACC*, Box 248.

129. Serge Koussevitzky, letter to Aaron Copland, March 20, 1943, *SKC*, Box 13.

130. Carl Sandburg's contribution to the Radio Script for CBS, "Coca Cola…'The Pause That Refreshes on the Air,'" August 16, 1942, *AKC*, Box 2.

131. Given in Nicolas Slonimsky, typescript for a biography of Roy Harris (1951), 76, *NSC*, Box 13.

132. Both comments are in "Concert and Opera Asides," *New York Times*, May 30, 1943.

133. For a brief description of the symphony, see Stehman, *Roy Harris*, 89–93; and Robertson, "Roy Harris's Symphonies," 13–14.

134. Harris (1943), given in Slonimsky, typescript for a biography of Roy Harris (1951), 76.

135. Roy Harris, letter to Archibald MacLeish, January 4, 1944. Records of the Librarian of Congress: The Central File (MacLeish–Evans), Library of Congress, Manuscript Division, Box 899.

136. Roy Harris, letter to Serge Koussevitzky, October 21, 1943, *SKC*, Box 27.

137. Roy Harris, letter to Serge Koussevitzky, February 7, 1944, *SKC*, Box 27. The program for the work's première presents Harris as "Born February 12, 1898, in Lincoln County, Oklahoma"; program for the première by the Boston Symphony Orchestra, April 14/15, 1944, Library of Congress, Music Division, MT125.B.

138. Roy Harris, letter to Nicolas Slonimsky, February 7, 1944, *SKC*, Box 43.

139. Several newspaper articles pointed to this constellation of dates; see Roy Harris's scrapbook for 1944, *RHP*, Box 42. The scrapbook contains a significant collection of reviews but does not indicate their source. Quotation from "Harris Writes Lincoln Symphony," *Ithaca Journal*, April 14, 1944. An unidentified press clipping makes the point clearly: "The first performance will be heard on the anniversary of the day Lincoln was shot, while the radio première will be heard on a nation-wide hook-up over the Blue Network on April 15th, the anniversary of Lincoln's death."

140. Roy Harris, letter to Archibald MacLeish, November 18, 1943. Records of the Librarian of Congress: The Central File (MacLeish–Evans), Library of Congress, Manuscript Division, Box 899.

141. All quotations from Roy Harris, letter to Serge Koussevitzky, December 20, 1943, *SKC*, Box 27.

142. Roy Harris, letter to Serge Koussevitzky, February 7, 1944, *SKC*, Box 27.

143. Roy Harris, letter to Virgil Thomson, January 27, 1944, *VTP*, Box 47.

144. Roy Harris, letter to Archibald MacLeish, January 4, 1944. Records of the Librarian of Congress: The Central File (MacLeish–Evans), Library of Congress, Manuscript Division, Box 899.

145. Both extracts from Roy Harris, letter to Serge Koussevitzky, December 20, 1943, *SKC*, Box 27.

146. Rudolph Elie, Jr. (*Boston Herald*, April 15, 1944), Warren Storey Smith (*Boston Post*, April 15, 1944), and Moses Smith (*Modern Music*, May–June 1944); all three in *RHP*, Box 32.

147. L. A. Sloper, "Roy Harris' Sixth Symphony Has Its First Performance," *Christian Science Monitor*, April 15, 1944. Sloper alludes to Léonide Massine's controversial ballet *Choreartium* (1933), choreographed to Brahms's Fourth Symphony.

148. Program for the première by the Boston Symphony Orchestra, April 14/15, 1944, Library of Congress, Music Division, MT125.B.

149. See Schnepel, "The Critical Pursuit of the Great American Symphony." For a presentation of nineteenth-century debates on the symphony in the United States, see Shadle, "Music of a More Perfect Union." For a series of short vignettes of American symphonies written between the late 1920s and the 1950s, see Tawa, *The Great American Symphony*.

150. Given in Slattery, "The Symphonic Works," 101. For a discussion of nationalist populism in Still's *Afro-American Symphony*, see Fauser, "'Presenting a Great Truth.'"

151. Buell, "The Unkillable Dream of the Great American Novel," 140.

152. On the concept of *Weltanschauung* in music, see Danuser, *Weltanschauungsmusik*.

153. On monumentality in the symphony, see Rehding, *Music and Monumentality*, especially his chapter on the Third Reich and Bruckner (169–96).

154. For one of the best overviews of the symphonic aesthetic in the nineteenth century, see Bonds, "Symphony. §II. 19th Century." The most in-depth overview of the symphony in the 1930s and '40s is Steinbeck and Blumenröder, eds., *Die Symphonie im 19. und 20. Jahrhundert*, vol. 2, *Stationen der Symphonik seit 1900*, especially 153–269; for discussions of the genre through a set of case studies, see Osthoff and Schubert, eds., *Symphonik, 1930–1950*.

155. "War Symphony Acclaimed," *Washington Post*, July 20, 1942; Nicolas Slonimsky, "Dmitri Dmitrievitch Shostakovitch," *Musical Quarterly* 28 (1942): 415–44, at 439. The

American reception of the Leningrad Symphony has been discussed in several publications, most prominently in Klefstad, "Reception in America of Dmitri Shostakovich"; Gibbs, "'The Phenomenon of the Seventh.'"

156. This was related to me by a witness who recalled vividly, after more than sixty years, how almost all the children in his neighborhood (including himself) were called away from their usual Sunday afternoon activities to join their families at home to listen to "something really important" on the radio—which turned out to be the NBC performance of Shostakovich's symphony.

157. Gibbs discusses how the U.S. reception foregrounded Beethoven even before the work's first American performance; see "'The Phenomenon of the Seventh,'" 62, 73.

158. Slonimsky, "Dmitri Dmitrievitch Shostakovitch," 417.

159. Klefstad discusses the dichotomy between professional criticism and enthusiastic audience response in "Reception in America of Dmitri Shostakovich," 191–92. The continued positive audience response was noted in the press (204–6).

160. Thomson (1942), given in Klefstad, "Reception in America of Dmitri Shostakovich," 210; Arthur Berger, "Music in Wartime," New Republic, February 7, 1944, 175–78, at 177.

161. Harold Clurman, letter to Aaron Copland, August 24, 1942, ACC, Box 251.

162. Roy Harris, undated letter to Virgil Thomson, VTP, Box 47.

163. Roy Harris, letter to Archibald MacLeish, January 4, 1944. Records of the Librarian of Congress: The Central File (MacLeish–Evans), Library of Congress, Manuscript Division, Box 899.

164. Dedication given in Olin Downes, "Harris Symphony Has Première Here," New York Times, March 12, 1943.

165. Both extracts from Roy Harris, letter to Serge Koussevitzky, January 26, 1943, SKC, Box 27.

166. Copland agreed to write the arrangement in a letter to Serge Koussevitzky, March 5, 1942, ACC, Box 13, though the score is not known.

167. Given in Slonimsky, typescript for a biography of Roy Harris (1951), 73.

168. Rudolph Elie, Jr., Boston Herald, February 27, 1943, copy in RHP, Box 32.

169. Rudolph Elie, Jr., Boston Herald, March 7, 1943, copy in RHP, Box 32.

170. For a good overview of Blitzstein's activities in London see Gordon, Mark the Music, 225–63. More detail is provided in Pollack, Marc Blitzstein, chapters 13–15. Chapter 15 contains a detailed account of the genesis, musical structure, and reception of the Airborne Symphony which in some areas overlaps with the one I have developed here.

171. Marc Blitzstein, letter to Josephine Davis, December 25, 1942, MBA.

172. Marc Blitzstein, Notebook, entry of December 9, 1942, n.p., MBA, Box 1.

173. Blitzstein, Notebook, entry of December 23, 1942, n.p., MBA, Box 1.

174. Blitzstein, Notebook, entry of January 5, 1943, n.p., MBA, Box 1.

175. Marc Blitzstein, Outline, dated "January 25, 1943" for "Symphony/THE AIRBORNE," MBA, Box 1.

176. Blitzstein, Outline, p. 4.

177. Ibid. This passage is also given in Gordon, Mark the Music, 232.

178. Gordon, Mark the Music, 232.

179. Undated note titled "Re 'The Airborne'—by Marc Blitzstein," MBA, Box 1.

180. For a detailed account of the genesis and reception of Barber's Second Symphony, see Wright, "The Enlisted Composer, " 68–97.

181. Marc Blitzstein, letter to Josephine Davis, February 16, 1943, *MBA*; also quoted in Gordon, *Mark the Music*, 234.

182. "Project for a lyrico-musical work: THE AIRBORNE," January 6, 1943, *MBA*, Box 1.

183. Blitzstein, Notebook, entry of January 7, 1943.

184. Blitzstein, Notebook, entry of January 26, 1943.

185. Blitzstein, "Symphony, 'THE AIRBORNE,'" *MBA*, Box 1.

186. Blitzstein, Notebook, entry of February 21, 1943. Pollack offers additional models for Blitzstein's formal decisions with Arthur Honegger's *Le roi David*, Aaron Copland's *Lincoln Portrait*, Gustav Mahler's *Das Lied von der Erde*, and Beethoven's String Quartet, op. 131; see Pollack, *Marc Blitzstein*, 285.

187. Outline, dated March 17, [1943], *MBA*, Box 1.

188. Blitzstein, untitled note, dated March 24, [1943].

189. Marc Blitzstein, letter to Aaron Copland, April 17, 1944, *ACC*, Box 246.

190. Given in Franklin, *Mahler: Symphony no. 3*, 37. Though Blitzstein was ambivalent about Mahler's music (see Pollack, *Marc Blitzstein*, 285), having studied with Nadia Boulanger he was very familiar with Mahler's symphonies.

191. Blitzstein, "Symphony, 'THE AIRBORNE,'" *MBA*, Box 1.

192. Pollack, *Marc Blitzstein*, 291.

193. Pollack, *Aaron Copland*, 410; "Aaron Copland's Program Notes from the Première" (October 19, 1946), reproduced as Appendix B in Crist, "Aaron Copland's Third Symphony (1946)," 239–40, at 240.

194. Pollack, *Aaron Copland*, 410.

195. Copland and Perlis, *Copland since 1943*, 67–68.

196. Fine and Koussevitzky both given in ibid., 68–69.

197. This is research by Crist, who—over the course of three studies—has explored the wartime context of Copland's Third Symphony: Crist, "Aaron Copland's Third Symphony (1946)"; Crist, "Aaron Copland's Third Symphony from Sketch to Score"; and Crist, *Music for the Common Man*, 176–91.

198. Howard Pollack, *Aaron Copland*, 412.

199. Schnepel, "Critical Pursuit of the Great American Symphony," 507.

200. Crist, "Aaron Copland's Third Symphony (1946)," 195.

201. I am borrowing Stanley Fish's term from Anne C. Shreffler's discussion of Shostakovich's "Leningrad" Symphony in "Denkmal wider Willen," 101.

202. Thomson's reviews are cited in Crist, *Music for the Common Man*, 193.

203. Stravinsky's First Symphony in E-flat (1905–7) was a student composition, and neither his Symphony for Wind Instruments (1920) nor his *Symphonie des Psaumes* (1930) is a symphony in the traditional concept of the genre to which both the Symphony in C (1940) and the Symphony in Three Movements (1942–45) refer.

204. Both works were premièred in New York on April 22, 1944, in a concert sponsored by the League of Composers. For a review, see R. L., "Unusual Program by Harry Partch," *New York Times*, 23 April 1944.

205. John Cage, "The Future of Music: Credo," given in DeLio, *Amores of John Cage*, 9.

206. The 1943 photo spread and article are reproduced in Kostelanetz, ed., *John Cage*, figure 7 (between pp. 78 and 79).

207. Both texts in ibid., 64–66, 71–72. Thomson's assessment comes from personal familiarity with Cage in the years between 1943 and 1945, when he, Cowell, Harrison, and Cage met regularly and "provided for one another, with Europe and the Orient cut off by war, a musical academy of theory and practice." Silverman, *Begin Again*, 59.

208. Silverman, *Begin Again*, 54. Cage's *Perilous Night* (1944) is about erotic perils, not those encountered in war. Another 1942 work, *Imaginary Landscape no. 3*, was—as Cage pointed out in a 1970 interview with Richard Kostelanetz—"perfectly hideous" because he sought to show that World War II was "lousy"; see Kostelanetz, *Conversing with John Cage*, 63. Cage did "library research work" for his father, who was engaged in developing military technology (according to Cage, "doing work in seeing through fog for airplanes"), but the composer considered it "pleasant for me not to have to get involved" with the war in any direct way (ibid., 11).

209. Cage, *Credo in US*, flyleaf.

210. Kostelanetz, *Conversing with John Cage*, 66.

211. Bernstein, "Music I," 76.

212. Cage, *Credo in US*, 25–26.

213. John Cage, "Lecture on Nothing," in Cage, *Silence: Lectures and Writings*, 109–28, at 117. I am grateful to Alex Ross for pointing me to this text.

214. Swayne, *Orpheus in Manhattan*, 296.

Archival Sources

Library of Congress, Manuscript Division, Washington D.C.
  Records of the Librarian of Congress: The Central File (MacLeish–Evans)
Library of Congress, Music Division, Washington, D.C.
  Victor Babin Collection [ML94.B2]
  Ernst Bacon Collection
  Mario Castelnuovo-Tedesco Papers
  Elizabeth Sprague Coolidge Collection
  Aaron Copland Collection
  Ross Lee Finney, Responses to Questionnaires [ML94.F55]
  Morton Gould Papers
  Oscar Hammerstein II Collection
  Roy Harris Papers
  Andre Kostelanetz Collection
  Serge Koussevitzky Collection
  National Negro Opera Collection
  Claire R. Reis, Responses to Questionnaires [ML390.L37]
  Nicolas Slonimsky Collection
  Harold Spivacke Collection
  Archives of the Subcommittee on Music, Joint Army and Navy Committee on
      Welfare and Recreation
National Archives, College Park, Maryland
  RG 59: State Department Decimal Files (1940–44)
  RG 160: Office of the Director of Personnel, Special Services Division, General
      Records (1941–45)
  RG 208: Archives of the Office of War Information
  RG 225: Records of the Joint Army and Navy Committee on Welfare and
      Recreation

RG 226: Archives of the Office of Strategic Services
RG 353.3: Records of Interdepartmental and Intradepartmental Committees
(State Department)
New York Public Library, Billy Rose Theater Division
Agnes de Mille Collection
Papers of Jerome Lawrence and Robert E. Lee
USO Papers
New York Public Library, Music Division
Henry Cowell Collection
Ross Lee Finney Papers
Clippings File "World War II"
State Historical Society, Madison, Wisconsin
Marc Blitzstein Archives
Yale University, Irving S. Gilmore Music Library
Lehman Engel Collection
Paul Hindemith Collection
Goddard Lieberson Papers
Deems Taylor Papers
Virgil Thomson Papers
Kurt Weill and Lotte Lenya Papers
Yale University, Beinecke Rare Book and Manuscript Library
Yale Collection of American Literature, Theatre Guild Archives
Weill-Lenya Research Center, New York

Musical and Visual Sources

Bacon, Ernst. *A Tree on the Plains*. Mimeographed manuscript, 1942. University of North Carolina at Chapel Hill, Folio M1503.B127.T7.1942a.

Bauer, Marion. *American Youth Concerto*. Opus 36. New York and London: Schirmer, 1946.

Cage, John. *Credo in US: Music for the Dance Which Was Made by Merce Cunningham and Jean Erdman*. New York: Henmar Press, 1962.

Carter, Elliott. *Warble for Lilac-Time*. New York: Peer International, 1956.

Copland, Aaron. *Lincoln Portrait*. For Speaker and Orchestra. Orchestral Score. New York: Boosey & Hawkes, 1943.

Copland, Aaron. *Four Dance Episodes from "Rodeo."* London: Boosey & Hawkes, 1946.

Cowell, Henry. *American Muse*. New York: Music Press, 1943.

Downes, Olin, and Elie Siegmeister. *A Treasury of American Song*. 2nd revised and enlarged ed. New York: A. A. Knopf, 1943.

Fassbinder, Rainer Werner, dir. *Lili Marleen*. 1981.

Finney, Ross Lee. *Hymn, Fuguing, and Holiday*. New York: Carl Fischer, 1965.

Gould, Morton. *American Salute*. New York: Mills Music, 1943.

Herrmann, Bernard. *For the Fallen*. New York: Broude Brothers, 1955.

Hewitt, James. *The Battle of Trenton: A Favorite Historical Military Sonata Dedicated to George Washington*, edited by Maurice Hinson. Miami: CPP/Belwin, 1989.

Kerr, Walter, and Elie Siegmeister. *Sing Out, Sweet Land! Selections from the Theatre Guild Musical Play*. New York: Northern Music, 1946.

Kerr, Walter, and Elie Siegmeister. *Sing Out, Sweet Land!* Theatre Guild Broadcast, October 21, 1945. http://www.archive.org/details/TheaterGuildontheAir (accessed June 6, 2010).

Latouche, John, and Earl Robinson. *Ballad for Americans.* Piano reduction by Domenico Savino. New York: Robbins Music, 1940.

Latouche, John, and Earl Robinson. *Ballad for Americans.* Recorded by Paul Robeson, the American People's Chorus and the Victor Symphony Orchestra. Conducted by Nathaniel Shilkret. 1940. Reissued as *Songs for Free Men*, Pearl CD 9264, 1997.

Lomax, John A., and Alan Lomax. *Our Singing Country: Folksongs and Ballads.* Music Editor Ruth Crawford Seeger. Introduction to the Dover ed. by Judith Tick. Mineola, NY: Dover, 2000.

Martinů, Bohuslav. *Memorial to Lidice.* Prague: Melantrich, 1944.

McDonald, Harl. *Bataan.* Philadelphia: Elkan Vogel, 1942.

Michell, Roger, dir. *Hyde Park on Hudson.* 2012.

Schoenberg, Arnold. *Ode to Napoleon Buonaparte (Lord Byron), Opus 41.* New York: Schirmer, 1944.

Sessions, Roger. *Turn O Libertad.* New York: Edward B. Marks, 1952.

Siegmeister, Elie. *Songs of Early America, 1620–1830.* New York: Edward B. Marks, 1944.

Singer, Bryan, dir. *Valkyrie.* 2008.

Spielberg, Steven, dir. *Saving Private Ryan.* 1998. DVD released by Dreamworks Video, 2004.

Still, William Grant. *In Memoriam: The Colored Soldiers Who Died for Democracy.* Los Angeles: Delkas, 1943.

Strauß, Johann. *Rosalinda (Fledermaus).* New English lyrics by Paul Kerby. Piano-vocal score. New York: Boosey & Hawkes, 1943.

Ten Fanfares by Ten Composers for Brass and Percussion. New York: Boosey & Hawkes, 1944.

Thompson, Randall. *The Testament of Freedom: A Setting of Four Passages from the Writings of Thomas Jefferson.* Boston: Schirmer, 1944.

Tuesday in November. OWI Documentary. Music by Virgil Thomson. Available at http://www.archive.org/details/Tuesdayi11945 (accessed April 12, 2010).

Verdi, Giuseppe. *Hymn of Nations.* Performed by Jan Peerce, the Westminster Choir, the NBC Symphony Orchestra. Conducted by Arturo Toscanini. OWI documentary added as bonus material to *The Internationale*, produced and directed by Peter Miller. First Run/Icarus Film Release NTSC FRF921357D, 2000.

Weill, Kurt. *Mine Eyes Have Seen the Glory.* Settings for Helen Hayes. Recorded 1942 by RCA. Papers of Lotte Lenya and Kurt Weill, Irving S. Gilmore Music Library, Yale University.

Weill, Kurt. *Johnny Johnson (1936)*, edited by Tim Carter. New York: Kurt Weill Foundation, 2012.

Weinberger, Jaromír. *The Lincoln Symphony.* New York: Carl Fischer, 1940.

Text Sources and Secondary Literature

N.B.: This list does not contain articles published during World War II in the daily press or in musical periodicals such as *Modern Music, Musical America, Musical Quarterly*, or *Proceedings of the Music Teachers National Association*.

Aciman, André, ed. *Letters of Transit: Reflections on Exile, Identity, Language, and Loss.* New York: Norton, 1999.

Adams, Byron. "Martinů and the American Critics." In *Martinů's Mysterious Accident: Essays in Honor of Michael Henderson*, edited by Michael Beckerman, 81–93. Hillsdale, NY: Pendragon Press, 2007.

Adler, Les K., and Thomas G. Paterson. "Red Fascism: The Merger of Nazi Germany and Soviet Russia in the American Image of Totalitarianism, 1930s–1950s." *American Historical Review* 75 (1970): 1046–64.

Adorno, Theodor W. *Minima Moralia: Reflexionen aus dem beschädigten Leben*. Vol. 4 of *Gesammelte Schriften*, edited by Rolf Tiedemann. Darmstadt: Wissenschaftliche Buchgesellschaft, 1998.

Adorno, Theodor W. "Schöne Stellen." In Adorno, *Gesammelte Schriften*, edited by Rolf Tiedemann, 18:695–718. Darmstadt: Wissenschaftliche Buchgesellschaft, 1998.

Allen, Warren Dwight. *Our Marching Civilization: An Introduction to the Study of Music and Society*. Stanford: Stanford University Press, 1943.

Alpert, Hollis. *The Life and Times of "Porgy and Bess": The Story of an American Classic*. New York: Alfred A. Knopf, 1990.

Anderson, Tim. "'Buried under the Fecundity of His Own Creations': Reconsidering the Recording Bans of the American Federation of Musicians, 1942–44 and 1948." *American Music* 22 (2004): 231–69.

Andraschke, Peter. "Bohuslav Martinů: Musik gegen Krieg und Zerstörung." In *Glasba in Družba v 20. Stoletju/Music and Society in the 20th Century: Ljubljana, Slovenske Konjice, 12.–15. V. 1998*, 128–39. Ljubljana: Festival Ljubljana, 1999.

Ansari, Emily Abrams. "'Masters of the President's Music': Cold War Composers and the United States Government." Ph.D. dissertation, Harvard University, 2009.

Applegate, Celia. *Bach in Berlin: Nation and Culture in Mendelssohn's Revival of the St. Matthew Passion*. Ithaca: Cornell University Press, 2005.

Auner, Joseph H., ed. *A Schoenberg Reader: Documents of His Life*. New Haven: Yale University Press, 2003.

Barg, Lisa. "National Voices/Modernist Histories: Race, Performance and Remembrance in American Music, 1927–1943." Ph.D. dissertation, State University of New York at Stony Brook, 2001.

Barg, Lisa. "Paul Robeson's Ballad for Americans: Race and the Cultural Politics of 'People's Music.'" *Journal of the Society for American Music* 2 (2008): 27–70.

Barlow, Michael, and Robert Barnett. "Stanley Bate: Forgotten International Composer." Musicweb International <http://www.musicweb-international.com/bate/index.htm> (accessed July 19, 2011).

Bartók, Béla. *Letters*, edited by János Demény. London: Faber & Faber, 1971.

Bartók, Peter. *My Father*. Homosassa, FL: Bartók Records, 2002.

Bauer, Marion, and Claire R. Reis. "Twenty-five Years with the League of Composers." *Musical Quarterly* 34 (1948): 1–14.

Beal, Amy C. "The Army, the Airwaves, and the Avant-Garde: American Classical Music in Postwar West Germany." *American Music* 21 (2003): 474–513.

Beal, Amy C. *New Music, New Allies: American Experimental Music in West Germany from the Hour Zero to Reunification*. Berkeley and Los Angeles: University of California Press, 2006.

Bennett, Rebecca Meador. "The Anxiety of Appreciation: Virgil Thomson Wrestles with a 'Racket.'" Ph.D. dissertation, Northwestern University, 2009.

Bennett, Todd. "Culture, Power, and *Mission to Moscow*: Film and Soviet-American Relations during World War II." *Journal of Film History* 88 (2001): 489–518.

Bentley, Christa Anne. "Finding *The Lost Colony* (1937): Paul Green, Symphonic Drama, and the History of a Collaboration." M.A. thesis, University of North Carolina at Chapel Hill, 2012.

Bernstein, David W. "Music I: To the Late 1940s." In *The Cambridge Companion to John Cage*, edited by David Nicholls, 63–84. Cambridge: Cambridge University Press, 2002.

Bérubé, Allan. *Coming Out under Fire: The History of Gay Men and Women in World War II*. New York: Free Press, 2000.

Bianchi, Carlo: "Musica e Guerra: Comporre all'epoca del secondo conflitto mondiale." Ph.D. dissertation, Università di Pavia-Cremona, 2006.

Bonds, Mark Evan. *After Beethoven: Imperatives of Originality in the Symphony*. Cambridge, MA: Harvard University Press, 1996.

Bonds, Mark Evan. "Symphony. §II. 19th Century." In *Grove Music Online. Oxford Music Online*, http://www.oxfordmusiconline.com.libproxy.lib.unc.edu/subscriber/article/grove/music/27254pg2 (accessed July 29, 2011).

Booker, Bryan D. *African Americans in the United States Army in World War II*. Jefferson, NC: McFarland, 2008.

Bork, Camilla, Tobias Klein, Burkhard Meischein, Andreas Meyer, and Tobias Plebuch, eds. *Ereignis und Exegese—Musikinterpretation und Interpretation der Musik: Festschrift für Hermann Danuser*. Schliengen: Edition Argus, 2011.

Botstein, Leon. "After Fifty Years: Thoughts on Music and the End of World War II." *Musical Quarterly* 79 (1995): 225–30.

Březina, Aleš. "*... the essential nobility of thoughts and things which are quiet simple...*: Martinůs Versuch einer Erneuerung der Symphonie." In Osthoff and Schubert, eds., *Symphonik, 1930–1950*, 224–42.

Briner, Andres, Dieter Rexroth, and Giselher Schubert. *Paul Hindemith: Leben und Werk in Bild und Text*. Zurich: Atlantis Musikbuch-Verlag, 1988.

Brinkmann, Reinhold. "Reading a Letter." In Brinkmann and Wolff, eds., *Driven into Paradise*, 3–20.

Brinkmann, Reinhold, and Christoph Wolff, eds. *Driven into Paradise: The Musical Migration from Nazi Germany to the United States*. Berkeley and Los Angeles: University of California Press, 1999.

Buell, Lawrence. "The Unkillable Dream of the Great American Novel: *Moby-Dick* as Test Case." *American Literary History* 20 (2008): 132–55.

Buhrmann, Dirk. *Arnold Schönbergs "Ode to Napoleon Buonaparte" op. 41 (1942)*. Diskordanzen: Studien zur neueren Musikgeschichte 11. Hildesheim and New York: Georg Olms Verlag, 2002.

Bunt, Leslie. "Music Therapy." In *Grove Music Online. Oxford Music Online*, http://www.oxfordmusiconline.com.libproxy.lib.unc.edu/subscriber/article/grove/music/19453 (accessed April 28, 2010).

Burlingame, John. "Williams' Music to Obama's Ears." *Variety*. January 15, 2009. http://www.variety.com/article/VR1117998645?refCatId=16 (accessed July 30, 2011).

Burton, Humphrey. *Yehudi Menuhin: A Life*. Boston: Northeastern University Press, 2001.

Cage, John. *Silence: Lectures and Writings*, 50th Anniversary Edition. Middletown, CT: Wesleyan University Press, 2011.

Campbell, Jennifer L. "Creating Something Out of Nothing: The Office of Inter-American Affairs Music Committee (1940–1941) and the Inception of a Policy for Musical Diplomacy." *Diplomatic History* 36 (2012): 29–39.

Carter, Tim. *"Oklahoma!" The Making of an American Musical*. New Haven: Yale University Press, 2007.

Carter, Tim. "Celebrating the Nation: Kurt Weill, Paul Green, and the Federal Theatre Project (1937)." *Journal of the Society for American Music* 5 (2011): 297–334.

Carter, Tim. "Schoenberg, Weill, and the Federal Arts Projects in Los Angeles, Spring 1937." In *Ereignis und Exegese*, edited by Bork, Klein, Meischein, Meyer, and Plebuch, 600–612.

Castelnuovo-Tedesco, Mario. *Una vita di musica (un libro di ricordi)*, edited by James Westby. Fiesole: Edizioni Cadmo, 2005.

Cherry, Paul Wyman. "The String Quartets of Darius Milhaud." Ph.D. dissertation, University of Colorado, Boulder, 1980.

Chimènes, Myriam, ed. *La vie musicale sous Vichy*. Brussels: Complexe, 2001.

Citron, Marcia J. *Gender and the Musical Canon*. Cambridge: Cambridge University Press, 1993.

Clark, Katerina. *Moscow, the Fourth Rome: Stalinism, Cosmopolitanism, and the Evolution of Soviet Culture, 1931–1941*. Cambridge, MA: Harvard University Press, 2011.

Clarke, Joseph. *Commemorating the Dead in Revolutionary France: Revolution and Remembrance, 1789–1799*. Cambridge: Cambridge University Press, 2007.

Cochran, Alfred W. "The Documentary Film Scores of Gail Kubik." In *Film Music: Critical Approaches*, edited by Kevin J. Donnelly, 117–28. New York: Continuum, 2001.

Cohen, Brigid. "Migrant Cosmopolitan Modern: Cultural Reconstruction in Stefan Wolpe's Musical Thought, 1919–1972." Ph.D. dissertation, Harvard University, 2007.

Cone, Edward T., ed. *Roger Sessions on Music: Collected Essays*. Princeton: Princeton University Press, 1979.

Conkle, Christian, "Building Our Cultural Defenses: The Noninterventionist Rhetoric of the National Federation of Music Clubs." M.A. thesis, University of North Carolina at Chapel Hill, 2009.

Conrad, Doda. *Dodascalies: Ma chronique du XXe siècle*. Arles: Actes Sud, 1997.

Cooper, David. *Bartók: Concerto for Orchestra*. Cambridge: Cambridge University Press, 1996.

Copland, Aaron. *Our New Music: Leading Composers in Europe and America*. New York: McGraw-Hill, 1941.

Copland, Aaron, and Vivian Perlis. *Copland: 1900 through 1942*. New York: St. Martin's Press, 1984.

Copland, Aaron, and Vivian Perlis. *Copland since 1943*. New York: St. Martin's Press, 1989.

Copland, Aaron. *What to Listen for in Music*. Foreword and epilogue by Alan Rich. New York: Signet, 1999.

Crist, Elizabeth B. "Aaron Copland's Third Symphony (1946): Context, Composition, and Consequence." Ph.D. dissertation, Yale University, 2000.

Crist, Elizabeth B. "Aaron Copland's Third Symphony from Sketch to Score." *Journal of Musicology* 18 (2001): 377–405.

Crist, Elizabeth B. *Music for the Common Man: Aaron Copland during the Depression and War.* Oxford and New York: Oxford University Press, 2005.

Crist, Elizabeth B., and Wayne Shirley, eds. *The Selected Correspondence of Aaron Copland.* New Haven: Yale University Press, 2006.

Cusick, Suzanne G. "'You Are in a Place That Is Out of the World…': Music in the Detention Camps of the 'Global War on Terror.'" *Journal of the Society for American Music* 2 (2008): 1–26.

Daniel, Peggy. *Tanglewood: A Group Memoir.* New York: Amadeus Press, 2008.

Daniels, Roger. "Immigration Policy in a Time of War: The United States, 1939–1945." In *Immigration, Incorporation and Transnationalism*, edited by Elliott R. Barkan, 95–103. New Brunswick, NJ: Transaction, 2007.

Danuser, Hermann. "Paul Hindemiths amerikanische Lieder." *Hindemith Jahrbuch/ Annales Hindemith* 27 (1998): 155–79.

Danuser, Hermann. "Composers in Exile: The Question of Musical Identity." In Brinkmann and Wolff, eds., *Driven into Paradise*, 155–71.

Danuser, Hermann. *Weltanschauungsmusik.* Schliengen: Edition Argus, 2009.

Davis, William B. "Music Therapy in 19th Century America." *Journal of Music Therapy* 24 (1987): 78–87.

Davis, William B. "Keeping the Dream Alive: Profiles of Three Early Twentieth-Century Music Therapists." *Journal of Music Therapy* 30 (1993): 34–45.

DeLapp, Jennifer Lois. "Copland in the Fifties: Music and Ideology in the McCarthy Era." Ph.D. dissertation, University of Michigan, 1997.

DeLio, Thomas. *The Amores of John Cage.* Hillsdale, NY: Pendragon Press, 2009.

De Mille, Agnes. *Dance to the Piper.* Boston: Little, Brown, 1951.

Denning, Michael. *The Cultural Front: The Laboring of American Culture in the Twentieth Century.* London and New York: Verso, 1997.

Dizikes, John. *Opera in America: A Cultural History.* New Haven: Yale University Press, 1993.

Döge, Klaus. "Das entsetzliche Grauen zum Ausdruck gebracht: Anmerkungen zu Martinůs *Memorial to Lidice*." In *Bohuslav Martinů*, edited by Ulrich Tadday, 78–91. Munich: Edition Text + Kritik, 2009.

Doherty, Thomas. *Projections of War: Hollywood, American Culture, and World War II.* New York: Columbia University Press, 1993.

Drake, Jeremy. *The Operas of Darius Milhaud.* New York: Garland, 1989.

Dreisziger, Nándor F. "A Hungarian Patriot in American Exile: Béla Bartók and Émigré Politics." *Journal of the Royal Musical Association* 130 (2005): 283–301.

Drew, David. *Kurt Weill: A Handbook.* Berkeley and Los Angeles: University of California Press, 1987.

Drot, Otniel E. "Dangerous Liaisons: Science, Amusement and the Civilizing Process." In Gouk and Hill, eds., *Representing Emotions*, 223–34.

Eckmann, Sabine, and Lutz Koepnick, eds. *Caught by Politics: Hitler Exiles and American Visual Culture.* New York: Palgrave Macmillan, 2007.

Ellis, Katharine. *Interpreting the Musical Past: Early Music in Nineteenth-Century France.* Oxford and New York: Oxford University Press, 2005.

Engel, Lehman. *This Bright Day: An Autobiography*. New York: Macmillan, 1974.

Erismann, Guy. *Martinů: un musicien à l'éveil des sources*. Arles: Actes Sud, 1990.

Ewen, David. *Music Comes to America*. New York: Thomas Y. Cromwell, 1942.

Farneth, David, with Elmar Juchem and Dave Stein. *Kurt Weill: A Life in Pictures and Documents*. Woodstock, NY: Overlock Press, 2000.

Fauser, Annegret. "Musik als 'Lesehilfe': Zur Rolle der Allusion in den Opern von Jules Massenet." In *Musik als Text: Bericht über den Internationalen Kongreß der Gesellschaft für Musikforschung Freiburg im Breisgau 1993*, edited by Hermann Danuser and Tobias Plebuch, 462–64. Kassel: Bärenreiter-Verlag, 1999.

Fauser, Annegret. "Gendering the Nations: The Ideologies of French Discourse on Music (1870–1914)." In *Musical Constructions of Nationalism: Essays on the History and Ideology of European Musical Culture, 1800–1945*, edited by Michael Murphy and Harry White, 72–103. Cork: Cork University Press, 2001.

Fauser, Annegret. *Musical Encounters at the 1889 Paris World's Fair*. Rochester, NY: University of Rochester Press, 2005.

Fauser, Annegret. "Creating Madame Landowska." *Women and Music: A Journal of Gender and Culture* 10 (2006): 1–23.

Fauser, Annegret. "Aaron Copland, Nadia Boulanger, and the Making of an 'American' Composer." *Musical Quarterly* 89 (2006): 524–55.

Fauser, Annegret. "'Dixie *Carmen*': War, Race, and Identity in Oscar Hammerstein's *Carmen Jones* (1943)." *Journal of the Society for American Music* 4 (2010): 127–74.

Fauser, Annegret. "Carmen in Khaki: Europäische Oper in den Vereinigten Staaten während des Zweiten Weltkrieges." In *Oper im Wandel der Gesellschaft: Kulturtransfers und Netzwerke des Musiktheaters im modernen Europa*, edited by Sven Oliver Müller, Philipp Ther, Jutta Toelle, and Gesa zur Nieden, 303–29. Vienna: Oldenbourg, 2010.

Fauser, Annegret. "Cultural Musicology: New Perspectives on World War II." *Zeithistorische Forschungen/Studies in Contemporary History* 8 (2011): 282–86.

Fauser, Annegret. "'Presenting a Great Truth': William Grant Still's *Afro-American Symphony* (1930)." In Bork, Klein, Meischein, Meyer, and Plebuch, eds., *Ereignis und Exegese*, 644–53.

Fauser, Annegret. "Music for the Allies: Representations of Nationhood during World War II." In *Crosscurrents: American and European Music In Interaction, 1900–2000*, edited by Felix Meyer, Carol Oja, Wolfgang Rathert, and Anne C. Shreffler. Basel: Paul Sacher Stiftung, forthcoming.

Fauser, Annegret, ed. *"Mon cher Copland": The Correspondence of Nadia Boulanger and Aaron Copland*. New York: Oxford University Press, forthcoming.

Feisst, Sabine. "Arnold Schoenberg in America Reconsidered: A Historiographic Investigation." In *Music's Intellectual History*, edited by Zdravko Blažeković and Barbara Dobbs Mackenzie, 409–25. New York: Répertoire International de la Littérature Musicale, 2009.

Feisst, Sabine. *Schoenberg's New World: The American Years*. Oxford and New York: Oxford University Press, 2011.

Filene, Benjamin. *Romancing the Folk: Public Memory and American Roots Music*. Chapel Hill: University of North Carolina Press, 2000.

Finney, Ross Lee. *Profile of a Lifetime: A Musical Autobiography*. New York: C. F. Peters, 1992.

Firme, Annemarie, and Ramona Hocker, eds. *Von Schlachthymnen und Protestsongs: Zur Kulturgeschichte des Verhältnisses von Musik und Krieg*. Bielefeld: Transcript Verlag, 2006.

Fischer, Heinz-Dietrich, ed. *Musical Composition Awards, 1943–1999: From Aaron Copland and Samuel Barber to Gian-Carlo Menotti and Melinda Wagner*. The Pulitzer Prize Archive 15. Munich: Saur, 2001.

Flynn, John J. "Americans at the Met: The Rise of Homegrown Opera Stars in the Twentieth Century." In *The Sounds of People and Places: A Geography of American Music from Country to Classical and Blues to Bebop*, edited by George O. Carney, 149–63. Lanham, MD: Rowan & Littlefield, 2003.

Foreman, Lewis. "Forging a Relationship and a Role: Michael Tippett and the BBC, 1928–51." In *Michael Tippett: Music and Literature*, edited by Suzanne Robinson, 122–50. Aldershot, UK: Ashgate, 2002.

Fosler-Lussier, Danielle. *Music Divided: Bartók's Legacy in Cold War Culture*. Berkeley and Los Angeles: University of California Press, 2007.

Francis, Kimberly. "Mediating Modern Music: Nadia Boulanger Constructs Igor Stravinsky," Ph.D. dissertation, University of North Carolina at Chapel Hill, 2010.

Franklin, Peter. *Mahler: Symphony no. 3*. Cambridge: Cambridge University Press, 1991.

Frevert, Ute. "Was haben Gefühle in der Geschichte zu suchen." *Geschichte und Gesellschaft: Zeitschrift für historische Sozialwissenschaft* 35 (2009): 183–208.

Frolova-Walker, Marina. *Russian Music and Nationalism from Glinka to Stalin*. New Haven: Yale University Press, 2008.

Gaines, Kevin. "Duke Ellington, *Black, Brown, and Beige*, and the Cultural Politics of Race." In *Music and the Racial Imagination*, edited by Ronald Radano and Philip V. Bohlman, 585–602. Chicago: University of Chicago Press, 2000.

Garafola, Lynn. "Making an American Dance: *Billy the Kid*, *Rodeo*, and *Appalachian Spring*." In Oja and Tick, eds., *Aaron Copland and His World*, 121–47.

Gelfand, Janelle Magnuson. "Germaine Tailleferre (1892–1983): Piano and Chamber Works." Ph.D. dissertation, University of Cincinnati, 1999.

Gibbs, Christopher H. "'The Phenomenon of the Seventh': A Documentary Essay on Shostakovich's 'War' Symphony." In *Shostakovich and His World*, edited by Laurel E. Fay, 59–113. Princeton: Princeton University Press, 2004.

Gienow-Hecht, Jessica C. E. *Sound Diplomacy: Music and Emotions in Transatlantic Relations, 1850–1920*. Chicago: University of Chicago Press, 2009.

Gillies, Malcolm. "Redrawing Bartók's Life." *Studia Musicologica Academiae Scientiarum Hungaricae* 36 (1995): 303–18.

Gillies, Malcolm. "Bartók in America." In *The Cambridge Companion to Bartók*, edited by Amanda Bayley, 190–201. Cambridge: Cambridge University Press, 2001.

Goebbels, Joseph. *Das eherne Herz: Reden und Aufsätze aus den Jahren 1941/42*. Munich: Zentralverlag der NSDAP, 1943.

Goebel, Stefan. "Re-membered and Re-mobilized: The 'Sleeping Dead' in Interwar Germany and Britain." *Journal of Contemporary History* 39 (2004): 473–85.

Goebel, Stefan. *The Great War and Medieval Memory: War, Remembrance and Medievalism in Britain and Germany, 1914–1940*. Cambridge: Cambridge University Press, 2007.

Goehr, Lydia. "Music and Musicians in Exile: The Romantic Legacy of a Double Life." In Brinkmann and Wolff, eds., *Driven into Paradise*, 66–91.

Goehr, Lydia. *Elective Affinities: Musical Essays on the History of Aesthetic Theory*. New York: Columbia University Press, 2008.

Goodman, Peter W. *Morton Gould: American Salute*. Portland, OR: Amadeus Press, 2000.

Gordon, Eric A. *Mark the Music: The Life and Work of Marc Blitzstein*. New York: St. Martin's Press, 1989.

Gouk, Penelope, and Helen Hill, eds. *Representing Emotions: New Connections in the Histories of Art, Music and Medicine*. Aldershot, UK: Ashgate, 2005.

Grant, Mark N. *Maestros of the Pen: A History of Classical Music Criticism in America*. Boston: Northeastern University Press, 1998.

Grieve, Victoria. *The Federal Art Project and the Creation of Middlebrow Culture*. Urbana: University of Illinois Press, 2009.

Grochulski, Michaela G., Oliver Kautny, and Helmke Jan Keden, eds. *Musik in Diktaturen des 20. Jahrhunderts*. Mainz: Are Musik Verlag, 2006.

Gruber, Gerold W. "Ode to Napoleon Buonaparte (Lord Byron) for String Quartet, Piano, and Reciter, op. 41." In *Arnold Schönberg: Interpretationen seiner Werke*, edited by Gerold W. Gruber, 2 vols., 2:81–94. Laaber: Laaber Verlag, 2002.

Grünzweig, Werner. "Propaganda der Trauer: Kurt Weills Whitman-Songs." In Kowalke and Edler, eds., *A Stranger Here Myself*, 297–325.

Haefeli, Anton. *Die internationale Gesellschaft für Neue Musik (IGNM): Ihre Geschichte von 1922 bis zur Gegenwart*. Zurich: Atlantis Musikbuch-Verlag, 1982.

Hagopian, Kevin Jack. "'You Know Who I Am!' Paul Robeson's Ballad for Americans and the Paradox of the Double V in American Popular Front Culture." In *Paul Robeson: Essays on His Life and Legacy*, edited by Joseph Dorinson and William Pencak, 167–79. Jefferson, NC: McFarland, 2002.

Hanheide, Stefan. *Pace: Musik zwischen Krieg und Frieden; Vierzig Werkporträts*. Kassel: Bärenreiter, 2007.

Hanson, Howard. "A Musician's Point of View toward Emotional Expression." *American Journal of Psychiatry* 99 (1942): 317–25.

Harding, Warren G. *Address of the President of the United States at the Ceremonies Attending the Burial of an Unknown American Soldier in Arlington Cemetery, November 11, 1921*. Washington, DC: Government Printing Office, 1921.

Hawes, Bess Lomax. *Sing It Pretty: A Memoir*. Urbana: University of Illinois Press, 2008.

Heinsheimer, Hans W. *Menagerie in F Sharp*. New York: Doubleday, 1947.

Helbig, Otto H. *A History of Music in the U.S. Armed Forces during World War II*. Philadelphia: M. W. Lads, 1966.

Heyman, Barbara B. *Samuel Barber: The Composer and His Music*. New York: Oxford University Press, 1992.

Hietala, Thomas R. *Manifest Design: American Exceptionalism and Empire*. Revised ed. Ithaca: Cornell University Press, 2003.

Higgins, Dick, ed. *Essential Cowell: Selected Writings on Music*. Kingston, NY: McPherson, 2001.

Hobson, Constance Tibbs, and Deborra A. Richardson. *Ulysses Kay: A Bio-Bibliography*. Westport, CT: Greenwood Press, 1994.

Hodgson, Godfrey. *The Myth of American Exceptionalism*. New Haven: Yale University Press, 2009.

Hoffman, Eva. "The New Nomads." In Aciman, ed., *Letters of Transit*, 35–63.

Holbrook, Susan, and Thomas Dilworth, eds. *The Letters of Gertrude Stein and Virgil Thomson: Composition as Conversation*. Oxford and New York: Oxford University Press, 2010.

Holden, Peregrine, ed. *Music as Medicine: The History of Music Therapy since Antiquity*. Aldershot, UK: Ashgate, 2000.

Horowitz, Joseph. *Understanding Toscanini: How He Became an American Culture-God and Helped Create a New Audience for Old Music*. New York: Alfred A. Knopf, 1987.

Horowitz, Joseph. *Artists in Exile: How Refugees from Twentieth-Century War and Revolution Transformed the American Performing Arts*. New York: Harper, 2008.

Huener, Jonathan, and Francis R. Nicosia, eds. *The Arts in Nazi Germany: Continuity, Conformity, Change*. New York: Berghahn Books, 2006.

Hughes, Catherine A. "Accented Cosmopolitanism: Reception of Ricardo Viñes, the Spanish Expatriate in Paris." Unpublished paper.

Illiano, Roberto, ed. *Italian Music during the Fascist Period*. Cremona: Brepolis, 2004.

Illiano, Roberto, and Massimiliano Sala, eds. *Music and Dictatorship in Europe and Latin America*. Turnhout: Brepols, 2009.

Jennert, Rüdiger. *Paul Hindemith und die neue Welt: Studien zur amerikanischen Hindemith-Rezeption*. Würzburger Musikhistorische Beiträge 26. Tutzing: Hans Schneider, 2005.

Johnson, John A. "Gershwin's 'American Folk Opera': The Genesis, Style, and Reputation of Porgy and Bess (1935)." Ph.D. dissertation, Harvard University, 1996.

Jones, John Busch. *The Songs That Fought the War: Popular Music and the Home Front, 1939–1945*. Waltham, MA: Brandeis University Press, 2006.

Josephson, David. "The Exile of European Music: Documentation of Upheaval and Immigration in the New York Times." In *Driven into Paradise*, ed. Brinkmann and Wolff, 92–152.

Juslin, Patrick N., and John A. Sloboda, eds. *Music and Emotion: Theory and Research*. Oxford and New York: Oxford University Press, 2001.

Kardon, Janet, ed. *Revivals! Diverse Traditions, 1920–1945: The History of Twentieth-Century American Craft*. New York: Harry N. Abrams, 1994.

Kárpáti, János. *Bartók's Chamber Music*. Stuyvesant, NY: Pendragon Press, 1994.

Katz, Mark. "Making America More Musical through the Phonograph, 1900–1930." *American Music* 16 (1998): 448–76.

Kelley, Bruce C., and Mark A. Snell, eds. *Bugle Resounding: Music and Musicians of the Civil War Era*. Columbia: University of Missouri Press, 2004.

Kennedy, David M. *Freedom from Fear: The American People in Depression and War, 1929–1945*. New York: Oxford University Press, 2005.

Kennicott, Philip. "Aaron Copland: Mythical America." *Dance Magazine* (November 1990): 64–65.

Kirsch, Winfried. "Brechungen symphonischer Tradition: Paul Hindemiths Symphonie in Es (1940)." In Osthoff and Schubert, eds., *Symphonik, 1930–1950*, 122–39.

Klefstad, Terry Wait. "The Reception in America of Dmitri Shostakovich, 1928–1946." Ph.D. dissertation, University of Texas at Austin, 2003.

Koppes, Clayton R., and Gregory D. Black. *Hollywood Goes to War: How Politics, Profits and Propaganda Shaped World War II Movies*. Berkeley and Los Angeles: University of California Press, 1987.

Kostelanetz, Richard, ed. *John Cage: An Anthology*. New York: Da Capo Press, 1991.

Kostelanetz, Richard. *Conversing with John Cage*. 2nd ed. New York: Routledge, 2003.

Kowalke, Kim H., and Horst Edler, eds. *A Stranger Here Myself: Kurt Weill-Studien*. Hildesheim: Georg Olms Verlag, 1993.

Kowalke, Kim H. "Formerly German: Kurt Weill in America." In Kowalke and Edler, eds., *A Stranger Here Myself*, 35–57.

Kowalke, Kim H."Kurt Weill, Moderne und populäre Kultur: Öffentlichkeit als Stil." In *Emigrierte Komponisten in der Medienlandschaft des Exils, 1933–1945*, edited by Nils Grosch, Joachim Lucchesi, and Jürgen Scherbera, 171–220. Stuttgart: M & P Verlag für Wissenschaft und Forschung, 1998.

Kowalke, Kim H. "Reading Whitman/Responding to America: Hindemith, Weill, and Others." In Brinkmann and Wolff, eds., *Driven into Paradise*, 194–220.

Kowalke, Kim H. "'I'm an American!' Whitman, Weill, and Cultural Identity." In *Walt Whitman and Modern Music: War, Desire, and the Trials of Nationhood*, edited by Lawrence Kramer, 109–31. New York and London: Garland, 2000.

Kraft, James P. *Stage to Studio: Musicians and the Sound Revolution, 1890–1950*. Baltimore: Johns Hopkins University Press, 1996.

Krenek, Ernst. *Die amerikanischen Tagebücher, 1937–1942: Dokumente aus dem Exil*, edited by Claudia Maurer Zenck. Vienna: Böhlau Verlag, 1992.

Kushner, David Z. "Jaromír Weinberger (1896–1967): From Bohemia to America." *American Music* 6 (1988): 293–313.

Lampert, Vera. "Bartók at Harvard as Witnessed in Unpublished Archival Documents." *Studia Musicologica Academiae Scientiarum Hungaricae* 35 (1993–94): 113–54.

Lang, Paul Henry. *Music in Western Civilization*. New York: Norton, 1941.

Langer, Suzanne K. *Philosophy in a New Key: A Study in the Symbolism of Reason, Rite, and Art*. Cambridge, MA: Harvard University Press, 1951.

Large, Brian. *Martinů*. New York: Holmes & Meier, 1976.

La Roe, Else K. *Woman Surgeon*. New York: Dial Press, 1957.

Laurie, Clayton D. *The Propaganda Warriors: America's Crusade against Nazi Germany*. Lawrence: University Press of Kansas, 1996.

Leibowitz, René. "Béla Bartók ou la possibilité du compromis dans la musique contemporaine." *Les temps modernes* 2 (1947): 705–34.

Lenoir, Yves "Folklore et transcendance dans l'œuvre américaine de Béla Bartók (1940–1945): contributions à l'étude de l'activité scientifique et créatrice du compositeur." Ph.D. dissertation, Université Louvain-la-Neuve, 1986.

Lepenies, Wolf. *Kultur und Politik: Deutsche Geschichten*. Munich: Karl Hanser Verlag, 2006.

Lerner, Neil. "The Classical Documentary Score in American Films of Persuasion: Contexts and Case Studies, 1936–1945." Ph.D. dissertation, Duke University, 1997.

Lerner, Neil. "Aaron Copland, Norman Rockwell, and the 'Four Freedoms': The Office of War Information's Vision and Sound in *The Cummington Story* (1945)." In *Aaron Copland and His World*, ed. Oja and Tick, 351–77.

Levi, Erik. *Mozart and the Nazis: How the Third Reich Abused a Cultural Icon*. New Haven: Yale University Press, 2010.

Levine, Lawrence W. *Highbrow/Lowbrow: The Emergence of Cultural Hierarchy in America*. Cambridge, MA: Harvard University Press, 1988.

Levy, Alan Howard. *Musical Nationalism: American Composers' Search for Identity*. Westport, CT: Greenwood Press, 1983.

Levy, Beth Ellen. "Frontier Figures: American Music and the Mythology of the American West, 1895–1945." Ph.D. dissertation, University of California at Berkeley, 2002.

Lowens, Irving. *Music in America and American Music*. I.S.A.M. Monographs 8. New York: Institute for Studies in American Music, 1978.

Lucas, John. *Thomas Beecham: An Obsession with Music*. Woodbridge, UK: Boydell, 2008.

Luening, Otto. *The Odyssey of an American Composer*. New York: Charles Scribner's Sons, 1980.

Lyall, Max. "The Piano Music of Gail Kubik." D.M.A. dissertation, Peabody Conservatory of Music, 1980.

Mann, Erika. *Blitze überm Ozean: Aufsätze, Reden, Reportagen*, edited by Irmela von der Lühe and Uwe Naumann. Hamburg: Rowohlt, 2000.

Martinů, Charlotte. *My Life with Bohuslav Martinů*. Prague: Orbis Press, 1978.

Martus, Steffen, Marina Münkler, and Werner Röcke, eds. *Schlachtfelder: Codierung von Gewalt im medialen Wandel*. Berlin: Akademie Verlag, 2003.

McKay, Leila A. "Music as a Group Therapeutic Agent in the Treatment of Convalescents." *Sociometry* 8 (1945): 233–37.

Menuhin, Yehudi. *Unfinished Journey*. London: Macdonald and Jane's, 1977.

Meyer, Felix, and Heidy Zimmermann, eds. *Edgard Varèse: Composer, Sound Sculptor, Visionary*. Woodbridge, UK: Boydell, 2006.

Meyer, Felix, and Anne C. Shreffler. *Elliott Carter: A Centennial Portrait in Letters and Documents*. Woodbridge, UK: Boydell, 2008.

Milhaud, Darius. *Notes sans musique*. Paris: René Julliard, 1949.

Milhaud, Darius. *Notes sur la musique: essais et chroniques*, edited by Jeremy Drake. Paris: Flammarion, 1982.

Milhaud, Darius, Madeleine Milhaud, Hélène Hoppenot, and Henri Hoppenot. *Conversation: Correspondance 1918–1974, complétée par des pages du journal d'Hélène Hoppenot*, edited by Marie France Mousli. Paris: Gallimard, 2006.

Mitchell, Donald, ed. *Letters from a Life: The Selected Letters and Diaries of Benjamin Britten, 1913–1976*. Vol. 2, *1939–1945*. Berkeley and Los Angeles: University of California Press, 1991.

Moe, Orin. "A Question of Value: Concert Music and Criticism." *Black Music Research Journal* 6 (1986): 57–66.

Mordden, Ethan. *Beautiful Mornin': The Broadway Musical in the 1940s*. New York: Oxford University Press, 1999.

Móricz, Klára. "New Aspects of the Genesis of Béla Bartók's Concerto for Orchestra: Concepts of 'Finality' and 'Intention.'" *Studia Musicologica Academiae Scientiarum Hungaricae* 35 (1993–94): 181–219.

Móricz, Klára. "Operating on a Fetus: Sketch Studies and Their Relevance to the Interpretation of the Finale of Bartók's Concerto for Orchestra." *Studia Musicologica Academiae Scientiarum Hungaricae* 36 (1995): 461–76.

Móricz, Klára. *Jewish Identities: Nationalism, Racism, and Utopianism in Twentieth-Century Music*. Berkeley and Los Angeles: University of California Press, 2008.

Mosse, George L. *Fallen Soldiers: Reshaping the Memory of World Wars*. Oxford and New York: Oxford University Press, 1990.

Mukherjee, Bharati. "Imagining Homelands." In Aciman, eds., *Letters of Transit*, 65–86.

Murchison, Gayle Minetta. "Nationalism in William Grant Still and Aaron Copland between the Wars: Style and Ideology." Ph.D. dissertation, Yale University, 1998.

Nathan, George Jean. *The Theatre Book of the Year 1942–1943: A Record and an Interpretation.* New York: Alfred Knopf, 1943.

Nettelbeck, Colin. *Forever French: Exile in the United States, 1939–1945.* New York: Berg, 1991.

Nichols, Roger. *Conversations with Madeleine Milhaud.* London: Faber & Faber, 1996.

Nicolodi, Fiamma. *Musica e musicisti nel ventennio fascista.* Fiesole: Discanto Edizioni, 1984.

Nicolodi, Fiamma. "Nationalistische Aspekte im Mythos von der 'alten Musik' in Italien und Frankreich." In *Nationaler Stil und europäische Dimension in der Musik der Jahrhundertwende*, edited by Helga de la Motte-Haber, 102–21. Darmstadt: Wissenschaftliche Buchgesellschaft, 1991.

Ninkovich, Frank A. *The Diplomacy of Ideas: U.S. Foreign Policy and Cultural Relations, 1938–1950.* Cambridge: Cambridge University Press, 1981.

Noss, Luther. *Paul Hindemith in the United States.* Urbana: University of Illinois Press, 1989.

O'Connell, Charles, *The Victor Book of the Symphony.* Revised edition. New York: Simon and Schuster, 1941.

Oja, Carol J. "Composer with a Conscience: Elie Siegmeister in Profile." *American Music* 6 (1988): 158–80.

Oja, Carol J. *Making Music Modern: New York in the 1920s.* New York: Oxford University Press, 2000.

Oja, Carol J., and Judith Tick, eds. *Aaron Copland and His World.* Princeton: Princeton University Press, 2005.

Olmstead, Andrea. *Conversations with Roger Sessions.* Boston: Northeastern University Press, 1987.

Olmstead, Andrea, ed. *The Correspondence of Roger Sessions.* Boston: Northeastern University Press, 1992.

Osthoff, Wolfgang, and Giselher Schubert, eds. *Symphonik, 1930–1950: Gattungsgeschichtliche und analytische Beiträge.* Frankfurter Studien 9. Mainz: Schott, 2003.

Paul, David C. "From American Ethnographer to Cold War Icon: Charles Ives through the Eyes of Henry and Sidney Cowell." *Journal of the American Musicological Society* 59 (2006): 399–458.

Pegolotti, James A. *Deems Taylor: A Biography.* Boston: Northeastern University Press, 2003.

Pernet, Corinne A. "'For the Genuine Culture of the Americas': Musical Folklore, Popular Arts, and the Musical Politics of Pan Americanism, 1933–50." In *Decentering America*, edited by Jessica C. E. Gienow-Hecht, 132–68. New York: Berghahn Books, 2007.

Perse, Saint-John. *Exile and Other Poems.* Bilingual ed. Translated by Denis Devlin. New York: Pantheon Books, 1949.

Peterson, Geoffrey R., ed. *Annals of the Metropolitan Opera: Performances and Artists, 1883–2000.* CD-ROM. New York: Metropolitan Opera Guild, 2002.

Petit, Jacques, ed. *Correspondance Paul Claudel–Darius Milhaud, 1912–1953*. Cahiers Paul Claudel 3. Paris: Gallimard, 1961.

Pinza, Ezio, with Robert Magidoff. *Ezio Pinza: An Autobiography*. New York: Reinhart, 1958.

Polisi, Joseph W. *American Muse: The Life and Times of William Schuman*. New York: Amadeus Press, 2008.

Pollack, Howard. *Aaron Copland: The Life and Work of an Uncommon Man*. Urbana and Chicago: University of Illinois Press, 1999.

Pollack, Howard. *George Gershwin: His Life and Work*. Berkeley and Los Angeles: University of California Press, 2006.

Pollack, Howard. *Marc Blitzstein*. Oxford and New York: Oxford University Press, 2012.

Portnow, Allison Kerbe. "Einstein, Modernism, and Musical Life in America, 1921–1945," Ph.D. dissertation, University of North Carolina at Chapel Hill, 2011.

Potter, Caroline. *Nadia and Lili Boulanger*. Aldershot, UK: Ashgate, 2006.

Potter, Pamela. "What Is 'Nazi Music'?" *Musical Quarterly* 88 (2005): 428–55.

Pound, Ezra. *Early Writings: Poems and Prose*, edited by Ira B. Nadel. New York: Penguin Books, 2005.

Pullen, John J. *Patriotism in America: A Study of Changing Devotions, 1770–1970*. New York: American Heritage Press, 1971.

Rathert, Wolfgang. "Die Sinfonien von Bohuslav Martinů: Ein Beitrag zur amerikanischen Musikgeschichte?" In *Bohuslav Martinů*, edited by Ulrich Tadday, 113–26. Munich: Edition Text + Kritik, 2009.

Rehding, Alexander. *Music and Monumentality: Commemoration and Wonderment in Nineteenth-Century Germany*. New York: Oxford University Press, 2009.

Reis, Claire R. *Composers, Conductors and Critics*. New York: Oxford University Press, 1955.

Renton, Barbara Hampton. "Martinů in the United States: Views of Critics and Students." In *Bohuslav Martinů Anno 1981: Papers from an International Musicological Conference, Prague, May 26–28, 1981*, edited by Jitka Brabcová, 268–76. Prague: Česká hudební společnost, 1990.

Richter, Petra. "A Music-Political Confession: Anmerkungen zu Martinů's *Memorial to Lidice*." *Czech Music* 3 (2008): 34–43.

Riethmüller, Albrecht, ed. *Geschichte der Musik im 20. Jahrhundert*. Vol. 2, *1925–1945*. Laaber: Laaber Verlag, 2006.

Roarty, Robert C. "The *Lunchtime Follies*: Food, Fun, and Propaganda in America's Wartime Workplace." *Journal of American Drama and Theatre* 11/1 (1999): 29–48.

Robertson, Malcolm D. "Roy Harris's Symphonies: An Introduction (I)." *Tempo* n.s. 207 (December 2008): 9–14.

Robinson, Suzanne. "'An English Composer Sees America': Benjamin Britten and the North American Press, 1939–42." *American Music* 15 (1997): 321–51.

Roosevelt, Eleanor. *My Day*. Online ed. The Eleanor Roosevelt Paper Project. http://www.gwu.edu/~erpapers/myday (accessed January 2–July 19, 2011).

Ross, Alex. *The Rest Is Noise: Listening to the Twentieth Century*. New York: Farrar, Straus and Giroux, 2007.

Ross, Alex. *Listen to This*. New York: Farrar, Straus and Giroux, 2010.

Rourke, Constance. *The Roots of American Culture and Other Essays*, edited and with a preface by Van Wyck Brooks. New York: Harcourt, Brace, 1942.

Rubin, Joan Shelley. *The Making of Middlebrow Culture*. Chapel Hill: University of North Carolina Press, 1992.

Ryan, Judith. "Schoenberg's Byron: The 'Ode to Napoleon Buonaparte,' the Antinomies of Modernism, and the Problem of German Imperialism." In *Music and the Aesthetics of Modernity: Essays*, edited by Karol Berger and Anthony Newcomb, 201–16. Harvard: Harvard University Press, 2005.

Saab, A. Joan. *For the Millions: American Art and Culture between the Wars*. Philadelphia: University of Pennsylvania Press, 2004.

Sachs, Harvey. *Music in Fascist Italy*. New York: Norton, 1987.

Sachs, Harvey, ed. *The Letters of Arturo Toscanini*. New York: Alfred A. Knopf, 2002.

Sachs, Joel. *Henry Cowell: A Man Made of Music*. Oxford and New York: Oxford University Press, 2012.

Šafránek, Miloš. *Bohuslav Martinů: The Man and His Music*. New York: Alfred A. Knopf, 1944.

Šafránek, Miloš. *Bohuslav Martinů: Leben und Werk*. Translated by Charlotte Kirschner, Ferdinand Kirschner, and Egon Siegmund. Kassel: Bärenreiter, 1961.

Said, Edward W. "No Reconciliation Allowed." In Aciman, ed., *Letters of Transit*, 87–113.

Schebera, Jürgen. "Der 'alien American' Kurt Weill und seine Aktivitäten für den War Effort der USA 1940–1945." In Kowalke and Edler, eds., *A Stranger Here Myself*, 267–83.

Schenbeck, Lawrence. *Racial Uplift and American Music, 1878–1943*. Jackson: University Press of Mississippi, 2012.

Schivelbusch, Wolfgang. *Entfernte Verwandtschaft: Faschismus, Nationalsozialismus, New Deal, 1933–1939*. Vienna: Carl Hanser Verlag, 2005.

Schmidt, Dörte. "Kulturelle Räume und ästhetische Universalität oder: Warum die Musik für die aktuelle Debatte über das Exil wichtig ist." In *Kulturelle Räume und ästhetische Universalität: Musik und Musiker im Exil*, edited by Claus-Dieter Krohn, Erwin Toermund, Lutz Winckler, and Wulf Koepke, in collaboration with Dörte Schmidt, 1–7. Exilforschung: Ein internationales Jahrbuch 26. Munich: Edition Text + Kritik, 2008.

Schneider, David E. *Bartók, Hungary, and the Renewal of Tradition: Case Studies in the Intersection of Modernity and Nationality*. Berkeley and Los Angeles: University of California Press, 2006.

Schnepel, Julie. "The Critical Pursuit of the Great American Symphony, 1893–1950." Ph.D. dissertation, Indiana University, 1995.

Schubert, Giselher. "'Amerikanismus' und 'Americanism': Hindemith und die Neue Welt." *Hindemith Jahrbuch/Annales Hindemith* 27 (1998): 80–101.

Schwartz, Barry. "Memory as a Cultural System: Abraham Lincoln in World War II." *American Sociological Review* 61 (1996): 908–27.

Schwartz, Barry. *Abraham Lincoln and the Forge of National Memory*. Chicago: University of Chicago Press, 2000.

Schwartz, Barry. *Abraham Lincoln in the Post-Heroic Era: History and Memory in Late Twentieth-Century America*. Chicago: University of Chicago Press, 2008.

Schwartz, Manuela. "Die Musikpolitik der Nationalsozialisten in Vichy-Frankreich." In *Kultur, Propaganda, Öffentlichkeit: Intentionen deutscher Besatzungspolitik und Reaktionen auf die Okkupation*, edited by Wolfgang Benz, Gerhard Otto, and Anabella Weismann, 55–78. Berlin: Metropol, 1998.

Scott, Ian. "From Toscanini to Tennessee: Robert Riskin, the OWI and the Construction of American Propaganda in World War II." *Journal of American Studies* 40 (2006): 347–66.

Seltzer, George. *Music Matters: The Performer and the American Federation of Musicians.* Metuchen, NJ: Scarecrow Press, 1989.

Shadle, Douglas. "Music of a More Perfect Union: Symphonic Constructions of American National Identity, 1840–1870." Ph.D. dissertation, University of North Carolina at Chapel Hill, 2010.

Shanken, Andrew M. "Planning Memory: Living Memorials in the United States during World War II." *Art Bulletin* 84 (2002): 130–47

Shepard, John. "The Legacy of Carleton Sprague Smith: Pan-American Holdings in the Music Division of the New York Public Library for the Performing Arts." *Notes* 62 (2006): 621–66.

Shirley, Wayne D. *Ballet for Martha: The Commissioning of "Appalachian Spring"; and, Ballets for Martha: The Creation of "Appalachian Spring," "Jeux de printemps," and "Hérodiade."* Washington, DC: Library of Congress, 1989.

Shirley, Wayne D. "The Hymns and Fuguing Tunes." In *The Whole World of Music: A Henry Cowell Symposium*, edited by David Nicholls, 95–143. Amsterdam: Harwood Academic, 1997.

Shirley, Wayne D. "Aaron Copland and Arthur Berger in Correspondence." In Oja and Tick, eds., *Aaron Copland and His World*, 179–229.

Shreffler, Anne C. "Denkmal wider Willen: Der Komponist der Leningrader Symphonie." In *Zwischen Bekenntnis und Verweigerung: Schostakowitsch und die Sinfonie im 20. Jahrhundert*, edited by Hans-Joachim Hinrichsen and Laurenz Lütteken, 98–121. Kassel: Bärenreiter, 2005.

Shulman, Holly Cowan. *The Voice of America: Propaganda and Democracy, 1941–1945.* Madison: University of Wisconsin Press, 1990.

Siegmeister, Elie. *The Music Lover's Handbook*. New York: William Morrow, 1943.

Silverman, Kenneth. *Begin Again: A Biography of John Cage*. New York: Alfred A. Knopf, 2010.

Simon, Yannick. *Composer sous Vichy*. Lyon: Symétrie, 2009.

Simonette, Lys, and Kim H. Kowalke, eds. and trans. *Speak Low (When You Speak Love): The Letters of Kurt Weill and Lotte Lenya*. Berkeley and Los Angeles: University of California Press, 1996.

Sklaroff, Lauren Rebecca. "Constructing G.I. Joe Louis: Cultural Solutions to the 'Negro Problem.'" *Journal of American History* 89 (2002): 958–83.

Slattery, Paul Harold. "The Symphonic Works." In *William Grant Still and the Fusion of Cultures in American Music*, 2nd, revised ed., edited by Judith Anne Still and Robert Bartlett Haas, 99–142. Flagstaff, AZ: Master-Player Library, 1995.

Smith, Catherine Parsons. "The Afro-American Symphony and Its Scherzo." In *William Grant Still: A Study in Contradictions*, edited by Catherine Parsons Smith, 114–51. Berkeley and Los Angeles: University of California Press, 2000.

Smith, Kathleen E. R. *God Bless America: Tin Pan Alley Goes to War*. Lexington: University Press of Kentucky, 2003.

Smolko, Joanna Ruth. "Reshaping American Music: The Quotation of Shape-Note Hymns by Twentieth-Century Composers." Ph.D. dissertation, University of Pittsburgh, 2009.

Sprout, Leslie A. "Music for a 'New Era': Composers and National Identity in France, 1936–1946." Ph.D. dissertation, University of California, Berkeley, 2000.

Stehman, Dan. *Roy Harris: An American Musical Pioneer*. Boston: Twayne, 1984.

Steinbeck, Wolfram, and Christoph von Blumenröder, eds. *Die Symphonie im 19. und 20. Jahrhundert*. Vol. 2: *Stationen der Symphonik seit 1900*. Laaber: Laaber Verlag, 2002.

Stenzl, Jürg. *Von Giacomo Puccini zu Luigi Nono: Italienische Musik 1922–1952; Faschismus, Resistenza, Republik*. Buren, The Netherlands: Frits Knuf, 1990.

Stern, Isaac, with Chaim Potok. *My First 79 Years*. New York: Alfred A. Knopf, 1999.

Stewart, John Lincoln. *Ernst Krenek: The Man and His Music*. Berkeley and Los Angeles: University of California Press, 1999.

Stone, Ellen, and Bonnie Smallwood Medin. *Musical Women Marines: The Marine Corps Women's Reserve Band in World War Two*. N.p.: The Authors, 1981.

Stowe, David W. *How Sweet the Sound: Music in the Spiritual Lives of Americans*. Cambridge, MA and London: Harvard University Press, 2004.

Suchoff, Benjamin. "Bartók in America." *Musical Times* 117 (1976): 123–24.

Svatos, Thomas D. "Martinů on Music and Culture: A View from His Parisian Criticism and 1940s Notes." Ph.D. dissertation, University of California, Santa Barbara, 2001.

Swayne, Steve. "William Schuman, World War II, and the Pulitzer Prize." *Musical Quarterly* 89 (2006): 273–320.

Swayne, Steve. *Orpheus in Manhattan: William Schuman and the Shaping of America's Musical Life*. New York: Oxford University Press, 2011.

Szwed, John. *Alan Lomax: The Man Who Recorded the World*. New York: Viking, 2010.

Tailleferre, Germaine. "Mémoires à l'emporte-pièce," edited by Frédéric Robert. *Revue internationale de musique française* 19 (February 1986): 7–82.

Tallián, Tibor. "Bartók's Reception in America, 1940–1945." Translated by Peter Laki. In *Bartók and His World*, edited by Peter Laki, 101–18. Princeton: Princeton University Press, 1995.

Taruskin, Richard. "The Darker Side of Modern Music." *The New Republic* 199 (September 5, 1988): 28–34.

Taruskin, Richard. *The Oxford History of Western Music*. Vol. 4, *The Early Twentieth Century*. Oxford and New York: Oxford University Press, 2005.

Tawa, Nicholas. *The Great American Symphony: Music, the Depression, and War*. Bloomington: Indiana University Press, 2009.

Thomson, Charles A., and Walther H. C. Laves. *Cultural Relations and U.S. Foreign Policy*. Bloomington: Indiana University Press, 1963.

Thomson, Virgil. *A Virgil Thomson Reader*. Introduction by John Rockwell. New York: Dutton, 1984.

Thym, Jürgen. "The Enigma of Kurt Weill's Whitman Songs." In Kowalke and Edler, eds., *A Stranger Here Myself*, 285–96.

Tick, Judith. *Ruth Crawford Seeger: A Composer's Search for American Music*. New York: Oxford University Press, 1997.

Tick, Judith, ed. *Music in the USA: A Documentary Companion*. Oxford and New York: Oxford University Press, 2008.

Tomoff, Kiril. *Creative Union: The Professional Organizations of Soviet Composers*. Ithaca: Cornell University Press, 2006.

Tucker, Sherrie. *Swing Shift: "All-Girl" Bands in the 1940s*. Durham, NC: Duke University Press, 2000.

Use of Mechanical Reproduction of Music. Hearings before a Subcommittee of the Committee on Interstate Commerce, United State Senate. Second Session Pursuant To S. Res. 286...September 17, 18, and 21, 1942. Washington: United States Government Printing Office, 1943.

Von der Lühe, Irmela. *Erika Mann: Eine Biographie*. Frankfurt and New York: Campus Verlag, 1994.

Von Glahn, Denise. *The Sounds of Place: Music and the American Landscape*. Boston: Northeastern University Press, 2003.

Walden, Joshua S. "'An Essential Expression of the People': Interpretations of Hasidic Song in the Composition and Performance History of Ernest Bloch's *Baal Shem*." *Journal of the American Musicological Society* 65 (2012): 777–820.

Walker, Robert Matthew. "Milhaud and America." *Musical Times* 133 (1992): 443–44.

Wall, Wendy L. *Inventing the "American Way": The Politics of Consensus from the New Deal to the Civil Rights Movement*. Oxford and New York: Oxford University Press, 2008.

Walsh, Stephen. *Stravinsky: The Second Exile; France and America, 1934–1971*. Berkeley and Los Angeles: University of California Press, 2006.

Wannamaker, John Samuel. "The Musical Settings of the Poetry of Walt Whitman: A Study of Theme, Structure, and Prosody." Ph.D. dissertation, University of Minnesota, 1971.

Watkins, Glenn. *Proof through the Night: Music and the Great War*. Berkeley and Los Angeles: University of California Press, 2003.

Watkins, Glenn. *The Gesualdo Hex: Music, Myth, and Memory*. New York and London: Norton, 2010.

Weber, Horst. "Exilforschung und Musikgeschichtsschreibung." In *Geächtet, verboten, vertrieben: Österreichische Musiker, 1938–1945*, edited by Hartmut Krones, forthcoming.

Wells, Christopher. "Grand Opera as Racial Uplift: The National Negro Opera Company, 1941–1962." M.A. thesis, University of North Carolina at Chapel Hill, 2009.

Whitman, Walt. *Leaves of Grass*. Boston: Small, Maynard, 1904.

Winkler, Allan M. *The Politics of Propaganda: The Office of War Information, 1942–1945*. New Haven: Yale University Press, 1978.

Winkler, Hans-Jürgen. "*La mélodie essentielle*: Zur Konzeption von Darius Milhauds frühen Symphonien für großes Orchester." In Osthoff and Schubert, eds., *Symphonik, 1930–1950*, 209–23.

Wolfe, Charles K., and James E. Akenson, eds. *Country Music Goes to War*. Lexington: University Press of Kentucky, 2005.

Wong, K. Scott. "From Pariah to Paragon: Shifting Images of Chinese Americans during World War II." In *Chinese Americans and the Politics of Race and Culture*, edited by Sucheng Chan and Madeline Y. Hsu, 153–72. Philadelphia: Temple University Press, 2008.

Woolley, John, and Gerhard Peters, eds. *American Presidency Project*. University of California at Santa Barbara. http://www.presidency.ucsb.edu/ws/print.php?pid=16273 (accessed January 27, 2008).

Wright, Jeffrey M., II. "The Enlisted Composer: Samuel Barber's Career, 1942–1945." Ph.D. dissertation, University of North Carolina at Chapel Hill, 2010.

Young, William H., and Nancy K. Young. *Music of the Great Depression.* Westport, CT: Greenwood Press, 2005.

Young, William H., and Nancy K. Young. *Music of the World War II Era.* Westport, CT: Greenwood Press, 2008.

Zuck, Barbara A. *A History of Musical Americanism.* Ann Arbor: UMI Research Press, 1978.

Bridge, Frank, 29
Briggs, Mrs. Whitney, 68
Britten, Benjamin, 159, 183–84, 205, 256
    Paul Bunyan, 170
Broadcasting, *see* Radio
Broman, Carl, 109
Bronson, Howard G., 106, 109, 116–17
Brooks, Van Wyck, 141
Brown, Ray C. B., 26, 245
Brown, William Theo, 215
Buchman, Carl
    Seven Songs of the Early Republic, 142
Buckley, Ann, 38
Budapest String Quartet, 105, 140, 242
Buell, Lawrence, 256
Bulliet, Clarence Joseph, 175
Burleigh, Henry Thacker (arr.)
    "De Gospel Train," 125
    "Every Time I Feel de Spirit," 125
    "Go Down, Moses," 125
    "I Want to Be Ready," 125
    "My Lord, What a Mornin'," 124
    "Oh, Didn't It Rain," 124
    "Weepin' Mary," 124
Burley, Dan, 174
Burma, 47, 49
Bush, George W., 14
Buttleman, Clifford V., 99
Byrd, William, 150
Byron, George Gordon Sixth Baron (Lord), 56,
    217

Cage, John, 18, 226, 268
    Credo in US, 57, 269–70
    The Harmony of Maine, 270
    Hymns and Variations, 270
    In the Name of the Holocaust, 269
Camp Lee, Virginia
    Camp Lee Symphony Orchestra, 5, 126
Camp Lejeune, North Carolina, 19
Camp Shanks, New York, 126
Camp Shelby, Michigan, 138
Campbell, George W., 109
Canada, 3, 185
"Canto di caccia," 125
Carissimi, Giacomo, 124
    Plorate, Filii Israel, 124
Carnegie Foundation, 95
Carpenter, John Alden
    The Anxious Bugler, 227, 236

Carr, George W., 109
Carter, Alan, 109
Carter, Elliott, 18, 57–58, 169, 236, 238
    "Music in America at War," 58, 91–92
    and OWI, 4, 15, 58, 84, 87
    Symphony no. 1, 267
    Warble for Lilac Time, 238–39
Carter, Elmer A., 40–41
Carter, John, 4
Casadesus, Robert, 181, 190
Cassel, Walter, 50–51, 166
Cassidy, Claudia, 155, 212, 232–33
Castelnuovo-Tedesco, Mario, 193, 221–23
    An American Rhapsody, 222
    Indian Songs and Dances, 222
    Sacred Service (for Sabbath Eve), 222
CBS (Columbia Broadcasting Society), 65, 69, 71,
    77, 101, 243
CBS Orchestra, 49
Central Intelligence Agency, 5
Chadwick, George, 88
Chanler, Theodore, 17
Chanute Air Field, Illinois, 125
Chase, Gilbert, 99
Chauvinism, 74, 136, 159–60, 165, 173, 179,
    183–84, 191, 224–25, 233, 258
Chávez, Carlos, 105
    Piano Concerto, 31
"Chee Lai," 86, 103
Chicago Civic Opera House, 164
Chile, 95, 97
China, 2, 34, 43–44, 47, 73, 86, 89, 100–105,
    116, 184, 215, 240, 262
China war relief, 35
Chinese Exclusions Acts, 101
Chopin, Frédéric, 29, 34, 103
    Ballade in G Minor, op. 23, 125
    Etude in E Major, op. 10, no. 3, 125
    Nocturne in F# Major, op. 15, 125
Churchill, Winston, 32
Chotzinoff, Samuel, 99
CIA, *see* Central Intelligence Agency
Cincinnati Symphony Orchestra, 5
The Circle of Chalk, 215
Civil rights, 2, 40, 173, 232
Civil war (U.S.), 14, 53, 149, 153, 219, 228,
    234, 240, 246, 248–52
Clark, Evans, 98–99
Clurman, Harold, 15, 258
Cold war, 6, 12, 89, 93, 105

WPA, *see* Works Progress (Projects)
    Administration
WQXR Radio Station (New York), 159, 224
Wright, Harold C., 112

Yale Glee Club, 97, 98
"Yankee Doodle," 230, 242
Yankee Tunesmiths, 147–51, 156, 169
YMCA, 37, 176

Young, Marvin, 40
Young, Victor, 5

Zakin, Alexander, 43
Zimbalist, Efrem, 180
Zionism, 59
Zobel, Edgar H., 112
Zuck, Barbara A.
    A History of Musical Americanism, 5